Statistics for Finance

CHAPMAN & HALL/CRC
Texts in Statistical Science Series

Statistical Theory: A Concise Introduction
F. Abramovich and Y. Ritov

Practical Multivariate Analysis, Fifth Edition
A. Afifi, S. May, and V.A. Clark

Practical Statistics for Medical Research
D.G. Altman

Interpreting Data: A First Course in Statistics
A.J.B. Anderson

Introduction to Probability with R
K. Baclawski

Linear Algebra and Matrix Analysis for Statistics
S. Banerjee and A. Roy

Mathematical Statistics: Basic Ideas and Selected Topics, Volume I, Second Edition
P. J. Bickel and K. A. Doksum

Analysis of Categorical Data with R
C. R. Bilder and T. M. Loughin

Statistical Methods for SPC and TQM
D. Bissell

Introduction to Probability
J. K. Blitzstein and J. Hwang

Bayesian Methods for Data Analysis, Third Edition
B.P. Carlin and T.A. Louis

Second Edition
R. Caulcutt

The Analysis of Time Series: An Introduction, Sixth Edition
C. Chatfield

Introduction to Multivariate Analysis
C. Chatfield and A.J. Collins

Problem Solving: A Statistician's Guide, Second Edition
C. Chatfield

Statistics for Technology: A Course in Applied Statistics, Third Edition
C. Chatfield

Bayesian Ideas and Data Analysis: An Introduction for Scientists and Statisticians
R. Christensen, W. Johnson, A. Branscum, and T.E. Hanson

Modelling Binary Data, Second Edition
D. Collett

Modelling Survival Data in Medical Research, Third Edition
D. Collett

Introduction to Statistical Methods for Clinical Trials
T.D. Cook and D.L. DeMets

Applied Statistics: Principles and Examples
D.R. Cox and E.J. Snell

Multivariate Survival Analysis and Competing Risks
M. Crowder

Statistical Analysis of Reliability Data
M.J. Crowder, A.C. Kimber, T.J. Sweeting, and R.L. Smith

An Introduction to Generalized Linear Models, Third Edition
A.J. Dobson and A.G. Barnett

Nonlinear Time Series: Theory, Methods, and Applications with R Examples
R. Douc, E. Moulines, and D.S. Stoffer

Introduction to Optimization Methods and Their Applications in Statistics
B.S. Everitt

Extending the Linear Model with R: Generalized Linear, Mixed Effects and Nonparametric Regression Models
J.J. Faraway

Linear Models with R, Second Edition
J.J. Faraway

A Course in Large Sample Theory
T.S. Ferguson

Multivariate Statistics: A Practical Approach
B. Flury and H. Riedwyl

Readings in Decision Analysis
S. French

Markov Chain Monte Carlo: Stochastic Simulation for Bayesian Inference, Second Edition
D. Gamerman and H.F. Lopes

Bayesian Data Analysis, Third Edition
A. Gelman, J.B. Carlin, H.S. Stern, D.B. Dunson, A. Vehtari, and D.B. Rubin

Multivariate Analysis of Variance and Repeated Measures: A Practical Approach for Behavioural Scientists
D.J. Hand and C.C. Taylor

Practical Longitudinal Data Analysis
D.J. Hand and M. Crowder

Logistic Regression Models
J.M. Hilbe

Richly Parameterized Linear Models: Additive, Time Series, and Spatial Models Using Random Effects
J.S. Hodges

Statistics for Epidemiology
N.P. Jewell

Stochastic Processes: An Introduction, Second Edition
P.W. Jones and P. Smith

The Theory of Linear Models
B. Jørgensen

Principles of Uncertainty
J.B. Kadane

Graphics for Statistics and Data Analysis with R
K.J. Keen

Mathematical Statistics
K. Knight

Introduction to Multivariate Analysis: Linear and Nonlinear Modeling
S. Konishi

Nonparametric Methods in Statistics with SAS Applications
O. Korosteleva

Modeling and Analysis of Stochastic Systems, Second Edition
V.G. Kulkarni

Exercises and Solutions in Biostatistical Theory
L.L. Kupper, B.H. Neelon, and S.M. O'Brien

Exercises and Solutions in Statistical Theory
L.L. Kupper, B.H. Neelon, and S.M. O'Brien

Design and Analysis of Experiments with R
J. Lawson

Design and Analysis of Experiments with SAS
J. Lawson

A Course in Categorical Data Analysis
T. Leonard

Statistics for Accountants
S. Letchford

Introduction to the Theory of Statistical Inference
H. Liero and S. Zwanzig

Statistical Theory, Fourth Edition
B.W. Lindgren

Stationary Stochastic Processes: Theory and Applications
G. Lindgren

Statistics for Finance
E. Lindström, H. Madsen, and J. N. Nielsen

The BUGS Book: A Practical Introduction to Bayesian Analysis
D. Lunn, C. Jackson, N. Best, A. Thomas, and D. Spiegelhalter

Introduction to General and Generalized Linear Models
H. Madsen and P. Thyregod

Time Series Analysis
H. Madsen

Pólya Urn Models
H. Mahmoud

Randomization, Bootstrap and Monte Carlo Methods in Biology, Third Edition
B.F.J. Manly

Introduction to Randomized Controlled Clinical Trials, Second Edition
J.N.S. Matthews

Statistical Methods in Agriculture and Experimental Biology, Second Edition
R. Mead, R.N. Curnow, and A.M. Hasted

Statistics in Engineering: A Practical Approach
A.V. Metcalfe

Statistical Inference: An Integrated Approach, Second Edition
H. S. Migon, D. Gamerman, and F. Louzada

Beyond ANOVA: Basics of Applied Statistics
R.G. Miller, Jr.

A Primer on Linear Models
J.F. Monahan

Applied Stochastic Modelling, Second Edition
B.J.T. Morgan

Elements of Simulation
B.J.T. Morgan

Probability: Methods and Measurement
A. O'Hagan

Introduction to Statistical Limit Theory
A.M. Polansky

Applied Bayesian Forecasting and Time Series Analysis
A. Pole, M. West, and J. Harrison

Statistics in Research and Development, Time Series: Modeling, Computation, and Inference
R. Prado and M. West

Introduction to Statistical Process Control
P. Qiu

Sampling Methodologies with Applications
P.S.R.S. Rao

A First Course in Linear Model Theory
N. Ravishanker and D.K. Dey

Essential Statistics, Fourth Edition
D.A.G. Rees

Stochastic Modeling and Mathematical Statistics: A Text for Statisticians and Quantitative Scientists
F.J. Samaniego

Statistical Methods for Spatial Data Analysis
O. Schabenberger and C.A. Gotway

Bayesian Networks: With Examples in R
M. Scutari and J.-B. Denis

Large Sample Methods in Statistics
P.K. Sen and J. da Motta Singer

Decision Analysis: A Bayesian Approach
J.Q. Smith

Analysis of Failure and Survival Data
P. J. Smith

Applied Statistics: Handbook of GENSTAT Analyses
E.J. Snell and H. Simpson

Applied Nonparametric Statistical Methods, Fourth Edition
P. Sprent and N.C. Smeeton

Data Driven Statistical Methods
P. Sprent

Generalized Linear Mixed Models: Modern Concepts, Methods and Applications
W. W. Stroup

Survival Analysis Using S: Analysis of Time-to-Event Data
M. Tableman and J.S. Kim

Applied Categorical and Count Data Analysis
W. Tang, H. He, and X.M. Tu

Elementary Applications of Probability Theory, Second Edition
H.C. Tuckwell

Introduction to Statistical Inference and Its Applications with R
M.W. Trosset

Understanding Advanced Statistical Methods
P.H. Westfall and K.S.S. Henning

Statistical Process Control: Theory and Practice, Third Edition
G.B. Wetherill and D.W. Brown

Generalized Additive Models: An Introduction with R
S. Wood

Epidemiology: Study Design and Data Analysis, Third Edition
M. Woodward

Practical Data Analysis for Designed Experiments
B.S. Yandell

Texts in Statistical Science

Statistics for Finance

Erik Lindström
Lund University
Sweden

Henrik Madsen
Technical University of Denmark
Lyngby, Denmark

Jan Nygaard Nielsen
Netcompany A/S, Copenhagen
Denmark

CRC Press
Taylor & Francis Group
Boca Raton London New York

CRC Press is an imprint of the
Taylor & Francis Group, an **informa** business
A CHAPMAN & HALL BOOK

Reprint 2025

CRC Press
Taylor & Francis Group
6000 Broken Sound Parkway NW, Suite 300
Boca Raton, FL 33487-2742

ISBN: 978-0-367-24141-4

Visit the Taylor & Francis Web site at
http://www.taylorandfrancis.com

and the CRC Press Web site at
http://www.crcpress.com

Printed and bound in India
For sale in India, Pakistan, Nepal, Bhutan, Bangladesh and Sri Lanka only.

Contents

Preface

This book is intended for students at the advanced undergraduate level or PhD level who want to develop professional skills in statistics with applications towards finance. The basis for this book is lecture notes written for a course "Statistics in Finance" at the Technical University of Denmark (DTU). Those notes were also used later in a related course at Lund University, now as a part of larger package of courses covering financial economics, risk management and financial mathematics.

The purpose of this book is to bridge the gap between on one hand classical books on financial mathematics that typically provide a rigorous treatment of the topic, but rarely connects the data, and on the other hand books on econometrics or time series analysis that do not cover the specific problems related to option valuation. We also include examples on how the statistical tools can be used to improve, e.g., Value at Risk calculations.

There is of course a risk that a book trying to cover several fields will become a "Jack of all trades, master of none", but our intention has been not only to cover different fields, but also to integrate them through examples, case studies and cross references throughout the book, thereby adding value beyond each part. In fact, the extended version of that quote is

Jack of all trades, master of none
Often times better than a master of one

A consequence of this design choice is that complete formal proofs seldom are presented. Instead, we either provide a reference to a source where the full proof can be found or try to make it plausible by presenting the main ideas of the proof, but skipping the technical details.

The book can be used for several different courses. It can be used for a course on *financial econometrics*, starting with a brief introduction of stylized facts in finance (Chapter 1), followed by statistical methods in discrete time (Chapters 4, 5 and 6), continuous time (Chapters 12, 13) and, finally, partially observed models in discrete and continuous time (Chapter 14).

It can also form the basis for a course on financial mathematics with an introduction to the problems (Chapters 1, 2 and 3) and then move over to continuous time problems using Brownian motions or jump process (Chapters 7 and 8), followed by applications in security markets (Chapter 9) and interest rate markets (Chapters 10 and 11). It would also be possible to include the numerical schemes in Chapter 12 if that course also has some computational elements. Chapter 14 also presents some cases on how options or bonds can be calibrated to market data.

We still believe, however, that the book as a whole contains values that are lost when using only a subset of the content. The integration of different topics leads to new insights and will ideally inspire new research. For example additional complexity in option valuation models can easily be motivated by statistical findings in Chapter 1, while advanced option valuation models are partly responsible for sparking an interest in statistics for partially observed models in Chapter 14.

Many people have helped with the development of the text over the years, Former students taking the course have been an especially excellent source of constructive feedback. The text has also been improved on by suggestions and feedback from former and current colleagues, where we especially would like to thank (in alphabetical order) Stefan I. Adalbjörnsson, Carl Åkerlindh, Mikkel Baadsgaard, Jan-Emil Banning-Iversen, Jingyi Guo, Jan Holst, Josef Höök, Michael Preisel, Johan Svärd, and Magnus Wiktorsson. Without their help, the text would not have been what it is today!

Author biographies

Erik Lindström

Dr. Lindström is an associate professor at the Centre for Mathematical Sciences at Lund University, Sweden, but substantial parts of the book were written when Erik was guest professor at the Technical University of Denmark.

His research ranges from statistical methodology (primarily time series analysis in discrete and continuous time), to financial mathematics as well as problems related to energy markets.

He earned his master's degree in engineering physics in 2000 and his master's degree in business and economics in 2001, followed by a PhD in mathematical statistics in 2004, all from Lund Institute of Technology (LTH)/Lund University, Sweden. He has a great interest in teaching, being part of LTH's Pedagogical Academy and has been awarded the distinction of Excellent Teaching Practitioner (ETP) in 2013.

Henrik Madsen

Dr. Madsen earned a PhD in statistics at the Technical University of Denmark (DTU) in 1986. He was appointed assistant professor in statistics in 1986, associate professor in 1989 and professor in mathematical statistics with a special focus on dynamical systems in 1999 also at DTU. He has authored or co-authored approximately 480 papers and 11 books, including books on mathematical statistics, time series analysis and on integration of renewables in electricity markets. He is an elected member of ISI and IEEE. He is currently section head at the Section for Dynamical Systems at the Department for Applied Mathematics and Computer Sciences at DTU.

Jan Nygaard Nielsen

Dr. Nielsen earned his master's degree at the Department of Mathematical Modelling at the Technical University in Denmark in 1996, and earned a PhD at the same department in 1999. He contributed to a set of lecture notes for a course in financial engineering that constitutes early versions of this manuscript while earning his PhD degree. He is currently employed as a principal architect at Netcompany (a Danish IT and Business Consulting firm).

Chapter 1

Introduction

In *Théorie de la Speculation* (1900), Louis Bachelier made the first attempt to model the inherent randomness in stock prices using a continuous-time counterpart of white noise, the Brownian Motion. For many years this modelling approach was of purely academic interest as financial institutions used less mathematically demanding methods. More than 70 years later the ideas proposed by Bachelier were used in two seminal papers by Robert Merton on continuous-time finance in general and Fischer Black and Myron Scholes on the pricing of options and corporate liabilities. Contrary to their own expectations, this area has expanded enormously during the last decades, and Merton and Scholes received the Nobel Prize in economics in 1997 for their research (Black passed away in 1995). The amount of money involved today is reported in Table 1.1, which can be compared to the US GDP which was about 15000 billion US dollar (USD) in 2012.

Companies use these new products to protect themselves against changes in interest rates, foreign exchange rates and commodities prices. Mutual funds and pension funds use them to protect their stocks and bond investments. Major banks, brokerage firms and insurance companies write them for customers, while inventing such exotic names as caps, collars and swaptions.

The complexity of the vast range of new financial products that are continuously being introduced on the financial markets and the inherent uncertainty associated with stock prices, interest rates and foreign exchange rates have given rise to the emergence of a new scientific field: *mathematical finance*. This area of research encompasses the theory of stochastic processes (stochastic

Contracts	Notional value	Market value
Foreign exchange	67358	2304
Interest rate	489703	18833
Equity-linked	6251	605
Commodity	2587	358
Credit default swaps	25069	848

Table 1.1: Notional and market value of outstanding OTC contracts in billions in US dollars December 2012. Data from Bank for International Settlements.

differential equations), partial differential equations, functional analysis and, last but not least, economics and finance.

In contrast to many other books on mathematical finance, this course will also cover the modern theory of financial derivatives from an empirical point of view. Thus identification and estimation theory play an integral part of the course. The reader should be able to utilize these methods in combination with methods in operations research for risk assessment, risk management and optimal portfolio selection. This combination of mathematical finance, statistics and operations research form the foundation of the science of *financial engineering*.

The ambitious and broad scope of the book can only be obtained at the expense of depth of coverage, so proofs and mathematical considerations of purely technical interest will be omitted for brevity. Nevertheless, it is our aim to bring the reader up to a level of understanding and managing empirical research in this area.

1.1 Introduction to financial derivatives

Let us introduce the merits of one of the most important financial derivatives, *the European call option*, by considering a fairly simple transaction between two companies. Assume that the Danish company IDEA A/S today ($t = 0$) orders 1 000 pieces of furniture from the American company Bench Inc. to be delivered in exactly 6 months' time ($t = T$). They have agreed upon a price of 500 000 USD, which should be paid upon delivery. We assume that the exchange rate today is 6 DKK/USD.

Due to the 6 months between the order and delivery date, IDEA A/S faces a serious *risk* regarding changes in the exchange rate between DKK and USD. Today ($t = 0$) they are unable to determine the exchange rate upon delivery ($t = T$) and hence the amount in DKK they are going to pay upon delivery is random. In the very unlikely case that the exchange rate should remain the same, they should pay 3 000 000 DKK, but if the exchange rate should go up to, say, 6.50 DKK/USD they will have to pay 3 250 000 DKK. From IDEA's point of view there is, of course, no problem associated with a possible lower exchange rate. Thus IDEA is exposed to an *asymmetrical risk*. There are at least three different ways of eliminating this risk.

I: The most naive approach would be to buy 500 000 USD today ($t = 0$) at the known exchange rate 6 DKK/USD, which would enable IDEA to avoid exposing themselves to a higher exchange rate at time $t = T$. This approach eliminates the risk, but there are a couple of noticeable drawbacks. First of all, a large amount of capital is tied up during the next 6 months, which might be put to more profitable uses. Second, they have lost the opportunity to take advantage of a lower exchange rate at time $t = T$.

II: A slightly more sophisticated approach would be to negotiate a *forward contract* with a participant on the foreign exchange (FX) markets that enables

IDEA to buy 500 000 USD at time $t = T$ at an exchange rate K determined at time $t = 0$. The exchange rate K (unit DKK/USD) is called the *strike price* and it is clearly specified in the contract.

No transactions are made at $t = 0$ and the amount to be paid at time $t = T$ is fixed at $K \times 500\,000$ DKK. As the writer of the contract is obliged to sell the predetermined amount of USD at the predetermined strike price at time $t = T$, no matter what the exchange rate will be, this contract represents a value, and it is possible to trade it as any commodity for $0 < t \leq T$.

Let us say that a contract with a strike price of $K = 6.2$ DKK/USD has been negotiated, and that IDEA is *obliged* to pay 3 100 000 DKK in 6 months' time to the writer of the contract. If the exchange rate S_T at time $t = T$ is 6.5 DKK/USD, IDEA may congratulate themselves by having (indirectly) earned 150 000 DKK, because they would have been forced to pay 3 250 000 DKK if they had not written the contract. On the other hand, should the exchange rate drop to, say, 5.9 DKK/USD, they lose 150 000 DKK.

Again, IDEA has eliminated the risk of a higher exchange rate, but they are still unable to take advantage of a lower exchange rate.

III: Thus the question remains: Is it possible to write a contract that allows the holder of the contract (IDEA) to eliminate the risk *and* at the same time take advantage of a possible lower exchange rate? The answer is yes, and such a contract is called a European call option.

Definition 1.1 (European call option). *A European call option on the amount of Y USD with exercise date T and strike or exercise price K is a contract, signed at time $t = 0$, that*

- *gives the holder of the contract the right to buy an amount Y dollars at the exchange rate K $[DKK/USD]$ at time $t = T$, and*
- *allows the holder of the contract not to buy any dollars if the holder of the contract does not want to.*

Options of this type (and a number of variations hereof) are traded on the international financial markets and the *underlying asset* can be anything from exchange rates to stocks, apples or oranges.

Note that purchasing an option on, say, an AP Møller stock is not the same as buying an AP Møller stock. The AP Møller stock is just the underlying asset that the holder has the right to buy if he finds it favourable.

Returning to IDEA, it now follows that they may buy a European call option on $Y = 500\,000$ USD with exercise date T and strike price $K = 6$ DKK/USD. Should the exchange rate at time $t = T$ exceed 6 DKK/USD, they may use (or *exercise*) the option and purchase the 500 000 USD at 6 DKK/USD from the writer of the contract. Conversely, should the exchange rate drop below 6 DKK/USD they can purchase the required amount of USD on the market and forget about the option.

Whereas the forward contract was, per definition, free, the option has a price. This price is determined by supply and demand on the option markets and it depends on the exercise date T and the strike price K. A higher strike price K gives rise to a lower price on the option, so IDEA is faced with the interesting problem of determining whether it is worth buying the option or not.

It is worth noting that this European call option is just one in an ever growing class of options that have at least two similarities:

1. An option is a *contingent claim* which means that the holder of the option owns an uncertain claim on an underlying asset and that the value of the contract is contingent (conditional) on the future development of the price of the underlying asset.
2. An option is a *financial derivative* as it exists solely in terms of the underlying asset and its value is derived from the (expected) value of this asset (in our case USD).

A major part of the course is to clarify what is meant by the fair, theoretical price of, e.g., a European call option and how to determine it. A brief overview of this project is as follows:

1. We are considering a market with a number of given assets, such as stocks. The prices of these assets are assumed to vary randomly in time.
2. We are going to introduce new financial products in terms of these given assets. These new products are called *derivatives* and typical examples are options, swaps, futures and forwards.
3. We will then examine how to price such derivatives. The clue is that the derivatives are introduced in terms of already given assets with their own price processes and markets, so the derivatives cannot be priced at will. The complete market consisting of the given assets and the new derivatives must be priced consistently. In other words, the market should be *efficient*.
4. It turns out that the valuation problem may be solved for a large number of derivatives such that each derivative is assigned a unique price. This price is called the *arbitrage-free price* of the financial derivative or *financial instrument*.

It is very important to remember that we are not going to determine the correct price, because the term "the correct price" of a derivative does not necessarily make any sense. We are just trying to determine the fair price in terms of the underlying assets.

Let us consider a very simple market where the uncertainty is limited to two different events in the sample space $\Omega = \{\omega_1, \omega_2\}$ with the probabilities $P(\omega_1) = 0.8$ and $P(\omega_2) = 0.2$. We are only considering the market at time $t = 0$ and $t = 1$ year. The market consists of two papers or so-called *securities*:

- A *bond* with a deterministic price process given by

$$B_0 = 100, \qquad B_1 = 110. \tag{1.1}$$

This implies that the deterministic annual rate r is 10%. This can be seen by solving

$$B_1 = (1+r)B_0 \tag{1.2}$$

with respect to r. Note that the price of the bond (which could be a Danish Government bond) is used to determine the interest rate.

- A *stock* with the price process S where $S_0 = 100$ and S_1 is given by

$$S_1(\omega) = \begin{cases} 125 & \text{if } \omega = \omega_1 \\ 90 & \text{if } \omega = \omega_2. \end{cases} \tag{1.3}$$

That is the initial price of the stock is 100. At time $t = 1$ the price will be 125, if the outcome ω of our random process is ω_1, or the price will be 90, if the outcome is ω_2. In other words, we know the values of the assets at time $t = 0$, but the value of the stock depends on the outcome ω of the stochastic process.

We are now going to introduce a European call option with exercise date $T = 1$ and strike price $K = 105$ DKK in this simple market. This implies that the holder of the option has the right, but not the obligation, to buy a stock for 105 DKK. Assume that at $t = 1$, the random process generates the outcome ω_1, then the value of the stock is 125 DKK and we exercise the option. Thus we have purchased a stock worth 125 DKK for 105 DDK and indirectly earned 20 DKK. Should the random process generate the outcome ω_2, the value of the stock is 90 DKK, so we buy the stock at 90 DKK and forget about the option.

By purchasing the option we are faced with the stochastic income at time $t = 1$

$$X = \max[S_1 - K_1, 0] = \max[S_1 - 105]. \tag{1.4}$$

This is illustrated in the *payoff diagram* in Figure 1.1.

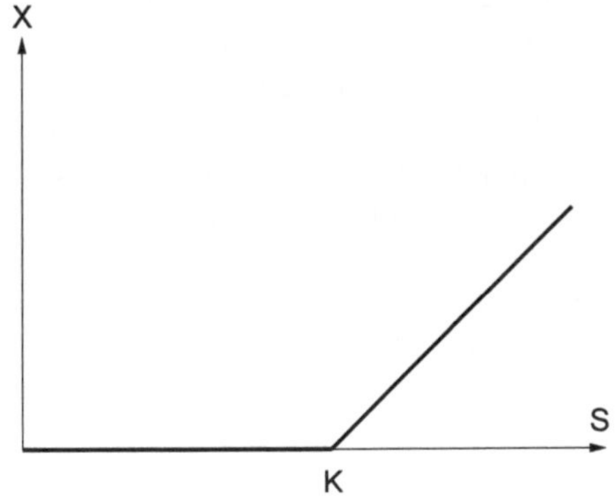

Figure 1.1: Payoff diagram for a European call option. For $S < K$, the option is not used. For $S > K$, the option is exercised and the amount $S - K$ is (indirectly) earned.

The question is now how to determine the price $\Pi(t,X)$ of the option at time $t=0$. Two reasonable answers come to mind:

1. It seems reasonable to price the option such that the value of the option equals expected value of the future incomes (properly discounted)

$$\Pi(0,X) = \beta \mathbf{E}^{\mathbb{P}}[X] \tag{1.5}$$

or equivalently

$$\frac{\Pi(0,X)}{B_0} = \mathbf{E}^{\mathbb{P}}\left[\frac{\Pi(1,X)}{B_1}\right] \tag{1.6}$$

where the $\beta = B_0/B_1 = 0.91$ is the discount factor determined by the bond prices. It is important to note that the paper with the deterministic price process, i.e., a paper where the price is known with certainty at all times, is used to determine the present value of the payoff function X at time $t=1$. We say that the future price ($t=1$) of the option is *discounted* to determine the present value ($t=0$) of this payoff. The discount factor β may be used to determine the so-called *implied interest rate* from the bond prices. We get the solution

$$\begin{aligned} \Pi(0,X) &= \beta\left(\mathbb{P}(\omega_1)(125-105)+\mathbb{P}(\omega_2)\cdot 0\right) \\ &= 0.91\,(0.8\cdot 20+0.2\cdot 0) = 14.5 \text{ DKK}. \end{aligned}$$

In other words, the value of the option is expressed in terms of the bond prices. In this case, we say that the bond is chosen as the *numeraire*.

2. From an economic point of view, it does not make any sense to talk about a correct price, because the price is determined by supply and demand on the market, and thus it depends on the perceptions of risk among the dealers on the market, which vary greatly among individuals as well as financial institutions.

As it will be shown later these answers are both right and wrong. Just to give the basic idea, the expected value in (1.5) should be taken with respect to another so called equivalent martingale measure $\mathbb{Q}$ than the objective probability measure $\mathbb{P}$ in order to obtain arbitrage-free prices, and this martingale measure is determined uniquely in complete markets and in incomplete markets by the market participants (although they are probably not aware of it). Besides these technicalities, it is obvious that the price should depend on the uncertainty in the markets. This uncertainty is usually called the *volatility* and it is associated with the standard deviation of the interest rates, foreign exchange rates or stock prices, e.g., pension funds tend to invest their members payments in bonds which are less volatile than stocks.

1.2 Financial derivatives — what's the big deal?

A large number of these exotic derivatives were developed by *quants* (a Wall Street jargon for quantitative analysts) in the 1980s, where money was moving around the world as never before. This may partly be explained by historical events: the demise of communism in Eastern Europe that expanded markets for investors, the progression towards free enterprise in China, the liberalization of economic policies in Latin America and the rapid economic growth of the countries in the Far East.

Trespassing in such unchartered markets is a very risky business for western European and American companies. It is very difficult to assess whether a newly established company in an Eastern European country is able to pay the promised amount. The inflation, interest and foreign exchange rates may vary enormously and in a manner that is essentially unpredictable. Thus, the demand for security blankets or financial derivatives that were particularly designed to protect companies against these uncertainties was high. Before 1973 all such derivative contracts were traded as "over-the-counter" (OTC) products, i.e., a new derivative contract was individually negotiated by a broker on behalf of two clients, one being the buyer and the other the seller. Trading on an official exchange began in 1973 on the Chicago Board Options Exchange (CBOE) with trading initially only in call options on some of the most heavily traded stocks. Nowadays options are traded as "off-the-shelf" products on all of the world's major exchanges. They are no longer restricted to stock options but include options on indices, futures, government bonds, commodities, currencies, etc. The OTC market stills exists, and specific options are written by institutions to meet a client's needs. This is where exotic options, such as Parisian, Asian, Barrier and multi-asset options are created; they are very rarely quoted on an exchange.

The fundamental advantage of derivatives is that you can buy the risk that you want and eliminate (or *hedge*) the risk you do not want. Because there are two sides of each transaction, one party will pass along the risk he or she does not want to someone who wants to speculate. This also explains that derivatives can be both conservative and highly speculative investments. Hedging is used to spread the risk, but the implemented hedging strategies generate interlocking commitments of trillions of dollars in a kind of *financial cyberspace*. If something goes wrong, it might spread fast due to the use of modern computers, and the entire market may crash like a house of cards. This has happened several times during the last decade, the most famous event being the *Flash Crash* that occurred on May 6, 2010. The Dow Jones Industrial Average plunged almost 9% only to recover the losses within minutes when many market participants realized something was seriously wrong with the market. Still crashes of this type causes a lot of trouble; see Easley et al. [2011] for a discussion.

It's one of the inherent paradoxes of derivatives that the market volatility increases when each market participant aims at minimizing the volatility of his portfolio.

Beside these speculative applications of financial derivatives, they may be very valuable for more productive enterprises. The basic idea is that you can buy, e.g., an option on a stock that you would like to purchase at some future date (maybe you do not have the money today) for only a limited amount of money compared to the actual price of the stock; but you can choose not to buy it if the price is not right.

Let us just for the sake of argument disregard the fact that the usual expected value of future payments is not an appropriate mean of computing the price of a European call option.

Example 1.1 (Leverage). *Assume that an investor would like to purchase an AP Møller stock in six months' time. He or she writes an European call option on the stock with exercise date T (in six months) and exercise price 250p.*[1]

If the AP Møller stock costs 270p at time T, then the investor would be able to purchase the stock for the exercise price 250p. Thus he has immediately made a profit of 20p, i.e., he or she can exercise the option and buy the stock at 250p and sell at the market value of 270p (assuming that there are no transaction costs associated with these trades). On the other hand, if the AP Møller stock is only worth 230p at time T, with equal probability, then the expected profit to be made is

$$\frac{1}{2}\cdot 0+\frac{1}{2}\cdot 20 = 10p$$

Ignoring interest rates for the moment, it seems reasonable that the order of magnitude for the value of the option is 10p.

Of course, valuing an option is not as simple as this, but let us suppose that the holder did indeed pay 10p for this option. Now if the stock price rises to 270p at expiry the investor has made a net profit of

profit on exercise	=	*20p*
cost of option	=	*-10p*
net profit	=	*10p*

This net profit of 10p is 100% of the upfront premium (the price paid at $t = 0$). The downside of this speculation is that if the stock price is less than 250p at expiry, the investor has lost all of the 10p invested in the option, giving a loss of 100%. If the investor had instead purchased the stock for 250p at time $t = 0$, the corresponding profit or loss of 20p would have been only ±8% of the original investment. Option prices thus respond in an exaggerated way to changes in the underlying asset price. This effect is called leverage.

Thus the price of the option may grossly affect the expected profit, and the idea behind *hedging* is to fence off the risk and avoid paying the price of the option by *option replication*. That is, we construct a collection or *a portfolio* of papers (stocks, bonds and money accounts in the bank) such that we get the same payoff diagram of this portfolio as the one associated with the call option without actually buying the option. Option replication may also be used to construct a portfolio that is less volatile (risky) than the original portfolio. In other words, the option is essentially redundant, and this observation will be

[1] This is short for pence, but the choice of unit ($, DKK, etc.) is not important for the argument.

used for valuation, because the price of the option should be the same as the price of the replicating portfolio.

The moral is that financial derivatives should be used with caution, but there are obvious advantages associated with their use. Otherwise they probably would not exist!

This discussion should demonstrate that there a number of important questions of technical interest that need to be addressed:

- *Identification:* We need statistical methods to identify the structure of the models from time series data, mathematical concepts to analyze these models and the statistical tools to apply these models to observed data sets. One of the most important concepts is the volatility.
- *Volatility:* We need to assess the volatility, i.e., we need to model the stock prices, foreign exchange rates, etc. such that we can quantify the market and portfolio volatility using statistical estimation methods.
- *Valuation:* We need to define markets where existing and new derivatives may be priced consistently.
- *Interest rates:* It should be clear by now that the interest rate plays a fundamental role in determining the present value of future payments. Thus we need to estimate the interest rates at these future dates using the information that is available today. The bond market is used to express the market participants' expectations and the future interest rates are derived from the bond prices. Hence, the modelling of bond prices and interest rates are inherently important.

1.3 Stylized facts

Financial data have some pretty universal properties that differ from what we know about data in physics, biology or engineering.

There are several nice papers summarizing these stylized facts (Rydén et al. [1998], Cont [2001]). The most commonly mentioned are

- No Autocorrelation in returns
- Unconditional heavy tails
- Gain/Loss asymmetry
- Aggregational Gaussianity
- Volatility clustering
- Conditional heavy tails
- Significant autocorrelation for absolute value of the returns
- Leverage effects

We evaluate these claims on daily OMXS30 data from 1991–2014. The OMXS30 is an index composed of the 30 largest companies on the Swedish Stock market.

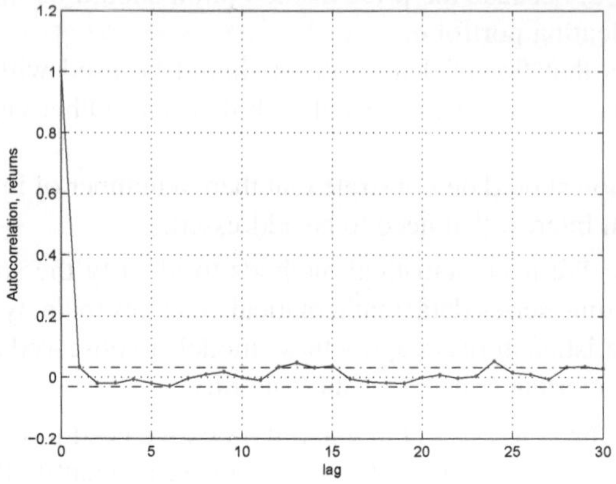

Figure 1.2: Sample autocorrelation for returns on the OMXS30 (solid line) and 95% confidence bands.

1.3.1 No autocorrelation in returns

There is very little (linear) autocorrelation in returns (Figure 1.2). This feature may not be surprising as investors being able to predict future values of assets would trade to benefit from the predictions. They would make a profit (on average) at the expense of their counterparties, who would then revise their forecasts or lose more money. The only long time surviving investors would be those who are able to predict well and revise their forecasts when new informations arrives.

Still some autocorrelation is often found in the first lags, due to trading friction, etc.

1.3.2 Unconditional heavy tails

The Gaussian distribution may be fine for many applications, but it does not represent the unconditional distribution of returns well. Large and extreme events are much more common than predicted by the normal distribution (Figure 1.3).

1.3.3 Gain/loss asymmetry

It is often claimed that losses are bigger in absolute value than gains (Figure 1.4). The losses (compared to the overall upward sloping trend) are bigger in amplitude and shorter in duration than the gains.

This would be consistent with risk averse investors and the leverage effect discussed below.

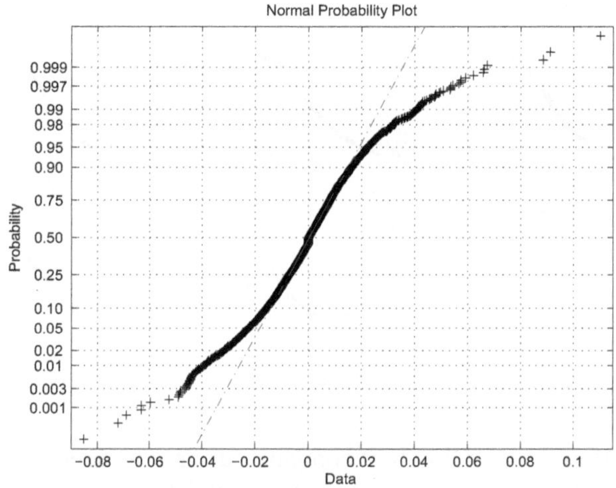

Figure 1.3: QQ-plot for the unconditional returns on the OMXS30.

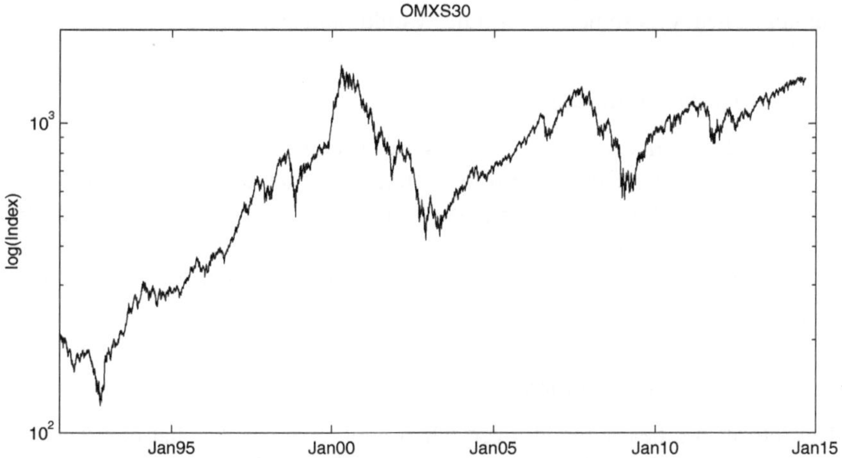

Figure 1.4: The evolution of the logarithm of OMXS30 between 1991 and 2014. Notice that losses are bigger and more rare than the gains.

1.3.4 Aggregational Gaussianity

Returns computed over long time periods are more Gaussian than returns computed for short time periods (Figure 1.5). The return over a long period can be written as a sum of returns over shorter periods. That suggests, under some conditions, that the return over long periods should become increasingly Gaussian.

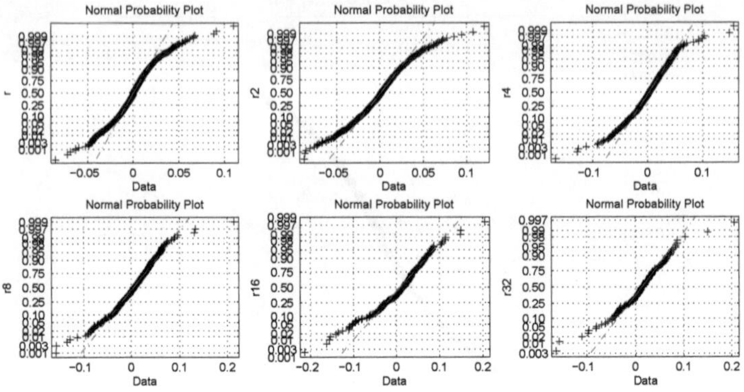

Figure 1.5: Returns the OMXS30 computed using one week (r), two weeks ($r2$), four, eight, sixteen and thirty-two weeks of data.

This Central limit theorem type behavior indicates that the tails are heavy, but not as heavy as some early studies would indicate.

1.3.5 Volatility clustering

The volatility in linear Gaussian time series is constant, meaning that the variability is the same. This is not true for financial data, as we are experiencing calm periods and more volatile periods (Figure 1.6). Time varying volatility contributes to the heavy tails.

Modeling time varying volatility is an important topic, and is covered in Chapter 5.

1.3.6 Conditional heavy tails

The returns are heavy-tailed, even when applying a model that compensates for the time varying volatility; cf. Figure 1.7. Events like earthquakes are extremely difficult to forecast, meaning that the volatility is going to be underestimated by virtually any volatility model during days when big unexpected events occur.

1.3.7 Significant autocorrelation for absolute returns

The volatility clustering clearly shows that returns $\{r(t)\}$ are not independent and identically distributed, *iid*. Computing the autocorrelation for $|r(t)|$ or $r^2(t)$ reveals a different story (Figure 1.8). The effect can be found for power transformations of the absolute returns $|r(t)|^\theta$, $\theta > 0$ but is most pronounced when $\theta = 1$. This is known as the *Taylor effect* (e.g., Granger and Ding [1995]).

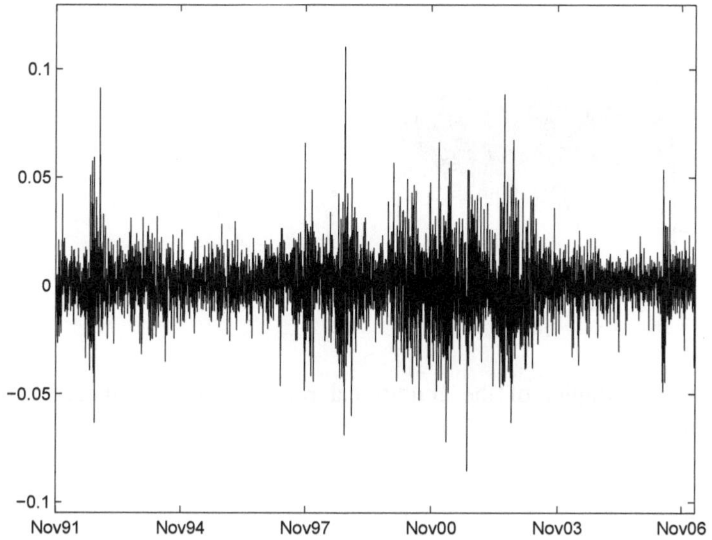

Figure 1.6: Returns of the OMXS30. It is clear that the variability varies over time.

There is a significant dependence in the volatility (ranging for at least 150 days), perhaps even long range dependence. Recent studies, however (e.g., Nystrup et al. [2014]), indicate that this is probably not the case, but rather due to lack of stationarity. This would also explain why the dependence does not drop to zero at any point in the Figure.

1.3.8 Leverage effects

The leverage effects are really due to bookkeeping in firms. A company experiencing bad times will either take up additional debt or live off savings. The financial status will deteriorate in either case, resulting in additional uncertainty in future earnings. A decrease in stock price means that the company is more leveraged since the relative value of their debt rises with respect to their equity. The effect due to good news on the other hand is rarely of the same magnitude as that of bad news (Christie [1982], for a through discussion).

All of this results in a negative correlation between returns and the volatility, known as the leverage effect. Several models in Chapter 5 will take this stylized fact into account.

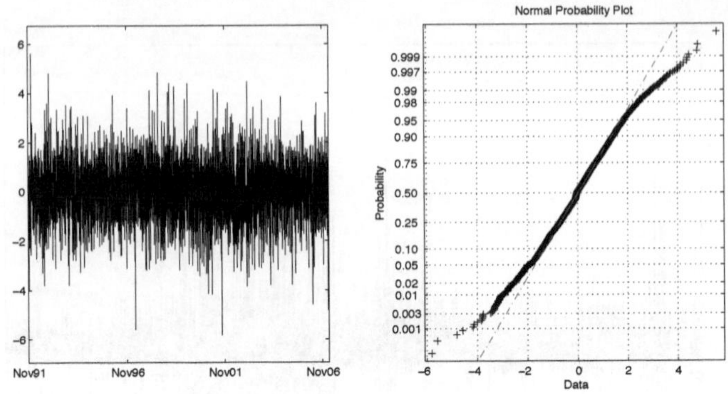

Figure 1.7: Normplot of the conditional returns when prefiltered using a GARCH(1,1) model.

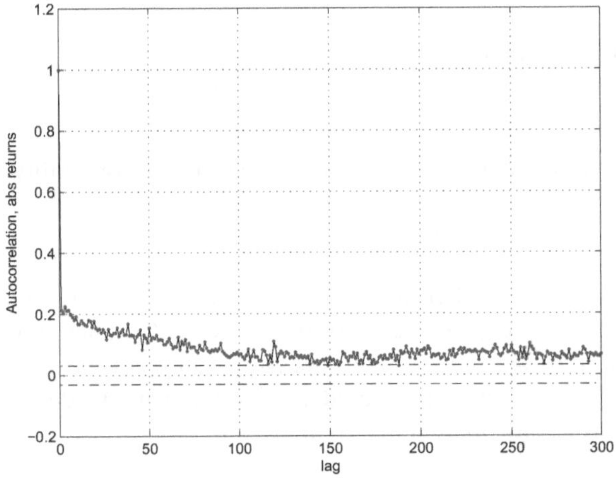

Figure 1.8: Sample autocorrelation for the absolute values of the returns, $|r(t)|$, showing significant dependence.

1.4 Overview

Now that we have established some of the fundamental terms in mathematical finance, we will sketch the contents of the remainder of this book.

Chapter 2, Fundamentals, will discuss applications of financial derivatives with respect to risk assessment and elimination. Some methods for computing the net present value of a future cash flow will be described using discount factors. Finally, continuously compounded interest rates, which provide the foundation of the remainder of the text, will be introduced.

Chapter 3, Discrete time finance, will introduce the concepts of arbitrage, probability measure transformations, self-financing portfolios and martingales in a simple financial market.

Chapter 4, Linear time series models, briefly reviews linear time series models and methods.

Chapter 5, Nonlinear time series models, extends the theory to nonlinear and/or nonstationary time series. An overview of a number of model classes is given. Emphasis will be placed on a description of the variance structure as the variance of, e.g., interest rates varies with time and depends on the current level of the interest rate. Such heteroscedastic behaviour cannot be described by linear models.

Chapter 6, Kernel estimators in time series analysis, describes some statistical methods for identification of discrete and continuous-time models of interest rates, foreign exchange rates, stock prices and other financial time series.

Chapter 7, Stochastic calculus, discusses the problem of introducing stochasticity in mathematical modelling of dynamical systems by means of the Wiener process. Focus is placed on Itō stochastic calculus.

Chapter 8, Stochastic differential equations, introduces stochastic differential equations (SDEs) and the important Itō formula is presented. The Feynman–Kac representation theorems establish a link between parabolic partial differential equations and SDEs, which may be used as a mean of computing prices of financial derivates and solving SDEs. Finally the Girsanov measure transformation is introduced. The concepts in this chapter may be used in many other areas of the natural and technical sciences.

Chapter 9, Continuous time security markets, provides a set of theoretical tools that makes it possible to determine the arbitrage-free price of the large variety of financial derivatives that are traded on the international markets. The celebrated Black & Scholes model is covered in detail, and a number of sensitivity parameters (the so called "Greeks") are discussed.

Chapter 10, Stochastic interest rate models, uses the concepts of the previous chapter to describe a number of famous interest rate models.

Chapter 11, The term structure of interest rates, discusses the valuation of bonds. Bonds are essentially simple options, but they are tremendeously important for estimating the interest rate over a long period of time. This is called the term structure of interest rates and it provides the foundation for computing the present value of future payments.

Chapter 12, Discrete time approximations, provides sampling or discretization schemes for computing a discrete-time approximation of SDEs, which is required in the following chapters.

Chapter 13, Parameter estimation in discretely observed SDEs, introduces a very general maximum likelihood method for parameter estimation in continuous/discrete-time state space models. In addition the generalized method-of-moments (GMM) is discussed. The last method encompasses both the well-known method-of-moments and nonlinear least squares methods.

Chapter 14, Inference in Partially Observed Processes, provides a considerable extension of the estimation methods listed above which makes it possible to estimate parameters in multidimensional state space models (e.g., multifactor interest rate models). The Kalman filter is introduced for linear and nonlinear continuous-time models. The topics covered in this chapter are of general interest.

Appendix A, Projections in Hilbert spaces, provides a unified introduction to a number of filtering and estimation methods, which may geometrically be viewed as projections in Hilbert spaces.

Appendix B, Probability theory, covers the fundamentals of probability theory from a measure-theoretical point of view.

Each chapter is closed with a number of problems that should support and extend the material covered in the text. It is advised to solve as many problems as possible while reading the text. Some problems in the early chapters require very little mathematical skill and are intended to develop your intuition for financial reasoning, which will be very important in later chapters, where the mathematical concepts are significantly more difficult.

Chapter 2

Fundamentals

A first-time home buyer is typically not able to pay the price of the new home up front, but will have to borrow against future income using the house as collateral. A company which sees a profitable investment opportunity may not have sufficient funds to launch the project (buy new machines, hire employees) and will seek to raise capital by issuing stocks and/or borrowing money from a bank. The home buyer and the company are both in need of money to invest now and are confident that they will earn enough in the future to pay back loans that they might receive.

Conversely, a pension fund receives payments from members and promises to pay a certain pension once their members retire. Insurance companies receive premiums on insurance contracts and deliver a promise of future payments in the case of property damage or other unpleasant events which people are willing to insure themselves against. The pension fund and the insurance company are both looking for profitable ways of placing current income in a way which provides income in the future.

Either way, a key role of financial markets is to find efficient ways of connecting the demand for capital with the supply of capital. The above examples should illustrate the desire of various economic agents to substitute income intertemporally (between now and some time in the future). Thus the chief mechanism by which the markets allocate capital is determined through prices. Prices govern the flow of capital.

The example on page 4 showed that interest rates play a fundamental role in the valuation of financial derivatives as interest rates are used to determine the *present value* of transactions, which will take place in the future, or the *future value* of some investments made today.

Even though the concept of interest rates is familiar to most people, the interest rate is not generally directly observable in the financial markets. Short term interest rates are quoted on a daily basis in the money markets for maturities up to approximately one year, but longer term interest rates are traded only indirectly through the bond market.

However, a lot of concepts need to be clarified before delving into this fundamental relationship between interest and (bond) prices from both a theoretical and practical point of view, but we will get back to that in later chapters.

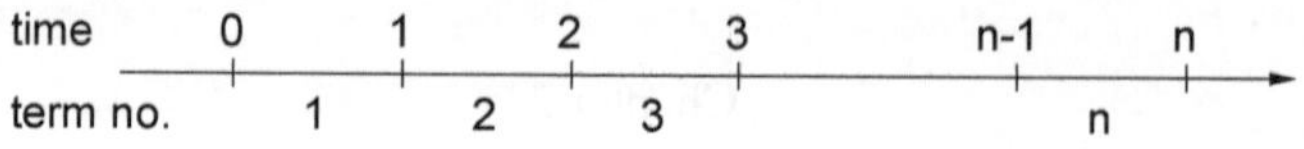

Figure 2.1: Naming conventions for terms.

2.1 Interest rates

Basically, an *interest rate* is the payment that the borrower (debtor) pays to the lender (creditor) at the end of each term for the right to use an amount that rightfully belongs to the lender.

A *term* is some time interval measured in days, months or years. The terms are numbered as shown in Figure 2.1. Usually transactions between the borrower and the lender are only made at the predetermined terms.

The rate of interest of one unit of account (e.g., 1 DKK) is called the interest rate, and it will henceforth be denoted by r. If $r = 0.06$, the borrower should pay the lender 0.06 unit of account at the end of the term per borrowed unit of account. Informally, the interest rate is the price of money.

In the following, we will assume that i) the interest rate r is deterministic and constant, ii) the number of terms n is a positive integer, iii) the interest rate is added to the capital instead of paid out at the end of the term and iv) the compounded interest is treated as the original amount.

2.1.1 *Future and present value of a single payment*

Assume that an initial capital c_0 is deposited in a bank account with the interest rate r in n terms. It is fairly obvious that the *future value* of this account is

$$c_n = c_0(1+r)^n. \tag{2.1}$$

Example 2.1 (Savings account). *Assume that a student deposits 1000 DKK in a savings account with the annual interest rate $r = 0.12$. Assuming that there are no taxes, this amounts to in 10 years' time*

$$1000 \cdot (1+0.06)^{10} = 1790.85 \; DKK\,.$$

Assuming that the semiannual interest rate is $r = 0.03$, we get

$$1000 \cdot (1.03)^{20} = 1806.11 \; DKK\,.$$

Notice the difference between these two results, which is due to the fact that the annual rate is not just twice the semiannual rate. For a semiannual rate of 3% the annual rate will be

$$((1.03)^2 - 1) \cdot 100\% = 6.09\%.$$

Please refer to Section 2.3 for a further discussion.

Assume that we are promised c_n unit of accounts at time n. The *present value* or *discounted value* of this amount at time 0 is

$$c_0 = c_n(1+r)^{-n}. \tag{2.2}$$

The factor $(1+r)^{-1}$ is called the *discount factor.*

Example 2.2. *Assume that you are promised 50000 DKK in 2 years' time and that the annual rate is $r = 0.06$. The present value is*

$$50000 \cdot (1+0.06)^{-2} = 44499.82 \; DKK \, .$$

2.1.2 Annuities

An *annuity* is defined as a series of equal payments that are due at some equidistant payment dates. Each payment consists of a *principal* and an *interest.* The principal accounts for the actual loan, whereas the interest accounts for the expenses associated with the loan. As we shall see in the following, Danish Government bonds and house loans, etc., are examples of annuities.

Consider an annuity with n terms. The duration of an annuity is the time elapsed from the time the loan contract has been negotiated to the last payment has been made (the n'th term). The first payments consist mainly of the principal, whereas the last payments consist mostly of the interest. Do note that the n payments are equal, but the distribution between principal and interest varies with time. The first payment of unit of account is made at the end of the first term.

2.1.3 Future value of an annuity

In the following, we will need the well-known result.

Proposition 2.1 (Finite geometric series)**.** *The sum of a finite geometric series in q is*

$$\sum_{i=0}^{n-1} q^i = 1 + q^1 + q^2 + \ldots + q^{(n-1)} = \begin{cases} \frac{1-q^n}{1-q} & \text{if } q \neq 1 \\ n & \text{if } q = 1. \end{cases} \tag{2.3}$$

Proof. By direct calculation, we get for $q \neq 1$

$$\sum_{i=0}^{n-1} q^i = \sum_{i=0}^{n-1} q^i \frac{1-q}{1-q} = \frac{1-q^n}{1-q}$$

where we used that the terms in the telescopic sum cancel out. Computing the sum when $q = 1$ is simply adding n terms. □

Theorem 2.1 (Future value of a unit annuity)**.** *The future value of a unit annuity as specified above is given by*

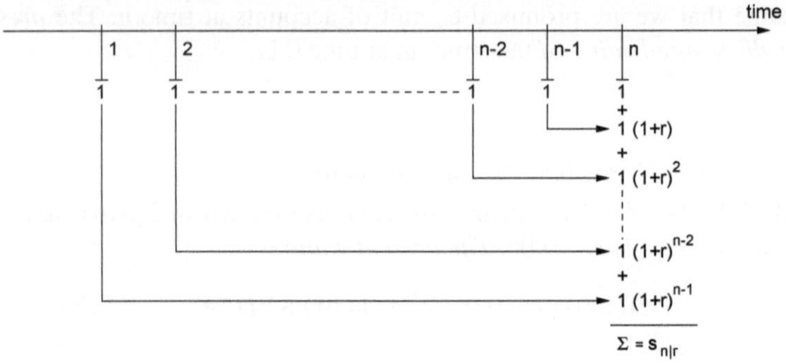

Figure 2.2: The evaluation of the future value of an annuity.

$$s_{n|r} = \begin{cases} \frac{(1+r)^n - 1}{r} & \text{if } r \neq 0 \\ n & \text{if } r = 0. \end{cases} \tag{2.4}$$

Proof. By referring to Figure 2.2, where all payments are transferred to time n using the interest rate r, we get

$$\begin{aligned} c_n &= s_{n|r} = 1 + 1(1+r) + 1(1+r)^2 + \ldots + 1(1+r)^{n-1} \\ &= \begin{cases} \frac{(1+r)^n - 1}{(1+r) - 1} & \text{if } r \neq 0 \\ n & \text{if } r = 0 \end{cases} \end{aligned} \tag{2.5}$$

where we have used Equation (2.3).

□

Corollary 2.1 (Future value of an annuity)**.** *The future value of an annuity with equal payments c per term is*

$$c_n = c s_{n|r}. \tag{2.6}$$

Proof. Follows readily from (2.5) by replacing the unit payments by payments of amount c. □

2.1.4 Present value of a unit annuity

Let us again consider an annuity with unit of account payments with a duration of n terms and a constant interest rate r.

Theorem 2.2 (Present value of a unit annuity)**.** *The present value of an annuity as specified above is*

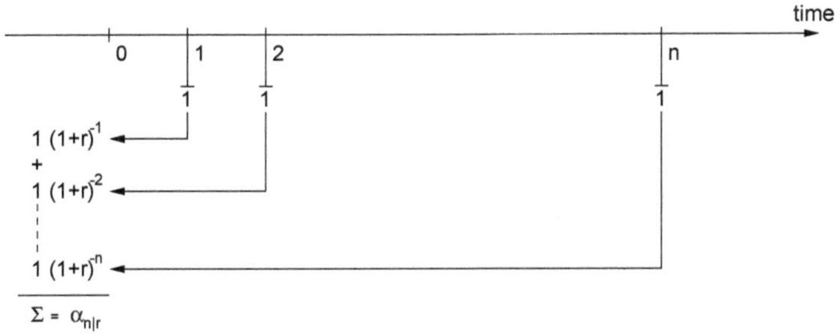

Figure 2.3: The evaluation of the present value of an annuity.

$$\alpha_{n|r} = \frac{1-(1+r)^{-n}}{r} = \frac{(1+r)^n - 1}{(1+r)^n \cdot r} \qquad r \neq 0 \tag{2.7}$$

where $\alpha_{n|r}$ is called the annuity discount factor.

Proof. By referring to Figure 2.3, where all the payments are transferred to time 0, we get

$$\begin{aligned} c_0 = \alpha_{n|r} &= 1(1+r)^{-1} + 1(1+r)^{-2} + \ldots + 1(1+r)^{-n} \qquad (2.8) \\ &= (1+r)^{-1}[1+(1+r)^{-1} + \ldots + (1+r)^{-(n-1)}] \\ &= (1+r)^{-1}\frac{1-(1+r)^{-n}}{1-(1+r)^{-1}} \qquad r \neq 0 \end{aligned}$$

using Equation (2.3).

□

Corollary 2.2 (Present value of an annuity). *The present value of an annuity with equal payments of c units of account is*

$$c_0 = c\alpha_{n|r}. \tag{2.9}$$

Proof. Follows readily from (2.7). □

Table 2.1 shows how $\alpha_{n|r}$ varies with n and r, where $1/r$ is called the *capitalization factor*.

2.2 Cash flows

In this section we will extend the annuities (with equal payments) from the previous section to more general *cash flows*, where the payments at time i,

	$\alpha_{n\|r}$
$n \to \infty$	$1/r$
$r \to 0$	n
$r \to \infty$	0

Table 2.1: Important limiting values of $\alpha_{n|r}$.

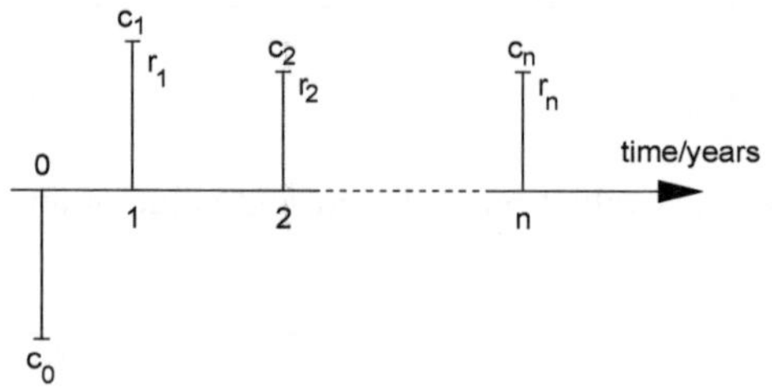

Figure 2.4: Naming conventions for cash flows and interest rates.

$i = 1, \ldots, n$, and the interest rates r_i may differ. Consider the cash flow diagram in Figure 2.4, which should be interpreted as follows: An initial investment c_0 is made at time $t = 0$. At time $t = 1$, an income c_1 is obtained, which should be discounted with the interest rate r_1 to determine its present value, at time $t = 2$, the income c_2 should be discounted with the interest rate r_2 for two time periods, etc.

Theorem 2.3 (Present Value and Future Value). *The present value (PV) of a cash flow* $\mathbf{c} = (c_1, \ldots, c_n)'$ *discounted by the interest rates* $\mathbf{r} = (r_1, \ldots, r_n)'$*, where n is the number of time periods, is*

$$PV(\mathbf{c}, \mathbf{r}) = \sum_{i=1}^{n} \frac{c_i}{(1+r_i)^i}. \tag{2.10}$$

The future value (FV) is given by

$$FV(\mathbf{c}, \mathbf{r}) = \sum_{i=1}^{n} c_i \cdot (1+r_i)^{n-i}. \tag{2.11}$$

Example 2.3 (Duration). *Let* $FV(\mathbf{c}, r, N)$ *denote the (future) value of the cash flow* $\mathbf{c}$ *at time N if the interest rate is fixed at level r. Then*

$$\begin{aligned} FV(\mathbf{c}, r, N) &= (1+r)^N PV(\mathbf{c}, r) & (2.12) \\ &= \sum_{i=1}^{N-1} c_i (1+r)^{N-i} + c_N \\ &\quad + \sum_{i=N+1}^{N} \frac{c_i}{(1+r)^{i-N}}. & (2.13) \end{aligned}$$

A reasonable question to pose is how a change in the interest rate immediately after time 0 will affect $FV(\mathbf{c}, r, N)$. There are important effects with opposite directions which influence the risk.

1. *Reinvestment risk: Assuming that r decreases, the first expression in the sum (2.13) will decrease. This decrease is caused by reinvestment risk which is due to the fact that the payments up to time N will have to be reinvested at a lower interest rate.*
2. *Price risk: Conversely, the last sum in (2.13) will increase when the interest rate r decreases. When the interest rate decreases the payments after time N will be discounted by a smaller factor and thus the payments will be higher. The payment af time N, c_N, is unaffected by changes in the interest rate.*

Theorem 2.4 (Net Present Value (NPV)). *The net present value (NPV) is given by*

$$NPV(\mathbf{c}, \mathbf{r}) = \sum_{i=1}^{n} \frac{c_i}{(1+r)^i} - c_0. \tag{2.14}$$

Proof. Straightforward. □

Example 2.4. *Consider the following cash flow and interest rates:*

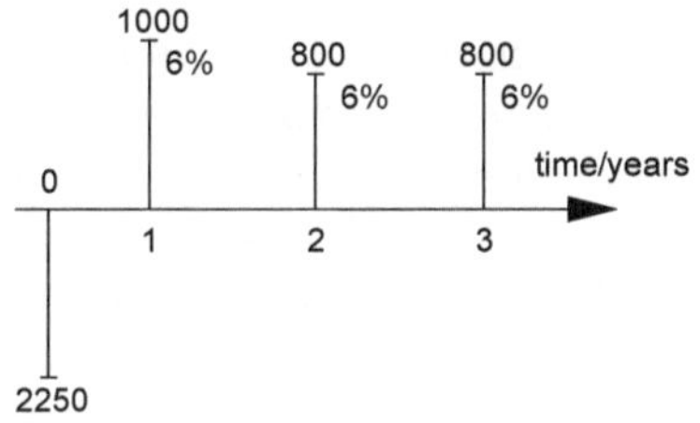

The present value is determined by (2.10)*;*

$$\begin{aligned} PV(\mathbf{c}, \mathbf{r}) &= \frac{1000}{1.06} + \frac{800}{(1.06)^2} + \frac{800}{(1.06)^3} \\ &= 943.40 + 712.00 + 671.70 = 2327.10 \end{aligned}$$

and the net present value follows from (2.14)

$$NPV(\mathbf{c}, \mathbf{r}) = PV(\mathbf{c}, \mathbf{r}) - c_0 = 2327.10 - 2250.00 = 77.10.$$

Thus by investing 2250 DKK we can make a profit of 77.10 DKK measured at time $t = 0$.

It is an interesting problem to determine the interest rate that implies that a given cash flow has the net present value 0. This implies that the present value of, e.g., a loan is zero such that it is merely an intertemporal substitution of money.

Definition 2.1 (Internal rate of return). *The internal rate of return (IRR) $y = IRR(c_0, \mathbf{c})$ of a cash flow $\mathbf{c}$ is a solution $y > -1$ of the equation*

$$c_0 = \sum_{i=1}^{n} \frac{c_i}{(1+y)^i}. \tag{2.15}$$

For $c_i > 0$, $i = 0, 1, \ldots, n$, the internal rate of return is called the yield.

Remark 2.1. *For a cash flow with both positive and negative future payments the IRR is not uniquely determined. In fact the polynomial* (2.15) *may have as many as $n-1$ roots. However, IRR is uniquely determined provided that the initial payment $c_0 > 0$ and $c_i > 0$, $i = 1, \ldots, n$.*

Remark 2.2. *Functions for determining $NPV(\mathbf{c}, \mathbf{r})$ and $IRR(c_0, \mathbf{c})$ for a given cash flow may be found in most spreadsheets, but can easily be computed using numerical methods (Quasi-Newton or Regula Falsi) in a general programming language.*

Example 2.5 (T-maturity bullet loan). *A T-maturity bullet loan with face value F and coupon rate c is essentially described by $\mathbf{c} = (cF, cF, \ldots, (1+c)F)'$.*

Assuming that the price of a bullet loan is given by $\pi = c_0$, we will show later that the internal rate of return y is not a reasonable choice of a discounting factor. It is unreasonable to assume that the interest rate will remain constant during the entire duration of the bond. The variation of the bond prices as a function of T is called the term structure of interest rates,[1] *and this subject will be studied in detail in later chapters. A primary goal will be to determine the interest rates $\mathbf{r}$ given an interest rate model and one (or possibly several) time series of bond prices.*

Note that an internal rate of return is defined without referring to the underlying term structure. The internal rate of return describes the level of a flat term structure (i.e., a constant interest rate) at which the NPV of the cash flow is 0.

An application of the internal rate of return in capital budgeting is to compare some projects that one may wish to initiate in order to choose the most profitable. When this criterion is used the better project is the one with the highest IRR. Another way of choosing among alternative projects could be to compare their net present values.

[1] A constant interest rate implies that the term structure is flat.

2.3 Continuously compounded interest rates

As the financial markets around the world trade continuously, a more frequent quotation (than on, say, a daily basis) of interest rates is called for. Thus we will introduce continuously compounded interest rates, i.e., interest rates in continuous time, which will be used extensively in the remainder of the text.

Assume that we deposit 1 000 DKK in a bank account with an annual rate of 6%. If the interest rate is calculated at the end of the year, the bank account will contain

$$FV = 1000 \cdot (1+0.06)^1 = 1060 \text{ DKK}$$

where (2.2) have been used.

Now assume that a semiannual rate of 6%/2=3% is added twice a year

$$FV = 1000 \cdot (1+0.03)^2 = 1060.90 \text{ DKK}.$$

If a quarterly rate of 6%/4=1.5% is used, we get

$$FV = 1000 \cdot (1+0.015)^4 = 1061.36 \text{ DKK}$$

and, if we use a monthly rate of 1% each month, we get

$$FV = 1000 \cdot (1+0.005)^{12} = 1061.68 \text{ DKK}.$$

Note that the number of interest additions during a year gives rise to a higher future value of our deposit although the annual rate remains the same.

In general, assume that the annual rate is fixed at r and that we add interest n times during a year. The future value of our deposit c_0 at time 0 will in a year be

$$FV = c_0 \left(1 + \frac{r}{n}\right)^n$$

which readily follows from the previous computations.

It is an interesting problem to determine the *compounded interest* if we let the number of interest additions tend to infinity. This implies that interest is added to your account at the end of every infinitesimally small time interval during the entire year.

Theorem 2.5 (Continuously compounded interest rate). *Let n denote the number of interest additions to an account with a fixed annual interest rate r and a unit deposit at time 0. The continuously compounded interest rate is given by*

$$\lim_{n\to\infty} \left(1 + \frac{r}{n}\right)^n = e^r \tag{2.16}$$

Proof. Consider the function

$$f(n) = \left(1+\frac{r}{n}\right)^n = \exp\left\{n\log\left(1+\frac{r}{n}\right)\right\} = \exp(g(n)).$$

Introduce the change of variable $t = \frac{1}{n}$ in $g(n)$ such that

$$g\left(\frac{1}{t}\right) = \frac{\log(1+rt)}{t}.$$

A first-order Taylor expansion of $\log(1+rt)$ yields

$$\frac{rt+o(t)}{t} \to r \text{ for } t \to 0^+.$$

This implies that $f(n) \to e^r$ for $n \to \infty$. □

Let us illustrate the use of the continuously compounded interest rate with a couple of examples.

Example 2.6. *Assume that you deposit 1 DKK in the bank at the continuously compounded interest rate r at time 0. The future value at time t is then* e^{rt}.

If you wish to use 1 DKK at time t you should deposit e^{-rt} *at time 0.*

Example 2.7. *Assume that you deposit 1 DKK on a bank account with the annual rate 6%. A year later this will be worth 1.06 DKK. The corresponding continuously compounded interest rate is then*

$$1.06 = e^r \quad \Leftrightarrow \quad r = \ln(1.06) = 0.0586 = 5.86\%.$$

This computation illustrates that one should carefully note whether it is the annual rate (a discrete time entity) or the annualized continuously compounded interest rate that is given in problems and other sources of information.

In the following we will need to be able to discount some amount C at time $t = T$ back to time t.

Let $M(t)$ denote the contents of a bank account with the continuously compounded interest rate r. At some time $t = T$, we know that the bank deposit will be C, and we need to determine its value at time t, $0 \leq t \leq T$.

The bank deposit will exhibit exponential growth with the growth rate r

$$\frac{\mathrm{d}M}{M} = r\mathrm{d}t \tag{2.17}$$

which has the solution

$$M(t) = ce^{rt} \tag{2.18}$$

where c is some constant. Using that $M(T) = C$, we get

$$M(t) = Ce^{-r(T-t)}. \tag{2.19}$$

Assuming that the continuously compounded interest rate varies deterministically with time, we get

$$M(t) = C\exp\left(-\int_t^T r(s)\mathrm{d}s\right). \tag{2.20}$$

We will also need to be able to determine the future value of some amount using the continuously compounded interest rate. For this purpose we introduce

Definition 2.2 (Money account). *The money account process is defined by*

$$B(t) = \exp\left(\int_0^t r(s)\mathrm{d}s\right) \tag{2.21}$$

or

$$\mathrm{d}B(t) = r(t)B(t)\mathrm{d}t \tag{2.22}$$
$$B(0) = 1 \tag{2.23}$$

where $r(t)$ denotes the continuously compounded interest rate at time t.

The money account is simply a formal way of saying "money in the bank," because the amount $B(t)$ is compounded continuously with the interest rate $r(t)$. Note, in particular, that the interest rate may be described by a stochastic process, and that we just plug in a given sample path of the interest rate in (2.21). By reverting the time in (2.21) (in which case we get (2.20)), it also serves as a simple model of bonds, such as Danish Government bonds or US Treasury bills.

2.4 Interest rate options: caps and floors

So far we have assumed interest rates to be deterministic, but this is clearly at odds with reality. Consider, e.g., the Copenhagen InterBank Offered Rate (CIBOR) in Figure 2.5, which is the interest rate banks use when they loan or borrow money from one another. These rates are quoted for a number of maturity dates, i.e., they are interest rates associated with loans on a 1, 3 or 6 months basis.

Referring to Figure 2.5, the first 600 observations (1/2 1990 to 1/7 1992) of the interest rates fluctuate around approximately 10% with slightly higher values at both ends of the period. Following this stable period, the currency turmoil begins in the fall of 1992. First, the pound drops out of the EMS (European Monetary System) on 22/9 1992 where the CIBOR 1M[2] is set at 35%,

[2]CIBOR 1M is short for the one-month CIBOR time series, etc.

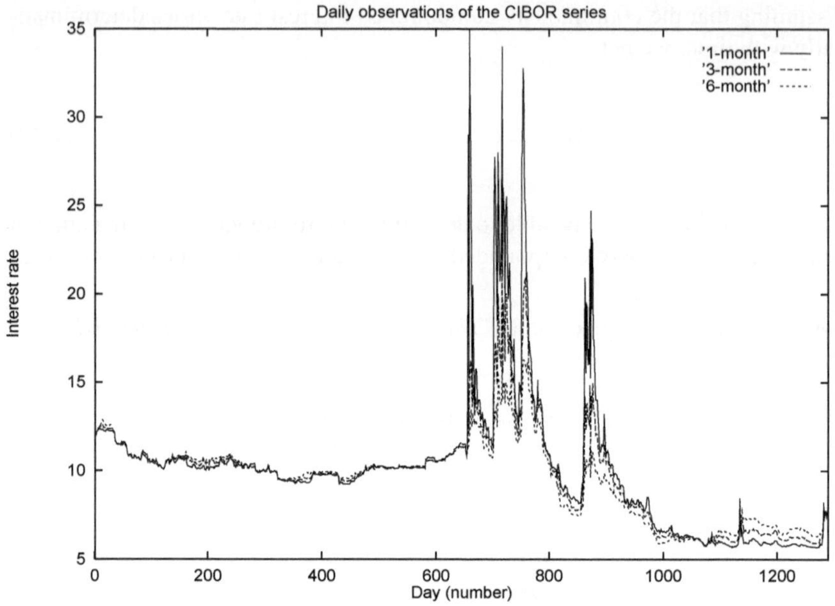

Figure 2.5: The complete data set for the period 1/2 1990 to 20/3 1995.

whereas the CIBOR 3M and 6M equal 14.875% and 12%, respectively. In November 1992, the international currency traders turned their attention towards the Scandinavian currencies. The first attack was on the Finnish markka on 8th September, that also influenced the Norwegian and Swedish currencies. This was followed by devaluations of the Italian lire on 14th September and the Spanish peseta on 17th September and the pound dropping out of the EMS on 22th September. Attention was the redirected towards the scandinavian currencies again, with the Swedish krona floating from 19th November an attacks on the Norwegian krone peaking at 23rd November (this is the first peak in Figure 2.5). The speculation continued through the year (the second cluster of peaks in Figure 2.5) with a third cluster in 2013. These attacks are easily seen in the group of observations numbered around 700–750, i.e., November-December 1992. The first peak on the November 11, 1992 was due to an attack on the Finnish markka, the second peak concerns the Norwegian Krone December 12 and finally attention was turned to the Swedish Krona around December 11. On this date, the CIBOR 1M was raised to 34%. During this period the National Banks in the Scandinavian countries spent large amounts of money trying to defend their currencies. Later, in February 1993, the Danish Krone came under attack and the CIBOR 1M was raised to 32.75% on February 8.

Following this turmoil, the interest rates drop exponentially until the

French Franc is brought into focus during July and August 1993, where the CIBOR 1M is raised to 24.7% on August 3, 1993. Although the figures in this last period do not seem to be as externally determined as the previous periods of currency turmoil, which might indicate that a very high level of volatility is present in the series/markets, it is deemed that some interventions are made by the National Banks.

By considering the three time series as a collection of three-dimensional stochastic variables, the correlation structure of the time series is easily obtained:

$$[\rho_{ij}] = \begin{pmatrix} 1.0000 & 0.9356 & 0.8311 \\ 0.9356 & 1.0000 & 0.9611 \\ 0.8311 & 0.9611 & 1.0000 \end{pmatrix}. \tag{2.24}$$

It is readily seen that the CIBOR interest rates for different maturities are strongly correlated, although it can be seen graphically that the correlation varies (decreases) over time. More specifically, the correlation between the interest rate was stronger prior to the events described in the text above.

Although some of the large variations in the CIBOR series may be explained by interventions from the National Banks, it is clear that market participants would like to protect themselves against such large variations in the interest rates. Indeed, a large number of *interest rate derivatives* have been derived with this application in mind. Some of these use the interest rate itself as the underlying asset. In the following we will consider two interest rate derivatives: The *cap* is a contract that can be used to protect a borrower against *floating* or stochastic interest rates being too high. A cap can be thought of as a series of interest rate options (these are called *caplets*.) Conversely, a *floor* is a contract that can be used to protect a lender against floating interest rates being too low.

Example 2.8 (A simple interest rate option). *We will consider a 6 Month European-style Call option on the 6 Month LIBOR*[3] *at a strike level of 8% and a face value of 10 Million USD. We will assume that this option costs 30 000 USD, which corresponds to 3% of the face value (or 30 basis points of the face value).*

Let us adapt a tabular form of specifying the details of the option:

Option type:	*European-style Call option*
Expiration date:	*6 Months (183 days)*
Underlying interest rate:	*6 Month LIBOR*
Strike level:	*8%*
Face value:	*10 Million USD*
Cost of the option:	*30 000 USD*
Current 6 month LIBOR interest rate:	*8%*

[3]LIBOR is short for London InterBank Offered Rate.

This call option gives the buyer the right but not the obligation to receive the difference between the 6 Month LIBOR interest rate (the underlying) prevailing in six months' time (the expiration date) and the 8% strike level, if the former happens to be greater. Thus the buyer of such an option receives a higher payoff as interest rates rise. The face value determines the size of the contract. The payoff function is as follows:

6 month LIBOR interest rate	*Call option payoff*
$\leq 8\%$	*0*
$>8\%$	$(r - 8\%) \cdot 182/360 \cdot$ *10 Million USD*

Thus, the payoff is determined by the difference between the actual interest rate r in 6 months (expressed as an annual rate in percent) and the strike level of 8%. This is multiplied by the actual number of days in the subsequent six months period as a proportion of the 360 days in a year (!), and the face value of the option. Note that this payoff is received on the maturity date of the underlying interest rate, i.e., 183+182=365 days from today. Thus, the current time ($t = 0$ days) is when the contract is written, the contract expires in 183 days and the payoff of the underlying face value will be received 365 days from today. Assuming that the actual interest rate in 183 days' time is 9%, the following payoff is obtained:

$$(9\% - 8\%) \cdot 182/360 \cdot 10 \textit{ Million USD } = 50555 \textit{ USD}$$

and this amount will be received 365 days from today. Let us compute the break-even point, i.e., the interest rate i, where the total borrowing cost would be the same with and without the call option. This is not the strike level of 8%, because we have to take the price of the option 30 000 USD into account.

Assuming that we didn't purchase the option, the cash flow on the repayment date of the loan of $10 million on the maturity date would be

$$10 \textit{ million USD } \cdot [1 + (i\% \cdot 182/360)].$$

Using the call option, the interest rate will be limited by the strike level. Thus the total payment on the loan on the maturity date would be

$$10 \textit{ million USD} \cdot [1 + (8\% \cdot 182/360)].$$

Recall that the option itself costs $30000 today, and we have to compute the future cost on the maturity date. The interest rate for the first six months (183 days) is known today, but the interest rate for the second six month period (182 days) is not known today. However this was denoted by i such that the compounded cost of the option is

$$30000 \, USD \cdot [1 + (8\% \cdot 183/360)][1 + (i\% \cdot 182/360)].$$

Thus the break-even point may be found from the equation

$$\begin{aligned}&10\ \textit{million USD}\cdot[1+(i\%\cdot 182/360)] =\\&10\ \textit{million USD}\ \cdot[1+(8\%\cdot 182/360)]\\&+30000\ USD\cdot[1+(8\%\cdot 183/360)][1+(i\%\cdot 182/360)].\end{aligned}$$

By solving this with respect to i, we get

$$i = 8.64\%.$$

This implies that the option starts to pay if the interest rate at the expiration date exceeds 8.64%. If the interest rate is lower at the expiration date, we would have been better off without the option.

An interest rate cap is a series of European call options. Let us consider an example.

Example 2.9 (Caps). *We consider a 5 year cap on 6 month LIBOR at 8% with a face value of 100 million USD*

Option type:	*Interest rate cap*
Term:	*5 years*
Underlying interest rate:	*6 Month LIBOR*
Reset dates:	*January 13, July 13*
Strike level:	*8%*
Trade date:	*January 13*
Settlement date:	*January 15*
Underlying amount:	*100 Million USD*
Upfront fee:	*3 million USD*

Essentially we wish to borrow 100 million USD and protect ourselves against interest rates above 8%. This protection is obtained by purchasing a cap at the cost of 3 million USD. Assume that we wish to pay this amount as a stream of periodic payments. Since the term of the cap is 5 years, there are 10 periods of 6 months involved. However, since the interest rate for the first period is known today, we need not purchase an option on this rate. Hence there are 9 options in the cap (each of these is called caplets) with payoffs to be determined on the reset dates: January 13 and July 13. The stream of periodic payments may be considered as a cash flow which should be balanced against the upfront fee of $3 million. Using a semiannual rate of 4%, we could determine the size of the 9 payments using (2.7)

$$c = \frac{c_0}{\alpha_{n|r}} = \frac{3\,000\,000}{\alpha_{9|4\%}} = \frac{3\,000\,000}{\frac{(1.04)^9-1}{(1.04)^9\cdot 0.04}} = 403\,479\ USD.$$

Thus we should pay 403 479 USD every 6 months for the next 4.5 years. However, these payments were computed under the assumption of equal interest rates during this period. We have to consider the multiperiod scenario of the cap spanning over 4.5 years, where the interest rate will be floating or vary randomly. If this is taken into account the payoffs from the cap depend on the whole sequence of future interest rates. Again, it turns out that we need to know something about future interest rates in order to price financial derivatives. An assessment of these future rates will be based on the term structure of interest rates.

2.5 Notes

The material in this chapter is based on Lynggaard [1993], which contains a number of examples and exercises. In addition in the lecture notes, Lando [1996] provides an excellent introduction to mathematical finance in general. An excellent introduction to a wide class of financial derivatives is Figlewski et al. [1991]. In particular, this book contains a large number of carefully worked examples.

2.6 Problems

Problem 2.1
1. Show the limits in Table 2.1.

Problem 2.2
Consider an European call option on the amount Y of USD with exercise date T and strike price K.
1. Explain why a higher strike price K gives rise to a lower price Π on the option.

Problem 2.3
Consider an European call option on the amount Y of USD with exercise date T and strike price K. Let c_o denote the arbitrage-free price of this option.
1. Draw the payoff diagram.

Problem 2.4
Consider the following cash flow:

Term	Payment
1	80000
2	80000
3	75000
4	65000
5	50000

Assume that the interest rate is $r = 0.12$.
1. Compute the present value $c_0 = PV(\mathbf{c}, r)$.
2. Compute the future value $c_5 = FV(\mathbf{c}, r)$.
3. Determine the initial payment c_0 for this cash flow such that the net present value is 0.

Problem 2.5
The Simpson family wish to have saved 100 000 in a bank account for a new car in 5 years.
1. Determine the monthly deposits to a bank account assuming that the monthly interest rate is $r = 1\%$.

Problem 2.6
A man borrows 10 000 DKK at time 0 for three years, which should be paid back as an annuity loan, i.e., as $n = 3$ equal payments a. The annual interest rate is $r = 0.06$.
1. Compute the payment c per term. Each payment of equal amount consists of a payment of principal and interest. The last two differ from one-period to another.
2. Complete the following table:

Time	Payment	Interest	Principal	Remaining debt
0				10000
1		600		
2				
3				

Problem 2.7
Show that

$$s_{\overline{n}|r}^{-1} = \alpha_{\overline{n}|r}^{-1} - r.$$

Problem 2.8
Consider the cash flow $\mathbf{c} = (c_0, c_1, c_2)'$. The internal rate of return y is the solution to the equation

$$c_0 = \frac{c_1}{1+y} + \frac{c_2}{(1+y)^2} \tag{2.25}$$

as stated in Definition 2.1.
1. Show that there may exist two solutions (y_1, y_2) such that the internal rate of return y is not uniquely specified.

Problem 2.9
Consider the following cash flow:

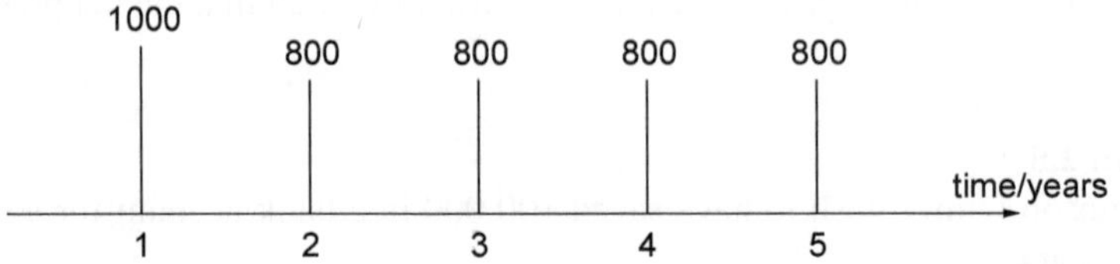

1. Assuming that the annual rate is 6%, what is the present value of this cash flow?

Consider the same cash flow with different interest rates as shown below:

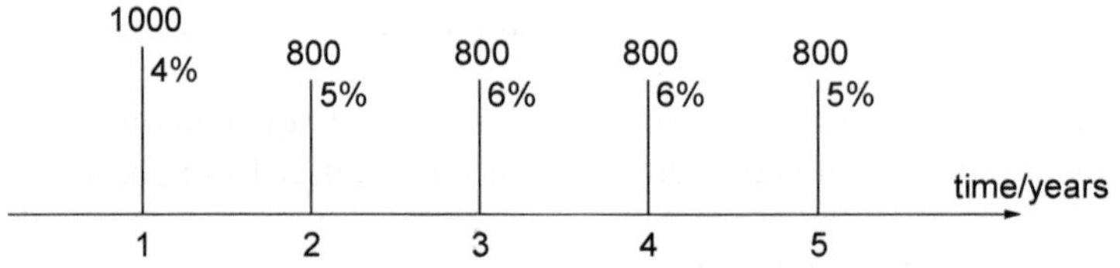

2. Determine the initial payment c_0 such that the present value is 0.

Consider the following cash flow with net present value 3600.78.

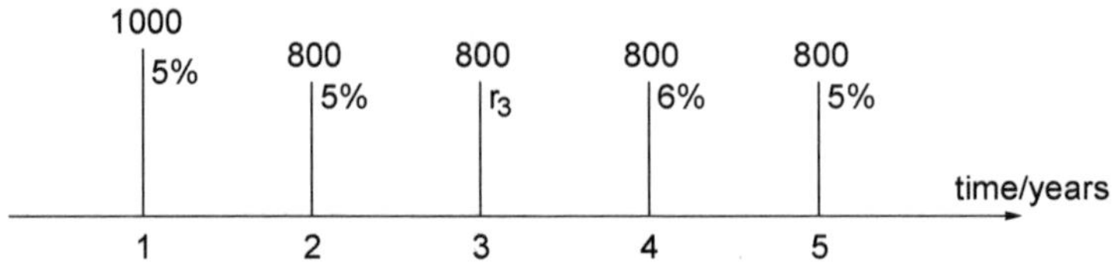

3. Determine the interest rate r_3.

Problem 2.10
Assume that you deposit 1 DKK in a bank account with an annual rate of 12%.
1. Determine the continuously compounded rate r.

Problem 2.11
Consider an annuity with n terms with equal payments c, a duration of n periods and the constant interest rate r.

If the first payment is made at the end of the first term the present value is given by (2.7). Consider the more general case, where the first payment is made at term k, where $0 < k < n$.
1. Plot the cash flow in a diagram similar to Figure 2.3.

2. Derive a formula for the present value in the more general case. The formula should contain $\alpha_{\cdot|r}$.

Problem 2.12
Consider the simple market on page 4.
1. Show that the discount factor $\beta = B_0/B_1$ is given by

$$\beta = (1+r)^{-1}$$

where r is the annual rate.
2. Now assume that the price of the bond at time $t = 1$ is fixed at B_1. Explain what will happen to the bond price at time $t = 0$, B_0, if the interest rate r goes up or down. Plot B_0 as a function of r for reasonable values of r.

Problem 2.13
1. Show that (2.20) simplifies to (2.19) for $r(t) = r$, i.e., a constant rate.

Chapter 3

Discrete time finance

This chapter will describe discrete time models in order to introduce the reader to some of the basic concepts to be used in subsequent chapters on continuous time. The theory in discrete time is simpler as the proofs only require linear algebra.

In this chapter we shall consider simple models of security markets and describe the basic principles of valuation of *contingent claims* (e.g., options, futures). The key idea behind valuation in markets with uncertainty is the notion of *absence of arbitrage*. Roughly speaking, an arbitrage is a situation where an investor, through buying and selling securities, takes a "position" in the market which has zero net cost and which guarantees 1) no losses in the future and 2) some chance of making a profit. In a model free of arbitrage such investments are not possible.

3.1 The binomial one-period model

Consider a financial market with two securities, a stock and a bond, and two time points $t = 0$ and $t = 1$. The bond is a riskless asset with initial price B_0, and price $(1+r)B_0$ at time $t = 1$, where $r > 0$ is the deterministic constant interest rate and $(1+r)^{-1}$ is the discounting factor. The initial stock price is given by S_0 and the price at time $t = 1$ is assumed to be unknown. At time $t = 1$ the market can be in either of two states. With probability p the stock price will be S_1^1 associated with state 1 (the upper index indicates the state), and with probability $1-p$ the stock price is S_1^2 at time $t = 1$.

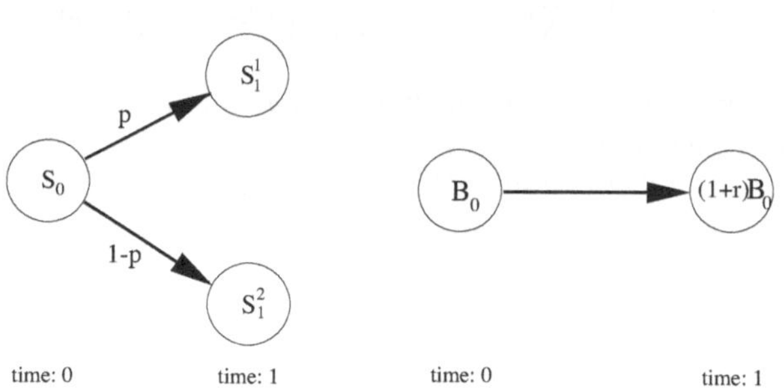

Figure 3.1: The binomial branch for the stock and the bond.

Suppose an investor is interested in a contract, e.g., an option which pays c_1 if state 1 is realized and c_2 if state 2 is realized. What should such a contract cost in the one-period financial market consisting of a stock and a bond? One suggestion would be to price the contract as the expected value of future payoffs, discounted by the factor $(1+r)^{-1}$. Let V denote the price of the contract. Then

$$\hat{V} = (1+r)^{-1}\mathbf{E}[C] = (1+r)^{-1}(pc_1 + (1-p)c_2). \tag{3.1}$$

We shall, however, see that this is not correct, at least not in the naive form; cf. Harrison and Pliska [1981], Biagini and Cont [2006].

Consider instead a general portfolio $(\phi, \psi) \in \mathbb{R}^2$, consisting of ϕ units of the stock and ψ units of the bond. The price of that portfolio at time $t = 0$ is $\phi S_0 + \psi B_0$.

At time $t = 1$ the value of that portfolio would be $\phi S_1^1 + \psi(1+r)B_0$ in state 1 and $\phi S_1^2 + \psi(1+r)B_0$ in state 2. To find the correct price of the contract we could choose the portfolio (ϕ, ψ) in a way that yields c_1 in state 1 and c_2 in state 2. The principle of buying a portfolio with the same cash flow/payoff as a contract is called *replication*. By solving the linear equations

$$\phi S_1^1 + \psi(1+r)B_0 = c_1 \tag{3.2}$$

$$\phi S_1^2 + \psi(1+r)B_0 = c_2 \tag{3.3}$$

the following portfolio is obtained

$$\phi = \frac{c_2 - c_1}{S_1^2 - S_1^1} \tag{3.4}$$

$$\psi = \frac{1}{(1+r)B_0}\left(c_2 - \frac{(c_2 - c_1)S_1^2}{S_1^2 - S_1^1}\right). \tag{3.5}$$

If this portfolio is bought, the payoff at time $t = 1$ would be c_j in state $j = 1, 2$. The price $\tilde{V}$ of the portfolio at time $t = 0$ is

$$\tilde{V} = \phi S_0 + \psi B_0 = S_0\left(\frac{c_2 - c_1}{S_1^2 - S_1^1}\right) + \frac{1}{(1+r)}\left(c_2 - \frac{(c_2 - c_1)S_1^2}{S_1^2 - S_1^1}\right). \tag{3.6}$$

This is an other candidate to the price of the contract which differs from (3.1), and this is the correct price as we shall see.

Consider some other market maker offering to buy or sell the contract for a price P less than $\tilde{V}$. Anyone could buy the contract in arbitrary quantity, and sell the portfolio (ϕ, ψ) above to replicate it. At time $t = 1$ the value of the contract would exactly cancel the value of the portfolio, whatever the stock price would be — thus this set of trades carries no risk. But the trades were carried out with a profit of $\tilde{V} - P$ per unit of contract. By buying arbitrary amounts anyone could make arbitrary risk-free profits, so P would not have been a rational/fair price for the market maker to quote.

Similarly if the market maker quotes a price P greater than $\tilde{V}$, anyone could again make arbitrary risk-free profits. Hence the price $\tilde{V}$ is the rational/fair price for that contract. In the next section a more general[1] model will be considered, which includes this model as a special case.

3.2 One-period model

The model considered in this section is the simplest possible model of a security market with uncertainty — the *Arrow–Debreu* model. We assume that there are N securities with the initial price vector $\mathbf{S_0} = (S_0^1, S_0^2, \ldots, S_0^N)^T$, which can be held in any positive or negative real number by any investor. An investor is said to hold a *short* position of a given security if he or she has a negative amount of that security, and the position is *long* if the investor has a positive amount. The security prices $\mathbf{S_0}$ are known at time $t = 0$ while the future prices $\mathbf{S_1}$ are unknown at time $t = 0$. It is assumed that the market can be in M different states ω_i at time $t = 1$, and the security prices at time $t = 1$ can be represented by the cash-flow matrix $\mathbf{D} \in \mathbb{R}^{N \times M}$ as follows

$$\begin{aligned}\mathbf{D} &= \begin{bmatrix} S_1^1(\omega_1) & S_1^1(\omega_2) & \cdots & S_1^1(\omega_M) \\ S_1^2(\omega_1) & S_1^2(\omega_2) & \cdots & S_1^2(\omega_M) \\ \vdots & \vdots & \ddots & \vdots \\ S_1^N(\omega_1) & S_1^N(\omega_2) & \cdots & S_1^N(\omega_M) \end{bmatrix} \\ &= \begin{bmatrix} \mathbf{S}_1(\omega_1) & \mathbf{S}_1(\omega_2) & \cdots & \mathbf{S}_1(\omega_M) \end{bmatrix}\end{aligned} \tag{3.7}$$

where ω_j is an outcome from the finite sample space $\Omega = \{\omega_1, \omega_2, \ldots, \omega_M\}$ and $\mathbf{S}_1(\omega_j) \in \mathbb{R}^N$ is the price vector at state j. Thus if the uncertainty in the market generates the outcome ω_j, the stock price will be $\mathbf{S}_1(\omega_j)$.

The jth column of D is the price vector $\mathbf{S}_1(\omega_j) \in \mathbb{R}^N$ associated with state j and the ith row is the possible payoffs which are associated with holding one unit of security j.

A *portfolio* of securities is represented by a column vector $\mathbf{h} = (h^1, h^2, \ldots, h^N)^T$, i.e., ($\mathbf{h} \in \mathbb{R}^N$), where h^i denotes the number of securities of type i bought at time $t = 0$. The portfolio $\mathbf{h}$ is defined on $\mathbb{R}^N$, i.e., $\mathbf{h} \in \mathbb{R}^N$. This implies that the investor is allowed both to go short in any security and own a noninteger number of any securities (e.g., 0.3). Assume, e.g., that $h^1 = -\sqrt{2}$. This means that at time $t = 0$ you get $\sqrt{2}S_0^1$ and at time $t = 1$ you owe $\sqrt{2}S_1^1(\omega)$, which is a stochastic variable.

The *wealth process* $V_t(\mathbf{h})$ is defined as

$$V_t(\mathbf{h}) = \sum_i^N h^i S_t^i = \mathbf{h}^T \mathbf{S}_t \qquad \text{for} \quad t = 0, 1 \tag{3.8}$$

[1] Although still very simple.

and it equals the value of a given portfolio as a function of the time ($t = 1,2$), of the initial price vector $\mathbf{S}_0$, and of the outcome of the stochastic variable $\mathbf{S}_1(\omega)$.

Definition 3.1 (Arbitrage in discrete time). *An arbitrage portfolio is a portfolio* $\mathbf{h}$ *such that* $\mathbf{h}^T\mathbf{S_0} = 0$ *and*

$$\mathbf{h}^T\mathbf{D}_{\cdot j} \geq 0 \quad \text{for all} \quad 1 \leq j \leq M \tag{3.9}$$

$$\mathbf{h}^T\mathbf{D}_{\cdot j} > 0 \quad \text{for some} \quad 1 \leq j \leq M \tag{3.10}$$

where $\mathbf{D}_{\cdot j}$ *denotes the* j^{th} *column of* $\mathbf{D}$.

This means that an arbitrage portfolio is a zero investment portfolio (at $t = 0$) where losses are impossible (at time $t = 1$) and there is a positive probability to make a profit (at time $t = 1$), provided that all $\omega_j > 0$.

3.2.1 Risk-neutral probabilities

As stated in the introduction, the value of a given security is in general not given by the discounted expected value of future cash flows. In the following we shall show that the right price of a security, in the sense of no arbitrage opportunities, is the discounted expected value of future cash flows. However, the expectation should be computed with respect to an other probability measure (possibly non-unique) called the *risk-neutral probabilities* $\mathbf{q}$, which in general differ from the objective probabilities $\mathbf{p}$.

Theorem 3.1 (State price vector). *If there exists a vector of strictly positive numbers* $\mathbf{q} \in \mathbb{R}^M_{++}$

$$\mathbf{q} = (q_1, q_2, \ldots, q_M)^T, \tag{3.11}$$

called a state price vector, such that

$$\mathbf{S}_0 = \mathbf{D}\mathbf{q} = \sum_{j=1}^{M} q_j \mathbf{D}_{\cdot \mathbf{j}} \tag{3.12}$$

then no arbitrage portfolios exist. Conversely, if there are no arbitrage portfolios, there exists a state price vector $\mathbf{q}$ *with positive entries satisfying* (3.12).

Proof. See Duffie [1996]. □

The theorem says that the initial price vector and the cash-flow matrix $\mathbf{D}$ must satisfy certain conditions in an arbitrage-free model. Given a state price vector π for the pair $(\mathbf{D}, \mathbf{S_0})$, let $q_0 = \sum_{i=1}^{M} q_i$, and for any state j, let $\hat{q}_j = q_j/q_0$. The vector $\hat{\mathbf{q}} = (\hat{q}_1, \hat{q}_2, \ldots, \hat{q}_M)^T$ has positive elements and the sum is 1 by construction; hence, it can be interpreted as a probability distribution.

By inserting $q_j = \hat{q}_j q_0$ in (3.12) we obtain

$$S_0^i = \sum_{j=1}^{M} q_0 \hat{q}_j D_{ij} = q_0 \sum_{j=1}^{M} \hat{q}_j D_{ij} = q_0 \mathbf{E}^{\mathbb{Q}}[D_{i\cdot}] \tag{3.13}$$

where $\mathbf{E}^{\mathbb{Q}}[\cdot]$ denotes the expectation operator with respect to the risk-neutral probabilities.

Suppose there exists an investment opportunity which guarantees a riskless payoff of 1 USD at time $t = 1$. In terms of the model the payoff of this riskless investment can be represented as a vector $(1, 1, \ldots, 1)$ in $\mathbb{R}^M$. According to Theorem 3.1 the value of such an investment must be $\sum_j^M q_j = q_0$. Since a bond basically is a security that pays a certain amount — say 1 USD without any loss of generality — at the expiry date ($t = 1$), the price of a bond in this one-period model is q_0. We call q_0 the discounting factor because it tells us how much 1 USD at time $t = 1$ is worth today $t = 0$.

Equation (3.13) states that the fair price of a security in a model free of arbitrage is the discounted expected payoff at time ($t = 1$), where the risk-neutral probabilities are used in the expectation. The change from the objective probabilities $\mathbf{p}$ to the risk-neutral "probabilities" $\mathbf{q}$ thus incorporates the discounting factor q_0, as well as the real risk-neutral probabilities $\hat{\mathbf{q}}$.

Remark 3.1. *We will see in the corresponding chapter on continuous-time models that a slightly more general formulation is used. The definition there is that a risk-neutral probability measure is a probability measure such that ratios of traded assets are martingales*

$$\frac{S_0}{B_0} = \mathbf{E}^{\mathbb{Q}}\left[\frac{S_1}{B_1}\right]. \tag{3.14}$$

This definition will be helpful when valuing, e.g., interest rate derivatives.

3.2.2 Complete and incomplete markets

In the binomial model (with two states) presented in the beginning of this chapter any vector of future cash flows, $\mathbf{c} = (c_1, c_2)$, can be replicated in terms of a portfolio of a stock and a riskless bond. This property can be generalized to the setting of N securities and M states.

Definition 3.2 (Complete market). *A securities market is said to be complete if, for any cash-flow vector $\mathbf{c} = (c_1, c_2, \ldots, c_M)$, there exists a portfolio $\mathbf{h} = (h_1, h_2, \ldots, h_N)^T$ of traded securities, which has a cash-flow c_j in state j, for all $1 \leq j \leq M$.*

Remark 3.2. *Market completeness is therefore equivalent to the existence of a solution $\mathbf{h} \in \mathbb{R}^N$ to the linear equations*

$$\mathbf{h}^T \mathbf{D} = \mathbf{c} \tag{3.15}$$

for any $\mathbf{c} \in \mathbb{R}^M$, where $\mathbf{D}$ is the cash-flow matrix defined in (3.7). *From linear algebra it is well known that this property is satisfied if and only if*

$$\operatorname{rank}(\mathbf{D}) = M \tag{3.16}$$

which is equivalent to saying that the rows of the matrix **D** *span the entire* $\mathbb{R}^M$ *space.*

Remark 3.3. *A necessary condition for market completeness is that the number of traded securities must be at least as large as the number of states.*

Proposition 3.1. *Suppose that the market is complete and the model is free of arbitrage. Then there exists a unique set of state prices* $(\pi_1, \pi_2, \ldots, \pi_M)$ *and hence a unique set of risk-neutral probabilities* $(\hat{\pi}_1, \hat{\pi}_2, \ldots, \hat{\pi}_M)$. *Conversely, if there exists a unique set of state prices, then the market is complete.*

Proof. Market completeness implies that the price of a contingent claim which pays \$1 in state j and 0 otherwise is determined for all j. Therefore, there can be at most one set of state prices. Hence, if they exist they are unique.

The converse statement, that if there exists a unique state price vector (with strictly positive elements) then the market is complete, is proved by a contradiction argument. Assume the market is not complete, then $\text{rank}(\mathbf{D}) < M$. From linear algebra, we know that the matrix **D** must have a non-empty nullspace, i.e., there exists a vector $\lambda = (\lambda_1, \lambda_2, \ldots, \lambda_M)$ such that

$$\mathbf{D}\lambda = \mathbf{0}.$$

Using the no arbitrage relation (3.12) we obtain

$$\mathbf{S}_0 = \mathbf{D}(\mathbf{q} + \rho\lambda)$$

for all real numbers ρ. Since the entries of **q** are strictly positive, we can choose ρ sufficiently small such that $q_j + \rho\lambda_j$ is positive for all j. Therefore we have constructed a new state price vector, contradicting the hypothesis. We conclude that in a market free of arbitrage, uniqueness of state prices implies that the market is complete. □

The concept of completeness is a convenient idealization of the behaviour of securities markets. However markets — with many possible price structures satisfying the no-arbitrage condition — are the rule rather than the exception.

Example 3.1 (The trinomial model)**.** *By adding one more state to the binomial model in Section 3.1 we obtain the so-called trinomial model, which is an incomplete market since the cash-flow matrix* **D** *is* 2×3. *Due to the fact that the state prices are not unique, the price of contingent claims can not in general be determined uniquely.*

Assuming that there is a riskless bond on the financial market, with a deterministic rate r *and a value of one at time* $t = 1$, *and assuming no arbitrage then we get from* (3.13) *that*

$$\frac{1}{1+r} = q_1 + q_2 + q_3 \qquad \textit{Bond price} \qquad (3.17)$$

$$S_0 = S_1^1 q_1 + S_1^2 q_2 + S_1^3 q_3 \qquad \textit{Stock price} \qquad (3.18)$$

where we assume that

$$S_1^1 < S_1^2 < S_1^3. \tag{3.19}$$

Admissible sets of state prices π *must satisfy Equations* (3.17)–(3.18) *and must have strictly positive entries. By subtracting* (3.18) *from* (3.17) *we obtain*

$$0 = \left(1 + r - \frac{S_1^1}{S_0}\right) q_1 + \left(1 + r - \frac{S_1^2}{S_0}\right) q_2 + \left(1 + r - \frac{S_1^3}{S_0}\right) q_3. \tag{3.20}$$

Since $\mathbf{q}$ *is strictly positive the equation above can only be fulfilled if*

$$\frac{S_1^1}{S_0} < 1 + r < \frac{S_1^3}{S_0}. \tag{3.21}$$

With this condition the model is free of arbitrage, and the set of admissible state prices can be visualized as a line segment corresponding to the intersection of the planes described by (3.17) *and* (3.18) *in the positive quadrant* $\mathbb{R}^3_{++}$.

Since the state prices are strictly positive in all coordinates, the extreme values at the line segments are

$$q_1 = \frac{\frac{S_1^3}{S_0} - (1+r)}{(1+r)(\frac{S_1^3}{S_0} - \frac{S_1^1}{S_0})}, \quad q_2 = 0, \quad q_3 = \frac{(1+r) - \frac{S_1^1}{S_0}}{(1+r)(\frac{S_1^3}{S_0} - \frac{S_1^1}{S_0})}, \tag{3.22}$$

and

$$q_1 = 0, \quad q_2 = \frac{\frac{S_1^3}{S_0} - (1+r)}{(1+r)(\frac{S_1^3}{S_0} - \frac{S_1^2}{S_0})}, \quad q_3 = \frac{(1+r) - \frac{S_2^1}{S_0}}{(1+r)(\frac{S_1^3}{S_0} - \frac{S_1^2}{S_0})} \tag{3.23}$$

if $\frac{S_1^2}{S_0} \leq (1+r)$, *or*

$$q_1 = \frac{\frac{S_1^2}{S_0} - (1+r)}{(1+r)(\frac{S_1^2}{S_0} - \frac{S_1^1}{S_0})}, \quad q_2 = \frac{(1+r) - \frac{S_1^1}{S_0}}{(1+r)(\frac{S_1^2}{S_0} - \frac{S_1^1}{S_0})}, \quad q_3 = 0 \tag{3.24}$$

if $S_1^2/S_0 > (1+r)$.

Due to the fact that the model is incomplete, the price of derivatives cannot be determined uniquely. However, since the set of admissible state prices is the line segment mentioned above, bounds on the value of derivatives can be calculated. Since the value of the derivative is a linear function, and the line segment is an open convex set, an infimum and supremum of the price can be found. To illustrate this, consider the case of a call option on the basic security S, *with strike price* K. *Assume that* $S_1^2 < K < S_1^3$. *Then the cash flows for this option are* $S_1^3 - K$ *in state* 3 *and* 0 *in state 1 and* 2. *Its no-arbitrage value is*

$C = \pi_3(S_1^3 - K)$. According to the extreme values of the admissible line segment the upper bound for the call option is

$$C^+ = \pi_3(s_1^3 - K) = \frac{(1+r) - \frac{S_1^1}{S_0}}{(1+r)(\frac{S_1^3}{S_0} - \frac{S_1^1}{S_0})}(S_1^3 - K). \tag{3.25}$$

If $S_1^2/S_0 > (1+r)$ the lower bound of the price is $C^- = 0$, and if $S_1^2/S_0 \leq (1+r)$ the lower bound is

$$C^- = \pi_3(s_1^3 - k) = \frac{(1+r) - \frac{S_1^2}{S_0}}{(1+r)(\frac{S_1^3}{S_0} - \frac{S_1^2}{S_0})}(S_1^3 - K). \tag{3.26}$$

This example addresses two subjects. First, the example shows an important application of state prices as a tool for valuation of derivatives in incomplete markets. State prices are not unique but they can nevertheless be used to obtain partial information about fair prices. Second, the example shows that in order to obtain complete markets, where the pricing of derivatives is uniquely determined, the number of stocks must be at least as large as the number of states.[2] To get more realism in a model of a financial stock market, the number of states must be large, because why should the stock take only two or three possible values? However the drawback by increasing the number of states is that the number of stocks must be increased as well. Fortunately, there is a clever way out of this problem.

3.3 Multiperiod model

The idea is to divide the interval from 0 to T into equidistant smaller subintervals, where T denotes the expiry date of a given derivative, and allow the stock price to move up and down in each subinterval; cf. Figure 3.2. With this setup the stock price can have 2^T different prices at time T, if none of the nodes at time $t = T$ coincide. However, often a so-called *recombinant* tree is used, where different branches can rejoin. Using the terminology of graph theory, a recombinant tree is a graph where a given node can have more than one predecessor. In the recombinant tree in Figure 3.2*b* the stock price can take $T+1$ possible values at time T.

Before we go into details with the mathematical technicalities, we provide an example to guide the intuition.

Example 3.2 (Two period model). *Consider a two period model consisting of a riskless security, with initial value* 1 *and a deterministic interest rate r, and a stock with uncertain values at time $t = 1, 2$. The uncertainty of the stock is modelled as a binomial tree, consisting of a binomial branch at the initial node*

[2]This follows from Remark 3.2.

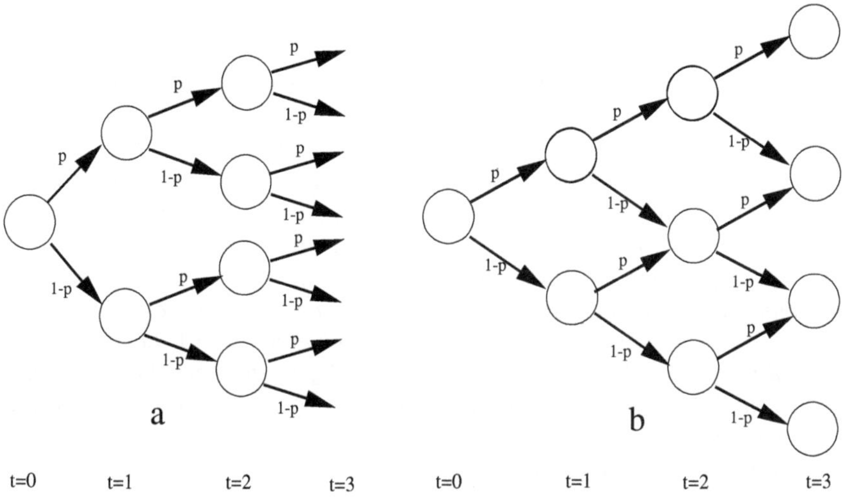

Figure 3.2: Two binomial trees — the one to the right is a so-called recombinant tree, where a given node can have two predecessors.

at time $t = 0$, and binomial branches at the two possible nodes at time $t = 1$. By truncating the tree in Figure 3.2 at time $t = 2$, the evolution of the value of the riskless security and the stock price is given in Figure 3.3.

The initial value of the stock is assumed to be S. At time $t = 1$ we know whether the state of the world is either (ω_1 or ω_2) or (ω_3 or ω_4). If the state

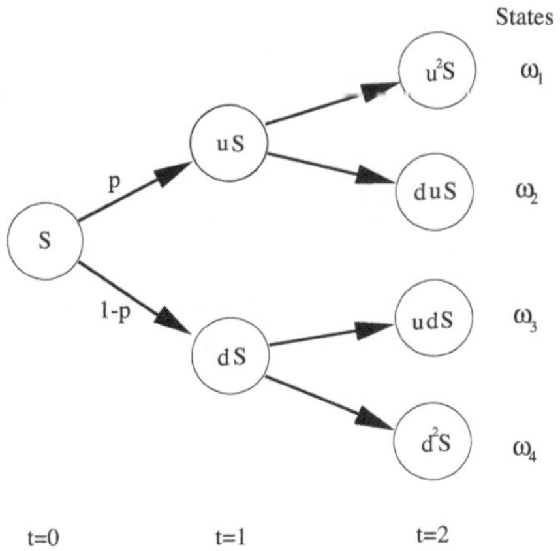

Figure 3.3: The evolution of the value of the stock price in a two period model.

of the world is (ω_1 or ω_2) the value of the stock is uS, and the value is dS if the state is (ω_3 or ω_4). The value of the money market account is $(1+r)$ independent of the state of the world. At time $t=2$ the state is known, and the value of the stock is listed in Figure 3.3. The value of the money market account is $(1+r)^2$.

Now suppose we want to price a European call option on the stock with exercise price K. The value of the option at time $t=2$ is $V=\max(S_2(\omega)-K,0)$, where ω indicates that the stock price depends on the state of the world.

In the one-period model the arbitrage-free price is found by the value of a replicating portfolio (with the same cash flow at the end of the period). This principle will be applied in a recursive manner to the two period binomial model. We begin with the upper binomial branch at time $t=1$. Let C_{uu} denote the value of the call option in state ω_1 and C_{du} in state ω_2. As in the one-period model we want to determine a portfolio (ϕ_u, ψ_u) in the stock and the money market account, which replicates the value of the option at time $t=2$. This is obtained by solving the linear system

$$\phi_u u^2 S + \psi_u (1+r)^2 = C_{uu}, \tag{3.27}$$

$$\phi_u du S + \psi_u (1+r)^2 = C_{du}. \tag{3.28}$$

The solution is

$$\phi_u = \frac{C_{uu}-C_{du}}{uS(u-d)}, \qquad \psi_u = \frac{uC_{du}-dC_{uu}}{(1+r)^2(u-d)}. \tag{3.29}$$

The value C_u of this portfolio is

$$\begin{aligned} C_u &= \phi_u uS + \psi_u(1+r) \\ &= \frac{1}{1+r}\left(\frac{(1+r)-d}{u-d}C_{uu} + \frac{u-(1+r)}{u-d}C_{du}\right), \end{aligned} \tag{3.30}$$

and this is what the call is worth at time $t=1$ if the first move was up. If the first move was down the value of the call C_d at time $t=1$ can be determined in a similar way, thus

$$C_d = \frac{1}{1+r}\left(\frac{(1+r)-d}{u-d}C_{ud} + \frac{u-(1+r)}{u-d}C_{dd}\right), \tag{3.31}$$

where C_{dd} and C_{ud} denote the value of the call at state ω_4 and ω_3 at time $t=2$. Now we know what the call is worth at time $t=1$ depending on which state we are in at that time. Looking at time $t=0$ we want to construct a portfolio which gives us C_u if we are in state (ω_1 or ω_2) at time $t=1$ and C_d is the state in (ω_3 or ω_4). Again we have a one-period problem, which we can easily solve, and the value of the replicating portfolio, which is equal to the value of the call C_0 at time $t=0$, is given by

$$C_0 = \frac{1}{1+r}\left(\frac{(1+r)-d}{u-d}C_u + \frac{u-(1+r)}{u-d}C_d\right). \tag{3.32}$$

By inserting (3.30) *and* (3.31) *in* (3.32), *and defining* $q = \frac{(1+r)-d}{u-d}$, *we get*

$$C_0 = \frac{1}{(1+r)^2}\left(q^2 C_{uu} + 2q(1-q)C_{ud} + (1-q)^2 C_{dd}\right). \tag{3.33}$$

We recognize that this expression shows that the value of a call option is found as the discounted value of the expected value of the payoff of the option at time $t = 2$*, where the expectation is taken with respect to the risk-neutral probabilities. The risk-neutral probabilities denote the probabilities under the equivalent martingale measure* $\mathbb{Q}$*, which we will discuss later. Formally we have*

$$C_0 = \frac{1}{(1+r)^2}\mathbf{E}^{\mathbb{Q}}[C_{t=2}]. \tag{3.34}$$

The important thing to learn from this example is the following: Starting out with the amount C_0*, an investor is able to form a portfolio of the stock and the money market account which produces the payoffs* C_u *or* C_d *at time* $t = 1$ *depending on where the stock goes. Now without any additional cost, the investor can rearrange his portfolio at time* $t = 1$*, such that the payoff at time* $t = 2$ *will match that of the option. Therefore, at time* $t = 0$ *the price of the option must be* C_0*.*

3.3.1 σ-algebras and information sets

In this section we shall present a general formula for derivative pricing in multiperiod models. Some important concepts from probability theory, like σ-algebras, probability spaces, partitions, etc., will be used. If the reader is not familiar with these concepts please consult Appendix B for a brief overview.

Given a probability space $(\Omega, \mathscr{F}, \mathbb{P})$ with a finite sample space Ω, and $\mathscr{F}$ the σ-algebra of all subsets of Ω, assume that $\mathbb{P}(\omega) > 0$ for all $\omega \in \Omega$ (no elements in Ω have probability zero). Also assume that there are $T+1$ dates, starting at date 0, ending at time T. In the general theory of multiperiods models it will be shown that the pricing of derivatives consists of a conditional expectation, where the conditioning argument is the "information set" up to the present time. It is therefore important to formalize the concept of information, which is done by introducing σ-algebras. However, to illustrate how information is revealed through time, we give an example.

Example 3.3 (Event tree). *Consider the event tree in Figure 3.4 with three periods. In this example we shall only consider how we can represent knowledge in terms of partitions/*σ*-algebras, and not study a particular financial market. Suppose that an outcome* $\omega \in \Omega$ *is chosen by "someone" or "something," but the chosen state is unknown to us at time* $t = 0$*. We only know that one state has been chosen. This is represented by a partition* $\mathscr{P}_0$ *containing one set, namely the entire sample space, which can be interpreted as no information. At time* $t = 1$*, we are in either state A or B, i.e., we know that the state is either (1)*

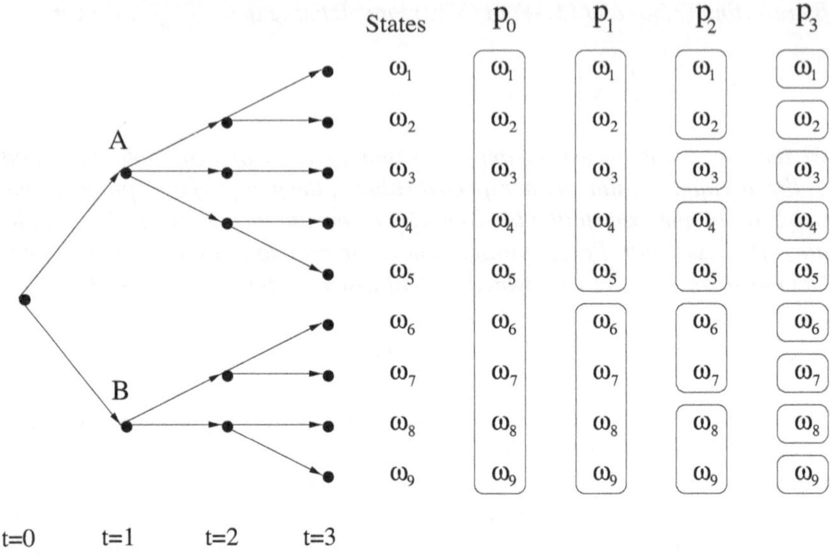

Figure 3.4: Event tree with three periods.

$\{\omega_1, \omega_2, \omega_3, \omega_4, \omega_5\}$ or (2) $\{\omega_6, \omega_7, \omega_8, \omega_9\}$, which is formalized by the partition $\mathscr{P}_1$ in Figure 3.4. At time $t = 2$ the partition is even richer. Thus, we know in which of the five subsets $\{\omega_1, \omega_2\}, \{\omega_3\}, \{\omega_4, \omega_5\}, \{\omega_6, \omega_7\}$ or $\{\omega_8, \omega_9\}$ the true state is. At time $t = 3$ we know exactly which of the states is the true state, and it is represented by a partition $\mathscr{P}_3$ where each of the elements of $\mathscr{P}_3$ contains one single state ω_i; cf. Figure 3.4. Thus as times goes by we obtain more information, and at time $t = 3$ we have complete information.

Although the "information set" from now on will be represented by σ-algebras, it is fruitful to think of it in terms of partitions and information sets that become more detailed as time goes by.

To formalize how information is revealed through time, we introduce the notion of a *filtration.*

Definition 3.3 (Filtration). *A filtration on $(\Omega, \mathscr{F})$ is a family $\{\mathscr{F}_i\}_{i=1}^T$ of σ-algebras in $\mathscr{F}$ such that*

$$\mathscr{F}_0 \subseteq \mathscr{F}_1 \subseteq \ldots \subseteq \mathscr{F}_T. \tag{3.35}$$

If $\mathscr{F}_0 = (\varnothing, \Omega)$ and $\mathscr{F}_T = \mathscr{F}$ the filtration may be considered as a sequence of information sets increasing from "no information" to "full information" — similar to the interpretation of partitions in Example 3.3.

Definition 3.4 (Adapted process). *A discrete time stochastic process $(X_t)_{t=0,\ldots,T}$ is a sequence of stochastic variables $X_0, X_1, \ldots, X_T$. The process* *is said to be adapted to the filtration $\mathscr{F}$ if X_s is $\mathscr{F}_s$-measurable, which is typically written as $X_s \in \mathscr{F}_s$.*

3.3.2 Financial multiperiod markets

We are now ready to model financial markets as multiperiod models. Let $\mathbf{S}_t(\omega) = (S_t^0, S_t^1, \ldots, S_t^N)$ be a vector of adapted processes of the securities available on the market. This means that $S_t^i(\omega)$ is the price of security i at time t in state ω. Suppose one of the securities S^0 is a money market account with initial value 1 and a deterministic interest rate r for all T periods. In the one-period model we defined a portfolio as an N-dimensional vector $\mathbf{h}$, where h^i denotes the number of security i bought at time $t = 0$. In a multiperiod model this concept ought to be generalized because the portfolio might change over time. Thus we obtain a portfolio vector at each time point. This is done in the following definition.

Definition 3.5 (Trading strategy). *A trading strategy is an (N)-dimensional vector of adapted processes*

$$\mathbf{h} = (\mathbf{h}^1, \mathbf{h}^2, \ldots, \mathbf{h}^N) \tag{3.36}$$

with the interpretation similar to that of a one-period model, so $h_t^i(\omega)$ denotes the number of security i held at time t in state ω.

The requirement that the trading strategy is adapted represents the very important idea that the strategy can only be based on the current level of knowledge. To illustrate this we assume we are in node A in Figure 3.4 at time $t = 1$. Then the trading strategy can base the number of securities on the fact that we are in node A and not in B. Notice that the number of securities may not be based on whether the true state is ω_1, ω_2, ω_3, ω_4 or ω_5 (i.e., it is not allowed to base a trading strategy on information released in the future, for example, future values of the stocks). From an economical point of view, it clearly makes sense to require that the trading strategy should be an adapted process.

Definition 3.6 (Value process). *The value process at time t corresponding to* $\mathbf{h}$ *is defined as*

$$V_t(\mathbf{h}) = \mathbf{h}_t\mathbf{S}_t = \sum_{i=1}^{N} h_t^i(\omega) S_t^i(\omega) \quad \textit{for } t = 0, 1, \ldots, T. \tag{3.37}$$

Definition 3.7 (Self-financing trading strategy). *A trading strategy* $\mathbf{h}$ *is self-financing if it satisfies*

$$\mathbf{h}_t\mathbf{S}_t = \mathbf{h}_{t-1}\mathbf{S}_t \quad \textit{for } t = 1, 2, \ldots, T. \tag{3.38}$$

The interpretation of a self-financing strategy is that it is only allowed to change the portfolio in a way such that the total value of the portfolio does not change. However, the value of the trading strategy can of course change over time due to changes in the stocks. The definition of arbitrage in multiperiods models is based on the definition of self-financing portfolios.

Definition 3.8 (Arbitrage). *An arbitrage is a self-financing strategy for which*

$$V_0(\mathbf{h}) = 0 \tag{3.39}$$

and

$$V_T(\mathbf{h}) \geq 0, \tag{3.40}$$

$$\mathbb{P}(V_T(\mathbf{h}) > 0) > 0. \tag{3.41}$$

In words this definition says that there are arbitrage possibilities in the model if there exists a trading strategy with zero cost at the initial time with the following two properties: (1) No risk of getting any losses at the future time T; (2) A positive probability of getting a strictly positive payoff. If no arbitrage possibilities exist in the model, we say that the model is free of arbitrage. Compared with the definition of arbitrage in the one-period model (3.1) it is readily seen, that the above definition is a generalization.[3]

3.3.3 Martingale measures

The pricing of derivatives in discrete and continuous-time models is built on so-called martingale measures which basically are probability distributions that are related to the historical or objective probability distribution. In the one-period model we saw that the price of a derivative, e.g., an option, was given by the discounted value of the expected value of the payoffs at time $t = 1$, where the expectation was taken with respect to the so-called risk-neutral probabilities. In multiperiod models as well as continuous models, we basically use the same procedure for pricing derivatives.

Since the pricing formulas stated in the following rely on conditional expectations it is necessary to be familiar with this concept, in the case where the conditioning argument is a σ-algebra. In Appendix B a brief overview is given.

Definition 3.9 (Martingale). *A stochastic process X is a martingale with respect to the filtration $\{\mathscr{F}_i\}_{i=1}^T$ if it satisfies*

1. The best prediction is the current value

$$\mathbf{E}\left[X_t | \mathscr{F}_{t-1}\right] = X_{t-1} \tag{3.42}$$

for all $t = 1, 2, \ldots, T$.

[3]In the one-period model two definitions of arbitrage were stated, where the first definition is directly comparable with the multiperiod definition of arbitrage.

2. X_t *is adapted to the filtration* $\mathscr{F}_t$ *for all* t.
3. *The process has finite expectation*

$$\mathbf{E}\left[|X_t|\right] < \infty \text{ for all } t. \tag{3.43}$$

Remark 3.4. *In applications we shall mainly be interested in the first property in Definition 3.9, and just assume that properties 2 and 3 are fulfilled.*

Let us consider two simple examples of martingales.

Example 3.4. *Consider a collection of independent and identically distributed stochastic variables* $X_1, X_2, \ldots$ *with mean zero* $\mathbf{E}[X_i] = 0$*. Let* $\mathscr{F}_n = \sigma\{X_1, X_2, \ldots, X_n\}$ *denote the* σ*-algebra generated by* $X_1, X_2, \ldots, X_n$*. Furthermore, we introduce the filtration* $\{\mathscr{F}_i\}_{i=1}^T = \{\mathscr{F}_1, \mathscr{F}_2, \mathscr{F}_3, \ldots\}$.

We wish to show that the sum

$$S_n = \sum_{i=1}^{n} X_i$$

is an $\mathbb{F}$*-martingale. From the linearity of the expectation operator, we get*

$$\mathbf{E}[S_n|\mathscr{F}_{n-1}] = \mathbf{E}[X_n|\mathscr{F}_{n-1}] + \mathbf{E}[S_{n-1}|\mathscr{F}_{n-1}]. \tag{3.44}$$

The latter S_{n-1} *is* $\mathscr{F}_{n-1}$*-measurable, and the former has expectation zero. Hence*

$$\mathbf{E}[S_n|\mathscr{F}_{n-1}] = S_{n-1} \tag{3.45}$$

which shows that S_n *is an* $\{\mathscr{F}_i\}_{i=1}^T$*-martingale.*

Example 3.5. *We consider the same setup as above with the exception that* $\mathbf{E}[X_i] = 1$ *and* $X_i > 0$ *for* $i = 1, 2, \ldots$.

We wish to show that the product

$$M_n = X_1 \cdot X_2 \cdot \ldots \cdot X_n$$

is a $\{\mathscr{F}_i\}_{i=1}^T$*-martingale. Thus we must show that*

$$\mathbf{E}[M_n|\mathscr{F}_{n-1}] = M_{n-1}.$$

As $X_1 \cdot X_2 \cdot \ldots \cdot X_{n-1}$ *is* $\mathscr{F}_{n-1}$*-measurable, we get*

$$\begin{aligned}
\mathbf{E}[M_n|\mathscr{F}_{n-1}] &= \mathbf{E}[X_1 \cdot X_2 \cdot \ldots \cdot X_n|\mathscr{F}_{n-1}] \\
&= X_1 \cdot X_2 \cdot \ldots \cdot X_{n-1}\mathbf{E}[X_n|\mathscr{F}_{n-1}] \\
&= M_{n-1}\mathbf{E}[X_n] = M_{n-1},
\end{aligned}$$

where the last equality sign follows from $\mathbf{E}[X_n] = 1$.

Definition 3.10 (Equivalent measures)**.** *Two probability measures* $\mathbb{P}$ *and* $\mathbb{Q}$ *are said to be equivalent if they assign zero probability to the same sets* A *in the* σ*-algebra*

$$\mathbb{P}(A) = 0 \iff \mathbb{Q}(A) = 0. \tag{3.46}$$

Definition 3.11 (Equivalent martingale measure). *An equivalent martingale measure for the security market model* $\mathbf{S}$*, defined on* $(\Omega, \mathscr{F}, \mathbb{P}, \{\mathscr{F}_i\}_{i=1}^T)$*, is a probability measure* $\mathbb{Q}$ *on* Ω *with* $\mathbb{Q}(\omega) > 0$ *for all* $\omega \in \Omega$ *such that each component in the vector of discounted price processes*

$$\mathbf{Z} = (Z^0, Z^1, \ldots, Z^N) = \left(1, \frac{S^1}{S^0}, \ldots, \frac{S^N}{S^0}\right) \tag{3.47}$$

is a martingale, i.e.,

$$\mathbf{E}^{\mathbb{Q}}[Z_t^i | \mathscr{F}_{t-1}] = Z_{t-1}^i \quad \textit{for } i = 1,2,\ldots,N \textit{ and } t = 1,2,\ldots,T. \tag{3.48}$$

For the one-period model it was stated in Theorem 3.1 that a financial model is free of arbitrage if and only if there exists a state price vector. Using the concept of martingale measures we can state a similar, but more general, theorem.

Theorem 3.2. *In a discrete time security market with finite sample space the following two statements are equivalent.*

1. *There are no arbitrage opportunities.*
2. *There exists an equivalent martingale measure.*

Proof. See Lando [1996]. □

Remark 3.5. *In Example 3.2 we found that the pricing formula for the call option was given by*

$$C_0 = \frac{C_0}{(1+r)^0} = \frac{1}{(1+r)^2}\left(q^2 C_{uu} + 2q(1-q)C_{ud} + (1-q)^2 C_{dd}\right), \tag{3.49}$$

which exactly shows that $\mathbb{Q} = (q^2, 2q(1-q), (1-q)^2)$ *is an equivalent martingale measure since*

1. *Strictly positive probabilities are assigned to the three final states.*
2. *The stochastic process* $Z_i = \frac{C_i}{(1+r)^i}$ *has the martingale property under the probability measure* $\mathbb{Q}$*,*

$$Z_0 = \mathbf{E}^{\mathbb{Q}}[Z_2 | \mathscr{F}_0]. \tag{3.50}$$

This leads us to the following theorem which is extremely useful for pricing various types of derivatives.

Theorem 3.3. *Let a security model* $\mathbf{S} = (S^0, \ldots, S^N)$ *be defined on* $(\Omega, \mathscr{F}, \mathbb{P}, \{\mathscr{F}_i\}_{i=1}^T)$*, where* S^0 *is a risk-free asset, and assume that* $\mathbf{S}$ *is arbitrage-free and complete. Let* $\mathbb{Q}$ *denote the unique martingale measure for* $\mathbf{S}$*. An extended model consisting of* $\mathbf{S}$ *and a new security price process* C *is free of arbitrage if and only if*

$$C_t = S_t^0 \mathbf{E}^{\mathbb{Q}}\left[\frac{C_T}{S_T^0} | \mathscr{F}_t\right]. \tag{3.51}$$

Proof. See Musiela and Rutkowski [1997]. □

In the case where the discount rate is deterministic and constant, $S_t^0 = (1+r)^t$, the expression simplifies somewhat.

$$C_t = \frac{1}{(1+r)^{T-t}} \mathbf{E}^{\mathbb{Q}} \left[C_T | \mathscr{F}_t \right]. \tag{3.52}$$

This arbitrage-free pricing formula can be applied to price options of various types, e.g., European call and put options, American options, etc. In the problems some of these are considered.

3.4 Notes

If the reader is further interested in the theory of discrete time finance Lando [1996] gives a excellent introduction and has some of the proofs that we have omitted, and a lot more. There are in Duffie [1996] a few chapters on discrete time finance which goes even further into the theory. This book is highly recommended, though it is written in a compact way.

3.5 Problems

Problem 3.1
Consider a one-period model with two states ($M = 2$) and the following three securities:

1. A stock with initial price S_0^1 and payoff $D_{11} = GS_0$ in state 1 and payoff $D_{12} = BS_0$ in state 2, where $G > B > 0$.
2. A riskless bond with initial price S_0^2 and payoff $D_{21} = D_{22} = (1+r)S_0^2$, where $(1+r)$ is the riskless return and $(1+r)^{-1}$ is the discounting factor.
3. A call option on the stock, with initial price $S_0^3 = C$ and payoffs $D_{3j} = \max[D_{1j} - K, 0]$ for both states, where $K \geq 0$ is the *exercise price* of the option. (The call option gives its holder the right, but not the obligation, to pay K for the stock, after the state is revealed.)

1. Show necessary and sufficient conditions on G, B and $(1+r)$ for the absence of arbitrage involving only the stock and the bond.
2. Assuming no arbitrage for the three securities, calculate the call-option price C explicitly in terms of S_0^1, G, $(1+r)$, B and K. Find the risk-neutral probabilities $\hat{q}_1$ and $\hat{q}_2$ in terms of G, B and R, and show that $C = (1+r)^{-1}\hat{E}[D_3]$, where $\hat{E}$ denotes the expectation with respect to $(\hat{q}_1, \hat{q}_2)$

Problem 3.2
Suppose we have a trinomial market free of arbitrage as described in Example 3.1. We have seen that this model is not complete since there are more

states than traded asset. Now assume that a European call option with the value $C_1^i = \max[S_1^1 - K_c, 0]$ at time $t = 1$ is added to the market.

1. Determine the values of K_c, which completes the market consisting of the bond, the stock and the European call option.

2. Now assume that the market is complete. Determine the price of a European put option with the value $P_1^i = \max[K_p - S_1^i, 0]$ at time time $t = 1$, in terms of the bond, the stock and the call option.

Problem 3.3

A stock index is a weighted sum over some of the most important stocks traded on a particular market. The C20-index is an example on the Danish stock market which includes the 20 most traded stocks.

$$C20_t = \sum_{i=1}^{20} w_i S_t^i \tag{3.53}$$

where $\sum_{i=1}^{20} w_i = 1$. Now assume we have a two period model with 20 states and with the 20 most traded assets, and that the market is complete and free of arbitrage. Assume that the following is known at time $t = 0$: the weights w_i, the initial prices of stocks $\mathbf{S_0}$, the payoff matrix $\mathbf{D}$ and a vector $\mathbf{v}$ indicating the number of stocks v_i that are currently on the market.

1. Determine the value of a future contract which gives the exact value of the C20-index at time $t = 1$.

Now assume that the weights are unknown at time $t = 0$, but determined at time $t = 1$ as the fraction of the total market value that at time $t = 1$ is placed in stock i.

Problem 3.4

Consider a one-period model of a financial market with two securities: a stock and a money market account with initial value B_0 and a constant interest rate

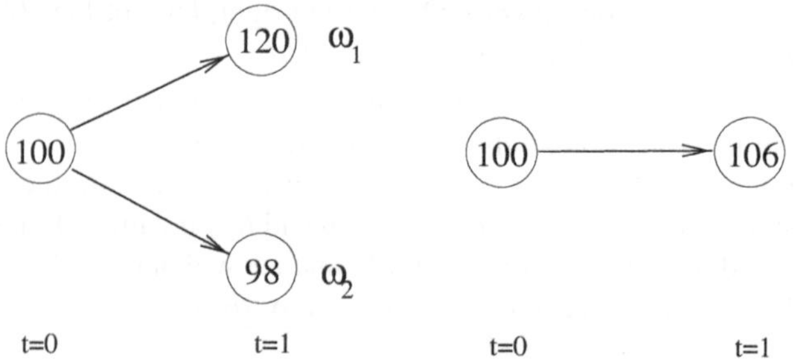

Figure 3.5: Event tree for Problem 3.4.

$r = 6\%$. Let S_t^i denote the value of the stock in state i $(i = 1,2)$ at time t $(t = 0,1)$.

We wish to replicate a contract that pays 115 in state 1 and 95 in state 2.

1. Determine the replicating portfolio (ϕ, ψ), i.e., a portfolio that contains ϕ units of the stock and ψ units of the bond.

2. Compute the fair price of the replicating portfolio at time 0.

3. Define the relative portfolio $(\phi', \psi') = \left(\frac{\phi}{\phi+\psi}, \frac{\psi}{\phi+\psi}\right)$ and fill out the table

r	2%	4%	6%	8%	10%
ϕ					
ψ					
ψ'					
V					

Comment on the results.

Problem 3.5

Consider a two period model of a financial model with a stock and a money market account with the constant interest rate $r = 8\%$. Referring to Figure 3.3, the initial stock price is $S = 100$, $S(\omega_1) = 121$ and $S(\omega_4) = 90.25$. The probability of an increasing stock price is $p = 0.70$ and $1 - p = 0.30$.

1. Determine the price in states 2 and 3. Is the event tree recombinant?

Now we wish to determine the arbitrage-free price of a European call option C_0 with strike price $K = 100$, i.e., the payoff function is $V = \max(S_2 - 100, 0) = (S_2 - 100)^+$, by constructing a replicating portfolio.

2. Assuming that the first stock price movement was upwards, determine the optimal portfolio.

3. Assuming that the first stock price movement was downwards, determine the value of the portfolio.

4. Compute the value of the replicating portfolio at time $t = 0$.

The following questions concern sensitivity analysis, i.e., an analysis of the changes in C_0 due to variations in K and r.

5. Repeat the previous question for the strike prices $K = 98$ and $K = 102$.

6. Compute the arbitrage-free price of the replicating portfolio for $r = 6\%$ and $r = 10\%$. You may assume that $K = 100$.

Chapter 4

Linear time series models

4.1 Introduction

In this chapter we introduce the concepts of linear stochastic processes and linear time series models. The description is rather condensed and far from complete. The justification for the non-completeness is that a lot of other books deal with the subjects, while the main motivation for including this chapter is for references as well as for a brief overview. For a more detailed treatment of linear time series models we refer to Box and Jenkins [1976], Brockwell and Davis [1991], Shumway [1988] and Madsen [2007].

Most of the attention is devoted to an introduction of linear time series models and a discussion of their characteristics and limitations. However, since the prediction concept is of high interest in finance, the use of linear time series models for prediction is also treated. The concept of modelling using linear time series models is only briefly mentioned.

Let us introduce some of the concepts by a very simple example.

Example 4.1 (Prediction models for wheat prices)**.** *In this example we assume that a model is needed for prediction of the monthly prices of wheat. Let P_t denote the price of wheat at time (month) t.*

The first naive guess would be to say that the price next month is the same as in this month. Hence, the predictor is

$$\hat{P}_{t+1|t} = P_t. \tag{4.1}$$

This predictor is called the naive predictor or the persistent predictor.

Next month, i.e., at time $t+1$, the actual price is P_{t+1}. This means that the prediction error or innovation may be computed as

$$\varepsilon_{t+1} = P_{t+1} - \hat{P}_{t+1|t}. \tag{4.2}$$

By combining Eq. (4.1) and (4.2) we obtain the stochastic model for the wheat price

$$P_t = P_{t-1} + \varepsilon_t. \tag{4.3}$$

If $\{\varepsilon_t\}$ is a sequence of uncorrelated random variables (white noise), the process (4.3) is called a random walk. The random walk model is very often seen in finance and econometrics. For this model the optimal predictor is the naive predictor (4.1).

The random walk can be rewritten as

$$P_t = \varepsilon_t + \varepsilon_{t-1} + \cdots \tag{4.4}$$

which shows that the random walk is an integration of the noise, and that the variance of P_t is infinity, and therefore no stationary distribution exists. This is an example of a non-stationary process.

However, it may be worthwhile to try to consider a more general model

$$P_t = \varphi P_{t-1} + \varepsilon_t, \tag{4.5}$$

called the AR(1) model (the autoregressive first-order model). A stationary distribution exists for this process when $|\varphi| < 1$. Notice that the random walk is obtained for $\varphi = 1$.

Another candidate for a model for wheat prices is

$$P_t = \psi P_{t-12} + \varepsilon_t, \tag{4.6}$$

which assumes that the price this month is explained by the price in the same month last year. This seems to be a reasonable guess for a simple model, since it is well known that wheat price exhibits a seasonal variation. (The noise processes in (4.5) and (4.6) are, despite of the notation used, of course not the same.)

For wheat prices it is obvious that both the actual price and the price in the same month in the previous year might be used in a description of the expected price next month. Such a model is obtained if we assume that the innovation ε_t in model (4.5) shows an annual variation, i.e., the combined model is

$$(P_t - \varphi P_{t-1}) - \psi(P_{t-12} - \varphi P_{t-13}) = \varepsilon_t. \tag{4.7}$$

Models like (4.6) and (4.7) are called seasonal models, and they are used very often in econometrics.

Notice, that for $\psi = 0$, we obtain the AR(1) model (4.5), while for $\varphi = 0$ the most simple seasonal model in (4.6) is obtained.

By introducing the back shift operator **B** *by*

$$\mathbf{B}^k P_t = P_{t-k} \tag{4.8}$$

the models can be written in a more compact form. The AR(1) model can be written as $(1 - \varphi\mathbf{B})P_t = \varepsilon_t$, and the seasonal model in (4.7) as

$$(1 - \varphi\mathbf{B})(1 - \varphi\mathbf{B}^{12})P_t = \varepsilon_t. \tag{4.9}$$

If we furthermore introduce the difference operator

$$\nabla = (1 - \mathbf{B}) \tag{4.10}$$

then the random walk can be written $\nabla P_t = \varepsilon_t$.

It is possible for a given time series of observed monthly wheat prices, $P_1, P_2, \ldots, P_T$ to identify the structure of the model and to estimate parameters in that model.

The model identification is most often based on the estimated autocovariance function, since, as it will be shown later in this chapter, the autocovariance function fulfils the same difference equation as the model.

The models considered in the example above will be generalized in Section 4.4. These processes all belong to the more general class of linear processes, which again is highly related to the theory of linear systems. Therefore linear systems and processes are briefly introduced in Section 4.2 and Section 4.3, respectively. The autocovariance function is considered in Section 4.5, and, finally, the use of the linear stochastic models for prediction is treated in Section 4.6.

4.2 Linear systems in the time domain

The definition of linear stochastic processes is highly related to the theory of linear systems (Lindgren [2012]). Therefore the most important theory for linear systems will be briefly reviewed.

The following functions are needed.

Definition 4.1 (Impulse functions). *(Continuous time) Dirac's delta function (or impulse function) $\delta(t)$ is defined by*

$$\int_{-\infty}^{\infty} f(t)\delta(t-t_0)\,dt = f(t_0). \tag{4.11}$$

(Discrete time) Kronecker's delta sequence (or impulse function) is

$$\delta_k = \begin{cases} 1 & \text{for } k=0 \\ 0 & \text{for } k=\pm 1, \pm 2, \cdots \end{cases}. \tag{4.12}$$

The following theorem is fundamental for the theory of linear dynamic systems.

Theorem 4.1 (Existence of impulse response functions). *For a linear, time-invariant system there exists a function h such that the output is obtained as the convolution integral*

$$y(t) = \int_{-\infty}^{\infty} h(u)x(t-u)\,du \tag{4.13}$$

in continuous time, or the convolution sum

$$y_t = \sum_{k=-\infty}^{\infty} h_k x_{t-k} \tag{4.14}$$

in discrete time. The weight function, h, is called the impulse response function, since the output of the system is $y = h$ if the input is the impulse function. Sometimes the weight function is called the filter weights.

Proof. Omitted (see Madsen [2007]). □

Often the *convolution operator* $*$ is used in both cases and the output is then written as $y = h * x$.

Theorem 4.2 (Properties of the convolution operator). *The convolution operator has the following properties:*

a) $h * g = g * h$ *(symmetric).*

b) $(h * g) * f = h * (g * f)$ *(associative).*

c) $h * \delta = h$*, where* δ *is the impulse function.*

Proof. Left for the reader. □

Remark 4.1. *For a given (parameterized) system the impulse response function is often found most conveniently by simply putting* $x = \delta$ *and then calculating the response,* $y = h$*; cf. Theorem 4.2. This is illustrated in Example 4.2.*

Definition 4.2 (Causality). *The system is said to be physically realizable or causal if*

$$h(u) = 0 \ \text{for } u < 0, \tag{4.15}$$

$$h_k = 0 \ \text{for } k < 0, \tag{4.16}$$

for systems in continuous and discrete time, respectively.

After introducing the impulse response function we have

Theorem 4.3 (Stability). *A sufficient condition for stability is that the impulse response function satisfy*

$$\int_{-\infty}^{\infty} |h(u)| \, du < \infty \tag{4.17}$$

or

$$\sum_{k=-\infty}^{\infty} |h_k| < \infty. \tag{4.18}$$

Proof. Omitted. □

Example 4.2 (Calculation of h_k). *Consider the linear, time-invariant system*

$$y_t - 0.8 y_{t-1} = 2x_t - x_{t-1}. \tag{4.19}$$

The impulse response is obtained by defining the external signal x *as an impulse function* δ*. We then see that* $y_k = h_k = 0$ *for* $k < 0$*. For* $k = 0$ *we get*

$$y_0 = 0.8 y_{-1} + 2\delta_0 - \delta_{-1} \tag{4.20}$$

$$= 0.8 \times 0 + 2 \times 1 - 0 = 2, \tag{4.21}$$

i.e., $h_0 = 2$. *Going on we get*

$$y_1 = 0.8y_0 + 2\delta_1 - \delta_0 \tag{4.22}$$

$$= 0.8 \times 2 + 2 \times 0 - 1 = 0.6 \tag{4.23}$$

$$y_2 = 0.8y_1 = 0.48 \tag{4.24}$$

$$\vdots \tag{4.25}$$

$$y_k = 0.8^{k-1}0.6 \ (k > 0). \tag{4.26}$$

Hence, the impulse response function is

$$h_k = \begin{cases} 0 & \text{for } k < 0 \\ 2 & \text{for } k = 0 \\ 0.8^{k-1}0.6 & \text{for } k > 0 \end{cases}$$

which clearly represents a causal system; cf. Definition 4.2. Furthermore, the system is stable since $\sum_0^\infty |h_k| = 2 + 0.6(1 + 0.8 + 0.8^2 + \cdots) = 5 < \infty$.

Theorem 4.4 (Difference and differential equations)**.** *The difference equation*

$$y_t + a_1 y_{t-1} + \cdots + a_p y_{t-p} = b_0 x_{t-\tau} + b_1 x_{t-\tau-1} + \cdots + b_q x_{t-\tau-q} \tag{4.27}$$

represents a linear, time-invariant system in discrete time with the input $\{x_t\}$ *and output* $\{y_t\}$, *where* τ *is an integer denoting the time-delay.*

The differential equation

$$\frac{d^p y(t)}{dt^p} + a_1 \frac{d^{p-1} y(t)}{dt^{p-1}} + \cdots + a_p y(t) = b_0 \frac{d^q x(t-\tau)}{dt^q} + b_1 \frac{d^{q-1} x(t-\tau)}{dt^{q-1}} + \cdots + b_q x(t-\tau) \tag{4.28}$$

represents a linear, time invariant system in continuous time. Here τ *is a time-delay from the input* $x(t)$ *to the output* $y(t)$.

Proof. The systems are linear because the difference/differential equation is linear, and time-invariant because the coefficients and the time-delay are constant. □

Linear systems are often most conveniently described by the transfer function, in the z-domain or in the s-domain for discrete time or continuous time systems, respectively.

Theorem 4.5 (Transfer function)**.** *A linear, time-invariant system in discrete time with input* $\{x_t\}$, *output* $\{y_t\}$ *and impulse function* $\{h_k\}$ *is described in the z-domain by*

$$Y(z) = H(z)X(z) \tag{4.29}$$

where $H(z) = \sum_{t=-\infty}^{\infty} h_t z^{-t}$ *is the transfer function. Here* $Y(z)$ *and* $X(z)$ *are the output and input in the z-domain, which are obtained by a z-transformation of the sequences, i.e.,* $Y(z) = \sum_{t=-\infty}^{\infty} y_t z^{-t}$ *and* $X(z) = \sum_{t=-\infty}^{\infty} x_t z^{-t}$.

Proof. Use the Z-transformation on $y_t = \sum_{k=-\infty}^{\infty} h_k x_{t-k}$. □

Notice that the convolution in the time domain becomes a multiplication in the Z-domain.

For continuous time systems the corresponding relation is

$$Y(s) = H(s)X(s) \tag{4.30}$$

where $Y(s) = \mathscr{L}\{y(t)\} = \int_{-\infty}^{\infty} e^{-st} y(t)dt$, $H(s) = \mathscr{L}\{h(t)\}$ and $X(s) = \mathscr{L}\{x(t)\}$, i.e., the Laplace transform of the various time domain functions. Again $H(s)$ is called the *transfer function*.

4.3 Linear stochastic processes

In the rest of this chapter we only consider stochastic processes in discrete time. Stochastic processes in continuous time will be considered later on.

A linear stochastic process can be considered as generated from a linear system where the input is *white noise*. White noise, which will be denoted $\{\varepsilon_t\}$, is a sequence of uncorrelated, identically distributed random variables. Discrete time white noise is therefore sometimes referred to as a *completely uncorrelated process* or a *pure random process*. We assume in the following that the mean of the white noise process is zero and the variance is σ_ε^2.

Definition 4.3 (The linear process). *A (general) linear process* $\{Y_t\}$ *is a process which can be written as*

$$Y_t - \mu = \sum_{i=0}^{\infty} \psi_i \varepsilon_{t-i}, \tag{4.31}$$

where $\{\varepsilon_t\}$ *is white noise, and* μ *is the mean of the process. (However, if the process is non-stationary then* μ *has no specific meaning except as a reference point for the level of the process.)*

By introducing the linear operator (see Madsen [2007])

$$\psi(\mathbf{B}) = 1 + \sum_{i=1}^{\infty} \psi_i \mathbf{B}^i, \tag{4.32}$$

then (4.31) can be written as

$$Y_t - \mu = \psi(\mathbf{B})\varepsilon_t. \tag{4.33}$$

Due to the close relation to linear systems $\psi(\mathbf{B})$ is called the transfer function for the process (Madsen [2007], Box and Jenkins [1976] and Lindgren [2012]).

Theorem 4.6 (Stationarity for linear processes). *The linear process given by (4.33) is stationary if the sum*

$$\psi(z) = \sum_{i=0}^{\infty} \psi_i z^{-i} \tag{4.34}$$

converges for $|z| \geq 1$.

Proof. Omitted. □

Notice the relation between stability of a linear system and Theorem 4.6.

Remark 4.2 (Cointegration). *If a time series* X_t *shows a linear trend and* $Z_t = (1-B)X_t = \nabla X_t$ *is stationary, then* X_t *is said to be an integrated process of order 1, which we write* $X_t \in I(1)$*. If a time series* X_t *shows a quadratic trend and* $Z_t = \nabla^2 X_t$ *is stationary, then* X_t *is said to be integrated of order 2, which similarly is written as* $X_t \in I(2)$.

In econometrics, additional variables are often introduced to model and, eventually, predict the variations in the process X_t*. Consider the case when* X_t *is an* $I(1)$ *process and an additional variable* Y_t *is also an* $I(1)$ *process. These are said to be cointegrated if* $X_t - \alpha Y_t$ *is stationary and process* $(X_t - \alpha Y_t)$ *is* $I(0)$ *(see e.g. Johansen [1995] for an introduction to cointegration analysis).*

Consider the data in Figure 4.1. It is clearly seen that the money series should be differenced once to obtain stationarity. This also pertains to the bond rate, although it is less clear. By comparing the plots to the left, it is seen that the money demand decreases when the bond rate increases and vice versa. Thus it is to be expected that these series are cointegrated.

4.4 Linear processes with a rational transfer function

A very useful class of linear processes consists of those which have a rational transfer function, i.e., where $\psi(z)$ is a rational function.

4.4.1 ARMA process

The most important process is probably the AutoRegressive-MovingAverage (ARMA) process.

Definition 4.4 (ARMA(p,q) process). *The process* $\{Y_t\}$ *defined by*

$$Y_t + \varphi_1 Y_{t-1} + \cdots + \varphi_p Y_{t-p} = \varepsilon_t + \theta_1 \varepsilon_{t-1} + \cdots + \theta_q \varepsilon_{t-q}, \tag{4.35}$$

where $\{\varepsilon_t\}$ *is white noise, is called an ARMA*(p,q)*-process.*

By introducing the following polynomials in **B**

$$\varphi(B) = (1 + \varphi_1 B + \cdots + \varphi_p B^p) \tag{4.36}$$

$$\theta(B) = (1 + \theta_1 B + \cdots + \theta_q B^q) \tag{4.37}$$

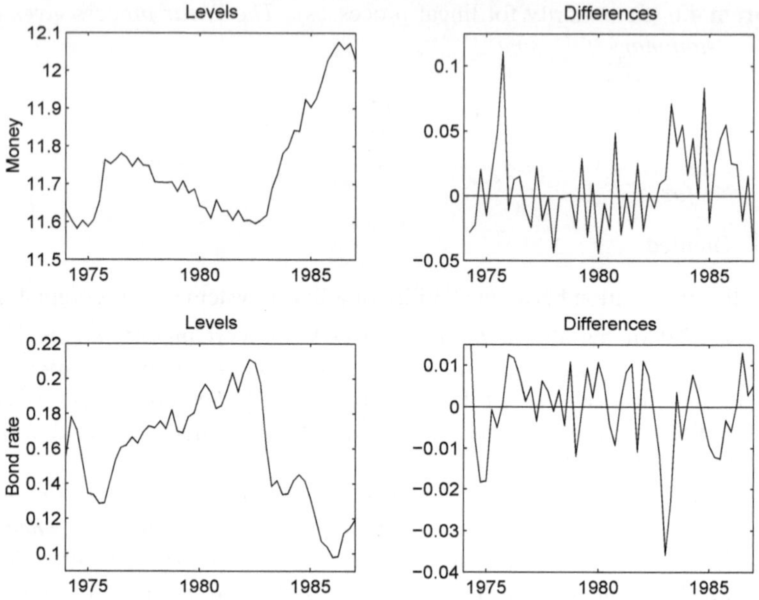

Figure 4.1: The upper-left plot shows observations from 1974:1 to 1987:3 of log real money (m2), where the log transformation has been applied to stabilize the variance. The upper-right plot shows the differenced series. The lower-left plot shows observations from the same time period of the bond rate, and the lower-right plot shows the differenced series.

the ARMA process can be written as

$$\varphi(B)Y_t = \theta(B)\varepsilon_t. \tag{4.38}$$

The ARMA(p,q) process is *stationary* if all the roots of $\varphi(z^{-1}) = 0$ lie inside the unit circle, and it is said to be *invertible* if all the roots of $\theta(z^{-1}) = 0$ lie inside the unit circle.

4.4.2 ARIMA process

As mentioned in the introductory example the random walk given by $(1 - \mathbf{B})Y_t = \varepsilon_t$ is a non-stationary process, since it is an integration of the white noise input.

The AutoRegressive-Integrated-MovingAverage (ARIMA) process is very useful for describing some non-stationary behaviours like stochastic trends.

Definition 4.5 (ARIMA(p,d,q) process). *The process $\{Y_t\}$ is called an ARIMA(p,d,q)-process, if it can be written in the form*

$$\varphi(B)\nabla^d Y_t = \theta(B)\varepsilon_t \qquad (d \in \mathbb{N}), \tag{4.39}$$

where $\{\varepsilon_t\}$ is white noise, $\varphi(B)$ and $\theta(B)$ are polynomials of the order p and q, respectively, and both polymials have all the roots inside the unit circle.

It is clear from the definition that the process

$$W_t = \nabla^d Y_t \tag{4.40}$$

is a stationary and invertible ARMA(p,q) process.

4.4.3 Seasonal models

As a suggestion for a very simple model for the monthly wheat prices in the introductory example we proposed to use the wheat price one year before as an explanatory variable. Assume that the seasonal period is s, then this type of seasonality can be introduced into the ARIMA model by making it *multiplicative*, as also illustrated in Eq. (4.9) in the case of the wheat price.

Definition 4.6 (The multiplicative $(p,d,q)\times(P,D,Q)_s$ model). *The process $\{Y_t\}$ is said to follow a multiplicative $(p,d,q)\times(P,D,Q)_s$ seasonal model if*

$$\varphi(B)\varphi(B^s)\nabla^d\nabla_s^D Y_t = \theta(B)\Theta(B^s)\varepsilon_t \tag{4.41}$$

where $\{\varepsilon_t\}$ is white noise, and φ and θ are polynomials of order p and q, respectively. Furthermore, φ and Θ are polynomials in B^s defined by

$$\varphi(B^s) = 1 + \varphi_1 B^s + \cdots + \varphi_P B^{sP}, \tag{4.42}$$
$$\Theta(B^s) = 1 + \Theta_1 B^s + \cdots + \Theta_Q B^{sQ}, \tag{4.43}$$

and the seasonal difference operator is

$$\nabla_s = (1 - B^s). \tag{4.44}$$

The roots of all the polynomials $(\varphi, \theta, \varphi, \Theta)$ are all inside the unit circle.

Example 4.3. *The number of new cars sold on a monthly basis in Denmark during the period 1955–1984 was investigated in Milhøj [1994]. The variance turned out to depend on the number of sold cars. Therefore, in order to stabilize the variance, the chosen dependent variable is*

$$Y_t = \ln(\textit{Number of sold new cars in month } t).$$

By considering, for instance, the autocovariance function, Milhøj [1994] found that the following $(0,1,1)\times(0,1,1)_{12}$ seasonal model

$$\nabla\nabla_{12} Y_t = (1 + \theta_1 B)(1 + \Theta_1 B^{12})\varepsilon_t \tag{4.45}$$

gave the best description of the observations.

4.5 Autocovariance functions

In this section it is assumed that the considered processes are stationary – and for simplicity it will also be assumed that the means of the involved processes are zero.

Definition 4.7 (Autocovariance function)**.** *The autocovariance function for the stationary process Y_t is*

$$\gamma(k) = \mathrm{Cov}[Y_t, Y_{t+k}] = \mathbf{E}[Y_t Y_{t+k}], \tag{4.46}$$

where the assumption about zero mean for Y_t is used in the last equality. In order to indicate to which process the autocovariance function belongs we shall often use an index, as for instance $\gamma_{YY}(k)$, for the autocovariance function for $\{Y_t\}$.

Definition 4.8 (Cross-covariance function)**.** *The cross-covariance function between two stationary processes X_t and Y_t is*

$$\gamma_{XY}(k) = \mathrm{Cov}[X_t, Y_{t+k}] = \mathbf{E}[X_t Y_{t+k}]. \tag{4.47}$$

The corresponding *autocorrelation function* $\rho(k)$ and *crosscorrelation function* $\rho_{XY}(k)$ are found by normalizing the covariance functions using the appropriate variances, i.e.,

$$\rho(k) = \gamma(k)/\gamma(0), \tag{4.48}$$

$$\rho_{XY}(k) = \frac{\gamma_{XY}(k)}{\sqrt{\gamma_{XX}(0)\gamma_{YY}(0)}}. \tag{4.49}$$

For a more thorough treatment of the covariance and correlation functions we refer to Madsen [2007].

4.5.1 *Autocovariance function for ARMA processes*

Consider the ARMA(p,q)-process:

$$Y_t + \varphi_1 Y_{t-1} + \cdots + \varphi_p Y_{t-p} = \varepsilon_t + \theta_1 \varepsilon_{t-1} + \cdots + \theta_q \varepsilon_{t-q}. \tag{4.50}$$

Remark 4.3. *Notice that by multiplying the relevant polynomials the above formulation also contains the (stationary) seasonal models.*

Theorem 4.7 (Difference equation for $\gamma(k)$)**.** *The autocovariance function $\gamma(k)$ for the ARMA-process in (4.50) satisfies the following inhomogeneous difference equation*

$$\begin{aligned} &\gamma(k) + \varphi_1 \gamma(k-1) + \cdots + \varphi_p \gamma(k-p) = \\ &\qquad \theta_k \gamma_{\varepsilon Y}(0) + \cdots + \theta_q \gamma_{\varepsilon Y}(q-k) \quad \text{for } k = 0, 1, \cdots \end{aligned} \tag{4.51}$$

where $\gamma_{\varepsilon Y}$ is the cross-covariance function between ε_t and Y_t.

Proof. Multiply by Y_{t-k} and take expectations on both sides of (4.50). □

It is noticed that for $p > q$

$$\gamma(k) + \varphi_1 \gamma(k-1) + \cdots + \varphi_p \gamma(k-p) = 0; \quad k = p, p+1, \cdots, \tag{4.52}$$

i.e., the entire autocovariance function fulfils a homogeneous difference equation.

In general it is seen that from lag $k = \max(0, q+1-p)$ the autocovariance function will fulfil the homogeneous difference equation in (4.52).

Remark 4.4. *Since the process is stationary all the roots of the characteristic equation corresponding to the difference equation for the autocovariance function are inside the unit circle. This means that the autocovariance (and the autocorrelation) function from lag* $k = \max(0, q+1-p)$ *consists of a linear combination of damped exponential and harmonic functions.*

4.6 Prediction in linear processes

Assume that an estimate of $Y_{t+k} (k > 0)$ is wanted given the observations available at time t, namely $Y_t, Y_{t-1}, \cdots$. The best estimate is then given by the conditional mean. We have the following fundamental result.

Theorem 4.8 (Optimal prediction)**.** *Assume that the conditional distribution of* Y_{t+k} *given the information set* $(Y_t, Y_{t-1}, \cdots)$ *is symmetric around the conditional mean m and nonincreasing for arguments larger than m. Let the loss function be symmetric and nondecreasing for positive arguments. Then the optimal estimate is given by the conditional mean*

$$\hat{Y}_{t+k|t} = \mathbf{E}[Y_{t+k} | Y_t, Y_{t-1}, \cdots]. \tag{4.53}$$

Proof. Omitted. See for instance Madsen [2007]. □

Consider now, as an example, the ARIMA(p, d, q)-process

$$\varphi(B) \nabla^d Y_t = \theta(B) \varepsilon_t, \tag{4.54}$$

where $\{\varepsilon_t\}$ is white noise with the variance σ^2. All what follows can easily be extended to, for instance, the seasonal ARIMA model.

By introducing $\varphi(\mathbf{B}) = \varphi(\mathbf{B}) \nabla^d$ the ARIMA-process is written

$$Y_t + \varphi_1 Y_{t-1} + \cdots + \varphi_{p+d} Y_{t-p-d} = \varepsilon_t + \theta_1 \varepsilon_{t-1} + \cdots + \theta_q \varepsilon_{t-q} \tag{4.55}$$

where the coefficients $\varphi_1, \ldots, \varphi_{p+d}$ are found from the identity (4.54).

If the k-step ahead forecast is wanted, we consider the equation

$$Y_{t+k} + \varphi_1 Y_{t+k-1} + \cdots + \varphi_{p+d} Y_{t+k-p-d} = \varepsilon_{t+k} + \theta_1 \varepsilon_{t+k-1} + \cdots + \theta_q \varepsilon_{t+k-q} \tag{4.56}$$

and simply take the conditional expectations (as prescribed by Theorem 4.8), i.e.,

$$\begin{aligned} \hat{Y}_{t+k|t} = & -\varphi_1 \mathbf{E}[Y_{t+k-1}|Y_t, Y_{t-1}, \cdots] - \cdots \\ & - \varphi_{p+d} \mathbf{E}[Y_{t+k-p-d}|Y_t, Y_{t-1}, \cdots] \\ & + \mathbf{E}[\varepsilon_{t+k}|Y_t, Y_{t-1}, \cdots] + \theta_1 \mathbf{E}[\varepsilon_{t+k-1}|Y_t, Y_{t-1}, \cdots] \\ & + \cdots + \theta_q \mathbf{E}[\varepsilon_{t+k-q}|Y_t, Y_{t-1}, \cdots]. \end{aligned} \tag{4.57}$$

In the evaluation of (4.57) we use that

$$\begin{aligned} \mathbf{E}[Y_{t-j}|Y_t, Y_{t-1}, \cdots] &= Y_{t-j} &&; \; j = 0, 1, 2, \cdots \\ \mathbf{E}[Y_{t+j}|Y_t, Y_{t-1}, \cdots] &= \hat{Y}_{t+j|t} &&; \; j = 1, 2, \cdots \\ \mathbf{E}[\varepsilon_{t-j}|Y_t, Y_{t-1}, \cdots] &= \varepsilon_{t-j} &&; \; j = 0, 1, 2, \cdots \\ \mathbf{E}[\varepsilon_{t+j}|Y_t, Y_{t-1}, \cdots] &= 0 &&; \; j = 1, 2, \cdots. \end{aligned}$$

Previously we have seen that the autocovariance function fulfils a homogeneous difference equation determined by the autogressive part of the model. Exactly the same holds for the predictor $Y_{t+k|t}$.

Theorem 4.9 (Difference equation for optimal predictor). *For the ARIMA(p,d,q)-process (4.54) the optimal predictor satisfies the homogeneous difference equation*

$$\varphi(B) \nabla^d \hat{Y}_{t+k|t} = 0 \tag{4.58}$$

for $k > q$.

Proof. Assume that we have observations until time t, write the ARIMA-process for Y_{t+k}, and take the expectations conditional on observations until time t. Doing this the MA-part of the model will vanish. □

This is illustrated in the following example

Example 4.4 (Prediction in the ARIMA($0,d,q$)-process). *Consider the ARIMA($0,d,q$)-process*

$$\nabla^d Y_t = \theta(B) \varepsilon_t. \tag{4.59}$$

For $k > q$ we obtain the homogeneous difference equation for the predictor

$$\nabla^d \hat{Y}_{t+k|t} = 0. \tag{4.60}$$

The characteristic equation for the difference equation has a d-double root in one. This means that the general solution is

$$\hat{Y}_{t+k|t} = A_0^t + A_1^t k + A_2^t k^2 + \cdots + A_{d-1}^t k^{d-1}, \tag{4.61}$$

where the superscript t on the coefficients indicates that the particular solution is found using the information set, $Y_t, Y_{t-1}, \cdots$ at time t. That is, the predictor is a polynomial of degree $d-1$.

4.7 Problems

Problem 4.1
Consider the linear, time-invariant system

$$(1-0.6\mathbf{B})(1-0.8\mathbf{B})y_k = (2-\mathbf{B})x_k$$

where it is assumed that $y_k = 0$ and $x_k = 0$ for $k < 0$.
1. Determine the impulse response function h_k for $k = 0, \ldots, 6$.
2. Is the system stable?

Problem 4.2
Consider the first-order autoregressive process

$$y_k - \varphi y_{k-1} = \varepsilon_k \tag{4.62}$$

where $|\varphi| < 1$ and $\{\varepsilon_k\}$ is zero mean white noise with variance σ_ε^2.
1. Determine the mean of y_k.
2. Determine the variance of y_k.
3. Determine the autocovariance function for (4.62).
Now assume that bond prices may be described by the ARI(1,2) process

$$(1+\varphi\mathbf{B})\nabla^2 y_k = \varepsilon_k. \tag{4.63}$$

4. To which order is y_k defined when (4.63) is integrated?

Problem 4.3
Consider the linear, time-invariant system

$$(1-0.8\mathbf{B})^2 y_t = (2-\mathbf{B})x_t$$

where it is assumed that $y_t = 0$ and $x_t = 0$ for $t < 0$.
1. Determine the impulse response function h_t for $t \geq 0$.
2. Is the system stable?

Problem 4.4
Consider the linear system

$$\varphi(\mathbf{B})y_t = \theta(\mathbf{B})x_t$$

where $\varphi(\mathbf{B}) = (0.8\mathbf{B})(1-7.7\mathbf{B})$ and $\theta(\mathbf{B}) = (4-\mathbf{B})(2-\mathbf{B})$. It is assumed that $y_t = 0$ and $x_t = 0$ for $t < 0$.

1. Determine the impulse response function h_t for $t \geq 0$.

2. Is the system stable?

Now consider the linear stochastic process

$$\varphi(\mathbf{B})Y_t = \theta(\mathbf{B})\varepsilon_t$$

where $\{\varepsilon_t\}$ is zero mean white noise with variance σ_ε^2.

3. What is this process called? Is it stationary and/or invertible?

4. Determine and solve the difference equation for the optimal predictor $\hat{Y}_{t+k|t}$ for $k > 2$.

Problem 4.5

1. Calculate the autocorrelation for an $AR(2)$-process

$$X_t + a_1 X_{t-1} + a_2 X_{t-2} = \varepsilon_t \tag{4.64}$$

where $\{\varepsilon_t\}$ is zero mean white noise with variance σ_ε^2.

2. Calculate the autocorrelation for a $MA(2)$-process

$$X_t = \varepsilon_t + c_1 \varepsilon_{t-1} + c_2 \varepsilon_{t-2}. \tag{4.65}$$

3. Calculate the autocorrelation for an $ARMA(1,1)$-process

$$X_t + a_1 X_{t-1} = \varepsilon_t + c_1 \varepsilon_{t-1}. \tag{4.66}$$

4. Determine a suitable model using the sample autocorrelogram below:

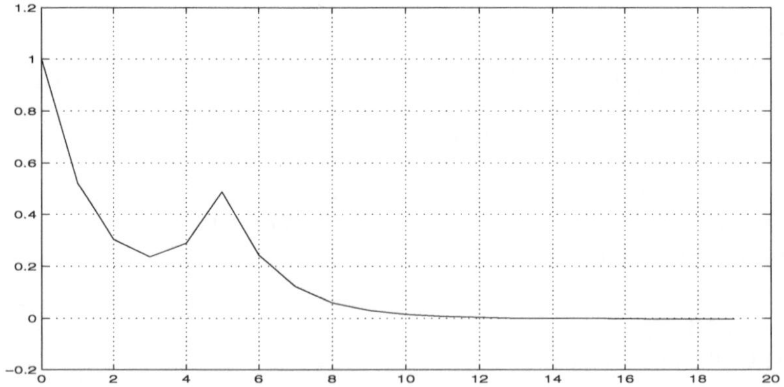

Figure 4.2: Autocorrelation for a linear process.

5. Guesstimate the parameter values (and model order) from the autocorrelation figure.

6. It is common in technical analysis when trying to predict trends to filter data using a short-length MA-filter (say an MA(5)) and a long-range MA filter (say an MA(50)). Trading strategies are subsequently triggered when these processes cross.

What are people relying on these technical analysis tools really doing in terms of linear filters?

Chapter 5

Nonlinear time series models

5.1 Introduction

The linear models have some characteristics, which have been discussed in Chapter 4, and which clearly might be a serious limitation. Some of the most important characteristics and limitations of the linear models are that the dynamics is constant for all values of the process and for all time. Furthermore, the variance of any forecast is constant. It is, however, well known that financial data tends to display *heteroscedasticity* (Section 1.3), which means that the (conditional) variance changes over time and typically depends on the past observations. In finance the variance is an expression of the *risk* or the *volatility*, and it is often found that large values of, for instance, interest rates lead to larger fluctuations in subsequent observations. The distributions (conditional and unconditional) are also often non-Gaussian; cf. Section 1.3.

In this chapter we only consider stationary discrete time models, as continuous-time non-linear models will be treated in some subsequent chapters. The focus will be on parametric models, even though some non-parametric models will be described in this chapter. The *non-parametric models* lead to a generalization of the impulse response function, whereas the *parametric models* can be seen as generalizations of the ARMA models. Several of the most important parametric non-linear models will be described, and it turns out to be convenient to divide the models into two main classes of models depending on the purpose of the model (conditional mean or conditional variance, although combinations are also possible).

Most of the attention in the Chapter will be devoted to models where the conditional mean and variance can be explicitly computed. The description takes place mostly in the time domain. Frequency domain methods, and further information about non-linear time series models, can be found in Priestley [1988], Tong [1990] and Madsen et al. [2007].

5.2 Aim of model building

A model should be able to extract or collect all the information given in the *information set*, i.e., all the past and present data. If this is the case, then the sequence of model's errors does not contain further information about the future, i.e., they should be stochastic independent.

Non-linear modelling: For a given time series $\{Y_t\}$ determine *a general function* f such that $\{\varepsilon_t\}$ defined by

$$f(\{Y_t\}) = \varepsilon_t \tag{5.1}$$

is a *strict white noise* i.e., a sequence of **independent** random variables.

If the strict white noise process is a sequence of identically distributed random variables, then the noise process is *strictly stationary*, or, if the mean and variance are constant, then the noise process is *weakly stationary* or *stationary*. Notice the difference between strict white noise and white noise, as defined on page 62.

The task in non-linear modelling is thus to find some relationship $f(\cdot)$ between the past, present and future observations which reduces the sequence of residuals to strict white noise. This relationship could be expressed using either non-parametric models as Volterra series (generalized impulse response functions), neural nets or using parametric models like the SETAR or STAR model.

5.3 Qualitative properties of the models

From Section 4.3 it is known that linear and stationary stochastic models (or processes) can be written

$$Y_t - \mu = \sum_{k=0}^{\infty} \psi_k \varepsilon_{t-k}, \tag{5.2}$$

where $\{\varepsilon_t\}$ is some white noise, and μ is the mean of the process. Suppose that $\pi(B) = \psi^{-1}(B)$ exists, then the function f is simply given by the non-parametric model $\pi(B)$.

In the linear and stationary case, the modelling may be performed either in the time domain or in the frequency domain (or z-domain). In the non-linear case this twofold possibility does not exist in general and the concept of a *transfer function* describing the system is therefore in general not defined.

However, in the following we shall see how (5.2) can be extended in order to cover non-linear (stationary) models.

5.3.1 Volterra series expansion

Suppose the system is *causal*. In that case (5.1) can be reduced to find a function f such that

$$f(Y_t, Y_{t-1}, \ldots) = \varepsilon_t. \tag{5.3}$$

Suppose also that the model is *causally invertible*, i.e., (5.3) may be "solved" such that we may write

$$Y_t = f^*(\varepsilon_t, \varepsilon_{t-1}, \ldots). \tag{5.4}$$

Furthermore, suppose that f^* is sufficiently well behaved, then there exists a sequence of bounded functions

$$\sum_{k=0}^{\infty} |\psi_k| < \infty, \ \sum_{k=0}^{\infty}\sum_{l=0}^{\infty} |\psi_{kl}| < \infty, \ \sum_{k=0}^{\infty}\sum_{l=0}^{\infty}\sum_{m=0}^{\infty} |\psi_{klm}| < \infty, \ldots$$

such that the right hand side of (5.4) can be expanded in a Taylor series:

$$\begin{aligned} Y_t &= \mu + \sum_{k=0}^{\infty} \psi_k \varepsilon_{t-k} + \sum_{k=0}^{\infty}\sum_{l=0}^{\infty} \psi_{kl} \varepsilon_{t-k}\varepsilon_{t-l} \\ &\quad + \sum_{k=0}^{\infty}\sum_{l=0}^{\infty}\sum_{m=0}^{\infty} \psi_{klm} \varepsilon_{t-k}\varepsilon_{t-l}\varepsilon_{t-m} + \ldots \end{aligned} \tag{5.5}$$

where

$$\mu = f^*(0), \ \psi_k = \left(\frac{\partial f^*}{\partial \varepsilon_{t-k}}\right), \ \psi_{kl} = \left(\frac{\partial^2 f^*}{\partial \varepsilon_{t-k} \partial \varepsilon_{t-l}}\right), \ldots. \tag{5.6}$$

This is called the *Volterra series* for the process $\{Y_t\}$. The sequences $\psi_k, \psi_{kl}, \ldots$ are called the *kernels* of the Volterra series. For the non-linear model the sequence is called the *sequence of generalized impulse response functions*. It is now clear that there is no single impulse response function for non-linear systems, but an infinite sequence of generalized impulse response functions.

Notice that the first two terms in Equation (5.5) correspond to a linear causally invertible model; cf. Equation (5.2).

5.3.2 Generalized transfer functions

The kernel based description in (5.5) is the basis for the derivation of a transfer function concept. Let U_t and Y_t denote the input and the output of a non-linear system respectively. By using the Volterra series representation of the dependence of $\{Y_t\}$ on $\{U_t\}$ and omitting any disturbance (or regarding them as a possible input signal) we get

$$\begin{aligned} Y_t &= \mu + \sum_{k=0}^{\infty} \psi_k U_{t-k} + \sum_{k=0}^{\infty}\sum_{l=0}^{\infty} \psi_{kl} U_{t-k} U_{t-l} \\ &\quad + \sum_{k=0}^{\infty}\sum_{l=0}^{\infty}\sum_{m=0}^{\infty} \psi_{klm} U_{t-k} U_{t-l} U_{t-m} + \ldots \end{aligned} \tag{5.7}$$

where the sequences $\{\psi_k\}, \{\psi_{kl}\}, \ldots$ are given by (5.6).

Recall that for a stationary *linear system* the *transfer function* is defined as

$$H(\omega) = \sum_{k=0}^{\infty} \psi_k e^{-i\omega k} \tag{5.8}$$

and it is completely characterizing the system.

For linear systems it is furthermore well known that

1. If the input is a single harmonic $U_t = A_0 e^{i\omega_0 t}$ then the output is a single harmonic of *the same frequency* with the amplitude scaled by $|H(\omega_0)|$ and the phase shifted by $\arg H(\omega_0)$.
2. Due to the linearity, the *principle of superposition* is valid, and the total output is the sum of the outputs corresponding to the individual frequency components of the input. Hence the system is completely described by knowing the response to all frequencies — that is what the transfer function supplies.

Notice that the above defined transfer function is often (more appropriately) called the *frequency response function.*

For *non-linear systems*, however, neither (1) or (2) holds. More specifically we have that

1. For an input with frequency ω_0, the output will, in general, also contain components at the frequencies $2\omega_0, 3\omega_0, \ldots$ (*frequency multiplication*).
2. For two inputs with frequencies ω_0 and ω_1, the output will contain components at frequencies $\omega_0, \omega_1, (\omega_0 + \omega_1)$ and all harmonics of the frequencies (*intermodulation distortion*).

Hence, in general there is *no such thing as a transfer function* for non-linear systems. However, an *infinite sequence of generalized transfer functions* may be defined as:

$$H_1(\omega_1) = \sum_{k=0}^{\infty} \psi_k e^{-i\omega_1 k} \tag{5.9}$$

$$H_2(\omega_1, \omega_2) = \sum_{k=0}^{\infty}\sum_{l=0}^{\infty} \psi_{kl} e^{-i(\omega_1 k + \omega_2 l)} \tag{5.10}$$

$$H_3(\omega_1, \omega_2, \omega_3) = \sum_{k=0}^{\infty}\sum_{l=0}^{\infty}\sum_{m=0}^{\infty} \psi_{klm} e^{-i(\omega_1 k + \omega_2 l + \omega_3 m)} \tag{5.11}$$

$$\vdots$$

In order to get a frequency interpretation of this sequence of functions, consider the input U_t to be a stationary process with *spectral representation*:

$$U_t = \int_{-\pi}^{\pi} e^{it\omega} dZ_U(\omega) \tag{5.12}$$

when $Z_u(\omega)$ is the spectrum of U. Using the Volterra series in (5.7) we may write the output as

$$\begin{aligned} Y_t &= \int_{-\pi}^{\pi} e^{it\omega_1} H_1(\omega_1) dZ_U(\omega_1) \\ &\quad + \int_{-\pi}^{\pi}\int_{-\pi}^{\pi} e^{it(\omega_1+\omega_2)} H_2(\omega_1, \omega_2) dZ_U(\omega_1) dZ_U(\omega_2) \\ &\quad + \ldots. \end{aligned} \tag{5.13}$$

When U_t is single harmonic, say $U_t = A_0 e^{i\omega_0 t}$, then $dZ_U(\omega) = A_0 dH(\omega - \omega_0)$, where $H(\omega) = 1$ for $\omega > \omega_0$ and $H(\omega) = 0$ for $\omega < \omega_0$. (Note that the Steiltjes integral is used here.) Hence Eq. (5.13) becomes

$$Y_t = A_0 H_1(\omega_0) e^{i\omega_0 t} + A_0^2 H_2(\omega_0, \omega_0) e^{2i\omega_0 t} + \dots. \tag{5.14}$$

The output thus consists of components with frequencies $\omega_0, 2\omega_0, 3\omega_0, \dots$, etc.

5.4 Parameter estimation

Most statistical software have routines for fitting linear time series models to data, but this is rarely the case for any larger class of non-linear models. The statistician must instead be prepared to implement the software him-/herself.

We will review some basic statistical theory in this section. Recall from basic courses in statistics that an estimator is a function of data

$$\hat{\theta}_N = T(X_1, \dots, X_N). \tag{5.15}$$

Estimators should ideally be *unbiased* $\mathbf{E}[\hat{\theta}_N] = \mathbf{E}[T(X_1, \dots, X_N)] = \theta_0$, where θ_0 is the true parameter, or at least *asymptotically unbiased* $\lim_{N\to\infty} \mathbf{E}[T(X_1, \dots, X_N)] = \theta_0$.

A related concept is consistency which means that

$$\hat{\theta}_N \xrightarrow{p} \theta_0 \text{ weak consistency} \tag{5.16}$$

or

$$\hat{\theta}_N \xrightarrow{a.s.} \theta_0 \text{ strong consistency} \tag{5.17}$$

where p mean convergence in probability and $a.s.$ convergence almost surely (see e.g. Shiryaev [1996] for definitions). Consistency is a stronger condition than asymptotic unbiasness, as it also implies that the variance (when it exists) of the estimator goes to zero; cf. the Chebyshev's inequality.

5.4.1 *Maximum likelihood estimation*

A good estimator should optimize the fit of the model to data. This is done in the least squares algorithm by minimizing the squared distance between observations and the model predictions. It turns out, however, that the least squares estimator is suboptimal in certain situation, such as Gaussian ARMA-processes (Madsen [2007]), or when the data is heavy-tailed.

An alternative is to use the maximum likelihood estimator defined as the argument that maximizes the joint likelihood

$$\hat{\theta}_{MLE} = \underset{\theta \in \Theta}{\operatorname{argmax}} L(\theta) \tag{5.18}$$

where

$$L(\theta) = p(x_0, \ldots, x_N | \theta) \quad (5.19)$$

$$= \left(\prod_{n=1}^{N} p(x_n | x_{n-1}, \ldots, x_0, \theta) \right) p(x_0 | \theta). \quad (5.20)$$

The argument maximizing $L(\theta)$ is not affected by a logarithmic transformation, $\ell(\theta) = \log L(\theta)$. The optimization problem can then be written as

$$\hat{\theta}_{MLE} = \underset{\theta \in \Theta}{\operatorname{argmax}} \log p(x_0 | \theta) + \sum_{n=1}^{N} \log p(x_n | x_1, \ldots, x_{n-1}, \theta) \quad (5.21)$$

which is much nicer when trying to compute derivatives with respect to the parameters. The maximum likelihood estimator is consistent under rather general conditions (see Van der Vaart [2000] for details). The estimates are asymptotically Gaussian converging according to

$$\sqrt{N} \left(\hat{\theta} - \theta_0 \right) \xrightarrow{d} N(0, I_F^{-1}), \quad (5.22)$$

where θ_0 is the true parameter and I_F is the so-called Fisher information matrix defined as

$$I_F = \mathbf{Var} \left[\nabla_\theta \log p(X | \theta_0) \right] \quad (5.23)$$

or equivalently

$$I_F = \mathbf{E} \left[(\nabla_\theta \log p(X | \theta_0))(\nabla_\theta \log p(X | \theta_0))^T \right] \quad (5.24)$$

and

$$I_F = -\mathbf{E} \left[\nabla_\theta \nabla_\theta \log p(X | \theta_0) \right] \quad (5.25)$$

where ∇_θ is the gradient and $\nabla_\theta \nabla_\theta$ is the Hessian with respect to the parameters.

A nice feature of the Maximum Likelihood estimator is that it is invariant under (nice) transformations, as the densities that are being used in the loss function are transformed simultaneously with the data. This means that you can typically transform log-Normal data (which can be hard to maximize the log-likelihood for) to Gaussian data, which results in a much simpler optimization problem.

5.4.1.1 Cramér–Rao bound

The maximum likelihood estimator is optimal among all asymptotically unbiased estimators as the variance of any estimator $\hat{\theta} = T(x_1, \ldots, x_N)$ can be bounded from below according to

$$\operatorname{Cov}(T(X)) \geq I_F^{-1}. \quad (5.26)$$

Some further analysis reveals that the only estimator achieving equality with the Fisher information is the maximum likelihood estimator.

5.4.1.2 *The likelihood ratio test*

It is well known how to use t-tests and F-tests when analysing linear, Gaussian regression models. There is a more general likelihood based theory that includes these tests as special cases.

Assume that we are interested in testing

$$H_0 : \theta_i = a_i \tag{5.27}$$

$$H_A : \text{some } \theta_i \neq a_i \tag{5.28}$$

where a_i are some predefined values, typically 0 (the parameter is not needed).

The Likelihood Ratio (LR) statistic is defined as the logarithm of ratio between the likelihood when all parameters are optimized over and the likelihood when some parameters are fixed (as in H_0)

$$\Lambda = \log\left(\frac{\sup_{H_0} L(\theta)}{\sup_{H_0 \cup H_A} L(\theta)}\right). \tag{5.29}$$

The intuition is that a large Λ close to one indicates that the models are similar while a Λ far from one suggests that the restriction of the parameter space is a bad idea.

It can be shown that

$$-2\log(\Lambda) \xrightarrow{d} \chi^2(d) \tag{5.30}$$

where d is the dimension of the parameter vector that is being restricted.

5.4.2 *Quasi-maximum likelihood*

The optimality of the maximum likelihood estimator is only valid when the correct distribution is being used. This is impossible to check empirically, which is why it is good to know what happens when this is not true.

Using a Gaussian likelihood function even when the data are non Gaussian is a kind of quasi-likelihood method. The general result is that estimates are *still consistent, but no longer efficient* in terms of the Cramér-Rao bound. If we denote the density used by $q(X|\theta)$, then it can be shown that the estimates converge according to

$$\sqrt{N}\left(\hat{\theta} - \theta_0\right) \xrightarrow{d} N(0, J^{-1}IJ^{-1}), \tag{5.31}$$

where $J = \mathbf{E}\left[\nabla_\theta \nabla_\theta \log q(X|\theta_0)\right]$ and $I = \mathbf{E}[(\nabla_\theta \log q(X|\theta_0))(\nabla_\theta \log q(X|\theta_0))^T]$. It can be seen that $J^{-1}I$ cancels out when the correct model is being used, but they will differ when $q(X|\theta)$ and $p(X|\theta)$ are different.

5.4.3 *Generalized method of moments*

The *generalized method of moments (GMM)* (Hansen [1982]), is often used in econometrics, but rather seldom within other fields. It is commonly said that GMM is the only development in econometrics in the 80s that might threaten the position of cointegration as the most important contribution to the theory in the field of econometrics. In fact, Lars Peter Hansen, who proposed the GMM framework, was awarded in 2013 The Sveriges Riksbank Prize in Economic Sciences in Memory of Alfred Nobel for his work (GMM and other results).

For the GMM method no explicit assumption about the distribution of the observations is made, but the method can include such assumptions. In fact, it is possible to derive the maximum likelihood estimator as a very special case of the GMM estimator.

5.4.3.1 *GMM and moment restrictions*

Assume that the observations are given as the following sequence of random vectors:

$$\{\mathbf{x}_t \; ; \; t = 1, \cdots, N\}$$

and let θ denote the unknown parameters ($\dim(\theta) = p$).

Let $\mathbf{f}(\mathbf{x}_t, \theta)$ be a q-dimensional zero mean function, which is chosen as some *moment restrictions* implied by the model of $\mathbf{x}_t$.

According to the law of large numbers the sample mean of $\mathbf{f}(\mathbf{x}_t, \theta)$ converges to its population mean

$$\lim_{N\to\infty} \frac{1}{N} \sum_{t=1}^{N} \mathbf{f}(\mathbf{x}_t; \theta) = E\left[\mathbf{f}(\mathbf{x}_t; \theta)\right]. \tag{5.32}$$

The GMM estimates are found by minimizing

$$J_N(\theta) = \left(\frac{1}{N}\sum_{t=1}^{N} \mathbf{f}(\mathbf{x}_t, \theta)\right)^T \mathbf{W}_N \left(\frac{1}{N}\sum_{t=1}^{N} \mathbf{f}(\mathbf{x}_t, \theta)\right) \tag{5.33}$$

where $\mathbf{W}_N \in \mathbb{R}^{q\times q}$ is a positive semidefinite *weight matrix*, which defines a metric subject to which the quadratic form has to be minimized.

Most often the number of restrictions is larger than the number of unknown parameters, i.e., $q > p$. This implies that different estimates are obtained by using different weighting matrices. It can, however, be shown (Hansen [1982]) that:

- Under fairly general regularity conditions the GMM estimator is asymptotically consistent for arbitrary positive definite weight matrices.
- The efficiency of the GMM estimator is dependent on the weight matrix. The optimal weight matrix is given by the inverse of the covariance matrix Ω of the disturbance terms $\mathbf{f}(\mathbf{x}_t, \theta)$.
- The efficiency can be highly dependent on the selected restrictions.

The simplest weight matrix is simply an identity matrix having suitable dimension. This would still lead to consistent estimates, and it is therefore common practice to start with this matrix in order to obtain a first guess.

The optimal or near optimal matrix depends on the parameters and can be computed (and recomputed) once estimates are available. This is either done offline (optimizing the J_N function with a fixed weight matrix) or with a matrix that depends explicitly on the parameters (that version of GMM is often called continuously updated GMM and is closely related to Martingale Estimation Functions; see Bibby and Sørensen [1995]).

5.4.3.2 Standard error of the estimates

Assume that Ω_N is a consistent estimator for the covariance matrix Ω (estimators for Ω are discussed in Section 5.4.3).

Let

$$\Gamma_N = \frac{1}{N}\sum_{t=1}^{N} \frac{\partial \mathbf{f}(\mathbf{x}_t,\theta)}{\partial \theta^T} \tag{5.34}$$

be an estimator for

$$\mathbf{E}\left[\left(\frac{\partial \mathbf{f}(\mathbf{x}_t,\theta)}{\partial \theta^T}\right)\right]. \tag{5.35}$$

It then holds that

$$\sqrt{N}\left(\hat{\theta}_N - \theta_0\right) \to N(\mathbf{0},\Sigma) \tag{5.36}$$

where

$$\Sigma = \left(\Gamma_N^T\, \Omega_N^{-1}\, \Gamma_N\right)^{-1}. \tag{5.37}$$

5.4.3.3 Estimation of the weight matrix

If the sequences of the disturbance terms $\mathbf{f}(\mathbf{x}_t,\theta)$ are serially uncorrelated then an estimate of the weight matrix $W = \Omega^{-1}$ is given by

$$\hat{\Omega}_N = \frac{1}{N}\sum_{t=1}^{N} \mathbf{f}(\mathbf{x}_t,\theta)\mathbf{f}(\mathbf{x}_t,\theta)^T. \tag{5.38}$$

In case of serial correlation (which is most often seen) we can use estimations of the form:

$$\hat{\Omega}_N = \frac{N}{N-p}\sum_{\tau=-N+1}^{N} k\left(\frac{\tau}{S_N}\right)\Phi(\tau) \tag{5.39}$$

where

$$\Phi(\tau) = \frac{1}{N}\sum_{t=\tau+1}^{N} \mathbf{f}(\mathbf{x}_t,\theta)\mathbf{f}^T(\mathbf{x}_{t-\tau},\theta) \tag{5.40}$$

and $k(\cdot)$ is a kernel function (cf. Chapter 6), and S_N is a bandwidth determining which values of the autocovariance function (cf. (5.40), that we are taking into account. The kernel acts as a lag window in spectrum analysis, and the purpose is to weigh down higher lags in the autocovariance function. Also the traditional lag windows, i.e., Bartlett, Parzen, Tukey-Hanning, may be used. See Chapter 6 for more information.

5.4.3.4 *Nested tests for model reduction*

As in traditional maximum likelihood theory, a likelihood ratio type test is also available in the GMM setup, to test nested models against each other. If one starts by estimating a larger/unrestricted model, the test measures to what extent the object function (5.41) is increased by considering a reduced model, where some of the parameters are fixed — often by putting them equal to zero. Formally the test is

$$\tilde{LR} = N\left(\mathrm{J_N}(\hat{\theta}^{\mathrm{r}}) - \mathrm{J_N}(\hat{\theta}^{\mathrm{u}})\right), \tag{5.41}$$

where $\mathrm{J_T}(\hat{\theta}^{\mathrm{r}})$ and $\mathrm{J_T}(\hat{\theta}^{\mathrm{u}})$ are the value of the objective function for the restricted and unrestricted model. Under a set of regularity conditions the likeliood ratio type test statistic has asymptotic chi-square distributions with s degrees of freedom, where s denotes the number of parameter restrictions imposed by the restricted model

$$\tilde{LR} \sim \chi^2(d), \tag{5.42}$$

where d is the dimension of the parameter space being restricted; cf. Equation (5.30).

5.5 Parametric models

The parametric models considered here belong all to various generalizations of the linear ARMA model, namely to models which are able to cover different aspects of non-linearity.

For Gaussian processes it is well known that the conditional mean is linear in the elements of the information set, i.e., it is linear in the past observations. Furthermore, it is known that the conditional variance is constant, and hence independent of the information set. It can be shown that *any Gaussian process conforms to a linear process.* See Chapter 1 in Madsen [2007] for a further description of the conditional mean and variance in the Gaussian case, and Madsen and Holst [1996] for a further discussion on the relation between Gaussian processes and linearity.

For a *non-linear process* the conditional mean is, in general, *not linear*, and the conditional variance is, in general, *not constant.*

The parametric non-linear models can be subdivided into three different classes which will be introduced below. This separation is related to how the *information set* enters the conditional mean and the conditional variance. The separation is useful for identification purposes which will be shown in Chapter 6, since the conditional mean and variance part of the model can be identified using non-parametric estimates of those quantities. Furthermore, the separation illustrates and introduces some of the various non-linear models.

1. *Conditional mean models*, where the conditional mean depends on some (external or internal) variables. This class of models contains the *threshold models* and *regime models*, which are motivated by a desire to describe changes in the dynamic part of the model.
   Consider for instance the first-order model

   $$Y_t = f(Y_{t-1}, \theta) + \varepsilon_t \tag{5.43}$$

   where f is a known function, θ an unknown parameter vector and $\{\varepsilon_t\}$ is a sequence of i.i.d. random variables. For this model the conditional mean is

   $$\mathbf{E}[Y_t | Y_{t-1} = y] = f(y, \theta). \tag{5.44}$$

   This model contains, for instance, first-order versions of some of the threshold models. Models belonging to this class are further described in Section 5.5.1.

2. *Conditional variance models*, where the conditional variance depends on some (external or internal) variables. This class of models contains the *conditional heteroscedastic model*, where the conditional variance depends on past observations

   $$Y_t = g(Y_{t-1}, \theta)\varepsilon_t. \tag{5.45}$$

   As an example Engle [1982] suggested the pure *AutoRegressive-Conditional-Heteroscedastic model* (*ARCH model*) given by

   $$Y_t = \varepsilon_t \sqrt{\theta_1 + \theta_2 Y_{t-1}^2}. \tag{5.46}$$

   For this model the conditional variance is

   $$\mathbf{Var}[Y_t | Y_{t-1} = y] = (\theta_1 + \theta_2 y^2)\sigma_\varepsilon^2. \tag{5.47}$$

   There is a considerable literature on various ARCH-like models, and in Section 5.5.2 we shall go into more details. A survey article is Bera and Higgins [1993] while Bollerslev [2008] provides a more updated overview of the family of ARCH models.

3. *Mixed models*, which contain both a conditional mean and a conditional variance component. A general model subclass consists of those models where the conditional mean and the conditional variance can be expressed using a simple and *finite* information set of past dependent variables, namely

   $$Y_t = f(Y_{t-1}, \ldots, Y_{t-p}; \theta_1) + g(Y_{t-1}, \ldots, Y_{t-p}; \theta_2)\varepsilon_t \tag{5.48}$$

where both functions are known. For these models

$$\mathbf{E}[Y_t|Y_{t-1}=y_1,\dots,Y_{t-p}=y_p]=f(y_1,\dots,y_p;\theta_1), \tag{5.49}$$

$$\mathbf{Var}[Y_t|Y_{t-1}=y_1,\dots,Y_{t-p}=y_p]=g^2(y_1,\dots,y_p;\theta_2)\sigma_\varepsilon^2. \tag{5.50}$$

The bilinear models, like $Y_t=\varepsilon_t+Y_{t-1}\varepsilon_{t-1}$, belong to the class of mixed models, though not to the subclass (5.48). For some models it is possible to establish an explicit expression for both the conditional mean and variance; but in some other cases, as, e.g., the *bilinear model*, this is not possible. The bilinear models are, however, very flexible models, and they have been used in several applications.

Given time series of observations, estimates for the conditional mean and variances in models like (5.43), (5.46) and (5.48) can be computed. These estimates can then be used for *identification of the structure* of the non-linear model. Non-parametric methods and their use for identification of non-linear models are described in Chapter 6.

5.5.1 *Threshold and regime models*

Most of the models described in this section belong to the class of conditional mean models; but some of them also show conditional heteroscedasticity, and these models then belong to the class of mixed models.

The threshold models belong to a very rich class of models, which have been discussed, e.g., in Tong [1983], and in the book Tong [1990]. It has proved to be useful if, for instance, the dynamical behaviour of the system depends on the actual state or process value. In such cases the threshold model may, for instance, approximate the dynamics in some *regimes* by "simple" models (usually linear). *Threshold* values determine the actual regime (or mix of regimes). We list and name below some versions of models with thresholds. The analysis of the probabilistic structure of these types of models including, e.g., discussions of stationarity and stability, is in general very complicated. Some results on stochastic stability may be found in Kushner [1971] and Tong [1990].

5.5.1.1 *Self-exciting threshold AR (SETAR)*

Define intervals $R_1,\dots,R_l$ such that $R_1\cup\dots\cup R_l=\mathbb{R}$ and $R_i\cap R_j=\emptyset$ for all i,j. Each interval R_i is given by $R_i=]r_{i-1};r_i]$, where $r_0=-\infty$ and $r_1,\dots,r_{l-1}\in R$ and $r_l=\infty$. The values $r_0,\dots,r_l$ are called *thresholds*.

The SETAR$(l;d;k_1,k_2,\dots,k_l)$ model is given by:

$$Y_t=a_0^{(J_t)}+\sum_{i=1}^{k_{J_t}}a_i^{(J_t)}Y_{t-i}+\varepsilon_t^{(J_t)} \tag{5.51}$$

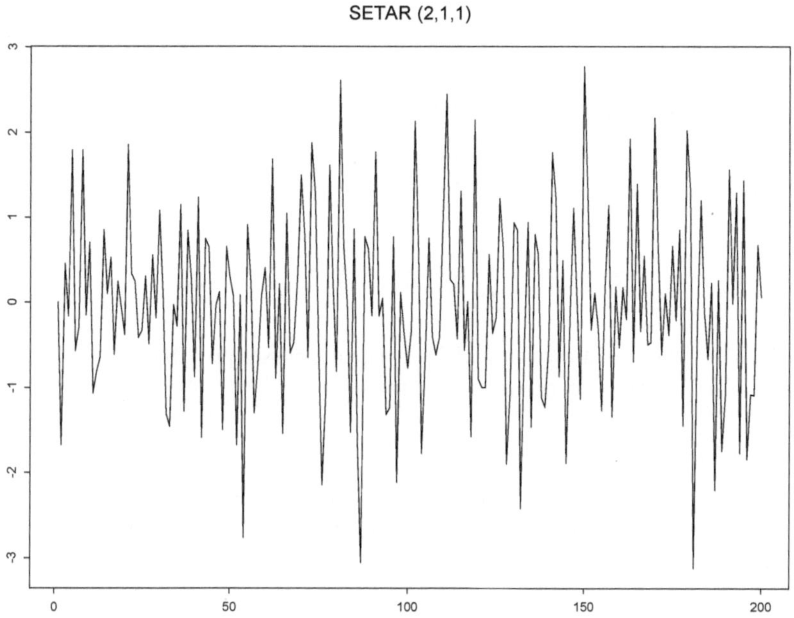

Figure 5.1: A simulation of a SETAR model with two regimes, SETAR(2;1;1).

where the index (J_t) is described by

$$J_t = \begin{cases} 1 & \text{for } Y_{t-d} \in R_1 \\ 2 & \text{for } Y_{t-d} \in R_2 \\ \vdots & \quad\vdots \\ l & \text{for } Y_{t-d} \in R_l. \end{cases} \tag{5.52}$$

The parameter d is the *delay parameter*. Hence the model has l regimes, a delay parameter d and in the j'th regime the process is simply an AR-process of order k_j.

If the AR-processes all have the same order k we often write SETAR$(l;d;k)$.

Example 5.1 (SETAR(2;1;1) model). *A simulation of the SETAR(2;1;1) model:*

$$Y_t = \begin{cases} 1.0 + 0.6Y_{t-1} + \varepsilon_t & \textit{for } Y_{t-1} \le 0 \\ -1.0 + 0.4Y_{t-1} + \varepsilon_t & \textit{for } Y_{t-1} > 0 \end{cases}$$

where $\varepsilon_t \in N(0,1)$ is shown in Figure 5.1.

One of the reasons why SETAR models are popular is due to the fact that the parameters in SETAR models are easy to estimate. The complexity is l

times that of an AR model (you will have to run l regressions instead of only one regression).

5.5.1.2 *Self-exciting threshold ARMA (SETARMA)*

The SETARMA model is an obvious generalization to different ARMA models in the different regimes. The SETARMA$(l;d;k_1,\ldots,k_l;k_1',\ldots,k_l')$ is:

$$Y_t = a_0^{(J_t)} + \sum_{i=1}^{k_{J_t}} a_i^{(J_t)} Y_{t-i} + \sum_{i=1}^{k_{J_t}'} b_i^{(J_t)} \varepsilon_{t-i} + \varepsilon_t \tag{5.53}$$

where J_t is given as above in (5.52). It is, of course, possible also to let the white noise process depend on the regime.

5.5.1.3 *Open loop threshold AR (TARSO)*

A second possible generalization of the basic SETAR structure above is to choose an input signal U_t and let that external signal determine the regime, as, e.g., in the TARSO$(l;(m_1,m_1'),\ldots,(m_l,m_l'))$ model:

$$Y_t = a_0^{(J_t)} + \sum_{i=1}^{k_{J_t}} a_i^{(J_t)} Y_{t-i} + \sum_{i=0}^{k_{J_t}'} b_i^{(J_t)} U_{t-i} + \varepsilon_t. \tag{5.54}$$

Now the regime shifts are governed by

$$J_t = \begin{cases} 1 & \text{for } U_{t-d} \in R_1 \\ 2 & \text{for } U_{t-d} \in R_2 \\ \vdots & \qquad \vdots \\ l & \text{for } U_{t-d} \in R_l \end{cases}, \tag{5.55}$$

i.e., for each value of the regime variable the system is described by an ordinary ARX model. The extension of this structure to, e.g., ARMAX performance in each regime, as well as to regime dependent white noise processes, is immediate.

5.5.1.4 *Smooth threshold AR (STAR)*

Now consider a class of models with a *smooth transition* between the regimes.

The STAR(k) model:

$$Y_t = a_0 + \sum_{j=1}^{k} a_j Y_{t-j} + \left(b_0 + \sum_{j=1}^{k} b_j Y_{t-j} \right) G(Y_{t-d}) + \varepsilon_t \tag{5.56}$$

where $G(Y_{t-d})$ now is the *transition function* lying between zero and one, as for instance the standard Gaussian distribution.

In the literature two specifications for $G(\cdot)$ are commonly considered, namely the logistic and exponential functions:

$$G(y) = (1+\exp(-\gamma_L(y-c_L)))^{-1}; \quad \gamma_L > 0 \tag{5.57}$$

$$G(y) = 1-\exp(-\gamma_E(y-c_E)^2); \quad \gamma_E > 0 \tag{5.58}$$

where γ_L and γ_E are transition parameters, c_L and c_E are threshold parameters (location parameters). The functions used in (5.56) lead to the LSTAR and ESTAR model, respectively.

5.5.1.5 Hidden Markov models and related models

In this variant of general threshold models the selection scheme for the regimes is determined by a stochastic variable $\{J_t\}$, which is independent of the noise sources in the various regimes.

A simple example is the *Independent Governed AR* model, where the selection of the regimes in the IGAR(l;k) model is given by:

$$Y_t = a_0^{(J_t)} + \sum_{i=1}^{k_{J_t}} a_i^{(J_t)} Y_{t-i} + \varepsilon_t^{(J_t)} \tag{5.59}$$

where

$$J_t = \begin{cases} 1 & \text{with prob. } p_1 \\ 2 & \text{with prob. } p_2 \\ \vdots & \vdots \\ l & \text{with prob. } 1-\sum_{i=1}^{l-1} p_i. \end{cases} \tag{5.60}$$

The sequence $\{J_t\}$ may be composed of independent random variables, in which case it is denoted *Exponential autoregressive model (EAR)* in Tong [1990], who also allows in an extension to *Newer Exponential autoregressive models (NEAR)* for a delay in the model to be regime variable dependent.

A particular case appears when the regime variable J_t is given by a stationary Markov chain, i.e., when there exists a matrix of stationary transition probabilities $\mathbf{P}$ describing the switches between the basic autoregressions. This type of l Markov modulated autogressive models of order k is denoted (MMAR(l;k)). Analysis and inference for this type of models is given in, e.g., Holst et al. [1994].

These types of Markov modulations are typically used in description of stochastic processes in telecommunication theory by giving a mechanism for switches between different Poisson processes (cf. Rydén [1993]), but the class is becoming increasingly popular (Cappé et al. [2005]).

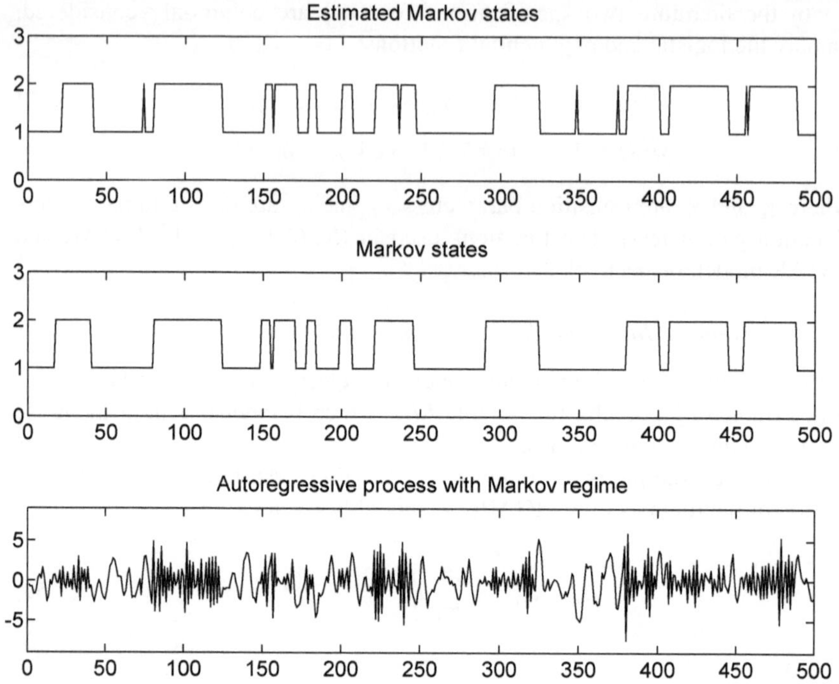

Figure 5.2: A Markov modulated regime model with two AR-processes and a rather inert Markov chain–MMAR(2;2)-process.

Example 5.2 (MMAR(2,2)-process). *Let the process be defined by*

$$
\begin{aligned}
(a_1^{(1)}, a_2^{(1)}) &= (1.1, -0.5) \\
(a_1^{(2)}, a_2^{(2)}) &= (-1.2, -0.5) \\
\varepsilon_t^{(1)} &\in N(0,1) \\
\varepsilon_t^{(2)} &\in N(0,1)
\end{aligned}
$$

and let the transitions between the different regimes be governed by the matrix

$$
\mathbf{P} = \begin{pmatrix} 0.95 & 0.05 \\ 0.05 & 0.95 \end{pmatrix}. \tag{5.61}
$$

The performance of this system is shown in Figure 5.2. The example and the figure are from Thuvesholmen [1994].

It is possible to extend the class further (MacDonald and Zucchini [1997]). Zucchini and MacDonald [2009] or Cappé et al. [2005] provides a nice overview on applications, theory and estimation methods for hidden Markov models.

Remark 5.1 (Transition mechanisms). *For various threshold models the most important difference is in the transition between the regimes:*

- *For SETAR the abrupt transition depends on X_{t-d}.*
- *For STAR the smooth transition depends on X_{t-d}.*
- *For HMM the transition is stochastic.*

5.5.2 *Models with conditional heteroscedasticity (ARCH)*

The ARCH process is introduced by Engle [1982] to allow the conditional variance to change over time as a function of past observations leaving the unconditional variance constant. Hence, the recent past gives information about the one-step prediction variance.

This type of model has proven to be very useful in finance and econometrics for modeling *conditional heteroscedasticity*, i.e., the conditional variance is not constant, but depends on past observations. In finance the *risk* is expressed using the actual (conditional) variability of, for instance, the interest rate. The actual variability is called the *volatility* of the phenomena.

Another reason for considering models for the volatility is that this will increase the statistical efficiency of the estimates in the conditional mean model; cf. weighted least squares.

The general formulation of non-linear, conditional models is the following class of models:

$$Y_t = f(Y_{t-1}, \varepsilon_{t-1}, \ldots, \theta_f) + g(Y_{t-1}, \varepsilon_{t-1}, \ldots, \theta_g)\varepsilon_t \tag{5.62}$$

where $f_t = f(\mathbf{Y}, \mathbf{w}, \theta_f)$ is the conditional mean, $g_t = g(\mathbf{Y}, \mathbf{w}, \theta_g)$ the conditional standard deviation and w_t is white noise having unit variance.

Adding the assumption of normality, the model can be more directly expressed as

$$Y_t | \mathscr{F}_{t-1} \sim N(f_t, g_t g_t^T) \tag{5.63}$$

where $\mathscr{F}_t$ is the information set available at time t, and N is the multivariate probability density function with mean f_t and variance $g_t g_t^T$.

5.5.2.1 *ARCH regression model*

The pure ARCH models belong to the class of conditional variance models, and the ARCH model suggested by Engle [1982] has been used in (5.46). The observation made in Engle [1982] was that volatility is clustering temporally.

The basic specification of the ARCH(p) model is written as:

$$Y_t = \sigma_t w_t,$$
$$\sigma_t^2 = \alpha_0 + \alpha_1 Y_{t-1}^2 + \cdots + \alpha_p Y_{t-p}^2,$$

where the strict white noise sequence $\{w_t\}$ satisfies $\mathbf{E}[w_t] = 0$, $\mathbf{Var}(w_t) = 1$ while $\alpha_i > 0$ is a sufficient but not necessary condition to ensure positive variances. Finally, $\sum \alpha_i < 1$ is required to ensure stationarity. Experience has shown that the number of lags, p, has to be fairly large to fit real data.

The model was used to test whether the conditional volatility depends on lagged values, i.e., if there is conditional heteroscedasticity. The tests are typically Lagrange multiplier or likelihood ratio type tests.

In the more general setup in Engle [1982] the following models are considered:

$$Y_t|\mathscr{F}_{t-1} \sim F(\mathbf{X}_t\beta_f, \sigma_t^2), \tag{5.64}$$

where $F(\cdot,\cdot)$ is some distribution (often but not exclusively Gaussian) with mean $\mathbf{X}_t\beta_f$ and variance σ_t^2, $\theta_f = [\alpha^T \ \beta_f^T]^T$ is a vector of unknown parameters, $\mathbf{X}$ a vector of variables included in the information set (lagged values of Y or external signals) and

$$\varepsilon_t = Y_t - \mathbf{X}_t\beta_f, \tag{5.65}$$

$$\sigma_t^2 = \alpha_0 + \sum_{i=1}^{p} \alpha_i \varepsilon_{t-i}^2. \tag{5.66}$$

Modelling the conditional mean is important as the variance is the second moment minus the first moment squared. Ignoring the conditional mean will therefore incorrectly inflate the conditional variance.

An appealing property due to the simplicity of the ARCH(p) model is that it can be estimated using ordinary least squares, but the least square estimates won't be efficient. Maximum likelihood estimation is therefore often the estimator of choice, using the least squares estimates as initial values for the numerical maximization. The likelihood function for conditional Gaussian models can be found in Engle [1982].

An interesting interpretation of ARCH regression models mentioned by Engle [1982] is that the model for the conditional variance picks up the effect of variables not recognized or otherwise not included in the model.

The ARCH regression model is very useful in monetary theory and finance theory. Portfolios of financial assets are often assumed to be functions of the expected means and variances of the rates of return.

5.5.2.2 GARCH model

The GARCH model, proposed by Bollerslev [1986], is an extension to ARMA-like structure for the model describing the conditional variance. For the ARCH process the conditional variance is specified as a linear function of past sample variances only, whereas for the GARCH process past values of the conditional variance are used as well. The Generalized ARCH (GARCH) model is given by

$$\varepsilon_t|\mathscr{F}_{t-1} \sim F(0, \sigma_t^2) \tag{5.67}$$

$$\sigma_t^2 = \omega + \sum_{i=1}^{q} \alpha_i \varepsilon_{t-i}^2 + \sum_{i=1}^{p} \beta_i \sigma_{t-i}^2 \tag{5.68}$$

where all the coefficients (α_i, β_i) must be non-negative to ensure positive variances, and $\sum_{i=1}^{p} a_i + \sum_{j=1}^{q} \beta_j < 1$ to preserve stability. It is also common to add additional explanatory variables to the σ^2 that are expected to be highly correlated with the variance; cf. Asgharian et al. [2013].

The GARCH(p,q) can be rewritten as an ARMA process. Introduce $\nu = \varepsilon_t^2 - \sigma_t^2 = \sigma_t^2(w_t^2 - 1)$ which is a sequence of white noise. The GARCH(p,q) process can then be written as

$$(1 - \psi(B))\,\varepsilon_t^2 = \omega + (1 - \beta(B))\,\nu_t \tag{5.69}$$

where $\psi(B) = \alpha(B) + \beta(B)$. The ARMA representation of the GARCH model can be used for identification of the order of the GARCH(p,q) model. It has been argued that a GARCH(1,1) is often sufficient for most data sets (Hansen and Lunde [2005]).

There are plenty of non-linear GARCH models (Bollerslev [2008]). Many of these are using the connection between ARMA and GARCH models, extending the ARMA structure by features originating from SETAR or STAR models.

Extending to the GARCH regression model is similar to the extension for the ARCH model

$$Y_t | \mathscr{F}_{t-1} \sim F(\mathbf{X}_t \beta_f, \sigma_t^2). \tag{5.70}$$

It has been argued that a GARCH(1,1) is sufficient; cf. Hansen and Lunde [2005]. They test a large number of alternative specifications and find, after compensating for the asymmetrical test procedure, that they are unable to reject the GARCH(1,1) in favor of more advanced ARCH/GARCH models.

5.5.2.3 EGARCH model

The GARCH model has a major limitation in that it is symmetric, i.e., it doesn't predict the volatility to behave differently depending on the sign of ε_t, contrary to empirical observations on real data.

Another problem with the GARCH model is the requirements on the parameters, making the numerical optimization difficult. These arguments were addressed in the introduction of the EGARCH model in Nelson [1991], specified as

$$\varepsilon_t = w_t \sigma_t, \tag{5.71}$$

$$\sigma_t = \exp\left(\frac{1}{2} h_t\right), \tag{5.72}$$

$$h_t = \omega + \sum_{i=1}^{p} \alpha_i w_{t-1} + \sum_{i=1}^{q} \beta_i h_{t-i}. \tag{5.73}$$

The EGARCH-process addresses the symmetry problems and does also impose less restrictions on the parameters, as the exponent of the conditional variance equation is an ARMA-process.

5.5.2.4 FIGARCH model

One of the more remarkable stylized facts is the dependence in squared or absolute returns (Section 1.3.7). Long range dependence in ordinary time series is often modeled using ARFIMA models (Granger and Joyeux [1980]). Their idea is introduce a fractional differentiation of the ARIMA model in Section 4.4.2 according to

$$\varphi(B)(1-B)^d Y_t = \theta(B)\varepsilon_t, \tag{5.74}$$

where d is some number between 0 and 1. This leads to a model that sits somewhere in between the stationary ARMA model and the non-stationary ARIMA model. They also show that the variance of the resulting process is finite if $d < 1/2$. Requirements for the volatility process to imposed positivity of the process can be found in Conrad and Haag [2006].

Similar ideas were employed on GARCH models in Baillie et al. [1996], Bollerslev and Ole Mikkelsen [1996], as the GARCH model can be written as an ARMA model (Equation (5.69)). Recall the ARMA representation of the GARCH model

$$(1-\psi(B))\,\varepsilon_t^2 = \omega + (1-\beta(B))\,v_t \tag{5.75}$$

while the IGARCH representation is given by

$$\Phi(B)(1-B)\varepsilon_t^2 = \omega + (1-\beta(B))\,v_t \tag{5.76}$$

where $\Phi(B) = (1-\alpha(B)-\beta(B))(1-B)^{-1}$ being of order $m-1$ with $m = \max(p,q)$. The FIGARCH is defined by replacing the first-order differentiation by a fractional differentiation

$$\Phi(B)(1-B)^d\varepsilon_t^2 = \omega + (1-\beta(B))\,v_t \tag{5.77}$$

with the process having finite variance if $-.5 < d < 0.5$. Fractional differentiation can be expressed by the hypergeometric function

$$(1-B)^d = \sum_{k=0}^{\infty} \frac{\Gamma(k-d)}{\Gamma(k+1)\Gamma(-d)} B^k. \tag{5.78}$$

The implications of the fractional integration in terms of memory of the process are analyzed in Davidson [2004].

5.5.2.5 ARCH-M model

Several extensions of the basic ARCH model are possible. In Engle et al. [1987] the ARCH model is extended to allow the conditional variance to affect the mean. In this way changing conditional (co-)variances directly affect, for instance, the expected return; cf. CAPM.

The models are called ARCH-in-Mean or ARCH-M models. The ARCH-M is obtained by a slight modification of Equation (5.63)

$$Y_t|\mathscr{F}_{t-1} \sim F(\mathbf{X}_t\theta_f + \delta\sigma_t^2, \sigma_t^2) \tag{5.79}$$

where the conditional variance σ_t^2 is given by the ARCH model. It is possible to generalize the ARCH-M models by replacing the ARCH model by arbitrary conditional variance models. Additionally, other mean specifications have also been suggested such as

$$Y_t|\mathscr{F}_{t-1} \sim F(\mathbf{X}_t\theta_f + \delta\sigma_t, \sigma_t^2) \tag{5.80}$$

or

$$Y_t|\mathscr{F}_{t-1} \sim F(\mathbf{X}_t\theta_f + \delta\log(\sigma_t^2), \sigma_t^2) \tag{5.81}$$

(Engle et al. [1987]).

5.5.2.6 SW-ARCH model

A further extension of the ARCH models is the switching ARCH model. The idea of the switching ARCH model is to use a combination of different ARCH models. One possible parametrisation is given by

$$\varepsilon_t = \sqrt{g(S_t)}\sigma_t w_t, \tag{5.82}$$

$$\sigma_t^2 = \alpha_0 + \sum_{i=1}^{p}(\alpha(S_t)_{t-i}\varepsilon_{t-i})^2 \tag{5.83}$$

where S_t is the state of a hidden Markov chain taking K different states, and $g(S_t)$ is a constant taking different values depending on S_t. The model can be interpreted as an extension of the ordinary ARCH(p) process by using different ARCH(p) processes for each state of the market.

Switching models are significantly more difficult to estimate than ordinary (G)-ARCH models due to the large number of additional parameters and complex likelihood function (see e.g. Henricsson [2002]), but it can be argued that the states can be interpreted as states of the market, e.g., recession or boom, giving an increased understanding of data.

5.5.2.7 General remarks on ARCH models

The performance of ARCH-like models can often be improved using a combination of the following three different strategies:

1. The AR or ARMA structure of the conditional variance can be extended by introducing external signals (ARX or ARMAX), e.g., it is commonly believed that the trading volume can be used to predict the volatility.

2. The distribution of w_t does not have to be Gaussian. In fact, it is often better to use the t-distribution or the *generalized error distribution*, the latter being specified (having zero mean and unit variance) as

$$f(x) = \frac{\nu \exp\left(-\frac{1}{2}\left|\frac{x}{\lambda}\right|^{\nu}\right)}{\lambda 2^{(\nu+1)/\nu}\Gamma(1/\nu)}, \tag{5.84}$$

where λ is a constant given by

$$\lambda = \left\{\frac{2^{-(2/\nu)}\Gamma(1/\nu)}{\Gamma(3/\nu)}\right\}^{1/2}. \tag{5.85}$$

Other alternatives include the *variance gamma* or the *normal inverse Gaussian* (henceforth called the NIG) distribution. The NIG distribution is a Gaussian mean variance mixture model (Barndorff-Nielsen [1977]), and has been popular in econometrics (Jensen and Lunde [2001], Kiliç [2007]) as well as in the option valuation literature (Cont and Tankov [2004] and Definition 7.11). The probability density function is given by

$$f_{NIG}(x) = \frac{\alpha\delta K_1(\alpha\sqrt{\delta^2+(x-\mu)^2})}{\pi\sqrt{\delta^2+(x-\mu)^2}} e^{\delta\gamma+\beta(x-\mu)}, \tag{5.86}$$

where μ is a location parameter, α controls the tail heaviness, β is an asymmetry parameter and δ is a scale parameter. Finally, K_1 is a modified Bessel function of the second kind.

3. Introducing a non-linear influence of old values of ε_{t-i} to account for the the asymmetric response of volatility shocks. This can be done by replacing lagged values of, e.g., ε_t^2 by a function $f(\varepsilon_{t-i}/\sigma_{t-i})$. The modified EGARCH model would then be specified as

$$\varepsilon_t = \sigma_t w_t \tag{5.87}$$

$$\sigma_t = \exp\left(\frac{1}{2}h_t\right) \tag{5.88}$$

$$h_t = \alpha_0 + \sum_{i=1}^{p} f(w_{t-i}) + \sum_{i=1}^{q} \beta_i h_{t-j} \tag{5.89}$$

where $f(w_{t-i}) = \lambda(|w_{t-i}| - \mathbf{E}[|w_{t-i}|]) + \gamma w_{t-i}$. The response will then depend on the sign of w_{t-i}, allowing for different response to good and bad news.

A related modification is the *Glosten-Jagannathan-Runkle* (GJR) GARCH model (Glosten et al. [1993]), where the conditional volatility is given by

$$\sigma_t^2 = \alpha_0 + \sum_{i=1}^{q}\left(\alpha_i\varepsilon_{t-i}^2 + \gamma_i \mathbf{1}_{\{\varepsilon_{t-i}<0\}}\varepsilon_{t-i}^2\right) + \sum_{i=1}^{p}\beta_i\sigma_{t-i}^2. \tag{5.90}$$

Estimating a positive γ_i parameter means that additional volatility is found due to bad news.

5.5.2.8 *Multivariate GARCH models*

The are many multivariate GARCH models; see Silvennoinen and Teräsvirta [2009b], for a review. These are defined similarly to the univariate models

$$r_t = H_t^{1/2}\eta_t, \tag{5.91}$$

where η_t is an *iid* zero mean, unit covariance random vector. The log-likelihood (when η is a Gaussian vector) for these models is given by

$$\ell_t(\theta) = -\frac{1}{2}\sum_{t=1}^{T}\ln|\det(2\pi H_t)| - \frac{1}{2}\sum_{t=1}^{T} r_t^T H_t^{-1} r_t. \tag{5.92}$$

It is rarely possible to write down closed form expressions for the parameter estimates. Equation (5.92) must therefore be maximized using numerical optimization. Many models are overparametrized from a practical point of view, which is why the CCC and DCC models (more on those below) are popular.

The first multivariate GARCH model was the VEC-GARCH model (Bollerslev et al. [1988]), which is a straightforward generalization of the univariate version. The model, for a N-dimensional problem, is given by

$$\mathrm{vech}(H_t) = c + \sum_{j=1}^{p} A_j \mathrm{vech}(r_{t-j}r_{t-j}^T) + \sum_{j=1}^{q} B_j \mathrm{vech}(H_{t-j}) \tag{5.93}$$

where the vech$(\cdot)$ operator stacks the columns of the lower triangular part of the matrix. Sufficient conditions for strictly positive variances are rather restrictive, and the model is also haunted by the shear number of parameters in it. It can be shown that the dimension of the A_i and B_i matrices is $N(N+1)/2 \times N(N+1)/2$ and hence that the total number of parameters is given by $(p+q)\,(N(N+1)/2)^2 + N(N+1)/2$.

A restricted version of the VEC-GARCH model is the BEKK model (Engle and Kroner [1995]). The number of parameters in this model is lower than for the VEC-GARCH model, and the conditional variances are always positive by construction. The conditional co-variance is given by

$$H_t = CC' + \sum_{j=1}^{q}\sum_{k=1}^{K} A_{kj}^T r_{t-j} r_{t-j}^T A_{kj} + \sum_{j=1}^{p}\sum_{k=1}^{K} B_{kj}^T H_{t-j} B_{kj}, \tag{5.94}$$

where A_{kj}, B_{kj} and C are $N \times N$ matrices, and C is lower triangular. The estimation is still rather complicated as the number of parameters is $(p+q)KN^2 + N(N+1)/2$.

A simpler model is the *Constant Conditional Correlation*-GARCH model due to Bollerslev [1990]. Here the conditional covariance matrix is defined as

$$H_t = D_t P D_t, \tag{5.95}$$

where $D_t = \text{diag}(h_{1t}^{1/2}, \ldots, h_{Nt}^{1/2})$ and P is a positive definite correlation matrix.

The models for the processes $\mathbf{r}_{it}$ are given by univariate models, which, in case of GARCH models, leads to the vector conditional variance process

$$\mathbf{h}_t = \omega + \sum_{j=1}^{q} \mathbf{A}_j \mathbf{r}_{t-j} \odot \mathbf{r}_{t-j} + \sum_{j=1}^{p} \mathbf{B}_j \mathbf{h}_{t-j}, \tag{5.96}$$

where ω is a $N \times 1$ vector, $\mathbf{A}$ and $\mathbf{B}$ are $N \times N$ matrices and $\odot$ is element-wise multiplication.

The CCC-GARCH is often considered to be too simple, as it is unable to capture varying correlations. The *Dynamic Conditional Correlation*-GARCH (see Engle [2002]) replaces the fixed correlation matrix with a dynamics matrix. Start by defining the matrix $\mathbf{Q}_t$ as

$$\mathbf{Q}_t = (1 - a - b)\mathbf{S} + a\varepsilon_{t-1}\varepsilon_{t-1}^T + b\mathbf{Q}_{t-1}. \tag{5.97}$$

The constants a and b are positive numbers satisfying $a + b < 1$, $\mathbf{S}$ is the unconditional correlation matrix of the standardized errors ε and the initial condition $\mathbf{Q}_0$ is some positive definite matrix. This matrix is rescaled to obtain a dynamic correlation matrix according to

$$\mathbf{P}_t = (\mathbf{I} \odot \mathbf{Q})^{-1/2} \mathbf{Q} (\mathbf{I} \odot \mathbf{Q})^{-1/2}. \tag{5.98}$$

The additional flexibility is inexpensive from a computational point of view as only two (a and b) new parameters were added. Several extensions of the DCC-GARCH have been proposed (see e.g. Cappiello et al. [2006] and references therein).

Another extension is the *Smooth Transition Conditional Correlation*-GARCH suggested by Silvennoinen and Teräsvirta [2005, 2009a]; cf. Section 5.5.1.4. Their idea is to use a smooth transition between fixed correlations

$$\mathbf{P}_t = (1 - G(s_t))\mathbf{P}^{(1)} + G(s_t)\mathbf{P}^{(2)}, \tag{5.99}$$

where $\mathbf{P}^{(1)}, \mathbf{P}^{(2)}$ are correlation matrices and $G(\cdot)$ is some smooth transition function. A particularly nice feature with the STCC-GARCH model is the possibility to test for smooth transition effects, by using a Lagrange multiplier test, starting from the standard CCC-GARCH (Silvennoinen and Teräsvirta [2009a]).

5.5.3 *Stochastic volatility models*

A different class of models describing volatility changing over time is the class of stochastic volatility models. The important difference between stochastic volatility models and the class of ARCH models is that the stochastic volatility models specify the volatility as a *latent* or unobservable process. This could be a significant advantage (but it is not for free as we will see soon) as the volatility at time $t+1$ is not completely determined at time t. This matters when there are unexpected shocks, such as terrorist attacks.

A simple stochastic volatility model (Taylor [1982]) is given by

$$Y_t = \exp(V_t/2)w_t, \tag{5.100}$$
$$V_t = \alpha + \beta V_{t-1} + e_t, \tag{5.101}$$

where w_t and e_t are white noise having unit variance. The class of stochastic volatility models can be generalized to continuous time models, where they are being used to derive improved option pricing formulas.

Parameters in discrete time stochastic volatility models can be approximately estimated using Kalman filters (Quasi-Maximum Likelihood), cf. Chapter 14, or using Monte Carlo methods, like MCMC or Sequential Monte Carlo methods (Lopes and Tsay [2011]).

The stochastic volatility can be transformed into a nicer problem by considering $\xi_t = \log(Y_t^2)$. This leads to

$$\xi_t = \log(\exp(V_t)) + \log(w_t^2), \tag{5.102}$$
$$V_t = \alpha + \beta V_{t-1} + e_t, \tag{5.103}$$

which is a linear model. The downside is that $\log(w_t^2)$ is non-Gaussian. It can be shown that $\mathbf{E}[\log(w_t^2)] \approx -1.27$ and $\mathbf{Var}[\log(w_t^2)] = \pi^2/2$. Using a Kalman filter to estimate the parameters is suboptimal (it is not a likelihood method), but the estimates will still be consistent. The Quasi-ML estimates are therefore useful as starting values for a likelihood based method, while modern Monte Carlo methods can provide an approximate maximum likelihood estimate; see Section 14.10 or (Cappé et al. [2005]).

Remark 5.2. *Recall that for a normal distributed stochastic variable, $X \in N(\mu, \sigma^2)$, it holds that*

$$\mathbf{E}[X] = \mu \tag{5.104}$$
$$\mathbf{E}[X^2] = \mu^2 + \sigma^2 \tag{5.105}$$
$$\mathbf{E}[X^3] = \mu^3 + 3\mu\sigma^2 \tag{5.106}$$
$$\mathbf{E}[X^4] = \mu^4 + 6\mu^2\sigma^2 + 3\sigma^4 \tag{5.107}$$
$$\mathbf{E}[X^5] = \mu^5 + 10\mu^3\sigma^2 + 15\mu\sigma^4 \tag{5.108}$$
$$\mathbf{E}[X^6] = \mu^6 + 15\mu^4\sigma^2 + 45\mu^2\sigma^2 + 15\sigma^6 \tag{5.109}$$
$$\mathbf{E}[(X - \mathbf{E}[X])^n] = \sigma^{2n}(2n-1)!! \tag{5.110}$$

for $n \in \mathbb{N}$ where $n!!$ denotes the double factorial, i.e., the product of every odd number from n to 1.

Recall also that $Y = \exp(X)$ *is lognormally distributed* $LN(\mu, \sigma^2)$*, and that*

$$\begin{aligned}
\mathbf{E}[Y] &= \exp(\mu + \sigma^2/2) && (5.111)\\
\mathbf{E}[Y^n] &= \exp(n\mu + n^2\sigma^2/2) && (5.112)\\
\mathbf{Var}[Y] &= \mathbf{E}[(Y - \mathbf{E}[Y])^2] = \exp(2\mu + \sigma^2)(\exp(\sigma^2) - 1) && (5.113)
\end{aligned}$$

for $n \in \mathbb{N}$.

5.6 Model identification

Model identification of non-linear models is almost an art, as the number of possible models grows rapidly with increasing dimension of the parameter vector. The mainstream approach to model identification is to discover the dominant features in data without going into specific models.

This is done in Nielsen and Madsen [2001] and Lindström [2013a] where it is shown how a linear model can be compared to a general non-linear model, defined either as a non-parametric model (Nielsen and Madsen [2001]) or semiparametric model (Lindström [2013a]). The latter even admits testing in terms of adjusted F-tests.

Modern variable selection techniques, such as Lasso, LARS or elastic net (Hastie et al. [2009]), make it possible to estimate and shrink complex models without thinking too much about the exact model structure. This presents a different approach as identification and model fitting procedure is merged into a single step.

5.7 Prediction in nonlinear models

Under exactly the same conditions as for linear models (see Madsen [2007]) the *optimal prediction* is given as the conditional mean, i.e.,

$$\hat{Y}_{t+k|t} = \mathbf{E}[Y_{t+k}|\mathscr{F}_t] \tag{5.114}$$

where $\mathscr{F}_t$ is the information set at time t.

One of the noticeable differences is, however, that the predictor is in general not linear in the elements of the information set. This is illustrated in the following simple example.

Example 5.3 (Prediction). *Consider the first-order model*

$$Y_t = f(Y_{t-1}, \theta) + \varepsilon_t \tag{5.115}$$

where $\{\varepsilon_t\}$ *is a strict white noise.*

For this model the optimal predictor is

$$\mathbf{E}[Y_{t+1}|\psi_t] = \mathbf{E}[Y_{t+1}|Y_t = y] = f(y, \theta) \tag{5.116}$$

where the fact that the model is a first-order Markov model has been used in the first equality.

The important difference between white noise and a strict white noise is illustrated in the next example.

Example 5.4. *Consider the process*

$$Y_t = \varepsilon_t + \theta \varepsilon_{t-1} \varepsilon_{t-2} \tag{5.117}$$

where $\{\varepsilon_t\}$ is strict white noise.

The one-step predictor is

$$\hat{Y}_{t+1|t} = \theta \varepsilon_{t-1} \varepsilon_{t-2}. \tag{5.118}$$

Let us for illustration consider the autocovariance function for $\{Y_t\}$

$$\begin{aligned} \gamma_k &= \mathbf{E}[Y_t Y_{t+k}] = \mathbf{E}[\varepsilon_t \varepsilon_{t+k} + \theta \varepsilon_{t-1} \varepsilon_{t-2} \varepsilon_{t+k} && (5.119)\\ &+ \theta \varepsilon_t \varepsilon_{t+k-1} \varepsilon_{t+k-2} + \theta^2 \varepsilon_{t-1} \varepsilon_{t-2} \varepsilon_{t+k-1} \varepsilon_{t+k-2}] && (5.120)\\ &= 0 \text{ for } k \neq 0, && (5.121) \end{aligned}$$

i.e., $\{Y_t\}$ is white noise. Hence, a non-linear predictor has to be used in order to use the information set for prediction.

5.8 Applications of nonlinear models

5.8.1 *Electricity spot prices*

Hidden Markov models are frequently used when modelling the electricity spot price (these models are often called Independent Spike Models; see Huisman and Mahieu [2003], Janczura and Weron [2010], Regland and Lindström [2012], Lindström and Regland [2012]) as these are often extremely volatile. Renewable energy (e.g. wind power) is less predictable than classical sources of energy. Surplus or lack of energy leads inevitably to large temporal variations in the price.

It is well known that electricity spot prices are mean-reverting and heteroscedastic, and there are also seasonal effects (yearly, weekly and daily) and jumps (Escribano et al. [2011]). The independent spike models provide a simple and very efficient solution to this problem by modelling the spread between the spot price and the forward price, as the forward price is essentially a robust, low-pass filtered version of the spot price (Figure 5.3).

The spread accounts for virtually all seasonality, but there are still bursts of volatility. The logarithm of the spot, y_t, was modeled in Regland and Lindström [2012] using a HMM regime switching model with three states, a normal state with mean-reverting dynamics, a spike (upward jumps) state and a drop (downward jumps) state. This is mathematically given by:

$$\Delta y_{t+1}^{(B)} = \alpha \left(\mu_t - y_t^{(B)} \right) + \sigma \varepsilon_t$$

$$y_{t+1}^{(S)} = Z_{S,t} + \mu_t, \quad Z_S \sim LogN(\mu_S, \sigma_S)$$

$$y_{t+1}^{(D)} = -Z_{D,t} + \mu_t, \quad Z_D \sim LogN(\mu_D, \sigma_D)$$

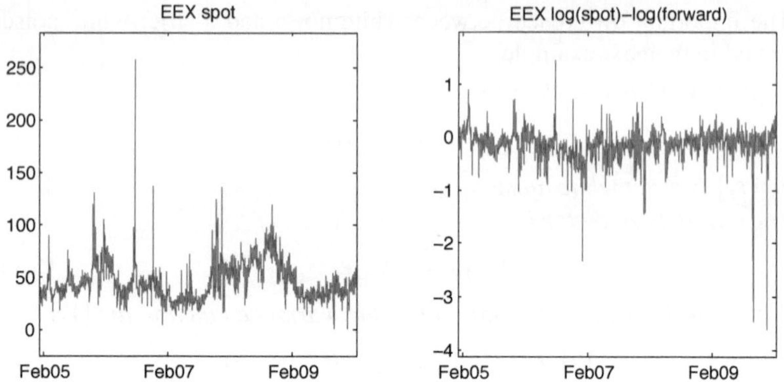

Figure 5.3: The electricity spot price (left) and spread, defined as the difference between the logarithm of the spot and the logarithm of the forward (right). Data from the German EEX market.

where μ_t is the logarithmic month ahead forward price.

The regimes are switching according to a Markov chain $R_t = \{B, S, D\}$ governed by the transition matrix

$$\Pi = \begin{bmatrix} 1 - \pi_{BU} - \pi_{BD} & \pi_{BS} & \pi_{BD} \\ \pi_{SB} & 1 - \pi_{SB} & 0 \\ \pi_{DB} & 0 & 1 - \pi_{DB} \end{bmatrix}.$$

The resulting fit of the model is presented in Figure 5.4, where we see that the regime switch captures the bursts well.

5.8.2 *Comparing ARCH models*

The performance of different models for conditional variance was evaluated in Henricsson [2002]. Different ARCH(p), GARCH(p,q) and SW-ARCH (with two regimes) models were evaluated on the Swedish stock index *Affärsvärldens generalindex* from 1980 to 2001 using a moving window of 4 years of data to estimate the models and the following year to evaluate the forecasting performance. Some observations generated by the study were:

- The standardized residuals are not Gaussian, but are more heavy-tailed, possibly even student-t distributed.
- It is important to include a term in the volatility equation that captures the asymmetric effect of lagged innovations ε_{t-i}.
- The persistence in volatility can only be captured in a satisfactory way using the GARCH model, although the improvement using SW-ARCH over an ordinary ARCH model is significant. Could a SW-GARCH capture both the persistence and the switching regimes?

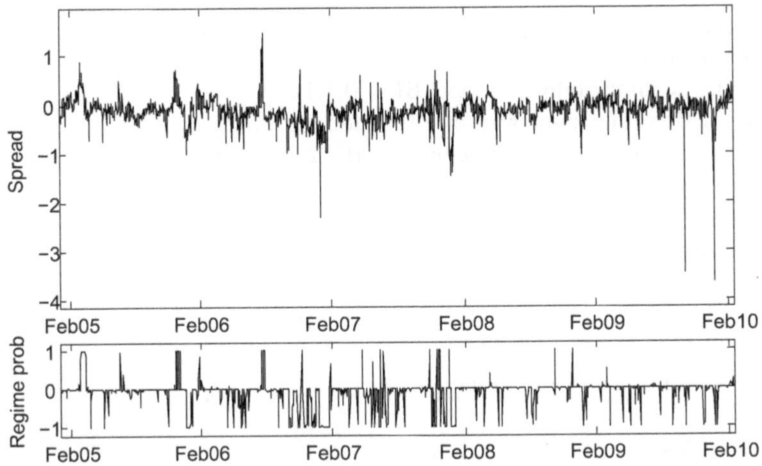

Figure 5.4: Fit of the independent spike model applied to EEX data.

Recent studies (Nystrup et al. [2014]) indicate that as many as four states are needed to to model equity returns, as two or three state regime switching models are unable to capture both the conditional distribution and the dependence structure found in market data.

5.9 Problems

Problem 5.1

Consider a SETAR(3;1;1,1,2) model for a univariate time series Y_t, where $R_1 =]-\infty, 0]$, $R_2 =]0, 15]$ and $R_3 =]15, \infty[$.

1. Specify the thresholds and the delay parameter.

2. Write down the model.

3. Does the model pertaining to the second regime R_2 need to be stable for the complete model to be stable?

Problem 5.2

Consider a STAR(2) with a delay parameter of 1.

1. Write down the model.

2. What is the major difference between SETAR and STAR models?

Problem 5.3

It is common to observe burst-like phenomena in financial time series, which may be due to governmental interventions in the market, attacks on some currency in the foreign exchange markets, the effects of earthquakes in California

and other unpredictable phenomena. Such phenomena may be described by bilinear models.
1. Write down the bilinear model BL(2,0,1,1).
2. Write down the autocovariance function for this particular model.
3. Is it possible to uniquely identify a BL(2,0,1,1) model using this autocovariance function?

Problem 5.4
Consider the *ARCH* model (5.46) as a model of interest rates r_t.
1. Which important characteristics do the *ARCH* models have compared to linear ARMA models?
2. Write down an *ARCH*(3) model.

Problem 5.5
Consider the *ARCH*(1) process

$$\begin{aligned} X_t &= \sqrt{h_t} Z_t \\ h_t &= a_0 + a_1 X_{t-1}^2. \end{aligned}$$

1. Calculate the p'th moment of X_t for $p \in \mathbb{N}$.
2. Can you use information about the moments to estimate parameters?
3. What about GARCH and EGARCH models?

Problem 5.6
Consider the *stochastic volatility model*

$$\begin{aligned} X_t &= \exp\{V_t/2\} Z_t, \\ V_t &= a_0 + a_1 V_{t-1} + e_t, \end{aligned}$$

and assume Z and e are zero mean, unit variance independent random variables.
1. Calculate mean, variance and covariance of V_t.
2. Calculate $\mathbf{E}[X_t^2]$.
Hint: We can write the model as

$$\ln X_t^2 = \ln Z_t^2 + V_t, \tag{5.122}$$

where $\mathbf{E}[\ln Z_t^2] = -(\ln(2) + \gamma) \approx -1.27$ and $\mathbf{Var}[\ln Z_t^2] = \pi^2/2$.
3. Calculate the autocovariance

$$Cov(\ln X_t^2, \ln X_{t+k}^2) = r_V(k) + \frac{\pi^2}{2} \mathbf{1}_{\{k=0\}}, \tag{5.123}$$

where $\mathbf{1}_{\{k=0\}}$ is an indicator function, being 1 if $k = 0$ and zero otherwise.

Chapter 6

Kernel estimators in time series analysis

6.1 Non-parametric estimation

Non-parametric methods are widely used in non-linear model building. Such methods are particularly useful if no prior information about the structure is available, since the estimation procedure is free of parameters and model structure (apart from a smoothing constant).

In this chapter we concentrate on *kernel estimation*. Some other non-parametric methods are based on *splines*, *k nearest neighbour (k-NN)* or *orthogonal series smoothing*. Each method has a specific weighting sequence $\{W_s(x); s = 1, \cdots, N\}$. These weighting sequences are related to each other and it can be argued (Härdle [1990]) that one of the simplest ways of computing a weighting sequence is kernel smoothing. For more information about non-parametric methods see Robinson [1983], Härdle [1990], Silverman [1986], Ruppert et al. [2003] or Hastie et al. [2011].

6.2 Kernel estimators for time series

6.2.1 Introduction

This chapter considers kernel estimation in general and its use in time series analysis. The *non-parametric estimators* are of particular relevance for non-Gaussian or non-linear time series. From kernel estimates of *probability density functions* Gaussianity can be verified or the nature of *non-Gaussianity* can be discovered. Thus non-parametric methods provide information that complements that given, for instance, by higher-order spectral analysis.

Non-parametric estimates of *the conditional expectation* can be used to detect non-linear structures and to *identify* a family of relevant time series models. Consider for instance the time series generated by the non-linear model:

$$Y_t = g(Y_{t-1}, \dots, Y_{t-p}) + h(Y_{t-1}, \dots, Y_{t-p})\varepsilon_t. \tag{6.1}$$

For this model

$$\mathbf{E}[Y_t | Y_{t-1}, \dots] = g(Y_{t-1}, \dots, Y_{t-p}) \tag{6.2}$$

$$\mathbf{Var}[Y_t | Y_{t-1}, \dots] = h^2(Y_{t-1}, \dots, Y_{t-p}) \tag{6.3}$$

where it is implicitly assumed that the variance of the white noise process ε_t is unity in order to avoid identifiability issues.

Thus the non-parametric methods can be used to estimate, e.g., $g(y) = \mathbf{E}[Y_{t+1}|Y_t = y]$ in the simple case $p = 1$. Using this non-parametric estimate a relevant parametrization of $g(\cdot)$ can be suggested.

Furthermore non-parametric estimates can be used to provide *predictors*, i.e., estimators of future values of the time series. Use of non-parametric estimators for getting insight in the *time-varying* behaviour and a complex *dependency on exogenous variables* will also be considered.

In this section we first introduce the most frequently considered non-parametric estimators for time series, the kernel estimators. Next the kernel estimators are described in more detail. Finally, some examples are given on how to use kernel estimation in time series analysis.

6.2.2 *Kernel estimator*

Let $\{Y_t; t = 0, \pm 1, \cdots\}$ be *a strictly stationary process*. A realization is given as a time series $\{y_t; t = 1, \cdots, N\}$, and that single realization of the process is the basis for inference about the process.

Introduce $Z_t = (Y_{t+j_1}, \cdots, Y_{t+j_n})$ and $Y_t^* = (Y_{t+h_1}, \cdots, Y_{t+h_m})$. In order to simplify the notation we consider the case $Y_t^* = (Y_t)$ in the rest of this section. It is obvious how to generalize the equations.

The basic estimated quantity is

$$\mathbf{E}[G(Z_t)|Y_t = y] f_Y(y) \tag{6.4}$$

where f_Y is the probability density function (pdf) of Y_t and G is a known function.

The estimator of (6.4) is

$$[G(Z_t); y] = (N'h)^{-1} \sum_{t=1}^{N'} G(Z_t) k(\frac{y - Y_t}{h}) \tag{6.5}$$

where $k(u)$ is a real bounded function such that $\int k(u) du = 1$, and h is a real number. Here, N' is some number which corrects for the fact that not all N observations can be used in the sum, typically $N' = N - j_n$, and $k(u)$ is the *kernel function* and h is the *bandwidth*.

Let us consider two examples of using Equation (6.5). In the first example it is illustrated that Equation (6.5) is a reasonable estimator.

Example 6.1 (Non-parametric estimation of a pdf)**.** *The pdf of Y_t at y is estimated by*

$$\hat{f}_Y(y) = [1; y] = \frac{1}{Nh} \sum_{t=1}^{N} k\left(\frac{y - Y_t}{h}\right). \tag{6.6}$$

Assume that Y has pdf $f(y)$, then

$$f(y) = \lim_{h \to 0} \frac{1}{2h} \mathbb{P}(y - h < Y \leq y + h) \tag{6.7}$$

when $\mathbb{P}$ *is the distribution function at* Y. *An estimator of* $f(y)$ *is*

$$\hat{f}(y) = \frac{1}{2hN}[\textit{Number of observations in } (y-h;y+h)]. \tag{6.8}$$

Define the rectangular kernel

$$w(u) = \begin{cases} \frac{1}{2} & \textit{if } |u| < 1 \\ 0 & \textit{otherwise.} \end{cases} \tag{6.9}$$

Then the estimator (6.8) *can be written as*

$$\hat{f}(y) = \frac{1}{N}\sum_{t=1}^{N}\frac{1}{h}w\left(\frac{y-Y_t}{h}\right).$$

Now consider the general kernel ($\int k(u)du = 1$*). Then the estimator is*

$$\hat{f}(y) = \frac{1}{Nh}\sum_{t=1}^{N}k\left(\frac{y-Y_t}{h}\right) \tag{6.10}$$

which clearly is equal to Equation (6.6).

Example 6.2. *The estimator of the conditional expectation of* $G(Z_t)$, *given* $Y_t = y$, *is*

$$\begin{aligned}\hat{\mathbf{E}}[G(Z_t)|Y_t = y] &= \frac{[G(Z_t);y]}{[1;y]} \\ &= \frac{\frac{1}{N'}\sum G(Z_t)k(\frac{y-Y_t}{h})}{\frac{1}{N}\sum k(\frac{y-Y_t}{h})} \end{aligned} \tag{6.11}$$

where $[1;y]$ *was found in the previous example.*

Of special interest is the case $G(Z_t) = Y_{t+1}$, *where* (6.11) *estimates* $\mathbf{E}[Y_{t+1}|Y_t = y]$.

6.2.3 Central limit theorems

Central limit theorems can be established under various weak dependence conditions on the process $\{Y_t\}$. Let $\mathscr{F}_u^v$ be the σ-field of events generated by $Y_t; u \le t \le v$. Then introduce the coefficient

$$\alpha_j = \sup_{A\in\mathscr{F}_{-\infty}^t, B\in\mathscr{F}_{t+j}^{\infty}} |P(A\cap B) - P(A)P(B)| : j > 0. \tag{6.12}$$

Definition 6.1 (Strong mixing condition). *The process* X_t *is said to be* strongly mixing *if* $\alpha_j \to 0$ *as* $j \to \infty$.

The strong mixing condition has been used frequently in the asymptotic theory of estimators for time series; but the condition is often very difficult to check.

Central limit theorems for non-parametric estimators of pdfs of a process $\{Y_t\}$, as well as of conditional pdfs and conditional expectations at continuity points, are given by Robinson [1983] under the strong mixing condition.

6.3 Kernel estimation for regression

This section describes in more detail the kernel estimation technique. Since the method is useful for non-parametric regression in general, a notation will be used which is related to non-parametric regression; however, the problem is highly related to the estimator in (6.11), and thus also useful in time series analysis.

6.3.1 *Estimator for regression*

The kernel based non-parametric regression was first proposed by Nadaraya [1964].

Assume that the theoretical relation is

$$Y = g(X^{(1)}, \ldots, X^{(q)}) + \varepsilon \tag{6.13}$$

where ε is a white noise, and g is a continuous function.

Given n observations

$$O = \{(X_1^{(1)}, \ldots, X_1^{(q)}, Y_1), \ldots, (X_n^{(1)}, \ldots, X_n^{(q)}, Y_n)\}$$

the goal is now to estimate the function g.

If $q = 1$, then the *kernel estimator* for g, given the observations, is

$$\hat{g}(x) = \frac{\frac{1}{n}\sum_{s=1}^{n} Y_s k\{h^{-1}(x - X_s)\}}{\frac{1}{n}\sum_{s=1}^{n} k\{h^{-1}(x - X_s)\}}. \tag{6.14}$$

Note that if we compare with Equation (6.5) then $G(Z_t) = Z_t = Y_t$ and the independent variable is now X.

The function k is the *kernel*, and h is the *bandwidth* of the kernel, where $h \to 0$ as $n \to \infty$. Various candidate functions for the kernel have been proposed, but it is shown in Härdle [1990] that the parabolic kernel with bounded support, called the Epanechnikov kernel, minimizes the mean square error among all kernels in which the bandwidth is optimally chosen.

The *Epanechnikov kernel* is given by

$$k_h^{Epa}(u) = \frac{3}{4h}\left(1 - \frac{u^2}{h^2}\right) I_{\{|u| \le h\}}. \tag{6.15}$$

Other possibilities are the rectangular, triangular or the *Gaussian kernel* given by:

$$k_h^{Gau}(u) = \frac{1}{h\sqrt{2\pi}} \exp\left(-\frac{u^2}{2h^2}\right). \tag{6.16}$$

These kernels are depicted in Figure 6.1. The Epanechnikov kernel is shown for $h = 1$, and the Gaussian kernel for $h = 0.45$.

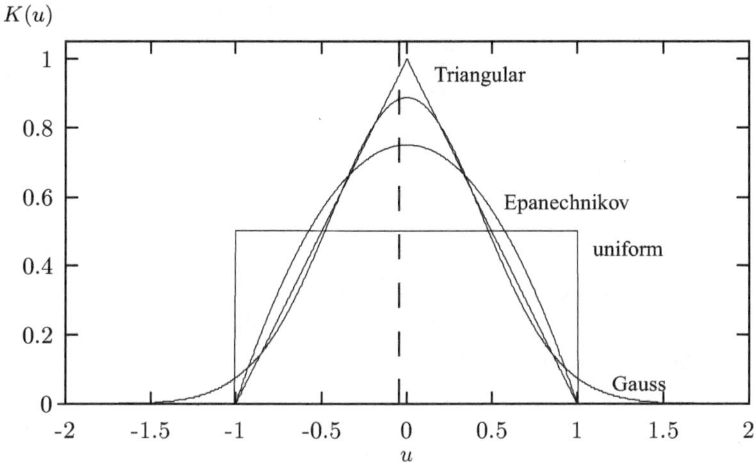

Figure 6.1: Different univariate kernel functions.

If we allow $q > 1$ in (6.14) a kernel of order q has to be used, i.e., a real bounded function $k_q(x_1, \ldots, x_q)$, where $\int k(\mathbf{u})d\mathbf{u} = 1$.

By a generalization of the bandwidth h to the quadratic matrix $\mathbf{h}$ with the dimension $q \times q$ the more general kernel estimator for $g(X^{(1)}, \ldots, X^{(q)})$ is

$$\hat{g}(\mathbf{x}) = \frac{\frac{1}{n}\sum_{s=1}^{n} Y_s k_q[\mathbf{h}^{-1}(\mathbf{x} - \mathbf{X_s})]}{\frac{1}{n}\sum_{s=1}^{n} k_q[\mathbf{h}^{-1}(\mathbf{x} - \mathbf{X_s})]} \tag{6.17}$$

where $\mathbf{x} = (x_1, \ldots, x_q)$ and $\mathbf{X_s} = (X_1^{(1)}, \ldots, X_1^{(q)})$. This is called the *Nadaraya-Watson estimator.*

6.3.2 Product kernel

In practice product kernels are used, i.e.,

$$k_q(\mathbf{h}^{-1}\mathbf{x}) = \prod_{i=1}^{q} k(x_i/h_i) \tag{6.18}$$

where k is a kernel of order 1.

Assuming that $h_i = h, \quad i = 1, \ldots, q$ the following generalization of the one-dimensional case in (6.14) is obtained

$$\hat{g}(x_1, \ldots, x_q) = \frac{\frac{1}{n}\sum_{s=1}^{n} Y_s \prod_{i=1}^{q} k\{h^{-1}(x_i - X_s^{(i)})\}}{\frac{1}{n}\sum_{s=1}^{n} \prod_{i=1}^{q} k\{h^{-1}(x_i - X_s^{(i)})\}}. \tag{6.19}$$

6.3.3 *Non-parametric estimation of the pdf*

An estimate of the probability density function (pdf) is Robinson [1983]

$$\hat{f}(x_{i_1},\ldots,x_{i_d}) = \frac{1}{n-i_d+i_1}\sum_{s=i_d+1}^{n+i_1}\prod_{j=1}^{d} h^{-1}k\{h^{-1}(x_{i_j}-X_{s-i_j})\}. \tag{6.20}$$

6.3.4 *Non-parametric LS*

If we define the weight $W_s(\mathbf{x})$ by

$$W_s(\mathbf{x}) = \frac{\prod_{i=1}^{q} k\{h^{-1}(x_i - X_s^{(i)})\}}{\frac{1}{n}\sum_{s=1}^{n}\prod_{i=1}^{q} k\{h^{-1}(x_i - X_s^{(i)})\}} \tag{6.21}$$

then it is seen that Equation (6.19) corresponds to the local average:

$$\hat{g}(x_1,\ldots,x_q) = \frac{1}{n}\sum_{s=1}^{n} W_s(\mathbf{x})Y_s. \tag{6.22}$$

The estimate is actually a *non-parametric least squares estimate* at the point $\mathbf{x}$. This is recognized from the fact that the solution to the least squares problem

$$\arg\min_{\theta} \frac{1}{n}\sum_{s=1}^{n} W_s(\mathbf{x})(Y_s-\theta)^2 \tag{6.23}$$

is given by

$$\hat{\theta}_{LS}(\mathbf{x}) = \frac{\sum_{s=1}^{n} W_s(\mathbf{x})Y_s}{\sum_{s=1}^{n} W_s(\mathbf{x})}. \tag{6.24}$$

This shows that at each $\mathbf{x}$, the estimate $\hat{g}$ is a scaled weighted LS location estimate, i.e.,

$$\hat{g}(\mathbf{x}) = \hat{\theta}_{LS}\frac{1}{n}\sum_{s=1}^{n} W_s(\mathbf{x}). \tag{6.25}$$

6.3.5 *Bandwidth*

The bandwidth h determines the smoothness of $\hat{g}$. In analogy with smoothing in spectrum analysis:

- If h is small the variance is large but the bias is small.
- If h is large the variance is small but the bias is large.

The limits provide some insight:

- As $h \to \infty$ it is seen that $\hat{g}(x_1,\ldots,x_q) = \bar{Y}$ as all data are included and given equal weights.
- As $h \to 0$ it is seen that $\hat{g}(x_1,\ldots,x_q) = Y_i$ for $(x_1,\ldots,x_q) = (X_i^{(1)},\ldots,X_i^{(q)})$ and otherwise undefined (or possibly 0 depending on how ratios of zeros are defined).

6.3.6 *Selection of bandwidth — cross validation*

The ultimate goal for the selection of h is to minimize the mean square error (MSE)(see Härdle [1990])

$$\text{MSE}(h) = \frac{1}{n}\sum_{i=1}^{n}[\hat{g}(X_i^{(1)},\ldots,X_i^{(q)}) - g(X_i^{(1)},\ldots,X_i^{(q)})]^2 \times \quad (6.26)$$

$$w(X_i^{(1)},\ldots,X_i^{(q)}) \quad (6.27)$$

where $w(\ldots)$ is a weight function which screens off some of the extreme observations, and g is the unknown function. A solution is the "plug-in" method, where Y_i is used as an estimate of $g(X_i^{(1)},\ldots,X_i^{(q)})$ in (6.26).

Hence, the criterion is

$$\widehat{\text{MSE}}(h) = \frac{1}{n}\sum_{i=1}^{n}[\hat{g}(X_i^{(1)},\ldots,X_i^{(q)}) - Y_i]^2 w(X_i^{(1)},\ldots,X_i^{(q)}) \quad (6.28)$$

but it is clear that $\widehat{\text{MSE}}(h) \to 0$ for $h \to 0$, since $y_i - \hat{g}(x_i^{(1)},\ldots,x_i^{(q)}) \to 0$ when $h \to 0$.

It is clear that a modification is needed! In the "leave one out" estimator the idea is to avoid that $(X_i^{(1)},\ldots,X_i^{(q)})$ is used in the estimate for Y_i. For every data $(X_i^{(1)},\ldots,X_i^{(q)},Y_i)$ we define an estimator $\hat{g}_{(i)}$ for Y_i based on all data except $(X_i^{(1)},\ldots,X_i^{(q)})$. The n estimators $\hat{g}_{(1)},\ldots,\hat{g}_{(n)}$ (called the "leave one out" estimators) are written

$$\hat{g}_{(j)}(x_1,\ldots,x_q) = \frac{\frac{1}{n-1}\sum_{s\neq j} Y_s \prod_{i=1}^{q} k\{h^{-1}(x_i - X_s^{(i)})\}}{\frac{1}{n-1}\sum_{s\neq j}\prod_{i=1}^{q} k\{h^{-1}(x_i - X_s^{(i)})\}}. \quad (6.29)$$

Now the cross-validation criterion using the "leave one out" estimates $\hat{g}_{(1)},\ldots,\hat{g}_{(n)}$ is

$$CV(h) = \frac{1}{n}\sum_{i=1}^{n}[\hat{g}_{(i)}(X_i^{(1)},\ldots,X_i^{(q)}) - Y_i]^2 w(X_i^{(1)},\ldots,X_i^{(q)}). \quad (6.30)$$

It can be shown that under weak assumptions the estimate of the bandwidth $\hat{h}$ that is obtained by minimizing the cross-validation criterion is asymptotic optimal, i.e., it minimizes (6.26) (Härdle [1990]). An example of using the CV procedure is shown in Figure 6.7.

6.3.7 *Variance of the non-parametric estimates*

To assess the variance of the curve estimate at point $\mathbf{x}$ Härdle [1990] proposes the pointwise estimator given by

$$\hat{\sigma}^2(\mathbf{x}) = \frac{1}{n}\sum_{s=1}^{n} W_s(\mathbf{x})\,(\hat{g}(\mathbf{X}_s) - Y_s)^2 \quad (6.31)$$

where the weights are given as shown previously by

$$W_s(\mathbf{x}) = \frac{\prod_{i=1}^{q} k\{h^{-1}(x_i - X_s^{(i)})\}}{\frac{1}{n}\sum_{s=1}^{n}\prod_{i=1}^{q} k\{h^{-1}(x_i - X_s^{(i)})\}}. \tag{6.32}$$

Remembering the WLS interpretation this estimate seems reasonable.

6.4 Applications of kernel estimators

6.4.1 *Non-parametric estimation of the conditional mean and variance*

Assume a realization of a stochastic process $\{X_1, \dots, X_n\}$.

Goal: Use the realization to estimate the functions $g(\cdot)$ and $h(\cdot)$ in the model

$$X_t = g(X_{t-1}, \dots, X_{t-p}) + h(X_{t-1}, \dots, X_{t-q})\varepsilon_t. \tag{6.33}$$

For the conditional mean and the conditional variance we shall use the notation

$$\begin{aligned} M(x_{i_1}, \dots, x_{i_d}) &= \mathbf{E}[X_t | X_{t-i_1} = x_{i_1}, \dots, X_{t-i_d} = x_{i_d}], & (6.34)\\ V(x_{i_1}, \dots, x_{i_d}) &= \mathbf{Var}[X_t | X_{t-i_1} = x_{i_1}, \dots, X_{t-i_d} = x_{i_d}]. & (6.35) \end{aligned}$$

One solution is to use the kernel estimator (other possibilities are splines, nearest neighbour or neural network estimates).

Using a product kernel we obtain

$$\hat{M}(x_{i_1}, \dots, x_{i_d}) = \frac{\frac{1}{n-i_d}\sum_{s=i_d+1}^{n} X_s \prod_{j=1}^{d} k\{h^{-1}(x_{i_j} - X_{s-i_j})\}}{\frac{1}{n-i_d+i_1}\sum_{s=i_d+1}^{n+i_1}\prod_{j=1}^{d} k\{h^{-1}(x_{i_j} - X_{s-i_j})\}}. \tag{6.36}$$

Assuming that $\mathbf{E}[X_t] = 0$ the estimator for $V(\cdot)$ is

$$\hat{V}(x_{i_1}, \dots, x_{i_d}) = \frac{\frac{1}{n-i_d}\sum_{s=i_d+1}^{n} X_s^2 \prod_{j=1}^{d} k\{h^{-1}(x_{i_j} - X_{s-i_j})\}}{\frac{1}{n-i_d+i_1}\sum_{s=i_d+1}^{n+i_1}\prod_{j=1}^{d} k\{h^{-1}(x_{i_j} - X_{s-i_j})\}}. \tag{6.37}$$

If $\mathbf{E}[X_t] \neq 0$ it is clear that the above estimator is changed to

$$\begin{aligned} \hat{V}(x_{i_1}, \dots, x_{i_d}) &= \frac{\frac{1}{n-i_d}\sum_{s=i_d+1}^{n} X_s^2 \prod_{j=1}^{d} k\{h^{-1}(x_{i_j} - X_{s-i_j})\}}{\frac{1}{n-i_d+i_1}\sum_{s=i_d+1}^{n+i_1}\prod_{j=1}^{d} k\{h^{-1}(x_{i_j} - X_{s-i_j})\}}\\ &\quad -\hat{M}^2(x_{i_1}, \dots, x_{i_d}). \end{aligned} \tag{6.38}$$

Example 6.3. *Simulations of 10 independent time series have been generated from the following non-linear models:*

$$\begin{aligned} A: \quad X_t &= \begin{cases} -0.8X_{t-1} + \varepsilon_t, & X_{t-1} \geq 0 \\ 0.8X_{t-1} + 1.5 + \varepsilon_t, & X_{t-1} < 0 \end{cases}\\ B: \quad X_t &= \sqrt{1 + X_{t-1}^2}\,\varepsilon_t. \end{aligned}$$

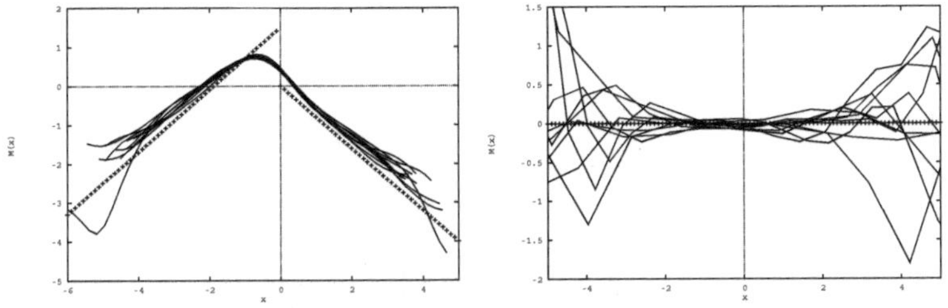

(a) Model A. SETAR(2,1,1) (b) Model B. ARCH(1)

Figure 6.2: Estimated conditional mean $M(x)$.

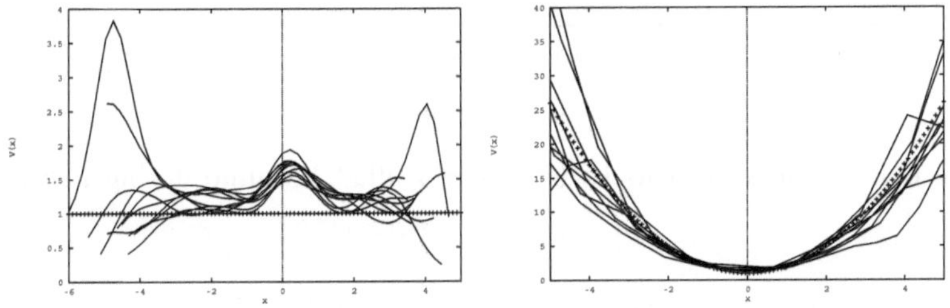

(a) Model A. SETAR(2,1,1) (b) Model B. ARCH(1)

Figure 6.3: Estimated conditional variance $V(x)$.

The first model is a SETAR model with non-linear conditional mean and constant conditional variance whereas the second model is an ARCH model with constant conditional mean and state dependent conditional variance.

A Gaussian kernel with $h = 0.6$ *is used to estimate the conditional mean (Figure 6.2) and variance (Figure 6.3) in order to detect the nonlinearities. The theoretical conditional mean and variance is shown with "+".*

6.4.2 *Non-parametric estimation of non-stationarity — an example*

Non-parametric methods can be applied to identify the structure of the existing relationships leading to proposals for parametric model classes. An example of identifying the diurnal dependence in a non-stationary time series is given in the following.

Measurements of heat supply from 16 terrace houses in Kulladal, a suburb of Malmö in Sweden, are used to estimate the heat load as a function of the time of the day.

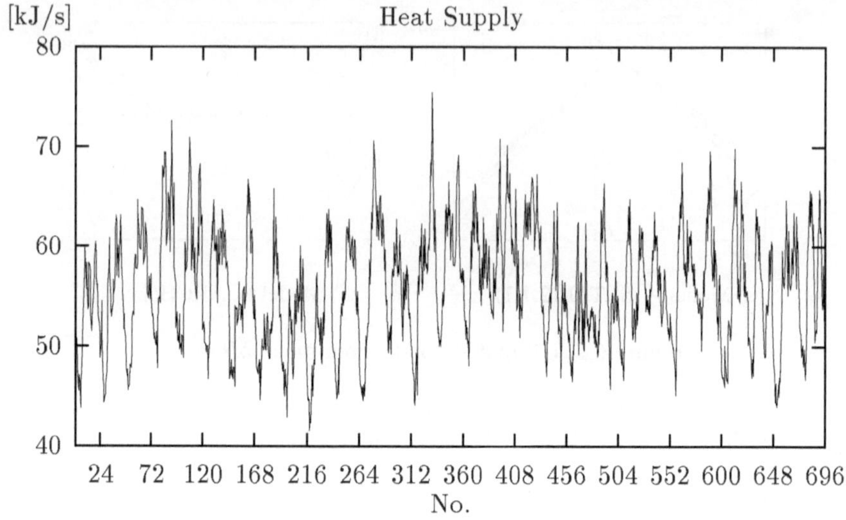

Figure 6.4: Supplied heat to 16 houses in Kulladal/Malmö during February 1989.

The heat supply was measured every 15 minutes for 27 days. The transport delay between the consumers and the measuring instruments is not more than a couple of minutes.

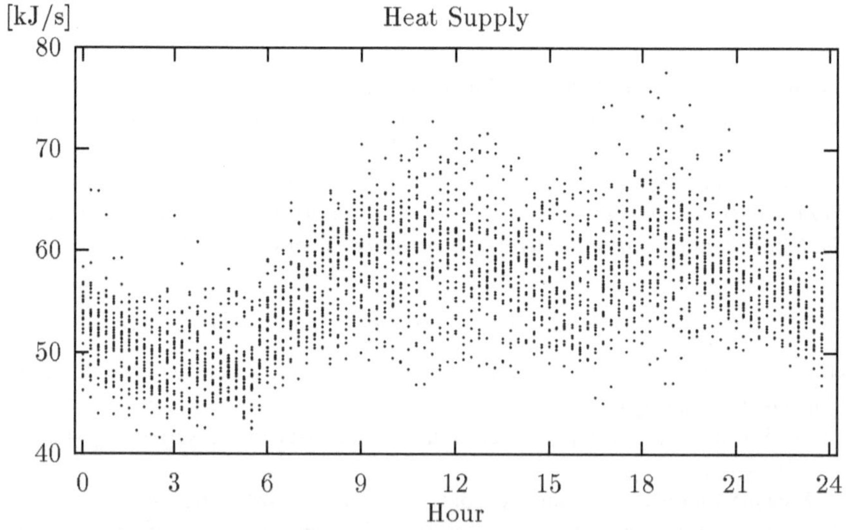

Figure 6.5: Supplied heat versus time of day and night.

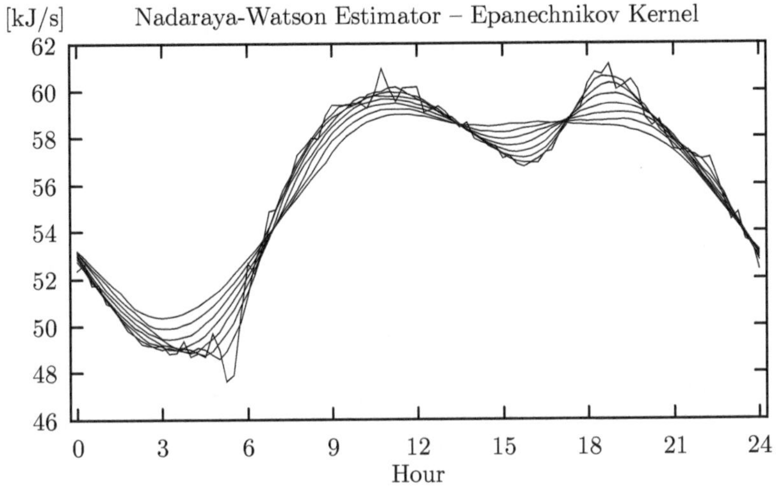

Figure 6.6: Smoothing of the diurnal power load curve using an Epanechnikov kernel and bandwidths 0.125, 0.625,... , 3.625.

It is assumed that the heat supply can be related to the time of day, and that there is no difference between the days for the considered period. Then the regression curve is a function only of the time of day, and it is this functional relationship, which will be considered.

Figure 6.6 shows the Epanechnikov curve estimate calculated for a spectrum of bandwidths. It is clear that the characteristics of the non-smoothed averages gradually disappear, when the bandwidth is increased.

When the cross-validation function is brought into action for bandwidth selection on the original data we get the result shown in Figure 6.7. Obviously the minimum of the CV-function is obtained for a bandwidth close to 1.3.

6.4.3 Non-parametric estimation of dependence on external variables — an example

This example illustrates the use of kernel estimators for exploring the (static) dependence on external variables. Data were collected in the district heating system in Esbjerg, Denmark, during the period August 14 to December 10, 1989.

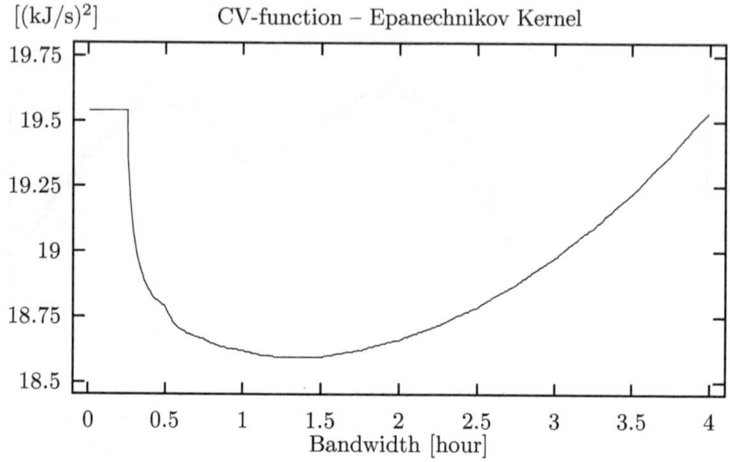

Figure 6.7: CV-function applied on the original district heating data (Kulladal/Malmö) using the Epanechnikov kernel.

The interest in this example is the heat load in a district heating system, when the two most influential explanatory variables in district heating systems, i.e., ambient air temperature and supply temperature, are included in the study.

For the estimation of the regression surface the kernel method is applied using the Epanechnikov kernel (6.15). A product kernel is used, i.e., the power load estimate, p, at time t, at ambient air temperature a and, for supply, temperature s is estimated as

$$\hat{p}_{h_t,h_a,h_s}(t,a,s) = \frac{\sum_{i=1009}^{3843} p(i) K_{h_t}(t-t(i)) K_{h_a}(a-a(i)) K_{h_s}(s-s(i))}{\sum_{i=1009}^{3843} K_{h_t}(t-t(i)) K_{h_a}(a-a(i)) K_{h_s}(s-s(i))} \tag{6.39}$$

where $K_h(u) = k(u/h)$. The bandwidths were chosen using a combination of Cross-Validation and visual inspection.

6.4.4 *Non-parametric GARCH models*

The very large number of parametric GARCH models makes model selection non-trivial (Bollerslev [2008] for a recent overview of different models).

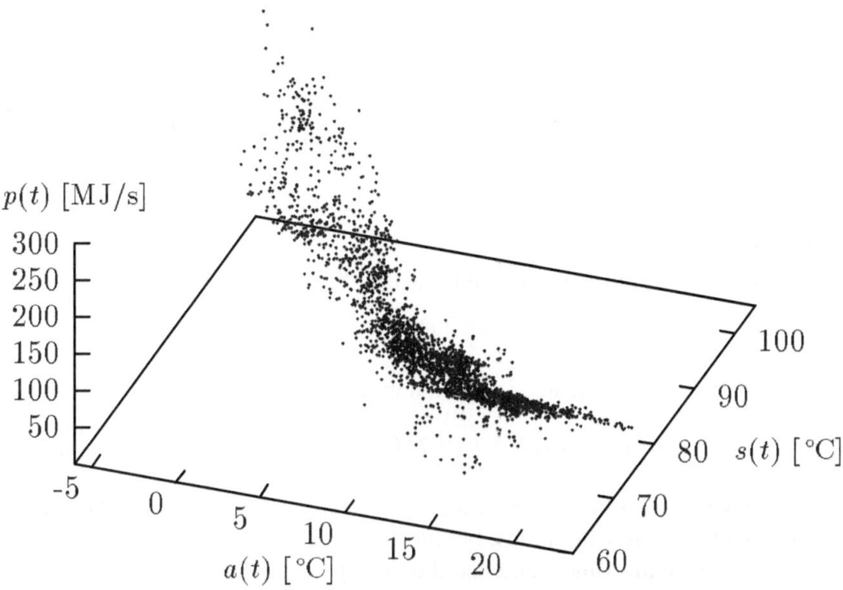

Figure 6.8: Heat load $p(t)$ versus ambient air temperature $a(t)$ and supply temperature $s(t)$ from August 14th to December 10th in Esbjerg, Denmark.

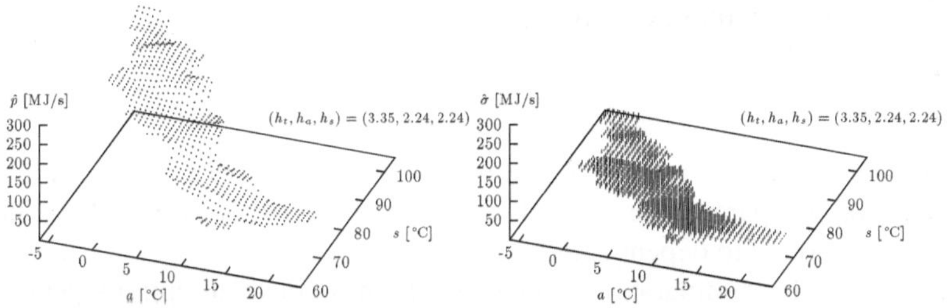

(a) Kernel estimate of the dependence on time of day, t_d, ambient air temperature, a, and supply temperature, s, shown at $t_d = 7$.

(b) Pointwise estimate of standard deviation of the surface estimates as a function of ambient air temperature, a, and supply temperature, s .

Non-parametric GARCH models were introduced by Bühlmann and McNeil [2002] as an alternative to the non-parametric models. Their model is defined as

$$X_t = \sigma_t Z_t \tag{6.40}$$

$$\sigma_t^2 = f(X_{t-1}, \sigma_{t-1}^2) \tag{6.41}$$

where $\{Z_t\}$ is an *iid* sequence of zero mean, unit variance random variables. Their basic idea is to start from a parametric GARCH model, and iteratively improve the estimate of the volatility function. Their algorithm is given by:

1. Estimate a simple GARCH model, recovering an approximation of the volatility $\{\sigma_{t,0} : 1 \leq t \leq n\}$.
2. Regress X_t^2 against X_{t-1} and $\sigma_{t-1,m-1}^2$ to estimate the unknown function $f(\cdot,\cdot)$, denoted $\hat{f}_m(\cdot,\cdot)$, for $m = 1,\ldots M$.
3. Calculate $\hat{\sigma}_{t,m}^2$ from the estimated function $\hat{f}_m(\cdot,\cdot)$.

The algorithm iterates between step 2 and 3 until the estimated function $\hat{f}(\cdot,\cdot)$ has converged.

The method was evaluated in a simulation, where the volatility is given by

$$f(x,\sigma^2) = 5 + 0.2x^2 + (0.75\mathbf{1}_{\{x>0\}} + 0.1 \cdot \mathbf{1}_{\{x<0\}})\sigma^2. \tag{6.42}$$

It was shown in Bühlmann and McNeil [2002] that the algorithm typically converges in just a few iterations, but they also argue that it can be worthwhile to iterate a few extra times, and use the average over the estimated volatility surfaces as the final volatility forecast.

The non-parametric GARCH model was successfully used to forecast crude oil price return volatility in Hou and Suardi [2012]. This is an excellent application of the model, as the price dynamics of many commodities often are more complex than those of, say, equities.

6.5 Notes

The reader is encouraged to dig into Härdle [1990] for a more complete overview of non-parametric methods and Robinson [1983] for details on how this can be applied to dependent data.

Alternatively, semiparametric methods are nowadays an options (Ruppert et al. [2003]). The explanatory properties of semiparametric methods are similar to non-parametric methods (Härdle [2004], Hastie et al. [2009]), but there are times when these are easier to apply to data.

Chapter 7

Stochastic calculus

In this and the following chapter, stochastic differential equations will be formally introduced. This exposition to stochastic calculus does not pretend to be complete. The presentation will be guided by intuition, and important topics and results from a practitioner's point of view will covered at a reasonable mathematical level. General measure theory and other technicalities of a (purely) mathematical interest will be kept at a minimum, but the reader is referred to Arnold [1974], Karatzas and Shreve [1996], Ikeda and Watanabe [1989] and Øksendal [2010] for a detailed account. It should be emphasized that the material in this chapter is not only of interest in mathematical finance. To stress the broad applicability, this chapter does not contain new financial concepts or ideas. A detailed account of these are deferred to the following chapters.

As the successful application of stochastic differential equations in mathematical modelling requires quite a substantial mathematical and statistical setup, we shall now argue why we should bother to consider them.

Application of the nonparametric methods (introduced in Chapter 6) on financial time series revealed some characteristics (e.g., heteroscedasticity) which linear time series models cannot explain, because their conditional mean functions are linear and their conditional variance functions are constants. This is clearly at odds with the small scale empirical studies reported in these notes (and the adjacent exercises) and the large scale studies reported in the open literature. A large number of nonlinear time series models were introduced (in Chapter 5) to model heteroscedasticity. In particular, the GARCH-type models and their numerous extensions performed reasonably well. However, there are a number of important reasons for using differential equations augmented by some kind of randomness or stochasticity.

- It is difficult to interpret the parameters of, say, an ARCH(3) model, whereas the embedded parameters in a stochastic differential equation model may have some physical or financial interpretation. A formal relationship between some SDEs and GARCH models may be derived, but that is outside the scope of this book.
- Numerous financial products (stocks, foreign exchange rates, etc.) are traded very often or very irregularly on the markets. Thus a reasonable

approximation is to use continuous-time models, and stochastic differential equations provide a framework for describing heteroscedasticity.

- Beside, being continuous in time, stochastic differential equations are also continuous in state, e.g., a stock price may be any positive, real number. As opposed to the finite number of states ω_i considered in Chapter 3, the uncertainty associated with a future stock price is modelled by considering a continuous distribution. Although stock prices are often quoted in *ticks* or units of, say, \$1/8, we shall consider the number of possible prices as being practically infinite. See Epps [1996] for a discussion of the discrete state case.

Stochastic differential equations entail the best of two worlds, i.e., a combination of physical knowledge (laws of motion, preservation of energy etc.) that may be used to develop a deterministic model of the system and statistical methods for parameter estimation and model validation. This allows the modeller to model causality as well as correlation, where causality may be considered as superior to the correlation functions used in traditional time series analysis. There are a number of disadvantages associated with the use of SDEs; one major disadvantage is the advanced probability theory involved. From an empirical point of view, it is by no means trivial to estimate parameters in SDEs, but we shall get back to that in later chapters.

The remainder of this chapter is organized as follows: Section 7.1 briefly considers adding stochasticity to dynamical systems. Section 7.2 informally introduces stochastic calculus while 7.3 considers stochastic integrals. Section 7.4 introduces concepts from stochastic processes and probability theory, and formally introduces Itō calculus. Finally, Section 7.5 provides a brief overview of jump processes and some convenient related mathematical tools.

7.1 Dynamical systems

Assume that we wish to model a general physical, chemical or technical system. Mathematical modelling of such systems often leads to the formulation of a system of coupled (nonlinear) differential equations, which may, in general, be written on the form

$$\frac{\mathrm{d}\mathbf{X}(t)}{\mathrm{d}t} = \dot{\mathbf{X}}(t) = \mathbf{f}(t, \mathbf{X}(t)), \tag{7.1}$$

where $\mathbf{f}(t, \mathbf{X}(t))$ describes the time-directed evolution of the so-called *state variables* $\mathbf{X}(t) \in \mathbb{R}^n$. The state variables describe the state of the system at time t in the *state space*.

The derivation of these equations is often based on a number of conceptual, mathematical and numerical approximations and the validity of these are difficult to evaluate per se.

By adding a stochastic term to (7.1) to account for these approximations *random differential equations* are obtained as illustrated in these examples.

Example 7.1 (Money market account). *Consider the simple money market account introduced in Definition 2.2 on page 27, i.e.,*

$$dB(t) = r(t)B(t)dt, \tag{7.2}$$
$$B(0) = 1, \tag{7.3}$$

where $B(t)$ is the value of the money account at time t, and $r(t)$ denotes the relevant (there are many different ones!) interest rate.

It is very likely that the interest rate evolves randomly over time, i.e., we have

$$r(t) = \tilde{r}(t) + \sigma"noise"(t) \tag{7.4}$$

where $\tilde{r}(t)$ is assumed to be deterministic. If we insert this in (7.2)*, we get*

$$dB(t) = (\tilde{r}(t) + \sigma"noise"(t))\,B(t)dt,\ B(0) = 1 \tag{7.5}$$

where σ denotes the standard deviation of the noise. The question is now how do we formalize the concept of "noise" such that (7.5) *makes sense and how do we solve it?*

Example 7.2 (Stock prices). *We have previously argued that the volatility of stock prices, foreign exchange rates and interest rates depend on the current level, i.e.,*

$$dS(t) = \alpha S(t)dt + "noise"(t)S(t)dt,\ S(0) = s \tag{7.6}$$

which is essentially similar to (7.5).

Example 7.3 (Simple Black–Scholes). *Consider a simple financial market with two assets:*

1. *A risky asset, where the price of the asset $S(t)$ at time t is described by* (7.6)*, and*
2. *a safe asset, namely the money market account* (7.2).

We propose the model

$$dS(t) = \alpha S(t)dt + "noise"(t)S(t)dt,\ S(0) = s \tag{7.7}$$
$$dB(t) = r(t)B(t)dt,\ B(0) = 1. \tag{7.8}$$

We get the celebrated Black–Scholes model, when we choose the so-called Brownian motion for the noise process in (7.7)*. This model will be described in detail later.*

The discussion above raises a number of questions about the mathematical and statistical nature of the added stochastic term. This chapter is devoted to answering these questions.

7.2 The Wiener process

The point of departure in our search for a formal definition of the noise terms in the previous examples will be the random difference equation (7.9) with $\Delta W(t) = W(t+\Delta t) - W(t)$.

$$X(t+\Delta t) - X(t) = \mu(t,X(t))\Delta t + \sigma(t,X(t))\Delta W(t) \tag{7.9}$$

where $W(t)$ is a normally distributed random variable with zero mean and a variance that is proportional to Δt. Furthermore $W(t)$ is assumed to be independent of all prior values of the process W_s, $s < t$, and $\mu(\cdot,\cdot)$ and $\sigma(\cdot,\cdot)$ are a priori known functions.

Remark 7.1 (Other driving processes). *The driving noise process $W(t)$ in the random difference equation* (7.9) *need not be a normally distributed random variable. It could easily be, say, a Poisson process or a compound Poisson process, which could account for completely unpredictable phenomena, such as attacks on some currency in the foreign exchange markets or the effects of earthquakes. We will present a brief introduction to jump processes in Section 7.5.*

In order to obtain a more mathematical description of (7.9), a more formal definition of the noise process $W(t)$ is required. In particular, we need a process that generates mutually independent and identically distributed normal random variables with zero mean and a variance that is proportional to Δt. A definition that also makes sense when we consider the limiting behaviour of (7.9) as Δt tends to 0.

One possibility is to consider a *Brownian motion*, named after the Scottish botanist Robert Brown, who used the process to describe the irregular movements of pollen suspended in water. This random movement, usually attributed to the buffeting of the pollen by water molecules, results in a *diffusion* of the pollen in the water. Brownian motion is thus a physical example of a random and continuous stochastic process.

A *standard Wiener process* is an abstract mathematical description of the physical process of Brownian motion. The mathematical properties defining a Wiener process, $\{W(t), t \geq 0\}$, are given in

Definition 7.1 (The Wiener process). *A stochastic process $[W(t); t \geq 0]$ is said to be a Wiener process if it satisfies the following conditions:*

1. $W(0) = 0$ *with probability 1 (w.p.1).*
2. *The increments $W(t_1) - W(t_0), W(t_2) - W(t_1), \ldots, W(t_n) - W(t_{n-1})$ of the process for any partitioning of the time interval $0 \leq t_0 < t_1 < \ldots < t_n < \infty$ are mutually independent.*

3. *The increments $W(t) - W(s)$ for any $0 \leq s < t$ are normally distributed with mean and variance, respectively,*

$$\begin{aligned} \mathbf{E}[W(t) - W(s)] &= 0, & (7.10) \\ \mathbf{Var}[W(t) - W(s)] &= t - s, & (7.11) \end{aligned}$$

i.e., $W(t) - W(s) \in N(0, t-s)$.

4. *$W(t)$ has continuous trajectories.*

It follows from (7.10) that the mean of the process is zero for any time interval, whereas the variance grows unboundedly as the length of the time interval $t - s$ is increased.

Using this definition of the Wiener process, we can write (7.9) as

$$X(t + \Delta t) - X(t) = \mu(t, X(t))\Delta t + \sigma(t, X(t))\Delta W(t) \tag{7.12}$$

where

$$\Delta W(t) = W(t + \Delta t) - W(t). \tag{7.13}$$

Let us now try to formalize (7.9) slightly by dividing through by Δt and then letting Δt tend to 0. Formally we should obtain

$$\dot{X}(t) = \mu(t, X(t)) + \sigma(t, X(t))V(t), \qquad X(0) = x \tag{7.14}$$

where we have added an initial value x and introduced $V(t)$ as the formal time derivative of the Wiener process.

Assuming that $V(t)$ is a well defined process, it should now be possible to solve (7.12) for every realization or trajectory of $V(t)$. It can be shown that the process $V(t)$ is unfortunately not well defined as the Wiener process is nowhere differentiable, although it is continuous. For illustration consider the limit

$$\lim_{h \to 0} \frac{\mathbf{E}\left[(W(t+h))^2\right] - \mathbf{E}\left[(W(t))^2\right]}{h} = \frac{t + h - t}{h} = 1.$$

Thus in a mean square sense the derivative of the Wiener process $W(t)$ is not the derivative process $V(t) = \dot{W}(t)$ as defined above.

The Wiener process is a Markov process as well as a martingale as we shall see later. The sample paths (realizations) of the process are continuous with probability one, but they are nowhere differentiable with probability 1 due to the (independent) increments (see e.g. Øksendal [2010] for a rigorous proof).

Another approach is to let Δt tend to zero in (7.12) without dividing through by Δt. Formally we get

$$\mathrm{d}X(t) = \mu(t, X(t))\mathrm{d}t + \sigma(t, X(t))\mathrm{d}W(t), \qquad X(0) = x \tag{7.15}$$

and it is natural to interpret (7.15) as a shorthand notation for the following integral equation

$$X(t) = x + \int_0^t \mu(s, X(s))\mathrm{d}s + \int_0^t \sigma(s, X(s))\mathrm{d}W(s). \tag{7.16}$$

The ds integral may be interpreted as an ordinary Riemann integral, whereas the natural interpretation of the d$W(s)$ integral is as an Riemann-Stieltjes integral for every trajectory of W. Unfortunately this is not reasonable as it can be shown that the process $W(t)$ is of unbounded variation, i.e. the d$W(s)$ integral in (7.16) is divergent.

Strictly speaking, the notation in (7.15) does not make any sense as it describes the infinitesimal evolution of $X(t)$, which is driven by a Wiener process with unbounded variation. We shall, however, use the notation (7.15) for convenience repeatedly in the following, but it should be remembered that it is only shorthand for (7.16).

The remaining questions are now

- how do we formalize the stochastic integral in (7.16),
- how do we define the adjacent stochastic calculus and
- how do we analyze (7.15) in this framework?

7.3 Stochastic Integrals

Although the Wiener process has some simple probabilistic properties it is by no means simple to define stochastic integration with respect to a Wiener process, because the trajectory of a Wiener process is very odd. Let us list some of its peculiar properties

- As a Wiener process is of unbounded variation, it will eventually hit every real value no matter how large or how negative.
- Once a Wiener process hits a value, it immediately hits it again infinitely often, and then again from time to time in the future.
- It does not matter what scale you examine a Wiener process on — it looks just the same. Thus a Wiener process or Brownian motion pertains to the same self-similarity property as fractals.

Nevertheless, we intend to introduce the stochastic integral

$$I(t, \omega) = \int_0^t g(s, \omega)\mathrm{d}W(s), \tag{7.17}$$

where $g(t, \omega)$ is some suitably, smooth (possibly random) function in the following scheme, which is identical to the definition of the Riemann integral:

1. Partition the time interval $[0,t]$ into n subintervals of equal length, i.e. define the time instants $0 = t_0 < t_1 < \ldots < t_n = t$.
2. Define for each trajectory ω an approximate integral $I_n(\omega)$ by

$$I_n(t,\omega) = \sum_{k=0}^{n-1} g(\tau_k,\omega)[W(t_{k+1},\omega) - W(t_k,\omega)] \tag{7.18}$$

   where τ_k is some arbitrarily chosen time in the interval $[t_k, t_{k+1})$.
3. Finally, we let n tend to infinity and hope that $I_n(\omega)$ to some limit I, which we shall use to define the integral (7.17).

The objective of the following discussion is to show that it is important where in the time interval $[t_k, t_{k+1}[$ the function $g(\tau_k, \omega)$ is evaluated. Recall that various choices of $\tau_k, \in [t_k, t_{k+1})$ yield the same results in ordinary calculus. We shall now show that this does not hold for stochastic calculus.

As an example, let us consider the case $g(t) = W(t)$, i.e. we wish to compute the stochastic integral

$$I(t) = \int_0^t W(s)\mathrm{d}W(s) \tag{7.19}$$

where we choose to compute the integral from $t_0 = 0$ instead of the more general t_0, because we may use that $W(0) = 0$ to obtain a shorter formula.

As a preparation it is convenient first to consider the quadratic variation of $W(t)$ on the interval $[0,t]$, i.e. we commence by considering the integral

$$\int_0^t (\mathrm{d}W(s))^2. \tag{7.20}$$

Thus we introduce the notation $\Delta W_k = W(t_{k+1}) - W(t_k)$ and define the stochastic variable

$$S_n = \sum_{k=0}^{n-1} (\Delta W_k)^2. \tag{7.21}$$

If the Wiener process was differentiable, we would expect that S_n would converge to zero as n tends to infinity, because the time interval $[0,t]$ is finite. Let us introduce the subintervals $\Delta t = t_{k+1} - t_k$, i.e. $\Delta t = t/n$. From Definition 7.1, it immediately follows that $\mathbf{E}\left[(\Delta W_k)^2\right] = \Delta t_k$ and thus

$$\mathbf{E}[S_n] = \sum_{k=0}^{n-1} \mathbf{E}\left[(\Delta W_k)^2\right] = \sum_{k=0}^{n-1} \Delta t_k = t.$$

The variance of S_n is found by direct calculation

$$\mathbf{Var}[S_n] = \sum_{k=0}^{n-1} \mathbf{Var}\left[(\Delta W_k)^2\right] = 2\sum_{k=0}^{n-1} (\Delta t_k)^2 = 2n\left(\frac{t}{n}\right)^2 = \frac{2t^2}{n}$$

where it is used that $(\Delta W_k)^2 \in \Delta t_k \chi^2(1)$. It is well known that a sum of N $\chi^2(1)$ distributed random variables is a $\chi^2(N)$ distributed variable with mean N and variance $2N$. In other words, we have

$$\mathbf{Var}[S_n] = \mathbf{E}\left[(S_n - \mathbf{E}[S_n])^2\right] = \mathbf{E}\left[(S_n - t)^2\right] = \frac{2t^2}{n}$$

and thus

$$\lim_{n\to\infty} \mathbf{E}\left[(S_n - t)^2\right] = 0.$$

In this case, we say that S_n converges towards t in a mean square sense or in the space $L^2(\mathrm{d}\mathbb{P} \times \mathrm{d}t)$. This result is the foundation of the so-called Itō *formula,* which plays a fundamental role in stochastic calculus as the stochastic counterpart of the well-known chain rule from ordinary calculus.

The main result may be restated in differential form as

$$(\mathrm{d}W(t))^2 = \mathrm{d}t. \tag{7.22}$$

Formally this metatheorem does not make any sense, but it is worth noticing that it states that the square of a stochastic increment yields a purely deterministic property. Do, please, remember this result.

Let us return to the evaluation of (7.19). We proceed in a similar fashion as above by constructing sums of the form (7.21). We consider two different sums which evaluate the $W(t)$ part at either the left hand side of the interval $[t_k, t_{k+1}[$, $\tau_k = t_k$, or the right hand side $\tau_k = t_{k+1}$, i.e.

$$A_n = \sum_{k=0}^{n-1} W(t_k)(W(t_{k+1}) - W(t_k)) \quad (\tau_k = t_k), \tag{7.23}$$

$$B_n = \sum_{k=0}^{n-1} W(t_{k+1})(W(t_{k+1}) - W(t_k)) \quad (\tau_k = t_{k+1}). \tag{7.24}$$

We immediately get the identities

$$A_n + B_n = W^2(t), \tag{7.25}$$

$$B_n - A_n = \sum_{k=0}^{n-1} (\Delta W_k)^2 = S_n, \tag{7.26}$$

for $n \to \infty$, where S_n is given by (7.21). It immediately follows that $B_n - A_n \to t$ in L^2 as $n \to \infty$. We therefore get the limits

$$A_n \to A,$$
$$B_n \to B,$$

where

$$A = \frac{W^2(t)}{2} - \frac{t}{2}, \tag{7.27}$$

$$B = \frac{W^2(t)}{2} + \frac{t}{2}. \tag{7.28}$$

These results show that the value of the stochastic integral (7.19) depends critically on the placement of τ_k in the interval $[t_k, t_{k+1})$, i.e. the integral depends on where the integrand is evaluated in the interval $[t_k, t_{k+1})$. Needless to say, this is not the case in ordinary calculus.

By choosing $\tau_k = t_k$, we get the enormously important Itō *integral*, which yields

$$\int_0^t W(s)\mathrm{d}W(s) = \frac{W^2(t)}{2} - \frac{t}{2}. \tag{7.29}$$

By choosing $\tau_k = t_{k+1}$, we get

$$\int_0^t W(s)\mathrm{d}W(s) = \frac{W^2(t)}{2} + \frac{t}{2}. \tag{7.30}$$

Note that in both cases, we get the additional term $t/2$ compared to ordinary calculus. Finally, choosing $t_k = (t_k + t_{k+1})/2$ yields the Stratonovich integral

$$\int_0^t W(s)\mathrm{d}W(s) = \frac{W^2(t)}{2}, \tag{7.31}$$

which is similar to classical calculus. However, there is a consensus that the Itō integral is the only appropriate integral for financial modelling.

7.4 Itō stochastic calculus

In this section we formally introduce the Itō stochastic integral. Therefore some concepts from probability theory will be repeated for convenience.

We assume the existence of a filtered probability space $(\Omega, \mathscr{F}, \mathbb{P})$, where $\mathscr{F}$ is a σ-algebra on the sample space Ω of possible outcomes, $(\Omega, \mathscr{F})$ is a measurable space and $\mathbb{P}\colon \mathscr{F} \mapsto [0,1]$ is some probability measure.

Definition 7.2 (Filtration). *A filtration on* $(\Omega, \mathscr{F})$ *is a family* $\{\mathscr{F}(t)\}_{t\geq 0}$ *of* σ*-algebras* $\mathscr{F}(t) \subset \mathscr{F}$ *such that*

$$\mathscr{F}(s) \subseteq \mathscr{F}(t) \text{ for } 0 \leq s < t.$$

Generally speaking, $\mathscr{F}(s)$ denotes the set of events (or the information set) up to time s. The *natural* filtration $\{\mathscr{F}(t)\}_{t\geq 0}$ is *increasing* and *right continuous*, i.e. at time t, $0 \leq s < t$, more information is available (or, at least, information is not lost) $\mathscr{F}(s) \subset \mathscr{F}(t)$ than at time s and in the limit complete information is obtained $\mathscr{F}(\infty) = \mathscr{F}$. Application of the natural filtration $\{\mathscr{F}(t)\}_{t\geq 0}$ implies that information about $X(t)$ in (7.15) must be deduced from observations of $X(t)$ as opposed to, e.g., $Y(t) = f(X(t))$, where $f\colon \mathbb{R} \mapsto \mathbb{R}$ is some nontrivial (possibly nonlinear) function.

Example 7.4. *Consider the function $Y(t) = |X(t)|$. Here, the value of $Y(t)$ is known when knowing $X(t)$, but the converse does not hold.*

Remark 7.2. *Consider a stochastic variable $X(t)$ as a function $X(t)\colon \Omega \mapsto \mathbb{R}$ that maps the sample space Ω into $\mathbb{R}$. If $\{\omega \in \Omega\colon X(t,\omega) \leq x\} \in \mathscr{F}$ for each $x \in \mathbb{R}$, then $X(t)$ is said to be $\mathscr{F}(t)$-measurable.*

Definition 7.3 (Martingale). *A stochastic process $\{X(t), t \geq 0\}$ on the probability space $(\Omega, \mathscr{F}, \mathbb{P})$ is called a martingale with respect to a filtration $\{\mathscr{F}(t)\}_{t\geq 0}$ if*

1. *$X(t)$ is $\mathscr{F}(t)$-measurable for all t*
2. *$\mathbf{E}[|X(t)|] < \infty$ for all t, and*
3. *$\mathbf{E}[X(t)|\mathscr{F}(s)] = X(s)$ for all $s \leq t$.*

Definition 7.4 (Adapted process). *The stochastic process $X(t)$ is adapted to the filtration $\mathscr{F}(t)$ if $X(t)$ is an $\mathscr{F}(t)$-measurable random variable for each $t \geq 0$.*

Remark 7.3 (Adaptedness). *It is instructive to think of measurability and adaptedness in the sense that if a function $g(t)$ is said to be $\mathscr{F}(t)$-measurable, then it essentially means that $g(t)$ is known at time t.*

Example 7.5. *A Wiener process $W(t)$ that is adapted to a given filtration $\mathscr{F}(t)$ possesses the property that*

$$W(t) - W(s) \text{ is independent of } \mathscr{F}_s. \tag{7.32}$$

The process $W(t)$ is then said to be a $\mathscr{F}_t$-Wiener process.

Please, refer to the Appendix for a more detailed exposition to these concepts or consult the references given in the introduction to this chapter.

Definition 7.5 (The class $\mathscr{L}^2$). *Let $\mathscr{L}^2[a,b]$ denote the class of processes $g(s,\omega)$ that satisfies the conditions:*

- *The function $g(s,\omega)$ is $\mathscr{F}(s)$-adapted.*
- *The integral*

$$\int_a^b \mathbf{E}\left[(g(s,\omega))^2\right] \mathrm{d}s < \infty \tag{7.33}$$

  is finite.

For some $a \leq b$ we now define the stochastic integral

$$\int_a^b g(s,\omega)\mathrm{d}W(s) \tag{7.34}$$

for all $g \in \mathscr{L}^2[a,b]$. We shall only consider simple functions (to be defined below) and leave the generalization to the interested reader.

Assume that g is simple, i.e. there exist deterministic time instants $a = t_0 < t_1 < \ldots < t_n = b$ such that

$$g(s,\omega) = g(t_k,\omega) \text{ for } s \in [t_k, t_{k+1}[$$

where

$$g(t_k,\omega) \in \mathscr{F}(t_k) \quad k = 0,\ldots,n.$$

In other words $g(t_k,\omega)$ is $\mathscr{F}(t_k)$-measurable, i.e. $g(t_k)$ is known at time t_k.

For a simple process g we define the stochastic integral by a sum similar to (7.23)

$$\int_a^b g(s,\omega)dW(s) = \sum_{k=0}^{n-1} g(t_k,\omega)(W(t_{k+1}) - W(t_k)). \tag{7.35}$$

It is inherently important that we define the incremental Wiener process in terms of the forward differences $W(t_{k+1}) - W(t_k)$.

Theorem 7.1 (Stochastic integration rules). *Let g and h be simple processes that satisfy* (7.33) *and let α, β be real numbers. The following rules apply*

- *Stochastic integrals are linear operators*

$$\int_a^b (\alpha g(s) + \beta h(s))\mathrm{d}W(s) = \alpha \int_a^b g(s)\mathrm{d}W(s) + \beta \int_a^b h(s)\mathrm{d}W(s). \tag{7.36}$$

- *The unconditional expectation of a stochastic integral when $g \in \mathscr{L}^2[a,b]$ is zero*

$$\mathbf{E}\left[\int_a^b g(s)\mathrm{d}W(s)\right] = 0. \tag{7.37}$$

- *Stochastic integrals are measurable with respect to the filtration generated by the Wiener process, i.e.*

$$\int_a^b g(s)\mathrm{d}W(s) \textit{ is } \mathscr{F}(b) - \textit{measurable}. \tag{7.38}$$

- *Stochastic integrals when $g \in \mathscr{L}^2[a,b]$ are martingales*

$$\mathbf{E}\left[\int_a^b g(s)\mathrm{d}W(s)\middle|\mathscr{F}(a)\right] = 0. \tag{7.39}$$

- *The Itō isometry is a convenient way of computing variances when $g \in \mathscr{L}^2[a,b]$*

$$\mathbf{E}\left[\left(\int_a^b g(s)\mathrm{d}W(s)\right)^2\right] = \int_a^b \mathbf{E}\left[g^2(s)\right]\mathrm{d}s \quad \textit{(Itō isometry)}. \tag{7.40}$$

- *It also applies to covariance*

$$\mathbf{E}\left[\left(\int_a^b g(s)\mathrm{d}W(s)\right)\left(\int_a^b h(s)\mathrm{d}W(s)\right)\right] = \int_a^b \mathbf{E}\left[g(s)h(s)\right]\mathrm{d}s. \tag{7.41}$$

Proof. That the Itō integral is a linear operator is trivial and is left as an exercise for the reader.

To make the notation less cumbersome, we introduce the entities

$$g_k = g(t_k),\ \Delta W_k = W(t_{k+1}) - W(t_k),\ \Delta t_k = t_{k+1} - t_k,\ \mathscr{F}_k = \mathscr{F}(t_k). \tag{7.42}$$

We get

$$\mathbf{E}\left[\int_a^b g(s)\mathrm{d}W(s)\right] = \sum_{k=0}^{n-1} \mathbf{E}\left[g_k \Delta W_k\right]. \tag{7.43}$$

If we use the fact that the process g_k is adapted to the filtration $\mathscr{F}(t_k)$, we get

$$\mathbf{E}\left[g_k \Delta W_k\right] = \mathbf{E}\left[\mathbf{E}\left[g_k \Delta W_k | \mathscr{F}(t_k)\right]\right] = \mathbf{E}\left[g_k \mathbf{E}\left[\Delta W_k | \mathscr{F}(t_k)\right]\right], \tag{7.44}$$

where we have used the standard trick (iterated expectations) of introducing a conditioning argument and taken the expectation with respect to that argument. As the Wiener process has independent increments, we get

$$\mathbf{E}\left[g_k \mathbf{E}\left[\Delta W_k | \mathscr{F}(t_k)\right]\right] = 0$$

and we have proved (7.37).

Next we shall prove (7.40). By introducing the well-known sum, we get

$$\mathbf{E}\left[\left(\int_a^b g(s)\mathrm{d}W(s)\right)^2\right] = \sum_{i,j} \mathbf{E}\left[g_i g_j (\Delta W_i)(\Delta W_j)\right]$$

where we need to consider two cases:

1. For $i = j$, we get

$$\begin{aligned}\mathbf{E}\left[g_i^2(\Delta W_i)^2\right] &= \mathbf{E}\left[\mathbf{E}\left[g_i^2(\Delta W_i)^2|\mathscr{F}_i\right]\right] \\ &= \mathbf{E}\left[g_i^2\mathbf{E}\left[(\Delta W_i)^2|\mathscr{F}_i\right]\right] = \mathbf{E}\left[g_i^2\Delta t_i\right] \\ &= \mathbf{E}\left[g_i^2\right]\Delta t.\end{aligned}$$

2. For $i \neq j$ with, say $i < j$, we get

$$\begin{aligned}\mathbf{E}\left[g_i g_j(\Delta W_i)(\Delta W_j)\right] &= \mathbf{E}\left[\mathbf{E}\left[g_i g_j(\Delta W_i)(\Delta W_j)|\mathscr{F}_j\right]\right] \\ &= \mathbf{E}\left[g_i g_j(\Delta W_i)\mathbf{E}\left[(\Delta W_j)|\mathscr{F}_j\right]\right] = 0\end{aligned}$$

as the Wiener increment has the conditional mean 0.

Thus we have

$$\mathbf{E}\left[\left(\int_a^b g(s)\mathrm{d}W(s)\right)^2\right] = \sum_{i,j}\mathbf{E}\left[g_i^2\right]\Delta t = \int_a^b \mathbf{E}\left[g_i^2(s)\right]\mathrm{d}s. \tag{7.45}$$

Equation (7.41) may be shown in a similar fashion. Eq. (7.38) follows immediately from the definition of the stochastic integral, and (7.39) is shown as (7.37). □

Remark 7.4 (Itō isometry). *Note that* (7.40) *establishes an isometry between stochastic integrals and deterministic integrals. This is very useful for the calculation of variances.*

Remark 7.5. *The rules in Theorem 7.1 may be extended to cover a larger class of functions than the simple functions considered above by considering Cauchy sequences in $\mathscr{L}^2$ of simple functions, but we will not go into the details here.*

Remark 7.6. *It is possible to extend stochastic integration to all adapted processes g which satisfy the condition*

$$\mathbb{P}\left[\int_0^t g^2(s)\mathrm{d}s < \infty\right] = 1.$$

For all such g it is not guaranteed that (7.37), (7.40) *and* (7.39) *are valid, but the properties* (7.38) *and* (7.36) *still hold. These stochastic integrals are known as local martingales.*

It is easy to show that the Wiener process is in itself an $\mathbb{P}$-martingale and it is a very important consequence of Theorem 7.1 that the martingale property is preserved with respect to integration of $\mathscr{L}^2$-processes.

Theorem 7.2 (Continuous trajectories). *Assume that $g \in \mathscr{L}^2[0,t]$ for all $t \geq 0$. Define the process X by*

$$X(t) = \int_0^t g(s) \mathrm{d}W(s). \tag{7.46}$$

Then $X(t)$ is a martingale with continuous trajectories.

Proof. By direct calculation we get

$$\begin{aligned} X(t) &= \int_0^t g(u) \mathrm{d}W(u) = \int_0^s g(u) \mathrm{d}W(u) + \int_s^t g(u) \mathrm{d}W(u) \\ &= X_s + \int_s^t g(u) \mathrm{d}W(u). \end{aligned}$$

Using (7.37) we get

$$\mathbf{E}[X(t)|\mathscr{F}(s)] = X_s + \mathbf{E}\left[\int_s^t g(u) \mathrm{d}W(u) \middle| \mathscr{F}(s)\right] = X(s).$$

The continuity of the trajectories is difficult to prove, but it should be intuitively clear as the Wiener process lacks jumps. □

7.5 Extensions to jump processes

It is possible to extend the theory on stochastic integration to discontinuous processes, Cont and Tankov [2004] being a good start. The simplest example of a discontinuous process with *iid* increments is the Poisson process.

Definition 7.6 (Poisson process). *A Poisson process is an integer-valued stochastic process $\{N(t), t \geq 0\}$ satisfying the following conditions:*

- *$N(0) = 0$ with probability 1 (w.p.1).*
- *The increments $N(t) - N(u)$ is independent of $N(s) - N(0)$ for $t > u \geq s > 0$.*
- *The distribution of $N(t) - N(s) \in Po(\lambda(t-s))$ where Po is the Poisson distribution and λ is the so-called intensity of the process.*
- *The process is continuous in probability.*

There are obvious similarities (and differences) between the Wiener process (7.1) and the Poisson process.

Jump processes are easier to analyse if we introduce some well-known transform methods (Fourier transforms, etc.).

Definition 7.7 (Characteristic function). *The Fourier transform of a random variable or process is called the* characteristic function

$$\psi_X(u) = \mathbf{E}\left[e^{iuX}\right]. \tag{7.47}$$

Characteristic functions are incredibly useful in probability, as, e.g., the distribution of sums of *iid* random variables is computed using convolution of the densities. A simpler alternative is to use Fourier methods. This can be seen by computing the characteristic function for the sum

$$\psi_{X_1+X_2}(u) = \mathbf{E}\left[e^{iu(X_1+X_2)}\right] = \mathbf{E}\left[e^{iuX_1}\right]\mathbf{E}\left[e^{iuX_2}\right] = \psi_{X_1}(u)\psi_{X_2}(u), \tag{7.48}$$

where we use the independence of the random variables to factor the expectation.

Example 7.6 (Gaussian). *The characteristic function for a Gaussian random variable X with mean μ and covariance Σ is given by*

$$\psi(u) = \mathbf{E}\left[e^{iuX}\right] = e^{i\mu^T u - \frac{1}{2}u^T\Sigma u}. \tag{7.49}$$

Example 7.7 (Poisson). *The characteristic function for a Poisson random variable with parameter λ is given by*

$$\psi(u) = e^{\lambda\left(e^{iu}-1\right)}. \tag{7.50}$$

Example 7.8 (Compound Poisson process). *A compound Poisson process is defined as*

$$S(t) = \sum_{n=1}^{N(t)} Y_n \tag{7.51}$$

where $N(t)$ is a Poisson process and $\{Y_n, n \in \mathbb{N}\}$ are iid *random variables independent of N. The convention is that no terms are included in the sum before $N(t)$ reaches one*

$$\sum_{n=1}^{0} Y_n = 0. \tag{7.52}$$

The compound Poisson process is a nice model for large, unexpected, rare events such as government interventions, earthquakes, etc.

Theorem 7.3. *The characteristic function for a compound Poisson process is given by*

$$\psi_{S(t)}(u) = e^{\lambda t(\psi_Y(u)-1)}, \tag{7.53}$$

where λ is the jump intensity and $\psi_Y(\cdot)$ is the characteristic function for the jumps Y.

Proof. The characteristic function is computed, using iterated expectations as

$$\psi_{S(t)}(u) = \mathbf{E}\left[e^{iuS(t)}\right] \tag{7.54}$$

$$= \mathbf{E}\left[\mathbf{E}\left[e^{iuS(t)}|N(t)\right]\right] = \mathbf{E}\left[\mathbf{E}\left[e^{iu(X_1(t)+\ldots+X_N(t))}|N(t)\right]\right] \tag{7.55}$$

$$= \mathbf{E}\left[(\psi_Y(u))^{N(t)}\right]. \tag{7.56}$$

Here, we recognize that this is in fact the probability generating function, $g(z) = \mathbf{E}[z^{N(t)}] = e^{\lambda t(z-1)}$, for a Poisson random variable, evaluated at $\psi_Y(u)$, concluding the proof. □

Compound Poisson processes, as well as Wiener processes, are special cases of a more general class of processes, namely Lévy processes.

Definition 7.8 (Lévy process). *A cadlag*[1] *process* $\{X(t), t \geq 0\}$ *is called a Lévy process if it satisfies the following conditions*

- $X(0) = 0$ *with probability* 1.
- *The increment* $X(t) - X(u)$ *is independent of* $X(s) - X(0)$ *for* $t > u \geq s > 0$.
- *The increments are strictly stationary, i.e.* $X(t+\delta t) - X(t) \stackrel{d}{=} X(t) - X(t-\delta t)$.
- *The paths are continuous in probability,*

$$\lim_{h \to 0} \mathbb{P}(|X(t+h) - X(t)| > \varepsilon) = 0. \tag{7.57}$$

Theorem 7.4 (Lévy-Khinchin representation). *Let* $\{X(t)\}$ *be a Lévy process with a characteristic triplet* (b, Σ, ν). *Then*

$$\mathbf{E}\left[e^{iuX(t)}\right] = e^{t\phi(u)} \tag{7.58}$$

with the characteristic exponent

$$\phi(u) = ib^T u - \frac{1}{2}u^T \Sigma u + \int \left(e^{iu^T x} - 1 - iu^T x \mathbf{1}_{\{|x|<1\}}\right) \nu(\mathrm{d}x) \tag{7.59}$$

where $u, b \in \mathbb{R}^d$, Σ *is a non-negative* $d \times d$ *matrix and* ν *is a measure on* $\mathbb{R}^d$ *with* $\nu(\{0\}) = 0$ *and* $\int \min(\|x\|, 1)\nu(\mathrm{d}x) < \infty$.

The first two parameters in characteristic triplet (b, Σ, ν) can be identified as the drift and diffusion in a Brownian motion with drift; cf. (7.49). The measure ν is called the Lévy measure and controls the jumps. It is defined, for some Borel set $A \in \mathscr{B}(\mathbb{R}^d)$, as

$$\nu(A) = \mathbf{E}\left[\#\{t \in [0,1] : \Delta X(t) \neq 0, \Delta X(t) \in A\}\right]. \tag{7.60}$$

We will see in Section 9.6 how characteristic functions can be used to value a large class of options, under rather general models.

[1]Right continuous with left limits.

Definition 7.9 (Merton). *The Merton model (Merton [1976]), is a simple jump process. The log spot price is modelled as a compound Poisson process with Gaussian $\mathcal{N}(\mu,\delta^2)$ jumps with intensity λ*

$$\log S(t) = X(t) = \log S(0) + \gamma t + \sigma W(t) + \sum_{n=0}^{N(t)} Y_n. \tag{7.61}$$

The conditional distribution generated by the Merton model is a mixture of Gaussians. Option prices computed using the Merton model will therefore be a mixture of Black & Scholes prices.

It follows from Equation (7.49) *and Equation* (7.53) *that the characteristic function (assuming $S(0)=1$) is given by*

$$\mathbf{E}\left[e^{iuX(t)}\right] = e^{i\gamma t u - \frac{\sigma^2 u^2}{2}t + \lambda t\left(e^{i\mu u - \frac{\delta^2 u^2}{2}} - 1\right)} \tag{7.62}$$

$$= e^{t\left(i\gamma u - \frac{\sigma^2 u^2}{2} + \lambda\left(e^{i\mu u - \frac{\delta^2 u^2}{2}} - 1\right)\right)} \tag{7.63}$$

where the second line presents the characteristic exponent.

We can easily find how to choose the parameter γ such that the discounted process becomes a martingale. Evaluating the characteristic function in $u=-i$ yields

$$\phi(-i) = \mathbf{E}\left[e^{iuX(t)}\right]\bigg|_{u=-i} = \mathbf{E}\left[e^{X(t)}\right] = \mathbf{E}\left[S(t)\right]. \tag{7.64}$$

Doing this for the Merton model gives

$$\mathbf{E}[e^{S(t)}] = \exp\left[t\left(\gamma + \frac{\sigma^2}{2} + \lambda\left(e^{\mu + \frac{\delta^2}{2}} - 1\right)\right)\right] \tag{7.65}$$

implying that

$$\gamma = \tilde{r} = r - \frac{\sigma^2}{2} - \lambda\left(e^{\mu + \frac{\delta^2}{2}} - 1\right) \tag{7.66}$$

transforms the discounted price process into a martingale.

Definition 7.10 (Variance Gamma process). *The Variance Gamma (VG) process (Madan and Seneta [1990]), is a time-shifted Wiener process, where the time shift is controlled by a Gamma process $\Gamma(t,1,\nu)$. The Variance Gamma process is then defined as*

$$X(t) = \theta\Gamma(t,1,\nu) + \sigma W(\Gamma(t,1,\nu)). \tag{7.67}$$

This definition is very useful for Monte Carlo simulations.

The characteristic function for a Variance Gamma process (Cont and Tankov [2004], Hirsa [2013]) is given by

$$\mathbf{E}\left[e^{iuX(t)}\right] = \left(\frac{1}{1 - iu\theta\nu + \sigma^2 u^2 \nu/2}\right)^{t/\nu}. \tag{7.68}$$

Lévy processes that are defined as time-shifted Brownian motions are commonly referred to as Subordinated Brownian motions.

Definition 7.11 (NIG process)**.** *The Normal Inverse Gaussian (NIG) (Barndorff-Nielsen [1997]), is similar to the VG process, the difference being that the time shift process is an Inverse Gaussian (IG) process, rather than a Gamma process. The corresponding characteristic function is given by*

$$\mathbf{E}\left[e^{iuX(t)}\right] = e^{\left(\kappa - \sigma\sqrt{\frac{\kappa^2}{\sigma^2} + \frac{\theta^2}{\sigma^4} - \left(\frac{\theta}{\sigma^2} + iu\right)^2}\right)t}. \tag{7.69}$$

Definition 7.12 (Time-shifted Lévy processes)**.** *The processes Defined in definition 7.9–7.11 all have* iid *increments, while it is well known that real world data typically exhibit time varying volatility. This can be achieved by another time shift, this time using an integrated, positive process. One of the most popular time shifts is to use an integrated Cox–Ingersoll-Ross (CIR) model (Cox et al. [1985]) (Stochastic differential equation will be introduced in Chapter 8). The Cox–Ingersoll-Ross model is given by the stochastic differential equation*

$$\mathrm{d}y(t) = \kappa(\eta - y(t))\mathrm{d}t + \lambda\sqrt{y(t)}\mathrm{d}W(t). \tag{7.70}$$

It is well known that this process is positive. Integrating this process

$$Y(t) = \int_0^t y(s)\mathrm{d}s \tag{7.71}$$

generates a time shift process.

A time-shifted Variance Gamma or NIG process would then be defined as

$$Z_{VG-CIR}(t) = X_{VG}(Y(t)). \tag{7.72}$$

The characteristic function can be derived (see Hirsa [2013]), arriving at

$$\mathbf{E}\left[e^{iuZ_{VG-CIR}(t)}\right] = \psi_{CIR}(-i\log\psi_{VG}(u)) \tag{7.73}$$

which is rather similar to Equation (7.53)*. Finally, the characteristic function for the integrated CIR process is given by*

$$\psi_{CIR}(u) = \mathbf{E}[e^{iuY(t)}] = A(t,u)e^{B(t,u)y(0)}, \tag{7.74}$$

where

$$A(t,u) = \frac{e^{\frac{\kappa^2 \eta t}{\lambda^2}}}{\left(\cosh(\frac{\gamma t}{2}) + \frac{\kappa}{\gamma}\sinh(\frac{\gamma t}{2})\right)^{\frac{2\kappa\eta}{\lambda^2}}} \tag{7.75}$$

$$B(t,u) = \frac{2iu}{\kappa + \gamma\coth(\frac{\gamma t}{2})} \tag{7.76}$$

with

$$\gamma = \sqrt{\kappa^2 - 2\lambda^2 iu}. \tag{7.77}$$

Time-shifted Lévy processes provide a very good fit to market data (Lindström et al. [2008]).

The characteristic function can also be derived for some stochastic volatility models, most notably the Heston model (Heston [1993]).

Definition 7.13. *The risk-neutral version of the Heston stochastic volatility model is given by*

$$\mathrm{d}S(t) = rS(t)\mathrm{d}t + \sqrt{V(t)}S(t)\mathrm{d}W^{(S)}(t) \tag{7.78}$$

$$\mathrm{d}V(t) = \kappa(\theta - V(t))\,\mathrm{d}t + \sigma_v\sqrt{V(t)}\mathrm{d}W^{(V)}(t) \tag{7.79}$$

where the driving Wiener processes are allowed to be correlated on an infinitesimal scale $\mathrm{d}W^{(S)}(t)\mathrm{d}W^{(V)}(t) = \rho\mathrm{d}t$.

It can be shown that the characteristic function for the logarithmic stock price, $X(t) = \log(S(t))$, *is given by*

$$\psi_{Heston}(u) = \exp\left(iu(\log(S(0)) + rt) + C(u) + D(u)V(0)\right) \tag{7.80}$$

where

$$C(u) = \frac{\kappa\theta}{\sigma_V^2}\left[(\kappa - \rho\sigma_V ui - d)t \right. \tag{7.81}$$

$$\left. -2\log\left(\frac{(\kappa - \rho\sigma_V ui)(1 - e^{-dt}) + d(e^{-dT} + 1)}{2d}\right)\right]$$

$$D(u) = (1 - e^{-dt})\frac{-iu - u^2}{(\kappa - \rho\sigma_V ui)(1 - e^{-dt}) + d(e^{-dt} + 1)} \tag{7.82}$$

$$d = \sqrt{(\rho\sigma_V ui - \kappa)^2 + \sigma_V^2(ui + u^2)}. \tag{7.83}$$

Extending the Heston characteristic function to the Bates model (Bates [1996]), is rather straightforward.

Definition 7.14. *The Bates model is a Heston model, with independent jumps in the S component, formally defined as*

$$\mathrm{d}S(t) = \gamma S(t)\mathrm{d}t + \sqrt{V(t)}S(t)\mathrm{d}W^{(S)}(t) + S_{t-}\mathrm{d}J(t) \tag{7.84}$$

$$\mathrm{d}V(t) = \kappa(\theta - V(t))\,\mathrm{d}t + \sigma_v\sqrt{V(t)}\mathrm{d}W^{(V)}(t) \tag{7.85}$$

where the driving Wiener processes once again are allowed to be correlated, $\mathrm{d}W^{(S)}(t)\mathrm{d}W^{(V)}(t) = \rho \mathrm{d}t$, while $J(t)$ is a compound Poisson process with intensity λ and lognormal distributed jumps of size k such that $\log(1+k) \in N(\mu, \delta^2)$. The jumps are independent of the diffusion part, although it is still possible to derive the joint characteristics function when the jump intensity is a linear function of the state variables (Duffie et al. [2003]).

Computing the logarithm of the stock price $X(t) = \log(S(t))$ leads to the dynamics

$$\mathrm{d}X(t) = \left(\gamma - \lambda\left(e^{\mu+\frac{\delta^2}{2}} - 1\right) - \tfrac{1}{2}V(t)\right)\mathrm{d}t + \sqrt{V(t)}\mathrm{d}W^{(S)}(t) + \mathrm{d}J(t). \tag{7.86}$$

The discounted price process will therefore be a risk-neutral martingale if the risk-free rate in the Heston models is replaced by

$$r' = r - \lambda\left(e^{\mu+\frac{\delta^2}{2}} - 1\right). \tag{7.87}$$

The characteristic function for the Bates model is, due to the independence between the jumps and the Wiener processes, given by a multiplication of the Heston characteristic function, replacing r with $r - \lambda\left(e^{\mu+\frac{\delta^2}{2}} - 1\right)$, while the jump term given by

$$\phi_{Jumps}(u) = e^{\lambda t\left(e^{i\mu u - \frac{\delta^2 u^2}{2}} - 1\right)}, \tag{7.88}$$

leads to the joint expression

$$\phi_{Bates}(u) = \phi_{Heston}(u)\phi_{Jumps}(u). \tag{7.89}$$

7.6 Problems

Problem 7.1

1. Show (7.25).
2. Show (7.27).

Problem 7.2

Referring to (7.18), the important Stratonovitch integrals are obtained by introducing

$$\xi_k = \frac{t_k + t_{k+1}}{2},$$

i.e. the integrand is evaluated at the midpoint of the interval $[t_k, t_{k+1}[$.

1. Compute the integral

$$\int_0^t W(s)\mathrm{d}W(s)$$

in the Stratonovitch sense.

Although it may be shown that Stratonovitch integrals are neither Markov processes nor martingales, they are important for theoretical work because the ordinary chain rule applies for variable transformations.

Problem 7.3

Let $B(t)$ denote a standard Brownian motion (a Wiener process) on the probability field $(\Omega, \mathscr{F}, \mathbb{P})$ and let $\mathscr{F}(t)$ be the natural filtration generated by $B(t)$.

1. Show that $B(t)$ is a martingale.

2. Show that only one of the following is a martingale

$$M(t) = B(t)^2,$$
$$\tilde{M}(t) = B(t)^2 - t.$$

3. Use this result to give an intuitive explanation of the martingale property. (*Hint:* Sketch a realization of the two processes.)

4. Show that $N(t) = B(t)^3 - 3tB(t)$ is a martingale.

Chapter 8

Stochastic differential equations

Having established stochastic calculus in the Itō sense in the last chapter, we are now prepared to consider stochastic differential equations. For ease of notation, we shall in general only state the important results for univariate SDEs, but a few results will be generalized to multivariate SDEs.

We repeat that the notion of stochastic differential equations (SDEs) is merely a shorthand notation for stochastic integral equations. The latter may be defined in several ways, but we restrict our discussion to stochastic integrals in the Itō sense. Unfortunately, this implies that the well-known chain rule for variable transformations must be replaced by the so-called *Itō formula*, which will be introduced in the multivariate case. This formula may be used to obtain closed form solutions of some SDEs. Besides, it just makes Itō stochastic calculus more tedious.

In the following exposition to stochastic differential equations, we shall only use the Wiener process as the driving noise process. We recall that the Wiener process is both a Markov process and a martingale, and that the mean of the stochastic integral (in the Itō sense) of any square integrable, adapted process with respect to a Wiener process, is zero.

Stochastic differential equations driven by, e.g., a Poisson process (or *jump processes*, *counting processes* or *marked point processes*) are gaining ground in the financial literature (Cont and Tankov [2004] for a gentle overview). However, a considerable extension of the measure-theoretical concepts of adaptedness and predictability is required, which is beyond the scope of this book. It is duly noted that the topics covered in this chapter may be generalized to cover the very general class of *square integrable* processes (see e.g. Björk [2009], Karatzas and Shreve [1996], Ikeda and Watanabe [1989] for details).

The remainder of this chapter is organized as follows: Section 8.1 introduces stochastic differential equations. Section 8.2 considers analytical solution methods. Section 8.3 considers a link between parabolic partial differential equations (PDEs) and SDEs, which we shall use later in order to avoid solving such PDEs. Section 8.4 introduces continuous measure transformations, which will be used in later chapters.

8.1 Stochastic Differential Equations

We assume the existence of a probability space $(\Omega, \mathscr{F}, \mathbb{P})$, where $\mathscr{F}$ is a σ-algebra on the sample space Ω of possible outcomes, and $(\Omega, \mathscr{F})$ is a measurable space and $\mathbb{P}\colon \mathscr{F} \mapsto [0,1]$ is a probability measure. Let the drift $\mu : \mathbb{R} \mapsto \mathbb{R}$ and the diffusion $\sigma\colon \mathbb{R} \mapsto \mathbb{R}$ be Borel-measurable functions[1] and assume that $X_t : \Omega \mapsto \mathbb{R}$ is a solution to the time-homogeneous Itō stochastic differential equation

$$\mathrm{d}X(t) = \mu(t, X(t))\mathrm{d}t + \sigma(t, X(t))\mathrm{d}W(t), \quad X(0) = x_0 \tag{8.1}$$

where $\{W(t), t \geq 0\}$ is a standard Wiener process defined on the probability space $(\Omega, \mathscr{F}, \mathbb{P})$ equipped with the natural filtration $\{\mathscr{F}(t)\}$ generated by $W(t)$.

The standard Wiener process is defined in Definition 7.1; the concepts of filtration, martingales and adaptedness are defined in Definitions 7.2, 7.3 and 7.4. Please refer to Appendix A for a detailed discussion of these concepts.

Let us give a number of examples to illustrate the following discussion.

Example 8.1 (The Wiener process)**.** *Consider the Wiener process*

$$\mathrm{d}X(t) = \sigma \mathrm{d}W(t), \qquad X(0) = x_0 \tag{8.2}$$

where σ is the standard deviation of the process and x_0 is a deterministic initial condition, which is short for

$$X(t) = x_0 + \int_0^t \sigma \mathrm{d}W(s).$$

From the definition of the Wiener process (Definition 7.1), it immediately follows that

$$X(t) = x_0 + \sigma(W(t) - W(0)) = x_0 + \sigma W(t).$$

Next we compute the mean of $X(t)$, i.e.

$$\mathbf{E}[X(t)] = \mathbf{E}\left[x_0 + \int_0^t \sigma \mathrm{d}W(s)\right] = x_0$$

[1] The functions μ and σ will, in general, depend on a p-dimensional parameter vector $\theta \in \Theta \subseteq \mathbb{R}^p$, where Θ may be some constrained subset of $\mathbb{R}^p$. For notational convenience this parameter dependency will be suppressed in this chapter.

which follows from (7.37)*. The variance is given by*

$$\mathbf{Var}\left[X(t)\right] = \mathbf{Var}\left[x_0 + \int_0^t \sigma \mathrm{d}W(s)\right] = \sigma^2 \mathbf{E}\left[\left(\int_0^t \mathrm{d}W(s)\right)^2\right]$$

$$= \sigma^2 \int_0^t \mathbf{E}\left[1^2\right] \mathrm{d}s = \sigma^2 t,$$

where we have used the Itō isometry property (7.40)*. This shows that* $\mathbf{Var}\left[X(t)\right] \to \infty$ *as* $t \to \infty$*. However the process is still bounded in finite time.*

Example 8.2 (Wiener process with drift)**.** *Let us compute the mean and variance of* $X(t)$*, where* $X(t)$ *is the solution to*

$$\mathrm{d}X(t) = \mu \mathrm{d}t + \sigma \mathrm{d}W(t), \qquad X(0) = x_0$$

where μ *and* σ *are some constants. This SDE corresponds to*

$$X(t) = x_0 + \int_0^t \mu \mathrm{d}s + \int_0^t \sigma \mathrm{d}W(s).$$

As in the previous example, we get

$$\mathbf{E}\left[X(t)\right] = x_0 + \mathbf{E}\left[\int_0^t \mu \mathrm{d}s\right] + \mathbf{E}\left[\int_0^t \sigma \mathrm{d}W(s)\right] = x_0 + \mu t,$$

$$\mathbf{Var}[X(t)] = \mathbf{Var}\left[\int_0^t \sigma \mathrm{d}W(s)\right] = \sigma^2 \mathbf{E}\left[\left(\int_0^t \mathrm{d}W(s)\right)^2\right] = \sigma^2 t.$$

We see that the mean of $X(t)$ *has a linear trend (or drift).*

Example 8.3 (Stochastic exponential growth)**.** *Consider the SDE*

$$\mathrm{d}X(t) = \mu X(t)\mathrm{d}t + \sigma \mathrm{d}W(t), \qquad X(0) = x_0 \tag{8.3}$$

where μ *and* σ *are constants, which may describe unlimited growth in biological systems or a stochastic money market account.*

If we take expectations in the adjacent stochastic integral equation, we get

$$\mathbf{E}[X(t)] = x_0 + \mathbf{E}\left[\int_0^t \mu X(s)\mathrm{d}s\right] + \mathbf{E}\left[\sigma \int_0^t \mathrm{d}W(s)\right].$$

Of course, the last term equals zero. Using Fubini's theorem (which we neither state nor prove here), we may exchange the expectation and integration operators, i.e.,

$$\mathbf{E}[X(t)] = x_0 + \mathbf{E}\left[\int_0^t \mu X(s)\mathrm{d}s\right] = x_0 + \mu \int_0^t \mathbf{E}[X(s)]\,\mathrm{d}s.$$

Compared to the last two examples the problem is now that $\mathbf{E}[X(t)]$ *exists on both sides of the equation. A standard trick is to introduce* $m(t) = \mathbf{E}[X(t)]$ *and then take the expectation and derivative with respect to time t on both sides, i.e.,*

$$\frac{\mathrm{d}m(t)}{\mathrm{d}t} = \dot{m}(t) = \mu m(t); \quad m(0) = \mathbf{E}[X(0)]$$

which clearly has the solution

$$\mathbf{E}[X(t)] = m(t) = m(0)e^{\mu t}.$$

We see that $\mathbf{E}[X(t)]$ *grows exponentially as* $t \to \infty$.

Considering the slightly more complicated *Geometric Brownian Motion (GBM)*

$$\mathrm{d}X(t) = \alpha X(t)\mathrm{d}t + \sigma X(t)\mathrm{d}W(t), \tag{8.4}$$

where α and σ are positive constants, it is not clear if there is existence and uniqueness of the solution for all $t \geq 0$ or if the solution might blow up with positive probability in finite time. Along the same lines we must examine whether it is possible to determine a closed form solution or not. In the former case, we may have to impose some restrictions on the functions μ and σ in (8.1) in order to obtain existence of the solution.

It is an interesting result that the answers to these questions only depend on the properties of the *infinitesimal characteristics* μ and σ in (8.1) (and possibly the initial condition $X(0)$).

8.1.1 Existence and uniqueness

As for ordinary differential equations (ODEs) Lipschitz and bounded growth conditions must be imposed on the drift and diffusion terms in order to obtain existence and uniqueness of solutions.

We must distinguish between *weak* and *strong* solutions to (8.1). A strong solution is obtained if the driving Wiener process is given in advance as a part of the problem such that the obtained solution to (8.1) is $\mathcal{F}(t)$-adapted, where $\mathcal{F}(t)$ is the σ-algebra generated by the Wiener process. On the other hand, if we are just given the infinitesimal characteristics μ and σ in advance and the solution should apply for all possible Wiener processes, then the obtained solution is called a weak solution. It is clear that a strong solution is also a weak solution, because the particular Wiener process $W(t)$ that resulted in the strong solution is just one of infinitely many Wiener processes that will give a weak solution. The converse is not true in general.

Theorem 8.1 (Strong uniqueness). *Suppose that the infinitesimal characteristics $\mu(x)$ and $\sigma(x)$ are locally Lipschitz-continuous in the state variable; i.e., for every integer $n \geq 1$ there exists a constant C_n such that for every $t \geq 0$, $|x| \leq n$ and $|y| \leq n$:*

$$|\mu(x) - \mu(y)| + |\sigma(x) - \sigma(y)| \leq C_n|x - y|. \tag{8.5}$$

Then strong uniqueness holds for (8.1).

Proof. Omitted. See Karatzas and Shreve [1996]. □

Let us consider an example that does not satisfy the condition (8.5).

Example 8.4. *It is easy to verify that the differential equation*

$$\frac{\mathrm{d}x}{\mathrm{d}t} = 3x^{2/3}$$

has several solutions, for any $a > 0$,

$$x(t) = \begin{cases} 0 & \text{for } t \leq a, \\ (t-a)^3 & \text{for } t > a. \end{cases}$$

This ODE is excluded as $\mu(x) = 3x^{2/3}$ does not satisfy (8.5) *for $x = 0$.*

We need an additional assumption in order to obtain existence and uniqueness of the solutions of (8.1).

Assumption 8.1 (Linear growth). *The functions μ and σ satisfy the usual linear growth condition*

$$|\mu(x)| + |\sigma(x)| \leq K(1 + |x|), \quad \forall x \in \mathbb{R} \tag{8.6}$$

where K is a positive, real constant.

Example 8.5. *The differential equation*

$$\frac{\mathrm{d}x}{\mathrm{d}t} = x^2(t), \quad x(0) = 1$$

corresponding to $\mu(x) = x^2$ has the solution

$$x(t) = \frac{1}{1-t}; \quad 0 \leq t < 1.$$

Thus it is impossible to find a solution for all t. This is due to the fact that $\mu(x) = x^2$ does not satisfy Assumption 8.1.

Next consider an example of a SDE.

Example 8.6 (Trespassing in a minefield). *Consider as an example of the process which satisfies* (8.5)*, but not* (8.6)

$$dX(t) = -\frac{1}{2}\exp(-2X(t))dt + \exp(-X(t))dW(t).$$

For $X(t) < 0$, we get exponential growth, which is faster than linear growth, and (8.6) *is not satisfied. It may be shown that the solution is given by*

$$X(t) = \ln\left(W(t) + \exp(X(0))\right).$$

It can be seen that the solution blows up when $W(t) < -\exp(X(0))$, as we would have to compute the natural logarithm of a negative number! If we define the (stopping) time $\tau(X(0), \omega)$ by

$$\tau(X(0), \omega) = \inf\{t \geq 0 : W(t, \omega) = -\exp(X(0, \omega))\}, \quad \omega \in \Omega$$

it is clear that the solution only exists up to time $\tau(X(0), \omega)$. This explosion time depends on the stochastic initial condition and the actual trajectory of the driving Wiener process.

Example 8.7 (Geometric Brownian motion). *Consider the process given in* (8.4)*. In this case an explosion time e may be defined by*

$$e = \inf\{t \geq 0 : X(t) \in \{0, \infty\}\} \tag{8.7}$$

which states that the explosion time e is the first (i.e., smallest) time, where the process $X(t)$ hits the boundary 0 or takes the value of ∞. Note that it is also critical if $X(t)$ attains the value 0 because the process $X(s)$ will remain at zero for $s \geq t$. The value of $X(t)$ as $t \to \infty$ depends on the parameters μ and σ as follows (this is illustrated in Example 8.10):

1. *If $\mu > \frac{1}{2}\sigma^2$ then $X(t) \to \infty$ a.s. as $t \to \infty$.*
2. *If $\mu < \frac{1}{2}\sigma^2$ then $X(t) \to 0$ a.s. as $t \to \infty$.*
3. *If $\mu = \frac{1}{2}\sigma^2$ then $X(t)$ will fluctuate between arbitrary large and arbitrary small values a.s. as $t \to \infty$,*

where a.s. is an abbreviation of almost surely. It may, however, be shown that $X(t)$ does not take either the value 0 or ∞ in finite time. Hence the geometric brownian Motion does not explode. This is also clear as the infinitesimal characteristics are linear in $X(t)$ and thus fulfils the Lipschitz condtions (8.5) *and, in particular, the linear growth condition* (8.6).

It may be shown that the conditions in Theorem 8.1 and Assumption 8.1 ensure the existence and uniqueness of solutions of (8.1). In particular (8.6) ensures that the solution does not explode in finite time. These assumptions may be generalized to the multivariate case (Karatzas and Shreve [1996]).

For one-dimensional processes (8.1), the assumptions (8.5) and (8.6) are not necessary to ensure nonexplosive solutions. The assumptions can be weakened to the following theorem.

Theorem 8.2 (The Yamada conditions). *Suppose that μ and σ are bounded. Assume further that the following conditions hold:*

1. *There exists a strictly increasing function $\nu(u)\colon \mathbb{R}_+ \mapsto \mathbb{R}$ such that $\nu(0) = 0$, and $\int_0^\infty \nu^{-2}(u)\mathrm{d}u = \infty$ and $|\sigma(x) - \sigma(y)| \leq \nu(|x-y|)$ for all $x, y \in \mathbb{R}$.*
2. *There exists an increasing and concave function $\kappa(u)\colon \mathbb{R}_+ \mapsto \mathbb{R}$ such that $\kappa(0) = 0$, $\int_0^\infty \kappa^{-1}(u)\mathrm{d}u = \infty$ and $|\mu(x) - \mu(y)| \leq \kappa(|x-y|)$ for all $x, y \in \mathbb{R}$.*

Then the pathwise uniqueness of solutions holds for (8.1) *and hence it has a unique strong solution.*

Proof. Omitted. See Ikeda and Watanabe [1989]. □

Remark 8.1. *The usual Lipschitz condition requires that $\nu(u) = K_1 u$ and $\kappa(u) = K_2 u$, where $K_1, K_2 \in \mathbb{R}_+$ are some constants, or even a unified condition for μ and σ as shown in, e.g. Rydberg [1997].*

There exist solutions to (8.1) which do not fulfil the linear growth condition (8.6). Thus we need to determine other conditions that ensure the nonexplosiveness of solutions, in particular conditions which are easier to check than those in Theorem 8.2.

Consider the *scale function*

$$s(x) = \int_c^x \exp\left(-\int_c^y \frac{2\mu(\xi)}{\sigma^2(\xi)}\mathrm{d}\xi\right)\mathrm{d}y \tag{8.8}$$

for some fixed $c \in \mathbb{R}_+$. This function may be used to establish sufficient conditions on the parameters $\theta \in \Theta \subset \mathbb{R}^p$ so that the explosion will never occur.

Theorem 8.3 (Probability of an explosion). *Let $X(t)$ be described by* (8.1), *the scale function $s(x)$ by* (8.8) *and the explosion time e by* (8.7).

1. *If $s(0) = -\infty$ and $s(\infty) = \infty$, then the probability for no explosion in finite time is one*
$$\mathbb{P}(e = \infty) = 1$$
for every $X(t)$.
2. *If $s(0) > -\infty$ and $s(\infty) = \infty$, then $\lim_{t\uparrow e} X(t)$ exists asymptotically and*
$$\mathbb{P}(\lim_{t\uparrow e} X(t) = 0) = \mathbb{P}(\sup_{t<e} X(t) < \infty) = 1$$
for every x. A similar assertion holds if the roles of 0 and ∞ are interchanged.

3. *If $s(0) > -\infty$ and $s(\infty) < \infty$, then $\lim_{t \uparrow e} X(t)$ exists asymptotically and*

$$\mathbb{P}(\lim_{t\uparrow e} X(t) = 0) = 1 - \mathbb{P}(\lim_{t\uparrow e} X(t) = \infty) = \frac{s(\infty) - s(x)}{s(\infty) - s(0)}.$$

Proof. Omitted. See e.g. Ikeda and Watanabe [1989]. □

Thus, if case 1) in Theorem 8.3 can be verified, the SDE in (8.1) does not explode with probability 1 and the solution exists for all t. On the other hand, if case 1) is not fulfilled, (8.1) may explode with positive probability in finite time. A further generalization is required, and this is called *Feller's test for explosions*. We refer the interested reader to, e.g., Karatzas and Shreve [1996, Section 5.1] for details.

Remark 8.2. *For specific choices of μ and σ in* (8.1) *the integral* (8.8) *may be difficult to evaluate. However, the computations may be simplified considerably by a change of measure using Girsanov's Theorem (see later) provided that a unique equivalent Martingale measure exists under the new measure (see e.g. Rydberg [1997] for the appropriate conditions in the one-dimensional case[2]). Informally speaking, Girsanov's Theorem simply introduces a measure that moves along with the deterministic drift and thus, under the equivalent martingale measure, the drift is removed.*

The following example illustrates the use of the scale function.

Example 8.8. *For the process* (8.2)*, there is no drift $\mu(X(t)) = 0$ and the diffusion is simply $\sigma(X(t)) = \sigma$, i.e.,*

$$s(x) = \int_c^x \exp\left(-\int_c^y 0 \, d\xi\right) dy = \int_c^x \exp(0) dy = x - c.$$

Thus we get $s(0) = -c$, which implies that

$$\lim_{c \to \infty} s(0) = -\infty$$

and

$$s(\infty) = \infty - c \quad \forall c \in \mathbb{R}_+.$$

Thus condition 1) in Theorem 8.3 is fulfilled and the Wiener process (8.2) *does not explode. This may seem contradictory, but it is important to stress that the trajectories of the Wiener process remain finite despite the fact that* **Var**$[X(t)] \to \infty$ *as $t \to \infty$. Note that ∞ does not belong to the real line $\mathbb{R}$.*

In the remainder of this book (and the problems), we simply assume that a unique solution exists. For brevity we shall not, in general, list the restrictions on the parameters that must be imposed to ensure nonexplosiveness.

[2]These conditions do not immediately generalize to higher dimensions.

8.1.2 Itō formula

An important feature of Itō stochastic differential equations is stated in the next theorem, but first we need a definition.

Definition 8.1 (The $C^{1,2}$ space). *Let $\varphi : \mathbb{R}^2 \mapsto \mathbb{R}$ be a function of two variables. The function φ is said to belong to the space $C^{1,2}(\mathbb{R} \times \mathbb{R})$ if φ is continuously differentiable w.r.t. the first variable and twice continuously differentiable w.r.t. the second variable.*

Theorem 8.4 (The Itō formula). *Let $X(t)$ be a solution to* (8.1) *and $\varphi : \mathbb{R}^2 \mapsto \mathbb{R}$ be a $C^{1,2}(\mathbb{R})$-function applied to $X(t)$*

$$Y(t) = \varphi(t, X(t)). \tag{8.9}$$

Then the following chain rule applies

$$\mathrm{d}Y(t) = \left[\frac{\partial \varphi}{\partial t} + \mu \frac{\partial \varphi}{\partial X(t)} + \frac{1}{2}\sigma^2 \frac{\partial^2 \varphi}{\partial X(t)^2} \right] \mathrm{d}t + \sigma \frac{\partial \varphi}{\partial X(t)} \mathrm{d}W(t) \tag{8.10}$$

where the functions μ and σ are as defined prior to (8.1).

Proof. For notational brevity, we will leave out the argument in $\varphi(t, X(t))$, $X(t)$ and $W(t)$ in this ad hoc proof. A second order Taylor expansion of $\mathrm{d}\varphi$ gives

$$\mathrm{d}\varphi = \frac{\partial \varphi}{\partial t}\mathrm{d}t + \frac{\partial \varphi}{\partial x}\mathrm{d}X + \frac{1}{2}\frac{\partial^2 \varphi}{\partial x^2}(\mathrm{d}X)^2 + \frac{1}{2}\frac{\partial^2 \varphi}{\partial t^2}(\mathrm{d}t)^2 + \frac{\partial^2 \varphi}{\partial t \partial x}\mathrm{d}t\mathrm{d}X.$$

From (8.1), we get

$$(\mathrm{d}X)^2 = \mu^2(\mathrm{d}t)^2 + \sigma^2(\mathrm{d}W)^2 + 2\mu\sigma(\mathrm{d}t)(\mathrm{d}W).$$

Compared to terms with $\mathrm{d}t$ and $\mathrm{d}W$, the terms containing $(\mathrm{d}t)^2$ and $(\mathrm{d}t)(\mathrm{d}W)$ are insignificant while $(\mathrm{d}W)^2 \sim \mathcal{O}(\mathrm{d}t)$. Thus we get

$$\begin{aligned}
\mathrm{d}\varphi &= \frac{\partial \varphi}{\partial t}\mathrm{d}t + \frac{\partial \varphi}{\partial x}(\mu \mathrm{d}t + \sigma \mathrm{d}W) + \frac{1}{2}\sigma^2 \frac{\partial^2 \varphi}{\partial x^2}(\mathrm{d}W)^2 \\
&= \frac{\partial \varphi}{\partial t}\mathrm{d}t + \mu \frac{\partial \varphi}{\partial x}\mathrm{d}t + \sigma \frac{\partial \varphi}{\partial x}\mathrm{d}W + \frac{1}{2}\sigma^2 \frac{\partial^2 \varphi}{\partial x^2}\mathrm{d}t \\
&= \left[\frac{\partial \varphi}{\partial t} + \mu \frac{\partial \varphi}{\partial x} + \frac{1}{2}\sigma^2 \frac{\partial^2 \varphi}{\partial x^2} \right] \mathrm{d}t + \sigma \frac{\partial \varphi}{\partial x}\mathrm{d}W
\end{aligned}$$

where we have also used Metatheorem 1. □

Remark 8.3 (Short form of the Itō formula). *By introducing the notation $\varphi_t = \partial \varphi / \partial t$, etc.,* (8.10) *may be written as*

$$\mathrm{d}\varphi = (\varphi_t + \mu \varphi_x + \frac{1}{2}\sigma^2 \varphi_{xx})\mathrm{d}t + \sigma \varphi_x \mathrm{d}W, \tag{8.11}$$

where we stress that φ_t should not be confused with $\varphi(t)$.

Remark 8.4 (Additional term in the Itō formula). *As opposed to classical calculus,* (8.10) *contains the additional term* $\frac{1}{2}\sigma^2\ \partial^2\varphi(X_t)/\partial X_t^2$, *which makes Itō calculus more complicated for theoretical considerations, although solutions to* (8.1) *are both Markov processes and martingales.*

Remark 8.5. *It follows from the last remark that the diffusion term from* (8.1) *enters the drift of* (8.10). *Another remarkable observation from* (8.10) *is that the transformed variable* $Y(t)$ *is also described by an Itō diffusion process.*

Example 8.9. *Consider the integral*

$$I(t) = \int_0^t W(s)\mathrm{d}W(s).$$

Choose $X(t) = W(t)$, *which implies that* $\mathrm{d}X(t) = \mathrm{d}W(t)$, *ie.* $\mu = 0$ *and* $\sigma = 1$. *In addition choose the transformation* $\varphi(t,x) = \frac{1}{2}x^2$. *Then*

$$Y(t) = \varphi(t, W(t)) = \frac{1}{2}W(t)^2.$$

Using (8.10), *we get*

$$\begin{aligned}
\mathrm{d}Y(t) &= \frac{\partial\varphi}{\partial t}\mathrm{d}t + \frac{\partial\varphi}{\partial x}\mathrm{d}W(t) + \frac{1}{2}\frac{\partial^2\varphi}{\partial x^2}(\mathrm{d}W(t))^2 \\
&= 0 + W(t)\cdot\mathrm{d}W(t) + \frac{1}{2}(\mathrm{d}W(t))^2 \\
&= W(t)\cdot\mathrm{d}W(t) + \frac{1}{2}\cdot\mathrm{d}t.
\end{aligned}$$

This implies that

$$\mathrm{d}(\frac{1}{2}(W(t))^2) = W(t)\cdot\mathrm{d}W(t) + \frac{1}{2}\mathrm{d}t$$

or in integral form

$$\frac{1}{2}(W(t))^2 = \int_0^t W(s)\mathrm{d}W(s) + \frac{1}{2}t$$

or

$$I = \int_0^t W(s)\mathrm{d}W(s) = \frac{1}{2}(W(t))^2 - \frac{1}{2}t.$$

Example 8.10 (Geometric Brownian motion). *We wish to solve the SDE given by*

$$\mathrm{d}X(t) = \mu X(t)\mathrm{d}t + \sigma X(t)\mathrm{d}W_t, \quad X_0 > 0. \tag{8.12}$$

This SDE is called the geometric Brownian motion and is considered extensively in mathematical finance as a model for interest rates and stock prices. This is mainly due to the fact that the solution $X(t)$ *is lognormally distributed and thus excludes negative interest rates (or populations in biology or concentrations in chemistry).*

By introducing the transformation $Y(t) = \varphi(t, X(t)) = \ln(X(t))$, *we get*

$$\frac{\partial \varphi}{\partial t} = 0, \quad \frac{\partial \varphi}{\partial X(t)} = \frac{1}{X(t)}, \quad \frac{\partial^2 \varphi}{\partial X(t)^2} = -\frac{1}{X(t)^2}.$$

Inserting these in (8.10) *we get*

$$\mathrm{d}Y_t = \left[\mu X(t)\frac{1}{X(t)} + \frac{1}{2}\sigma^2 X(t)^2 \left(-\frac{1}{X(t)^2}\right)\right]\mathrm{d}t + \sigma X(t)\frac{1}{X(t)}\mathrm{d}W(t)$$

or

$$\mathrm{d}(\ln X(t)) = (\mu - \frac{1}{2}\sigma^2)\mathrm{d}t + \sigma \mathrm{d}W(t)$$

and, finally,

$$X(t) = X_0 \exp((\mu - \frac{1}{2}\sigma^2)t + \sigma W(t)). \tag{8.13}$$

8.1.3 Multivariate SDEs

Let the state variable $\mathbf{X}(t) \in \mathbb{R}^n$ be described by the multivariate SDE

$$\mathrm{d}\mathbf{X}(t) = \mu(t, \mathbf{X}(t))\mathrm{d}t + \sigma(t, \mathbf{X}(t))\mathrm{d}\mathbf{W}(t) \tag{8.14}$$

where $\mu(t, \mathbf{X}(t))\colon \mathbb{R} \times \mathbb{R}^n \to \mathbb{R}^n$, $\sigma(t, \mathbf{X}(t))\colon \mathbb{R} \times \mathbb{R}^n \to \mathbb{R}^n \times \mathbb{R}^m$ and $\mathbf{W}(t)$ is an m-dimensional standard Wiener process. Note that n need not equal m.

Alternatively, Eq. (8.14) may be written as

$$\mathrm{d}X_i(t) = \mu_i(t, \mathbf{X}(t))\mathrm{d}t + \sum_{j=1}^{m} \sigma_{ij}(t, \mathbf{X}(t))\mathrm{d}W_j(t); \quad i = 1, \ldots, n. \tag{8.15}$$

For this process, we define the instantaneous covariances as

$$\Sigma(t, \mathbf{X}(t)) = \sigma(t, \mathbf{X}(t))\sigma^T(t, \mathbf{X}(t)). \tag{8.16}$$

Consider the following generalization of Theorem 8.4.

Theorem 8.5 (The multivariate Itō formula). *Let* $\mathbf{X}(t)$ *be a solution to* (8.14) *and* $\varphi\colon \mathbb{R}^n \mapsto \mathbb{R}^k$ *be a* $C^{1,2}(\mathbb{R})$*-function applied to* $\mathbf{X}(t)$

$$\mathbf{Y}(t) = \varphi(t, \mathbf{X}(t)). \tag{8.17}$$

Then the following chain rule applies

$$\mathrm{d}\varphi = \left[\frac{\partial \varphi}{\partial t} + \frac{\partial \varphi}{\partial \mathbf{X}}\mu + \frac{1}{2}\mathit{trace}\left(\sigma\sigma^T \frac{\partial^2 \varphi}{\partial \mathbf{X}\partial \mathbf{X}^T}\right)\right]\mathrm{d}t + \frac{\partial \varphi}{\partial \mathbf{X}^T}\sigma \mathrm{d}\mathbf{W}(t) \tag{8.18}$$

where $\varphi = \varphi(t, \mathbf{X}(t))$, $\mu = \mu(t, \mathbf{X}(t))$, *etc.*

Proof. Omitted, but it is similar to the proof of Theorem 8.4. □

Remark 8.6. *The multivariate Itō formula may also be written as*

$$d\varphi = \frac{\partial \varphi}{\partial t}dt + \sum_{i=1}^{n} \frac{\partial \varphi}{\partial X_i}dX_i + \frac{1}{2}\sum_{i=1}^{n}\sum_{j=1}^{m} \frac{\partial^2 \varphi}{\partial X_i \partial X_j}(dX_i)(dX_j) \tag{8.19}$$

where $(dW_i)(dW_j) = \delta_{ij}dt$ *(Kronecker's delta), i.e.,*

$$(dW_i)(dW_j) = 0 \quad i \neq j, \tag{8.20}$$
$$(dW_i)(dW_i) = dt, \tag{8.21}$$
$$(dW_i)(dt) = (dt)(dW_i) = 0. \tag{8.22}$$

The following example illustrates the use of Itō 's formula.

Example 8.11. *Consider the two-dimensional SDE*

$$dS_1 = \alpha_1 S_1 dt + \sigma_1 S_1 dW_1 \quad S_1(0) = S_{10}, \tag{8.23}$$
$$dS_2 = \alpha_2 S_2 dt + \sigma_2 S_2 dW_2 \quad S_2(0) = S_{20}, \tag{8.24}$$

where $\alpha_1, \alpha_2, \sigma_1$ *and* σ_2 *are constants, and* W_1, W_2 *are two uncorrelated, standard Wiener processes. (We have left out the time argument* t *for brevity.)*

By introducing the transformation

$$\varphi = \varphi(S_1, S_2) = \frac{S_1}{S_2}$$

in (8.19)*, we get*

$$\begin{aligned} d\varphi &= 0 \cdot dt + \frac{1}{S_2}(\alpha_1 S_1 dt + \sigma_1 S_1 dW_1) - \frac{S_1}{S_2^2}(\alpha_2 S_2 dt + \sigma_2 S_2 dW_2) \\ &\quad + \frac{1}{2} 0 \cdot dS_1 dS_1 + \frac{1}{2} S_1(-(-2S_2^{-3}))dS_2 dS_2 \\ &\quad + \frac{1}{2}\left(-\frac{1}{S_2^2}\right) dS_1 dS_2 + \frac{1}{2}\left(-\frac{1}{S_2^2}\right) dS_2 dS_1 \\ &= (\alpha_1 - \alpha_2 + \sigma_2^2)\frac{S_1}{S_2}dt + (\sigma_1 dW_1 - \sigma_2 dW_2)\frac{S_1}{S_2}. \end{aligned}$$

The difference between two uncorrelated Wiener processes W_1 *and* W_2 *with standard deviations* σ_1 *and* σ_2*, respectively, may be expressed as one Wiener process* W *with the standard deviation* $\sigma = \sqrt{\sigma_1^2 + \sigma_2^2}$ *(as for normally distributed random variables). Thus*

$$d\left(\frac{S_1}{S_2}\right) = (\alpha_1 - \alpha_2 + \sigma_2^2)\frac{S_1}{S_2}dt + \sigma\frac{S_1}{S_2}dW.$$

Note that (8.23) *may be solved independently and the solutions are given on the form* (8.13). *Thus*

$$\frac{S_1(t)}{S_2(t)} = \frac{S_{10}}{S_{20}} \exp\left[\left((\alpha_1 - \alpha_2) + \sigma_2^2 - \frac{\sigma_2^2 + \sigma_1^2}{2}\right)t + \sqrt{\sigma_1^2 + \sigma_2^2}W(t)\right].$$

Remark 8.7 (The sum of two Wiener processes). *From the Example, it follows that the sum of two standard Wiener processes $W_1(t)$ and $W_2(t)$ may be written as one Wiener process*

$$\sigma_1 W_1(t) + \sigma_2 W_2(t) \equiv \sqrt{\sigma_1^2 + \sigma_2^2}\, W(t). \tag{8.25}$$

This important result, which we state here without a formal proof, also applies to the increments of the Wiener process, i.e.,

$$\sigma_1 S(t)\mathrm{d}W_1(t) + \sigma_2 S(t)\mathrm{d}W_2(t) = \sqrt{\sigma_1^2 + \sigma_2^2} S(t)\mathrm{d}W(t). \tag{8.26}$$

These results will be very useful in some problems and applications.

8.1.4 Stratonovitch SDE

An alternative definition of SDEs that adhere to the classical calculus (e.g., the chain rule) is given by the Stratonovitch SDE

$$\mathrm{d}X(t) = \tilde{\mu}(X(t))\mathrm{d}t + \tilde{\sigma}(X(t)) \circ \mathrm{d}W(t) \tag{8.27}$$

where $\tilde{\mu}: \mathbb{R} \mapsto \mathbb{R}$ and $\tilde{\sigma}: \mathbb{R} \mapsto \mathbb{R}$ are Borel-measurable functions and the $\circ$-symbol is used to distinguish the Stratonovitch SDE from the Itō SDE (8.1). Although (8.27) does not define neither a Markov process nor a martingale (due to the definition of the Stratonovitch integral), this fact makes it unsuitable for, e.g., prediction and estimation purposes and it is more appropriate for theoretical work, such as existence and uniqueness theorems, stability analysis, bifurcation analysis (Baxendale [1994]) or Taylor series expansions (Kloeden and Platen [1995]).

Fortunately there is a link between the stochastic integrals in the Itō and Stratonovitch senses, namely

$$\tilde{\mu}(X(t)) = \mu(X(t)) - \frac{1}{2}\sigma(X(t))\frac{\partial \sigma(X(t))}{\partial X(t)}$$

where μ, σ and $\tilde{\mu}$ are defined by (8.1) and (8.27), respectively. See, e.g., Kloeden and Platen [1995], Pugachev and Sinitsyn [1987], Øksendal [2010] for further mathematical details, and Wang [1994], Nielsen [1996] for a discussion of the appropriate application of SDEs (Itō or Stratonovitch) in mathematical modelling.

Remark 8.8. *Note that* (8.1) *and* (8.27) *coincide provided that $\sigma(X(t)) = \tilde{\sigma}(X(t))$ is independent of $X(t)$, because $\partial\sigma(X(t))/\partial X(t) = 0$ in this special, but important, case.*

8.2 Analytical solution methods

Generally, it is difficult to obtain closed form solutions to stochastic differential equations. However, the Itō formula, that in all other aspects complicates analytical calculations considerably, may be valuable as an intermediary step in obtaining closed form solutions to (8.1). Some examples along these lines will be given. As with linear ordinary differential equations, the general solution of a linear stochastic differential equation can be found explicitly.

Closed form solutions for a number of SDEs (linear and nonlinear) are listed in Kloeden and Platen [1995], where a very elaborate discussion of numerical solutions may be found as well.

8.2.1 Linear, univariate SDEs

The general form of a *univariate linear stochastic differential equation* is

$$dX(t) = (\mu_1(t)X(t) + \mu_2(t))dt + (\sigma_1(t)X(t) + \sigma_2(t))dW(t) \tag{8.28}$$
$$X(t_0) = X_0 \tag{8.29}$$

where the coefficients μ_1, μ_2, σ_1 and σ_2 are given functions of time t or constants. We assume that these functions are measurable and bounded on an interval $0 \le t \le T$ such that the existence and uniqueness theorem from the preceding section applies and ensures the existence of a strong solution $X(t)$ on $t_0 \le t \le T$ for each $0 \le t_0 < T$.

When all the functions are constant the SDE is said to be *autonomous* and its solutions are homogeneous Markov processes. Otherwise, the SDE is said to be *nonautonomous*. When $\mu_2(t) \equiv 0$ and $\sigma_2(t) \equiv 0$, the Equations (8.28) reduce to the *homogenous* linear SDE

$$dX(t) = \mu_1(t)X(t)dt + \sigma_1(t)X(t)dW(t); \quad X(t_0) = X_0 \tag{8.30}$$

which clearly has the solution $X(t) \equiv 0$. The so-called *fundamental solution* Φ_{t,t_0} which satisfies the initial condition $\Phi_{t_0,t_0} = 1$ is much more important, because any other solution may be expressed in terms of the fundamental solution. To determine Φ_{t,t_0}, we consider the simple case where $\sigma_1(t) \equiv 0$, i.e.,

$$dX(t) = (\mu_1(t)X(t) + \mu_2(t))dt + \sigma_2(t)dW(t); \quad X(t_0) = X_0 \tag{8.31}$$

where the Wiener process appears additively. In this case we say that the SDE is *linear in the narrow sense.*

Theorem 8.6 (Solution to a linear SDE in the narrow sense). *The solution of* (8.31) *is given by*

$$X(t) = \Phi_{t,t_0}\left(X_{t_0} + \int_{t_0}^{t} \mu_2(s)\Phi_{s,t_0}^{-1}ds + \int_{t_0}^{t} \sigma_2(s)\Phi_{s,t_0}^{-1}dW(s)\right) \tag{8.32}$$

where

$$\Phi_{t,t_0} = \exp\left(\int_{t_0}^{t} \mu_1(s)\mathrm{d}s\right). \tag{8.33}$$

Proof. The homogenous version ($\sigma_2(t) \equiv 0$) of (8.31) is an ordinary differential equation

$$\dot{X}(t) = \mu_1(t)X(t) \tag{8.34}$$

with the fundamental solution

$$\Phi_{t,t_0} = \exp\left(\int_{t_0}^{t} \mu_1(s)\mathrm{d}s\right).$$

Applying the Itō formula (8.10) to the transformation $\varphi(t,x) = x/\Phi_{t,t_0} = \Phi_{t,t_0}^{-1}x$ and the solution $X(t)$ of (8.34), we get

$$\begin{aligned}
\mathrm{d}(\Phi_{t,t_0}^{-1}X(t)) &= \left(\frac{\mathrm{d}\Phi_{t,t_0}^{-1}}{\mathrm{d}t}X(t) + (\mu_1(t)X(t) + \mu_2(t))\Phi_{t,t_0}^{-1}\right)\mathrm{d}t \\
&\quad + \sigma_2(t)\Phi_{t,t_0}^{-1}\mathrm{d}W(t) \\
&= \mu_2(s)\Phi_{t,t_0}^{-1}\mathrm{d}t + \sigma_2(t)\Phi_{t,t_0}^{-1}\mathrm{d}W(t)
\end{aligned} \tag{8.35}$$

as

$$\frac{\mathrm{d}\Phi_{t,t_0}^{-1}}{\mathrm{d}t} = -\Phi_{t,t_0}^{-1}\mu_1(t).$$

The right hand side of (8.35) can be integrated giving

$$\Phi_{t,t_0}^{-1}X(t) = \Phi_{t,t_0}^{-1}X(t_0) + \int_{t_0}^{t} \mu_2(s)\Phi_{s,t_0}^{-1}\mathrm{d}s + \int_{t_0}^{t} \sigma_2(s)\Phi_{s,t_0}^{-1}\mathrm{d}W(s).$$

We have thus obtained the solution (8.32) as $\Phi_{t_0,t_0}^{-1} = 1$. □

Remark 8.9. *Notice again that* Φ_{t,t_0}^{-1} *means* $1/\Phi_{t,t_0}$ *and not the inverse function.*

Theorem 8.7 (Solution to a linear SDE in the wide sense)**.** *The solution to* (8.28) *is given by*

$$\begin{aligned}
X(t) = \Phi_{t,t_0}\Bigg(X_{t_0} &+ \int_{t_0}^{t} (\mu_2(s) - \sigma_1(s)\sigma_2(s))\Phi_{s,t_0}^{-1}\mathrm{d}s \\
&+ \int_{t_0}^{t} \sigma_2(s)\Phi_{s,t_0}^{-1}\mathrm{d}W(s)\Bigg)
\end{aligned} \tag{8.36}$$

where Φ_{t,t_0} is given as the solution to the SDE

$$\mathrm{d}\Phi_{t,t_0} = \mu_1(t)\Phi_{t,t_0}\mathrm{d}t + \sigma_1(t)\Phi_{t,t_0}\mathrm{d}W(t); \quad \Phi_{t_0,t_0} = 1. \tag{8.37}$$

Proof. Omitted. See Kloeden and Platen [1995, Section 4.3]. □

Theorem 8.8 (Moments of a linear SDE in the wide sense). *The mean $m(t) = \mathbf{E}[X(t)]$ of (8.28) satisfies the ordinary differential equation*

$$\dot{m}(t) = \mu_1(t)m(t) + \mu_2(t); \quad m(0) = m_0 \tag{8.38}$$

and the second order moment $P(t) = \mathbf{E}\left[X^2(t)\right]$ satisfies

$$\dot{P}(t) = (2\mu_1(t) + \sigma_1^2(t))P(t) + 2m(t)(\mu_2(t) + \sigma_1(t)\sigma_2(t)) + \sigma_2^2(t), \tag{8.39}$$

$$P(0) = P. \tag{8.40}$$

Proof. By proceeding as in Example 8.3, Equation (8.38) is readily seen. In order to show (8.39), we apply the Itō formula (8.10) to the transformation $\varphi(t,x) = x^2$, i.e.,

$$\begin{aligned} \mathrm{d}\varphi &= \left(0 + (\mu_1 X + \mu_2)2X + \frac{1}{2}(\sigma_1 X + \sigma_2)^2 \cdot 2\right)\mathrm{d}t \\ &\quad + (\sigma_1 X + \sigma_2)2X\mathrm{d}W \\ &= \left(2(\mu_1 X^2 + \mu_2 X) + \sigma_1^2 X^2 + \sigma_2^2 + 2\sigma_1\sigma_2 X\right)\mathrm{d}t \\ &\quad + 2(\sigma_1 X^2 + \sigma_2 X)\mathrm{d}W \end{aligned}$$

where the arguments have been left out for brevity as in the following equivalent stochastic integral formulation

$$\begin{aligned} X^2(t) = & X^2(t_0) + \int_{t_0}^{t} \left(2(\mu_1 X^2 + \mu_2 X) + \sigma_1^2 X^2 + \sigma_2^2 + 2\sigma_1\sigma_2 X\right)\mathrm{d}s \\ & + \int_{t_0}^{t} 2(\sigma_1 X^2 + \sigma_2 X)\mathrm{d}W. \end{aligned}$$

By taking expectations the last term drops out; cf. (7.37). If we define $P(t) = \mathbf{E}\left[X^2(t)\right]$ and take derivatives, we obtain

$$\frac{P(t)}{\mathrm{d}t} = 2\mu_1(t)P(t) + 2\mu_2(t)m(t) + \sigma_1^2(t)P(t) + \sigma_2^2(t) + 2\sigma_1(t)\sigma_2(t)m(t)$$

which equals (8.39). □

Remark 8.10. *Recall that the variance $\mathbf{Var}[X(t)]$ may be determined from*

$$\mathbf{Var}[X(t)] = P(t) - (m(t))^2. \tag{8.41}$$

In order to solve (8.39) the following result from calculus may be useful.

Remark 8.11 (A formula for solution of ODEs). *The solution to the ODE*

$$\dot{x}(t) + \psi(t)x(t) = \vartheta(t), \quad t \in \mathscr{I}, \tag{8.42}$$

where $\psi, \vartheta : \mathscr{I} \to \mathbb{R}$ *are continuous in the interval* $\mathscr{I}$*, is given by*

$$x(t) = \exp(-\Psi(t)) \left(\int \exp(\Psi(t))\vartheta(t)\mathrm{d}t + c \right), \quad t \in \mathscr{I}, c \in \mathbb{R} \tag{8.43}$$

where

$$\Psi(t) = \int \psi(t)\mathrm{d}t.$$

As an example consider the SDE from Example 8.3 again.

Example 8.12. *Consider the Langevin equation*

$$\mathrm{d}X(t) = -\mu X(t)\mathrm{d}t + \sigma \mathrm{d}W(t); \quad X(0) = X_0. \tag{8.44}$$

Without loss of generality, we assume that $t_0 = 0$*. From* (8.33)*, we immediately get*

$$\Phi_{t,0} = \exp\left(-\int_0^t \mu \mathrm{d}s \right) = \exp(-\mu t)$$

and thus (8.32) *yields the solution*

$$X(t) = \exp(-\mu t)\left(X_0 + \sigma \int_0^t \exp(\mu s)\mathrm{d}W(s) \right)$$

which is called the Ornstein-Uhlenbeck process.

The mean $m(t) = \mathbf{E}[X(t)]$ *is obtained from* (8.38)*, i.e.,*

$$m(t) = m_0 \exp(-\mu t).$$

The second moment $P(t)$ *should fulfill*

$$\dot{P}(t) + 2\mu P = \sigma^2.$$

Using Remark 8.11, we get

$$\Psi(t) = \int_0^t 2\mu \mathrm{d}t = 2\mu t$$

and insertion into (8.43) *yields*

$$X(t) = \exp(-2\mu t)\left(\int_0^t \exp(2\mu s)\sigma^2 \mathrm{d}s + P_0\right)$$

$$= \underbrace{P_0 \exp(-2\mu t)}_{\textit{Impact from initial variance}} + \underbrace{\frac{\sigma^2}{2\mu}(1-\exp(-2\mu t))}_{\textit{Response of the system}}.$$

The variance may be found as stated in Remark 8.10, i.e.,

$$\mathbf{Var}[X(t)] = P_0 \exp(-2\mu t) + \frac{\sigma^2}{2\mu}(1-\exp(-2\mu t)) - m_0^2 \exp(-2\mu t)$$

and the stationary value is

$$\lim_{t\to\infty} \mathbf{Var}[X(t)] = \frac{\sigma^2}{2\mu}.$$

Note that it is not just σ^2.

8.3 Feynman–Kac representation

In this section we shall describe a close relationship between stochastic differential equations and parabolic partial differential equations (PDEs).

Consider the following *Cauchy problem*

$$\frac{\partial F}{\partial t}(t,x) + \mu(t,x)\frac{\partial F}{\partial x}(t,x) + \frac{1}{2}\sigma^2(t,x)\frac{\partial^2 F}{\partial x^2}(t,x) = 0 \quad (8.45)$$

$$F(T,X) = \Phi(X) \quad (8.46)$$

where the functions $\mu(t,x)$, $\sigma(t,x)$ and $\Phi(T,x)$ are given and we wish to determine the function $F(t,x)$

As opposed to solving (8.45) analytically, we shall consider a representation formula for the solution $F(t,x)$ in terms of an associated stochastic differential equation.

Assume that there exists a solution to (8.45). Fix the time t and the state x. Let the stochastic process $X(t)$ be a solution to the SDE

$$\mathrm{d}X(s) = \mu(s,X(s))\mathrm{d}s + \sigma(s,X(s))\mathrm{d}W(s), \quad X(t) = x \quad (8.47)$$

where s is now the running time.

Remark 8.12 (Same $\mu(\cdot)$ and $\sigma(\cdot)$). *The functions* $\mu(t,X(t))$ *and* $\sigma(t,X(t))$ *in* (8.45) *and* (8.47) *are the same — except for the fact that the running time variable in* (8.47) *is* s.

If we apply the Itō formula (8.10) to the process $F(s,X(s))$ and write the result in stochastic integral form, we get

$$\begin{aligned} F(T,X(T)) &= F(t,X(t)) \\ &+ \int_t^T \left(\frac{\partial F}{\partial t}(s,X(s)) + \mu(s,X(s)) \frac{\partial F}{\partial x}(s,X(s)) \right. \\ &\qquad \left. + \frac{1}{2}\sigma^2(s,X(s)) \frac{\partial^2 F}{\partial x^2}(s,X(s)) \right) \mathrm{d}s \\ &+ \int_t^T \sigma(s,X(s)) \frac{\partial F}{\partial x}(s,X(s)) \mathrm{d}W(s). \end{aligned} \tag{8.48}$$

Let us further assume that the process

$$\sigma(s,X(s)) \frac{\partial F}{\partial x}(s,X(s))$$

belongs to the space $\mathscr{L}^2[t,T]$; see Definition 7.5. If we use that $F(t,x)$ solves (8.45), then the ds integral drops out of (8.48). If we apply the boundary condition $F(T,x) = \Phi(x)$, and the initial condition $X(t) = x$, and take the expected value of the remaining parts of (8.48) then the last term also drops out; cf. (7.37). The only remaining term is

$$F(t,x) = \mathbf{E}_{t,x}\left[\Phi(X(T))\right] \tag{8.49}$$

where the subscript t,x on the expectation operator is used to emphasize the fixed initial condition $X(t) = x$.

We state this important result in a theorem.

Theorem 8.9 (The Feynman–Kac representation). *Assume that F solves the boundary problem* (8.45) *and that the process*

$$\sigma(s,X(s)) \frac{\partial F}{\partial x}(s,X(s)) \in \mathscr{L}^2 \; \mathit{for} \; t \leq T, x \in \mathbb{R} \tag{8.50}$$

where $X(t)$ is defined by (8.47). *Then F has the stochastic Feynman–Kac representation*

$$F(t,x) = \mathbf{E}_{t,x}\left[\Phi(X(T))\right]. \tag{8.51}$$

Proof. Follows from the preceding derivation. □

Note that the theorem simply states that the solution to (8.45) is obtained as the expected value of the boundary condition.

Remark 8.13. *A major problem with this approach is that it is impossible to check the assumption* (8.50) *in advance as it requires some a priori information about the solution F to do so. At least two things can go wrong:*

1. *Eq.* (8.45) *does not have a "sufficiently integrable" solution, i.e., the process* (8.50) *does not belong to the class* $\mathscr{L}^2$*. If the latter is the case, the solution offered by the Feynman–Kac representation is pure nonsense.*
2. *The solution of* (8.45) *is not unique. If there are more solutions, the Feynman–Kac approach just supplies the "sufficiently integrable" solution. The remaining solutions must be found using another technique.*

In this book, we shall assume that all the functions in question are "sufficiently integrable." We shall not go into all the technical details (see e.g. Björk [2009], Øksendal [2010]).

Let us consider an example of this remarkable approach.

Example 8.13. *We wish to solve the following boundary problem in the domain* $[0,T]\times\mathbb{R}$*:*

$$\begin{aligned}\frac{\partial F}{\partial t}+\mu x\frac{\partial F}{\partial x}+\frac{1}{2}\sigma^2x^2\frac{\partial^2 F}{\partial x^2} &= 0\\ F(T,x) &= \ln(x^2)\end{aligned}$$

where μ *and* σ *are assumed to be constants.*

It is readily seen that the associated SDE is given by

$$\mathrm{d}X(s)=\mu X(s)\mathrm{d}s+\sigma X(s)\mathrm{d}W(s);\quad X(t)=x.$$

We recognize this as the geometric Brownian motion from Example 8.10 on page 148, where the solution was found to be

$$X(T)=\exp\left(\ln(x)+(\mu-\frac{1}{2}\sigma^2)(T-t)+\sigma[W(T)-W(t)]\right).$$

Using Theorem 8.9, we get the result

$$\begin{aligned}F(t,x) &= \mathbf{E}_{t,x}[2\ln(X(T))]\\ &= 2\ln(x)+2(\mu-\frac{1}{2}\sigma^2)(T-t)\end{aligned}$$

as the expected value of the Wiener increment $W(T)-W(t)$ *is zero.*

We shall now consider a more general case.

Theorem 8.10 (The Feynman–Kac representation with discounting)**.** *Let the functions* μ*,* σ *and* Φ *be given as above, and let* r *be a constant. The solution to*

$$\begin{aligned}\frac{\partial F}{\partial t}(t,x)+\mu(t,x)\frac{\partial F}{\partial x}(t,x)+\frac{1}{2}\sigma^2(t,x)\frac{\partial^2 F}{\partial x^2}(t,x)-rF(t,x)=0\\ F(T,x)=\Phi(x)\end{aligned}$$

is given by

$$F(t,x)=\exp(r(T-t))\mathbf{E}_{t,x}[\Phi(X(T))] \tag{8.52}$$

where the process $X(t)$ *is given by* (8.47).

Proof. Omitted. See e.g. Björk [2009]. □

The Feynman–Kac representation theorems will be used extensively in the following chapters. Further generalizations and examples are to be found in the problems.

These theorems may be used to solve for the transition probabilities for SDEs in order to obtain the conditional and unconditional probability density functions (pdf) of $X(t)$, where $X(t)$ is the solution of (8.47). This is outside the scope of this book.

8.4 Girsanov measure transformation

In this section we introduce the concepts of (probability) measures, the *Radon–Nikodym derivative* and the *Girsanov theorem*, which enables us to change (probability) measures in continuous-time models. The theory is much more complicated than in the discrete time case (as described in Chapter 3), so this exposition does not pretend to be complete. Whenever possible, mathematical rigour will be substituted by intuitive arguments.

Note that a measure transformation is an inherently mathematical concept, which greatly simplifies the pricing of financial derivatives, but it is very difficult to fully comprehend the concept.

The objective of this section is to provide the reader with an elementary understanding of the concept of absolute continuous measure transformations, which will be used extensively later to determine arbitrage-free prices of a large class of financial derivatives. This is due to the fact that there exists an intimate relation between arbitrage-free markets and absolute continuous measure transformations. A particularly interesting problem is the existence of *equivalent martingale measures* (EMM), because it may be shown that the existence of an EMM yields arbitrage-free markets and vice versa.

8.4.1 Measure theory

Intuitively, a *measure* is a notion that generalizes those of the length, the area of figures and the volume of bodies, and that corresponds to the mass of a set for some mass distribution throughout the space. Please refer to Appendix B for details.

Example 8.14 (Does 2 equal 1?). *Consider two independent, normally distributed stochastic variables X,Y with zero mean and variance 1. If we interpret (X,Y) as a point in $\mathbb{R}^2$ then we can introduce polar coordinates (R,ϕ), which are also independent.*

Consider the conditional mean

$$\begin{aligned}\mathbf{E}\left[R^2|X=Y\right] &= \mathbf{E}\left[R^2|\phi=\frac{\pi}{4}\ or\ \frac{5\pi}{4}\right]=\mathbf{E}\left[R^2\right]\\ &= \mathbf{E}\left[X^2+Y^2\right]=1+1=2.\end{aligned}$$

Now introduce the new variables $Z=\frac{X+Y}{\sqrt{2}}$ *and* $W=\frac{X-Y}{\sqrt{2}}$ *which are both* $N(0,1)$*-distributed. It is clear that* $Z^2+W^2=X^2+Y^2=R^2$ *such that*

$$\mathbf{E}\left[R^2|X=Y\right]=\mathbf{E}\left[Z^2+W^2|W=0\right]=\mathbf{E}\left[Z^2\right]=1.$$

Obviously $2\neq 1$ *so there must be something wrong! The problem is that in both conditional expectations we condition on a null set,* $W=0$*, which does not make any sense, whereas the expectation* $\mathbf{E}\left[R^2|X-Y=\nu\right]$ *makes sense for almost all* ν*, i.e., we should consider the expectation as an integral with respect to* $\mathrm{d}\nu$ *(as usual). Thus we need to consider conditional expectations in a wider sense, and this is exactly what measure theory and the Radon–Nikodym derivative enable us to do.*

Let $(X,\mathscr{F},\mu)$ be a *measurable* space and let $f\colon X\to\mathbb{R}$ be a positive $\mathscr{F}$-measurable function such that

$$\int_X f(x)\mathrm{d}\mu(x)<\infty. \tag{8.53}$$

As an example consider a continuous stochastic variable X with the probability density function $f(x)$. We may define the Lebesgue measure by $\mathrm{d}\mu(x)=f(x)\mathrm{d}x$ such that (8.53) takes the form

$$\int_X f(x)\mathrm{d}x<\infty.$$

We may now define a new function $\nu\colon\mathscr{F}\to\mathbb{R}$ by

$$\nu(E)=\int_E f(x)\mathrm{d}\mu(x)\quad\text{for all } E\in\mathscr{F} \tag{8.54}$$

which is also a measure on $(X,\mathscr{F})$.

It follows directly that the measure ν has the property

$$\text{if } E\in\mathscr{F} \textit{ and } \mu(E)=0 \text{ then also } \nu(E)=0 \tag{8.55}$$

which means that the ν has at least the same null sets as μ.

Definition 8.2 (Equivalent measures). *Let* $(X,\mathscr{F})$ *be a measurable space, and let* μ *and* ν *be measures on* $(X,\mathscr{F})$*. The measure* ν *is said to be absolute continuous with respect to* μ *if* (8.55) *is fulfilled. In short, we write* $\nu\ll\mu$*. If both* $\nu\ll\mu$ *and* $\mu\ll\nu$ *are true, the measures are said to be equivalent and we write* $\nu\sim\mu$*.*

Remark 8.14. *That two measures are equivalent simply means that they have the same null sets. Beside that there need not be any similarities.*

Example 8.15. *As an example consider an oil tanker that has run aground and starts to leak oil. Let the space X be some limited area of the ocean (a subset of $\mathbb{R}^2$). At each location $x \in X$, we define $f(x)$ as the density of the oil and the measure $\mu(x)$ as the depth of the oil. Then the measure $\nu(x)$ defined by* (8.54) *measures the amount of oil at location x. These measures are equivalent, because if there is not any oil at any depth at location x, expressed by $\mu(x) = 0$, then there is indeed no oil at location x, which means that $\nu(x) = 0$, and vice versa. As there is a limited amount of oil in the tanker,* (8.53) *is obviously fulfilled.*

8.4.2 Radon–Nikodym theorem

Assuming that μ is given and we define the new measure ν by (8.54), then ν is absolute continuous with respect to μ. A very important result attributable to Radon–Nikodym states that the converse is also true, namely that any measure ν, where $\nu \ll \mu$, can be written on the form (8.54). We state this as a theorem without proof.

Theorem 8.11 (Radon–Nikodym). *Let $(X, \mathscr{F}, \mu)$ be a finite measurable space and let ν be a finite measure on $(X, \mathscr{F})$ such that $\nu \ll \mu$. Then there exists a positive function $f\colon X \to \mathbb{R}$ which satisfies*

$$f \text{ is } \mathscr{F}\text{-measurable} \tag{8.56}$$

$$\int_X f(x)\mathrm{d}\mu(x) < \infty \tag{8.57}$$

$$\nu(E) = \int_E f(x)\mathrm{d}\mu(x); \quad \text{for all Borel sets } E \in \mathscr{F}. \tag{8.58}$$

The function f is called the Radon–Nikodym derivative of ν with respect to μ (on the σ-algebra $\mathscr{F}$). It is uniquely determined almost everywhere and we write

$$f = \frac{\mathrm{d}\nu}{\mathrm{d}\mu} \quad \text{or} \quad \mathrm{d}\nu(x) = f(x)\mathrm{d}\mu(x). \tag{8.59}$$

Example 8.16. *A simple example of absolute continuity is obtained if we let X be a finite set, i.e., $X = [1, \ldots, N]$ and define the σ-algebra by $\mathscr{F} = 2^X$, i.e., the family of all subsets of X. Let the measure μ on $(X, \mathscr{F})$ be given by the point masses $\mu(n = ([n]))$, $n = 1, \ldots, N$. The relation $\nu \ll \mu$ means that $\nu(n) = 0$ for all n where $\mu(n) = 0$. If we assume that ν and μ are given and that $\nu \ll \mu$ then the Radon–Nikodym derivative is simply found from*

$$\nu(n) = f(n)\mu(n), \quad n = 1, \ldots, N$$

or

$$f(n) = \frac{\nu(n)}{\mu(n)}.$$

Note that the special case $\mu(n) = 0$ and $\nu(n) \neq 0$ is excluded by $\nu \ll \mu$. If, however, both $\mu(n) = \nu(n) = 0$ then we may define $f(n)$ by

$$f(n) = \begin{cases} \frac{\nu(n)}{\mu(n)} & \text{for } \mu(n) \neq 0, \\ \text{Not defined} & \text{for } \mu(n) = 0. \end{cases}$$

The function $f(n)$ is not uniquely defined for the n where $\mu(n) = 0$, but the set of these null point has the measure 0. We say that $f(n)$ is uniquely determined almost everywhere (with respect to μ).

It is important to note that the concept of absolute continuity is linked to the specific σ-algebra that we are considering. If for example μ is defined on $(X, \mathscr{F})$ and $\mathscr{F} \supseteq \mathscr{G}$ then it is possible that $\nu \ll \mu$ on $(X, \mathscr{G})$ is true, while it is not true that $\nu \ll \mu$ on $(X, \mathscr{F})$.

Example 8.17. *Consider the set $X = [1,2,3]$ and the measure*

$$\mu(1) = 2, \quad \mu(2) = 0, \quad \mu(3) = 2$$

$$\nu(1) = 8, \quad \nu(2) = 5, \quad \nu(3) = 13$$

and the σ-algebras $\mathscr{F} = 2^X$ and $\mathscr{G} = [X, \emptyset, [1], [2,3]]$. It is clear that $\nu \ll \mu$ is not true on $\mathscr{F}$ because $\nu(2) \neq 0$ while $\mu(2) = 0$. On the other hand, we have $\nu \ll \mu$ on $\mathscr{G}$ with the Radon–Nikodym derivative

$$f(n) = \begin{cases} 8/2 = 4 & \text{for } n = 1 \\ (5+13)/(0+2) = 9 & \text{for } n = 2,3. \end{cases}$$

By comparing $\mathscr{F}$ and $\mathscr{G}$, it is clear that the absolute continuity property may be lost, if we consider a finer σ-algebra. The σ-algebra $\mathscr{G}$ cannot distinguish between $[2]$ and $[3]$.

We shall now consider measure transformations on filtered probability spaces and we assume that the probability space $(\Omega, \mathscr{F}, \mathbb{P})$ augmented by the filtration $\mathscr{F}(t)$ is given on the time interval $[0, T]$, where T is some fixed time. Assuming that we have a non-negative $\mathscr{F}(T)$-measurable stochastic variable L_T, we may construct a new measure $\mathbb{Q}$ on $(X, \mathscr{F}_T)$ by

$$\mathrm{d}\mathbb{Q} = L_T \mathrm{d}\mathbb{P} \tag{8.60}$$

and if we further have that

$$\mathbf{E}^{\mathbb{P}}[L_T] = 1 \tag{8.61}$$

then $\mathbb{Q}$ is a new *probability measure* on $(X, \mathscr{F}(T))$.

Measure transformations of this kind are closely related to martingale theory. Let $\mathbb{P}_t$ and $\mathbb{Q}_t$ denote the restrictions of $\mathbb{P}$ and $\mathbb{Q}$ on $\mathscr{F}(t)$, which implies that knowledge about the probability measures is only based on information up to and including time t. Then $\mathbb{Q}_t$ is absolute continuous with respect to $\mathbb{P}_t$ for all t, and the Radon–Nikodym Theorem 8.11 guarantees the existence of a stochastic process $[L_t; 0 \leq t \leq T]$ defined by

$$L_t = \frac{d\mathbb{Q}_t}{d\mathbb{P}_t} \quad \text{or} \quad d\mathbb{Q}_t = L_t d\mathbb{P}_t. \tag{8.62}$$

It also follows that L_t is adapted. Furthermore, we shall now show that L_t is also a martingale with respect to $(\mathscr{F}(t), \mathbb{P})$.

Theorem 8.12. *The stochastic process L_t is a $(\mathscr{F}(t), \mathbb{P})$-martingale.*

Proof. We need to show that

$$L_t = \mathbf{E}^{\mathbb{P}}[L_T | \mathscr{F}(t)] \quad \forall t \leq T \tag{8.63}$$

which is indeed the martingale property; namely that the expected value at time t of a stochastic variable L at some future time T, $t \leq T$, is simply the expected value of L based on the information up to time t.

In other words we need to show that for all $F \in \mathscr{F}_t$, we have

$$\int_F L_t d\mathbb{P} = \int_F L_T d\mathbb{P} \tag{8.64}$$

which follows from the following argument: As $F \in \mathscr{F}(t)$ it follows from (8.62) that

$$\int_F L_t d\mathbb{P} = \mathbb{Q}_t(F) = \mathbb{Q}_T(F)$$

where the latter is due to $\mathbb{Q}_t = \mathbb{Q}_T$ on $\mathscr{F}(t)$. This simply states that our information about the probability measure $\mathbb{Q}_T$ given the information set $\mathscr{F}(t)$ is limited to the restricted probability measure $\mathbb{Q}_t$. As the filtration is increasing $F \in \mathscr{F}_t \subseteq \mathscr{F}_T$, we finally get (8.64). □

Remark 8.15 (Restricted probability measures). *Think of a restricted probability measure $\mathbb{P}_t$ in the following way: Assume that we gather information about, say, stock prices in time. Each time we observe a price we obtain more information about the probability density function (pdf) of stock prices (by e.g., drawing a histogram). As $t \to \infty$, we obtain complete information about the pdf and our knowledge is no longer restricted to $\mathbb{P}_t$.*

It is sometimes convenient to exchange probability measures as we did in Chapter 3 to compute arbitrage-free prices. We recall that the price of any financial derivative may be expressed as the expected value of a (properly discounted) payoff function under an equivalent martingale measure $\mathbb{Q}$, Thus we need to establish a relation between expectations under different measures. We will need an important term before we can state the main result.

Definition 8.3 (The L^1-space). *Let an integrable stochastic variable X be defined on the probability space $(\Omega, \mathscr{F}, \mathbb{P})$. If*

$$\mathbf{E}^{\mathbb{P}}[X] < \infty \tag{8.65}$$

then X is said to belong to the class L^1. We write $X \in L^1(\Omega, \mathscr{F}, \mathbb{P})$.

Theorem 8.13 (Expectation under the $\mathbb{Q}$-measure). *Let the probability space $(\Omega, \mathscr{F}, \mathbb{P})$ and a stochastic variable $X \in L^1(\Omega, \mathscr{F}, \mathbb{P})$ be given. Let $\mathbb{Q}$ be another probability measure on $(X, \mathscr{F})$ where $\mathbb{Q} \ll \mathbb{P}$ with the Radon–Nikodym derivative given by*

$$L = \frac{\mathrm{d}\mathbb{Q}}{\mathrm{d}\mathbb{P}}.$$

Assume that X also belongs to $L^1(\Omega, \mathscr{F}, \mathbb{Q})$ and that a $\mathscr{G}$ is a σ-algebra such that $\mathscr{G} \subseteq \mathscr{F}$. Then

$$\mathbf{E}^{\mathbb{Q}}[X|\mathscr{G}] = \frac{\mathbf{E}^{\mathbb{P}}[LX|\mathscr{G}]}{\mathbf{E}^{\mathbb{P}}[L|\mathscr{G}]} \quad \mathbb{Q}-\textit{almost surely}. \tag{8.66}$$

Proof. Omitted. See Björk [2009]. □

We may apply this theorem to characterize martingales under the $\mathbb{Q}$-measure in terms of the characteristics under the $\mathbb{P}$-measure.

Theorem 8.14. *Consider the probability space $(\Omega, \mathscr{F}, \mathbb{P})$ augmented by the filtration $\mathscr{F}(t)$ on the time interval $[0,T]$. Let $\mathbb{Q}$ be another probability measure such that $\mathbb{Q}_T \ll \mathbb{P}_T$ and define the process L as in* (8.62). *Assume that M is an $\mathscr{F}(t)$-adapted process with $\mathbf{E}^{\mathbb{Q}}[M(t)] < \infty$ for all $t \in [0,T]$ such that*

$$L \cdot M \textit{ is a } (\mathbb{P}, \mathscr{F}(t))\textit{-martingale}. \tag{8.67}$$

Then M is a $(\mathbb{Q}, \mathscr{F}(t))$-martingale.

Proof. Omitted. See Björk [2009]. □

Remark 8.16. *The theorem simply states (under some additional conditions) that if we apply the Radon–Nikodym derivative to a $\mathbb{P}$-martingale M then we get a $\mathbb{Q}$-martingale. Thus (under some conditions) the martingale property is preserved. This is a very important result.*

8.4.3 Girsanov transformation

So far we have shown that is possible to introduce absolute continuous measure transformations from the objective probability measure $\mathbb{P}$ (the real-world measure) to an equivalent martingale measure $\mathbb{Q}$ such that we can obtain arbitrage-free prices of financial derivatives. We now show that such measure transformations affect the properties of the driving Wiener process and the infinitesimal characteristics of a stochastic differential equation.

As the mathematics is fairly complicated, one should at all times keep in mind that the objective is to choose a particular new measure $\mathbb{Q}$ such that we can obtain arbitrage-free prices.

The mathematical framework is as follows: We consider a Wiener process $X(t)$ defined on the probability space $(\Omega, \mathscr{F}, \mathbb{P})$ augmented by the natural filtration $\mathscr{F}(t)$ for $0 \leq t \leq T$, where T is some fixed time T (e.g., the maturity time of a bond or the exercise date of a call option on a stock). We introduce a nonnegative $\mathscr{F}(t)$-measurable stochastic variable L_T with $\mathbf{E}[L_T] = 1$. We wish to exchange measures by

$$\mathrm{d}\mathbb{Q} = L_T \mathrm{d}\mathbb{P} \quad (\text{on } \mathscr{F}(T))$$

and consider the problem how this change of measure affects the $\mathbb{P}$-Wiener process.

Let us consider a univariate stochastic differential equation (defined on some probability space)

$$\mathrm{d}Y(t) = \mu(t)\mathrm{d}t + \sigma(t)\mathrm{d}X(t) \tag{8.68}$$

where $X(t)$ is a $\mathbb{P}$-Wiener process.

Heuristically, the functions μ and σ may be interpreted as

$$\mu(t)\mathrm{d}t = \mathbf{E}[\mathrm{d}Y(t)|\mathscr{F}(t)] \quad \text{(drift)} \tag{8.69}$$

$$\sigma^2(t)\mathrm{d}t = \mathbf{E}\left[(\mathrm{d}Y(t))^2|\mathscr{F}(t)\right] \quad \text{(diffusion)} \tag{8.70}$$

where $\mathrm{d}Y(t)$ is short for $Y(t+\mathrm{d}t) - Y(t)$. In particular for the $\mathbb{P}$-Wiener process we have

$$\mathbf{E}^{\mathbb{P}}[\mathrm{d}X(t)|\mathscr{F}(t)] = 0 \cdot \mathrm{d}t \tag{8.71}$$

$$\mathbf{E}^{\mathbb{P}}\left[(\mathrm{d}X(t))^2|\mathscr{F}(t)\right] = 1 \cdot \mathrm{d}t \tag{8.72}$$

under the $\mathbb{P}$-measure. We wish to determine

$$\mathbf{E}^{\mathbb{Q}}[\mathrm{d}X(t)|\mathscr{F}(t)] \tag{8.73}$$

$$\mathbf{E}^{\mathbb{Q}}\left[(\mathrm{d}X(t))^2|\mathscr{F}(t)\right] \tag{8.74}$$

under the $\mathbb{Q}$-measure. To this end, we may use (8.66) from Theorem 8.13

$$\mathbf{E}^{\mathbb{Q}}[\mathrm{d}X(t)|\mathscr{F}(t)] = \frac{\mathbf{E}^{\mathbb{P}}[L(t+\mathrm{d}t)\mathrm{d}X(t)|\mathscr{F}(t)]}{\mathbf{E}^{\mathbb{P}}[L(t+\mathrm{d}t)|\mathscr{F}(t)]} \tag{8.75}$$

where we must evaluate L at time $t + \mathrm{d}t$, because we have defined $\mathrm{d}X(t) = X(t+\mathrm{d}t) - X(t)$. From Theorem 8.12, we know that L is a $\mathbb{P}$-martingale such that the denominator in (8.75) is simply $L(t)$. For the numerator we get

$$\begin{aligned}\mathbf{E}^{\mathbb{P}}[L(t+\mathrm{d}t)\mathrm{d}X(t)|\mathscr{F}(t)] &= \mathbf{E}^{\mathbb{P}}[(L(t)+\mathrm{d}L(t))\mathrm{d}X(t)|\mathscr{F}(t)] \\ &= \mathbf{E}^{\mathbb{P}}[L(t)\mathrm{d}X(t)|\mathscr{F}(t)] + \mathbf{E}^{\mathbb{P}}[\mathrm{d}L(t)\mathrm{d}X(t)|\mathscr{F}(t)].\end{aligned}$$

As $L(t)$ is $\mathscr{F}(t)$-measurable, $L(t)$ can move out of the first expectation, i.e.,

$$\mathbf{E}^{\mathbb{P}}\left[L(t+\mathrm{d}t)\mathrm{d}X(t)|\mathscr{F}(t)\right] = L(t)\mathbf{E}^{\mathbb{P}}\left[\mathrm{d}X(t)|\mathscr{F}(t)\right] + \mathbf{E}^{\mathbb{P}}\left[\mathrm{d}L(t)\mathrm{d}X(t)|\mathscr{F}(t)\right]$$

As $\mathrm{d}X(t)$ is a Wiener-increment with zero mean, we finally get

$$\mathbf{E}^{\mathbb{P}}\left[L(t+\mathrm{d}t)\mathrm{d}X(t)|\mathscr{F}(t)\right] = \mathbf{E}^{\mathbb{P}}\left[\mathrm{d}L(t)\mathrm{d}X(t)|\mathscr{F}(t)\right].$$

Thus (8.75) may be written as

$$\mathbf{E}^{\mathbb{Q}}\left[\mathrm{d}X(t)|\mathscr{F}(t)\right] = \frac{\mathbf{E}^{\mathbb{P}}\left[\mathrm{d}L(t)\mathrm{d}X(t)|\mathscr{F}(t)\right]}{L(t)}. \tag{8.76}$$

This is as far as we can get in general, but for very particular choices of the *likelihood process* $L(t)$, Equation (8.76) may be simplified considerably. We recall that $L(t)$ is a $\mathbb{P}$-martingale and that we know the properties of the $\mathbb{P}$-Wiener process X. It is to be expected that (8.76) may be simplified if the likelihood process takes the form

$$\mathrm{d}L(t) = f(t)\mathrm{d}X(t), \quad L(0) = 1. \tag{8.77}$$

It is by no means clear if there exist likelihood processes of the form (8.77). The process $L(t)$ does indeed become a martingale if $f \in \mathscr{L}^2$, but we have no a priori guarantee that $L(t)$ remains non-negative for some choice of f. For now we shall just assume that an $f(t)$ process exists and that $L(t)$ remains non-negative. If we use (8.77) in (8.76), we get

$$\begin{aligned}
\mathbf{E}^{\mathbb{P}}\left[\mathrm{d}L(t)|\mathscr{F}(t)\right] &= \mathbf{E}^{\mathbb{P}}\left[f(t)(\mathrm{d}X(t))^2|\mathscr{F}(t)\right] \\
&= f(t)\mathbf{E}^{\mathbb{P}}\left[(\mathrm{d}X(t))^2|\mathscr{F}(t)\right] = f(t)\mathrm{d}t
\end{aligned}$$

where we have used that $f(t)$ is $\mathscr{F}(t)$-measurable and that

$$\mathbf{E}^{\mathbb{P}}\left[(\mathrm{d}X(t))^2|\mathscr{F}(t)\right] = \mathrm{d}t$$

because $X(t)$ is a $\mathbb{P}$-Wiener process. If we now choose $f(t)$ of the form

$$f(t) = g(t)L(t)$$

and insert this into (8.76), we get

$$\begin{aligned}
\mathbf{E}^{\mathbb{Q}}\left[\mathrm{d}X(t)|\mathscr{F}(t)\right] &= \frac{\mathbf{E}^{\mathbb{P}}\left[\mathrm{d}L(t)\mathrm{d}X(t)|\mathscr{F}(t)\right]}{L(t)} \\
&= \frac{\mathbf{E}^{\mathbb{P}}\left[g(t)L(t)(\mathrm{d}X(t))^2|\mathscr{F}(t)\right]}{L(t)} \\
&= \frac{L(t)\mathbf{E}^{\mathbb{P}}\left[g(t)(\mathrm{d}X(t))^2|\mathscr{F}(t)\right]}{L(t)} = g(t)\mathrm{d}t
\end{aligned}$$

as $g(t)$ is also $\mathscr{F}(t)$-measurable.

Using a similar argument, it may be shown that

$$\mathbf{E}^{\mathbb{Q}}\left[(\mathrm{d}X(t))^2|\mathscr{F}(t)\right] = \mathrm{d}t.$$

By comparing these last results with (8.69), we see that the process X has the infinitesimal characteristics $\mu(t) = g(t)$ and $\sigma(t) = 1$ under the $\mathbb{Q}$-measure. Thus under the $\mathbb{Q}$-measure, $X(t)$ may be described by

$$\mathrm{d}X(t) = g(t)\mathrm{d}t + \mathrm{d}W(t) \tag{8.78}$$

where $W(t)$ is a $\mathbb{Q}$-Wiener process.

It is seen that the $\mathbb{P}$-wiener process obtains a drift term $g(t)\mathrm{d}t$ and a diffusion term $\mathrm{d}W(t)$ which is a $\mathbb{Q}$-Wiener process. The function $g(t)$ is called *the Girsanov kernel*. It plays a very important role in mathematical finance as we shall see.

We shall now formalize these results. We start with a small lemma.

Lemma 8.1. *Let $g(t)$ be an $\mathscr{F}(t)$-adapted process that satisfies*

$$\mathbb{P}\left[\int_0^T g^2(t)\mathrm{d}t < \infty\right] = 1. \tag{8.79}$$

Then the equation

$$\mathrm{d}L(t) = g(t)L(t)\mathrm{d}X(t), \quad L(0) = 1 \tag{8.80}$$

has the unique and strictly positive solution

$$L(t) = \exp\left(\int_0^t g(s)\mathrm{d}X(s) - \frac{1}{2}\int_0^t g^2(s)\mathrm{d}s\right). \tag{8.81}$$

Proof. Omitted. We leave it as an exercise for the reader. □

Recall that it is important that $\mathbf{E}^{\mathbb{P}}[L(T)] = 1$ for $\mathbb{Q}$ to be a probability measure. It is also important to note that it is not guaranteed that $L(t)$ defined by (8.80)–(8.81) may be applied as a Radon–Nikodym derivative because we do not know if $L(t)$ satisfies the condition $\mathbf{E}^{\mathbb{P}}[L(T)] = 1$. If $L(t)$ was a martingale (i.e., if we knew a priori that $g(t)L(t) \in \mathscr{L}^2$) then the initial condition $L(0) = 1$ would ensure that $L(t)$ is a martingale. Unfortunately, we can only state that $L(t)$ is a *supermartingale*, i.e., $\mathbf{E}^{\mathbb{P}}[L(T)] \leq 1$ for functions satisfying Lemma 8.1. We now state the main result in this section.

Theorem 8.15 (The Girsanov theorem)**.** *Let $X(t)$ be a $(\mathbb{P}, \mathscr{F}(t))$-Wiener process and let $g(t)$ and $L(t)$ be as defined in Lemma 8.1. Assume that*

$$\mathbf{E}^{\mathbb{P}}[L(T)] = 1 \tag{8.82}$$

and define the probability measure $\mathbb{Q}$ *by* $\mathrm{d}\mathbb{Q} = L(T)\mathrm{d}\mathbb{P}$ *on* $\mathscr{F}(t)$*. Then the process* $W(t)$ *defined by*

$$W(t) = X(t) - \int_0^t g(s)\mathrm{d}s \tag{8.83}$$

becomes a $(\mathbb{Q}, \mathscr{F}(t))$*-Wiener process.*

Proof. Omitted. See e.g. Björk [2009]. □

Remark 8.17. *Note that* (8.83) *on differential form is*

$$\mathrm{d}W(t) = \mathrm{d}X(t) - g(t)\mathrm{d}t$$

or

$$\mathrm{d}X(t) = g(t)\mathrm{d}t + \mathrm{d}W(t),$$

which is similar to (8.78).

The assumption (8.82) is obviously very important and we now state a theorem (without a very difficult proof) that establishes necessary and sufficient conditions for $g(t)$ such that (8.82) is satisfied.

Theorem 8.16 (The Novikov condition)**.** *Assume that* $g(t)$ *satisfies*

$$\mathbf{E}^{\mathbb{P}}\left[\exp\left(\frac{1}{2}\int_0^T g^2(t)\mathrm{d}t\right)\right] < \infty \tag{8.84}$$

then $L(t)$ *becomes a* $\mathbb{P}$*-martingale and, in particular, we have*

$$\mathbf{E}^{\mathbb{P}}[L(T)] = 1. \tag{8.85}$$

8.4.4 *Maximum likelihood estimation for continuously observed diffusions*

In this section, we introduce the Girsanov measure transformation as the theoretical foundation of a modern application of the well-known Maximum Likelihood method.

The intuition behind the *classical* maximum likelihood approach is that

- there is one measure (or one probability density function parametrized by a parameter θ and we wish to estimate this θ),
- there is one Wiener process or driving noise process and
- there are many processes $X(t)$ and that we have only observed one of these.

The *modern* view is that

- there are several measures (one measure for each admissible parameter θ),
- there are equally many Wiener processes and
- there is just one $X(t)$ process, namely the one that we have observed.

In the modern view the problem is thus to determine the measure given only one set of observations $X(t)$. To be specific, we fix the probability space $(\Omega, \mathscr{F}, \mathbb{P})$, where the process $X(t)$ is a Wiener process under the $\mathbb{P}$-measure. For each $\theta \in \Theta \subseteq \mathbb{R}$, where Θ is the admissible parameter set (for e.g., the exponential distribution only positive parameters are allowed $\Theta = \mathbb{R}_+$), we define the measure transformation

$$\begin{aligned} \mathrm{d}L_\theta(t) &= \theta L_\theta(t)\mathrm{d}X(t), & (8.86)\\ L_\theta(0) &= 1. & (8.87) \end{aligned}$$

Next we define the measure P_θ by the Radon–Nikodym derivative

$$\mathrm{d}\mathbb{P}_\theta = L_\theta(t)\mathrm{d}\mathbb{P} \quad \text{on } \mathscr{F}(t)^X, \tag{8.88}$$

where $\mathscr{F}(t)^X$ is the natural filtration generated by the process $X(t)$ up to and including time t. This is essentially the likelihood ratio as given in Newman-Pearsons lemma. We see that the likelihood ratio should be evaluated using our observations $\mathscr{F}(t)^X$. To be specific, the quantity $L_\theta(t)$ should be maximized with respect to θ and we interpret the solution $\hat{\theta}$ as the most probable or the most likely parameter given the observations.[3]

Our process $X(t)$ is no longer a Wiener process under the $\mathbb{P}$-measure, but it is a Wiener process under the new $\mathbb{P}_\theta$-measure. We say that $X(t)$ is a $\mathbb{P}_\theta$-Wiener process.

The Girsanov theorem with the Girsanov kernel $\theta = g$ states that these two measures are connected by

$$\mathrm{d}X(t) = \theta \mathrm{d}t + \mathrm{d}W_\theta(t); \quad W_\theta(t) \equiv X(t) - \int_0^t \theta \mathrm{d}s \tag{8.89}$$

where $W_\theta(t)$ is a $\mathbb{P}_\theta$-Wiener process, and that

$$\mathrm{d}\mathbb{P}_\theta(t) = L_\theta(t)\mathrm{d}\mathbb{P}.$$

Thus there is one measure associated with each $\mathbb{P}_\theta$-Wiener process for $\theta \in \Theta$, but there is only *one* observed process $X(t)$, $0 \leq t \leq T$, where T is some finite time.

Example 8.18 (Maximum likelihood estimation 1). *Assume that we wish to estimate the parameter θ in the process*

$$\mathrm{d}X(t) = \theta \mathrm{d}t + \mathrm{d}W(t).$$

The $L(t)$-process is given by

$$\mathrm{d}L_\theta(t) = \theta L_\theta(t)\mathrm{d}X(t)$$

[3]In compact form our statistical model can be expressed as $\langle [\mathbb{P}_\theta]_{\theta \in \Theta \subseteq R}, \Omega, \mathscr{F}, X \rangle$.

which according to (8.81) *has the solution*

$$\begin{aligned} L_\theta(t) &= \exp\left(\int_0^t \theta \mathrm{d}X(s) - \frac{1}{2}\int_0^t \theta^2 \mathrm{d}s\right) \\ &= \exp\left(\theta X(t) - \frac{1}{2}\theta^2 t\right). \end{aligned}$$

As usual, we compute

$$l_\theta(t) = \ln L_\theta(t) = \theta X(t) - \frac{\theta^2}{2}t$$

and solve

$$\frac{\partial l_\theta(t)}{\partial \theta}\Big|_{\theta=\hat{\theta}} = 0 \Leftrightarrow X(t) - \hat{\theta}t = 0;$$

thus the maximum likelihood estimate of θ *is*

$$\hat{\theta}(t) = \frac{X(t)}{t}$$

where the notation $\hat{\theta}(t)$ *emphasizes that the estimate of* θ *is based on* $\mathscr{F}(t)$.

Consider a slightly more complicated example.

Example 8.19 (Maximum likelihood estimation 2)**.** *Consider the Langevin equation*

$$\mathrm{d}X(t) = \theta X(t)\mathrm{d}t + \mathrm{d}W(t) \tag{8.90}$$

where $W(t)$ *is a* $\mathbb{P}$*-Wiener process. Assuming that we have observations of* $X(t)$ *for* $0 \le t \le T$*, we wish to estimate the parameter* θ.

The associated likelihood process ($g(t) = \theta X(t)$) *is*

$$\mathrm{d}L_\theta(t) \equiv \theta X(t)L_\theta(t)\mathrm{d}X(t), \quad L_\theta(0) = 1. \tag{8.91}$$

Another way of posing the estimation problem is to state that we wish to determine the measure P_θ *that maximizes the likelihood ratio*

$$L_\theta(T) = \frac{\mathrm{d}\mathbb{P}_\theta}{\mathrm{d}\mathbb{P}}.$$

The likelihood process $L_\theta(t)$ *should fulfill the condition* (8.82)*, i.e.,*

$$\mathbf{E}^{\mathbb{P}}\left[L_\theta(T)\right] = 1$$

in order for $L_\theta(t)$ *to be a probability density function. In addition the process should fulfil the square integrability condition*

$$\mathbf{E}^{\mathbb{P}}\left[\exp\left(\frac{1}{2}\int_0^T \theta^2 X^2(t)\mathrm{d}t\right)\right] < \infty.$$

This condition is fulfilled under the assumption that $X(t) \in \mathcal{L}^2$.

The Girsanov theorem 8.15 states that

$$\mathrm{d}X(t) = \theta X(t)\mathrm{d}t + \mathrm{d}W_\theta(t)$$

where $W_\theta(t)$ *is a* $\mathbb{P}_\theta$*-Wiener process.*

The solution to (8.91) *is, cf.* (8.81),

$$\begin{aligned} L_\theta(t) &= \exp\left(\int_0^t \theta X(s)\mathrm{d}X(s) - \frac{1}{2}\int_0^t \theta^2 X^2(s)\mathrm{d}s\right) \\ &= \exp\left(\theta\int_0^t X(s)\mathrm{d}X(s) - \frac{1}{2}\theta^2\int_0^t X^2(s)\mathrm{d}s\right). \end{aligned}$$

Using the standard ML-approach, we get

$$\frac{\partial \ln L_\theta(t)}{\partial\theta} = \int_0^t X(s)\mathrm{d}X(s) - \theta\int_o^t X^2(s)\mathrm{d}s = 0$$

which has the solution

$$\hat{\theta}(t) = \frac{\int_0^t X(s)dX(s)}{\int_0^t X^2(s)\mathrm{d}s} = \frac{\frac{X^2(t)}{2} - \frac{t}{2}}{\int_0^t X^2(s)\mathrm{d}s} = \frac{X^2(t) - t}{2\int_0^t X^2(s)\mathrm{d}s}$$

where we have used the result from Example 8.9. The notation $\hat{\theta}(t)$ *is used to emphasize that the estimate of* θ *is based on information up to time* t.

These examples should just illustrate an application of the Radon–Nikodym derivative and the Girsanov theorem. From these examples, it should also be clear that this approach is not immediately applicable for empirical work when dealing with more complicated models, although the approach in Beskos et al. [2006] is building on this idea. More general methods will be introduced in Chapter 13.

8.5 Notes

Some of the material in this chapter is inspired by the very readable Björk [2009]. A more thorough treatment is given by, e.g. Arnold [1974], Kloeden and Platen [1995], Øksendal [2010]. In particular the monograph by Kloeden and Platen [1995] covers a large number of interesting topics – also of practical interest. The often referenced books by Karatzas and Shreve [1996], Ikeda and Watanabe [1989], Doob [1990] are also recommended, although they require some understanding of measure theory and other rather technical subjects. It should, however, be clear from the preceding section that absolute continuous measure transformations have some interesting applications, albeit the transformations are a purely abstract mathematical concept. Thus, measure theory is inherently important if one wishes to obtain a deeper understanding of the theory of modern mathematical finance.

8.6 Problems

Problem 8.1

Compute the stochastic differential $\mathrm{d}X$ in the following cases:

1. $X(t) = \exp(\alpha t)$.

2. $X(t) = \int_0^t g(s)\mathrm{d}W(s)$, where g is an adapted stochastic process.

3. $X(t) = \exp(\alpha W(t))$.

Problem 8.2

Use the Itō formula (8.10) to show that

$$\int_0^t W^2(s)\mathrm{d}W(s) = \frac{1}{3}W^3(t) - \int_0^t W(s)\mathrm{d}s. \tag{8.92}$$

Problem 8.3

Let $X(t)$ be a solution of (8.1).

1. Assuming that $\sigma(x)^2 > 0$, for all x, determine a transformation $\varphi(X(t))$ using Itō 's formula such that the diffusion term in the SDE for $\mathrm{d}Y(t) = \mathrm{d}\varphi(X(t))$ is constant.

Problem 8.4

Consider the two SDEs

$$\begin{aligned} \mathrm{d}X(t) &= \alpha X(t)\mathrm{d}t + \sigma X(t)\mathrm{d}W^{(1)}(t), & (8.93)\\ \mathrm{d}Y(t) &= \beta Y(t)\mathrm{d}t + \delta Y(t)\mathrm{d}W^{(2)}(t). & (8.94) \end{aligned}$$

Compute the SDE for $\mathrm{d}\varphi(X,Y)$ in the following case:

$$\varphi(X,Y) = X\sqrt{Y}.$$

Problem 8.5

Let $\mathbf{W}(t) = (W_1(t), W_2(t))$ be a two-dimensional Wiener process and define the distance from the origin

$$R(t) = |\mathbf{W}(t)| = (W_1^2(t) + W_2^2(t))^{1/2}.$$

Assuming that $\mathbf{W}(0) = \mathbf{0}$, show that

$$\mathrm{d}R(t) = \frac{W_1(t)\mathrm{d}W_1(t) + W_2(t)\mathrm{d}W_2(t)}{R(t)} + \frac{1}{2R(t)}\mathrm{d}t.$$

This process is called a *Bessel process of order 2*.

Problem 8.6
Consider the geometric Brownian motion

$$\mathrm{d}X_t = \mu X_t \mathrm{d}t + \sigma X_t \mathrm{d}W_t, \quad X_0 > 0. \tag{8.95}$$

1. Determine the solution to (8.95).
2. Determine the mean.
3. Determine the variance.

Problem 8.7
Consider the one-dimensional SDE

$$\mathrm{d}X_t = (\theta + \eta X_t)\mathrm{d}t + \rho \mathrm{d}W_t. \tag{8.96}$$

1. Solve this SDE.
2. Determine the mean.
3. Determine the variance.

Problem 8.8
Consider the nonautonomous SDE

$$\mathrm{d}X(t) = \left(\frac{2}{1+t}X(t) + \sigma(1+t)^2\right)\mathrm{d}t + \sigma(1+t)^2\mathrm{d}W(t); \quad X(t_0) = a. \tag{8.97}$$

1. Show that the fundamental solution to (8.97) is

$$\Phi_{t,t_0} = \left(\frac{1+t}{1+t_0}\right)^2.$$

2. Determine the general solution to (8.97).

Problem 8.9
Consider the SDE on $t \in [0,T]$ defined by

$$\mathrm{d}X(t) = \mu(t,X(t))\mathrm{d}t + \sigma(t,X(t))\mathrm{d}W(t) \tag{8.98}$$

with starting value $X(0) = u$. Show that the dynamics of the *Bridge Diffusion Process* when $X(T) = v$ is given by

$$\mathrm{d}X(t) = \big(\mu(t,X(t)) + [\sigma\sigma^T](t,X(t))\nabla_x \log p_{t,T}(X(T) = v|x)\big)\,\mathrm{d}t \tag{8.99}$$
$$+\sigma(t,X(t))\mathrm{d}W(t). \tag{8.100}$$

Bridge processes are very useful when deriving Monte Carlo-based estimators for parameters; cf. Section 13.5.1.

Chapter 9

Continuous-time security markets

In this chapter we consider financial markets in continuous time, contrary to the discrete time approach in Chapter 3. The multiperiod binomial model considered in Chapter 3 allowed the asset prices to take only one of two values in the next period, which certainly contradicts the actual behaviour of stock prices. In real financial markets, trading is not restricted only to take place at a limited number of time points; hence, it seems reasonable to model the financial market in continuous time where the prices are allowed to change at any time.[1] The mathematical description of a stochastic process in continuous time presented in Chapter 8 will be used to model the price of securities.

9.1 From discrete to continuous time

Consider a financial market with n securities, e.g., stocks. The objective of this section is to derive, in an ad hoc manner, a formula for the wealth process of a self-financing portfolio in the n securities in continuous time. However, in order to obtain a formulation that is consistent with the definition of Itō stochastic integrals in Chapter 7, the discrete time model of Chapter 3 is restated. Let

1. $h^i(t)$ = the number of stocks of type i held in the period $[t, t+k[$.
2. $V(t, \mathbf{h})$ = the value of the portfolio h at time t.
3. $S^i(t)$ = price for one stock of type i in period $[t, t+k[$.

The interpretation is as follows:

1. At time t, i.e., at the beginning of period t, we are equipped with the portfolio $\mathbf{h}(t-k) \in \mathbb{R}^n$ from period $t-k$.
2. At time t we observe the stock prices $S^i(t) \in \mathbb{R}^n$ for all i.
3. After observing the stock price, we decide the portfolio $\mathbf{h}(t)$ for the next period t.

[1] It may be argued that it is misleading to model prices in continuous time as stock exchanges are closed at night and during the weekends and that there is only a finite number of trades each day. However, as the financial markets are becoming more internationalized and computerized, there always exists an open stock exchange somewhere around the globe where the trading can be effected.

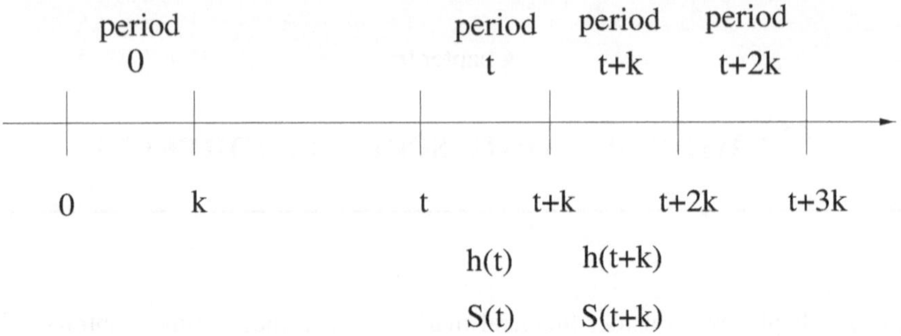

Figure 9.1: Illustration of how the periods are related to the time points.

At time t the value of the portfolio $h(t-k)$ is given by

$$V(t,\mathbf{h}) = \mathbf{h}^T(t-k)\mathbf{S}(t) = \sum_{i=1}^{n} h^i(t-k)S^i(t) \tag{9.1}$$

and the value of the new portfolio bought at time t is

$$V(t,\mathbf{h}) = \mathbf{h}^T(t)\mathbf{S}(t) = \sum_{i=1}^{n} h^i(t)S^i(t). \tag{9.2}$$

If we assume that the portfolio is self-financing we have the following equality according to the Definition 3.7.

$$\mathbf{h}^T(t-k)\mathbf{S}(t) = \mathbf{h}^T(t)\mathbf{S}(t). \tag{9.3}$$

By introducing the lag operator $\Delta X(t) = X(t) - X(t-k)$ formula (9.3) may be written as

$$\mathbf{S}^T(t)\Delta\mathbf{h}(t) = 0. \tag{9.4}$$

Since our aim is to obtain a model in continuous time, we consider $\mathbf{S}^T(t+k)\Delta\mathbf{h}(t+k) = 0$ and let $k \to 0$. We then get that

$$\mathbf{S}^T(t)\mathrm{d}\mathbf{h}(t) = 0. \tag{9.5}$$

In Chapter 7 where Itō stochastic calculus was introduced, it was shown that the value of a certain stochastic integral depends critically on where the integrand is evaluated in the interval $[t, t+k[$. In the formulation above the integrand is evaluated at the right endpoint of the interval, which means that the results will be inconsistent with the definition of Itō integrals (and differentials). In order to obtain Itō differentials the integral must be evaluated at the left endpoint. By adding and subtracting $\mathbf{S}(t)\Delta\mathbf{h}(t+k)$ in (9.4) we get

$$\begin{aligned} 0 &= \mathbf{S}^T(t)\Delta\mathbf{h}(t) + \mathbf{S}^T(t)\Delta\mathbf{h}(t+k) - \mathbf{S}^T(t)\Delta\mathbf{h}(t+k) && (9.6) \\ &= \mathbf{S}^T(t)\Delta\mathbf{h}(t+k) + \Delta\mathbf{S}^T(t+k)\Delta\mathbf{h}(t). && (9.7) \end{aligned}$$

For $k \to 0$ we obtain

$$0 = \mathbf{S}^T(t)\mathrm{d}\mathbf{h}(t) + \mathrm{d}\mathbf{h}^T(t)\mathrm{d}\mathbf{S}(t) \tag{9.8}$$

which might be interpreted as an infinitesimal budget restriction, since it says that one is only allowed to change the portfolio according to (9.8). Otherwise the portfolio (trading strategy) would not be self-financing. In order to obtain a stochastic differential equation for the wealth process $V(t,\mathbf{h})$ we apply the Itō formula (8.10)

$$\mathrm{d}V(t,\mathbf{h}) = \mathbf{h}^T(t)\mathrm{d}\mathbf{S}(t) + \mathbf{S}^T(t)\mathrm{d}\mathbf{h}(t) + \mathrm{d}\mathbf{h}^T(t)\mathrm{d}\mathbf{S}(t). \tag{9.9}$$

For self-financing trading strategies the last two terms cancel out and we get

$$\mathrm{d}V(t,\mathbf{h}) = \mathbf{h}^T(t)\mathrm{d}\mathbf{S}(t), \qquad V(t) = \int_0^t \mathbf{h}^T(u)\mathrm{d}\mathbf{S}(u). \tag{9.10}$$

The interpretation of the equation is that changes in the total value are generated by changes of the asset prices $\mathbf{S}(t)$. It is important to understand that the differentials and the integral should be interpreted in the Itō sense, because if we instead had used the concept of, e.g., Stratonovitch integrals, the SDE for the wealth process would not be the same as (9.10).

Define the relative portfolio strategy as

$$u^i(t) = \frac{h^i(t)S^i(t)}{V(t,\mathbf{h})}, \quad \text{for all } i = 1,\dots,n \tag{9.11}$$

where

$$\sum_{i=1}^{n} u^i(t) = 1 \tag{9.12}$$

and where $u^i(t)$ denotes the fraction of the total wealth that is placed in asset i. By substitution of $h^i(t)$ into the wealth process (9.2) we get

$$\mathrm{d}V(t,\mathbf{h}) = V(t,\mathbf{h}) \sum_{i=1}^{n} u^i(t) \frac{\mathrm{d}S^i(t)}{S^i(t)} \tag{9.13}$$

which gives an expression of the wealth process we shall need in the following.

9.2 Classical arbitrage theory

In this section we consider a financial market consisting of a riskless asset with a deterministic price process B_t, and a stock with the stochastic price process S_t. The model we shall consider is the famous Black–Scholes model and we will derive the Black–Scholes formula for pricing European call options.

The riskless asset is assumed to follow the following differential equation

$$\mathrm{d}B(t) = rB(t)\mathrm{d}t \tag{9.14}$$

where r is a constant interest rate. This asset is called the money market account. The solution is

$$B(t) = B(0)\exp\left(\int_0^t r\mathrm{d}s\right) = B(0)\exp(rt). \tag{9.15}$$

The corresponding solution, if the short term interest rate was varying deterministically, is simply given by

$$B(t) = B(0)\exp\left(\int_0^t r(s)\mathrm{d}s\right). \tag{9.16}$$

The price process of the stock is assumed to be stochastic in the following way

$$\mathrm{d}S(t) = \alpha S(t)\mathrm{d}t + \sigma S(t)\mathrm{d}W_t \tag{9.17}$$

where α and σ are constants. Note that the price process has a deterministic drift of magnitude $\alpha S(t)$. In Example 8.10 we found that the solution to (9.17) is given by

$$S(t) = S(0)\exp\left((\alpha - \frac{1}{2}\sigma^2)t + \sigma W(t)\right). \tag{9.18}$$

It seems like the growth rate is reduced to $\alpha - \frac{1}{2}\sigma^2$ plus some random noise. However by computation of the expected value we get

$$\mathbf{E}[S(t)] = S(0)\exp\left((\alpha - \frac{1}{2}\sigma^2)t\right)\mathbf{E}[\exp(\sigma W(t))] = S(0)\exp(\alpha t) \tag{9.19}$$

because $\exp\{\sigma W(t)\}$ is lognormally distributed with mean $\exp\{\sigma^2 t/2\}$. Thus the solution gives a trajectory with random fluctuations around the deterministic growth curve $S(0)\exp\{\alpha t\}$.

Remark 9.1 (Lognormal distribution)**.** *Assume that $X(t)$ is normally distributed. Then* $\mathbf{E}[\exp(X(t))] = \exp(\mathbf{E}[X(t)] + \mathbf{Var}[X(t)]/2)$.

The objective is now to find the "correct" price $P(t)$ for a European call option at time $t \leq T$. As we have seen in a previous chapter, the value at time $t = T$ is given by $P(T) = \max[S(T) - K, 0]$ where K is the exercise price. However it is not obvious what the price of a call option should be at time $t < T$.

Since the solution of the SDE for the stock price is a Markov process it is natural to assume that the price of a European call option is a function of time and the actual stock price $P(t) = F(t, S(t))$. Similar to the approach taken in the discrete time framework we now want to price the call option by constructing a replicating trading strategy.

Since the price of the option is a function of the stock price, we can apply the Itō formula to obtain a stochastic differential equation for the price of the call option.

$$\mathrm{d}P(t) = [F_t + \alpha S(t)F_s + \frac{1}{2}\sigma^2 S(t)^2 F_{ss}]\mathrm{d}t + \sigma S(t)F_s \mathrm{d}W(t) \tag{9.20}$$

where

$$F_t = \frac{\partial F(t,S(t))}{\partial t}, \quad F_s = \frac{\partial F(t,S(t))}{\partial S(t)}, \quad F_{ss} = \frac{\partial^2 F(t,S(t))}{\partial S(t)^2}. \tag{9.21}$$

By defining

$$\alpha_P = \frac{F_t + \alpha S(t)F_s + \frac{1}{2}\sigma^2 S(t)^2 F_{ss}}{P(t)} \text{ and } \sigma_P = \frac{\sigma S(t)F_s}{P(t)} \tag{9.22}$$

we get

$$\mathrm{d}P(t) = \alpha_P P(t)\mathrm{d}t + \sigma_P P(t)\mathrm{d}W(t). \tag{9.23}$$

Consider a trading strategy in the stock with price process (9.17) and the option with the above price process. According to (9.13), the total wealth process of such a trading strategy is given by

$$\mathrm{d}V(t) = V(t)\Big(\big[u^1\alpha + u^2\alpha_P\big]\mathrm{d}t + \big[u^1\sigma + u^2\sigma_P\big]\mathrm{d}W(t)\Big) \tag{9.24}$$

where u^1 and u^2 denote the fraction of the total wealth placed in the stock and the option. If u^1 and u^2 are chosen such that

$$u^1\sigma + u^2\sigma_P = 0 \tag{9.25}$$

it is readily seen that the stochastic part of the wealth process (9.24) cancels, and the wealth process then becomes deterministic with the drift term $(u^1\alpha + u^2\alpha_p)$. Since we know that $u^1 + u^2 = 1$ we can express the relative trading strategy as

$$u^1 = \frac{S(t)F_s(t,S(t))}{S(t)F_s(t,S(t)) - F(t,S(t))}, \tag{9.26}$$

$$u^2 = -\frac{F(t,S(t))}{S(t)F_s(t,S(t)) - F(t,S(t))}. \tag{9.27}$$

Since the stock price as well as the option price is a stochastic process, it is obvious that the relative trading strategy is a stochastic process as well. By choosing the trading strategy above we obtain a riskless return of $u^1\alpha + u^2\alpha_p$. Since the market consists of a riskless asset with interest rate r the riskless return of the trading strategy above must be the same as the riskless asset;

otherwise arbitrage is possible in the market. The argument goes like this: If $u^1\alpha + u^2\alpha_p > r$ you borrow money in the bank (the riskless asset) at the interest rate r, and reinvest the money in the trading strategy (u^1, u^2) with the riskless return $u^1\alpha + u^2\alpha_P$. Thus the trading strategy is an arbitrage. If $u^1\alpha + u^2\alpha_p < r$, a similar argument gives that the trading strategy is an arbitrage. This gives us the following restriction

$$u^1\alpha + u^2\alpha_P = r. \tag{9.28}$$

By inserting u^1 and u^2 from (9.26) we get

$$\frac{1}{2}\sigma^2 S(t)^2 F_{ss}(t,S(t)) + S(t)rF_s(t,S(t)) + F_t(t,S(t)) - rF(t,S(t)) = 0. \tag{9.29}$$

We have now derived a parabolic partial differential equation (PDE) which the price process $F(t,S(t))$ for the call option must fulfil in order to exclude arbitrage possibilities in the market consisting of the riskless asset, the stock and the call option. The boundary condition is

$$F(T,S(T)) = \max(S(T) - K, 0) \tag{9.30}$$

where T denotes the time of exercise. Notice that the PDE and the boundary condition do not involve the drift parameter α of the stock price. Contrary to most PDEs it is possible to give an analytic solution, which we shall return to later. In the derivation of the PDE above we did not use the fact that the price process $F(t,S(t))$ was the price process of a call option. We only use it in the boundary condition at time T. This gives rise to the following generalization:

Theorem 9.1 (Arbitrage-free pricing). *Consider the financial market given by* (9.14) *and* (9.17) *and a contingent claim with payoff* $\Phi(S(T))$ *at time* T. *If the market is free of arbitrage, the price* $P_t = F(t,S(t))$ *is given by the solution to the following PDE:*

$$\frac{1}{2}\sigma^2 S(t)^2 F_{ss}(t,S(t)) + S(t)rF_s(t,S(t)) + F_t(t,S(t)) - rF(t,S(t)) = 0 \tag{9.31}$$

with the boundary condition

$$F(T,S(T)) = \Phi(S(T)). \tag{9.32}$$

Proof. Follows from the above. □

The theorem enables us to price contingent claims $X = \Phi(S(T))$, where the value at the exercise price T is a function $\Phi(\cdot)$ of the underlying stock S. The reader will now notice that the boundary value problem stated in Theorem 9.1 is similar to the Cauchy problem considered in Section 8.3 where some Feynman–Kac representation theorems were stated. According to Theorem 8.10 the solution of the boundary value problem is given by

$$F(t,S(t)) = e^{-r(T-t)}\mathbf{E}^{\mathbb{Q}}\left[\Phi(S(T)|S(t) = s)\right] \tag{9.33}$$

where $S(u)$ has the following dynamics

$$dS(u) = rS(u)dt + \sigma S(u)d\tilde{W}(u) \tag{9.34}$$

$$S(t) = s \tag{9.35}$$

where s denotes the value of the underlying stock at time t and $\tilde{W}(u)$ is a standard Wiener process.

9.2.1 *Black–Scholes formula*

We will now apply this representation theorem to derive the famous Black–Scholes formula for pricing European call options, where $\Phi(S(T)) = \max(S(T) - K, 0)$. The solution to the SDE for the stock (9.34) is given by

$$S(T) = se^{\left((r-\frac{1}{2}\sigma^2)(T-t)+\sigma(\tilde{W}(T)-\tilde{W}(t))\right)}. \tag{9.36}$$

Since increments of the standard Wiener process are normally distributed with zero mean and variance $T-t$, the exponent $(r-\frac{1}{2}\sigma^2)(T-t)+\sigma(\tilde{W}(T)-\tilde{W}(t))$ has the distribution $N((r-\frac{1}{2}\sigma^2)(T-t), \sigma^2(T-t))$. Let $\xi \in N(0,1)$ be a standard Gaussian random variable, then the value of the stock at time $t = T$ is given by

$$S(T) = se^{\left((r-\frac{1}{2}\sigma^2)(T-t)+\sigma\sqrt{T-t}\xi\right)}. \tag{9.37}$$

We now want to find which values of the random variable ξ give the call option a positive value at the time of expiry.

$$S(T) > K \tag{9.38}$$

$$\Leftrightarrow \quad se^{\left((r-\frac{1}{2}\sigma^2)(T-t)+\sigma\sqrt{T-t}\xi\right)} > K \tag{9.39}$$

$$\Leftrightarrow \quad \left(r - \frac{1}{2}\sigma^2\right)(T-t) + \sigma\sqrt{T-t}\xi > \ln\left(\frac{K}{s}\right) \tag{9.40}$$

$$\Leftrightarrow \quad \xi > \frac{\ln(K/s) - (r - \frac{\sigma^2}{2})(T-t)}{\sigma\sqrt{T-t}} = -d. \tag{9.41}$$

In this case we say that the call option is *in the money*. Later on it will become clear why the entity $-d$ is introduced. The price of the call option at time t is given by

$$\begin{aligned} F(t,S(t)) &= e^{-r(T-t)}\mathbf{E}^{\mathbb{Q}}[\max(S(T)-K,0)] \\ &= e^{-r(T-t)}\int_{-\infty}^{\infty}\max(S(T)-K,0)\frac{1}{\sqrt{2\pi}}e^{-\frac{\xi^2}{2}}d\xi \\ &= e^{-r(T-t)}\int_{-d}^{\infty}(S(T)-K)\frac{1}{\sqrt{2\pi}}e^{-\frac{\xi^2}{2}}d\xi \\ &= e^{-r(T-t)}\left[\int_{-d}^{\infty}S(T)\frac{1}{\sqrt{2\pi}}e^{-\frac{\xi^2}{2}}d\xi - \int_{-d}^{\infty}K\frac{1}{\sqrt{2\pi}}e^{-\frac{\xi^2}{2}}d\xi\right]. \end{aligned} \tag{9.42}$$

The last term is given by

$$e^{-r(T-t)} \int_{-d}^{\infty} K \frac{1}{\sqrt{2\pi}} e^{-\frac{\xi^2}{2}} \mathrm{d}\xi = e^{-r(T-t)} K\Phi(d) \tag{9.43}$$

where $\Phi(\cdot)$ is the cumulative normal distribution function. By inserting the solution (9.37) into the first term in (9.42) we get

$$\begin{aligned}
& e^{-r(T-t)} \int_{-d}^{\infty} S(T) \frac{1}{\sqrt{2\pi}} e^{-\frac{\xi^2}{2}} \mathrm{d}\xi \\
= \; & e^{-r(T-t)} \int_{-d}^{\infty} s e^{\left((r-\frac{\sigma^2}{2})(T-t)+\sigma\sqrt{T-t}\xi\right)} \frac{1}{\sqrt{2\pi}} e^{-\frac{\xi^2}{2}} \mathrm{d}\xi \\
= \; & s \int_{-d}^{\infty} \frac{1}{\sqrt{2\pi}} e^{\left(-\frac{\sigma^2}{2}(T-t)+\sigma\sqrt{T-t}\xi-\frac{\xi^2}{2}\right)} \mathrm{d}\xi \\
= \; & s \int_{-d}^{\infty} \frac{1}{\sqrt{2\pi}} e^{-\frac{1}{2}\left(\xi-\sigma\sqrt{T-t}\right)^2} \mathrm{d}\xi \\
= \; & s\Phi(d+\sigma\sqrt{T-t}).
\end{aligned} \tag{9.44}$$

From the calculations above we get the following theorem:

Theorem 9.2 (Black–Scholes formula for European call options). *In the Black–Scholes model the price of a European call option with strike price K and time of expiry T is given by*

$$P_t = F(t, S(t)) = s\Phi(d+\sigma\sqrt{T-t}) - e^{-r(T-t)} K\Phi(d) \tag{9.45}$$

where

$$d = \frac{\ln(s/K) + (r-\frac{\sigma^2}{2})(T-t)}{\sigma\sqrt{T-t}}. \tag{9.46}$$

From this formula it is seen that the price of a European call option depends on

1. Time to expiry $T-t$.
2. The actual value of the underlying stock s.
3. The strike price K.
4. The deterministic interest rate r.
5. The volatility parameter σ. Notice once again that the pricing formula does not depend on the drift parameter α.

In Figure 9.2 the price of the call option is plotted for some specific choice of the parameters. It is readily seen that the price of a call option with strike price $K = 100$ is increasing in the actual price of the underlying asset, which could be expected because as the actual price of the stock increases so does the probability that the stock price at the time of expiry exceeds the strike

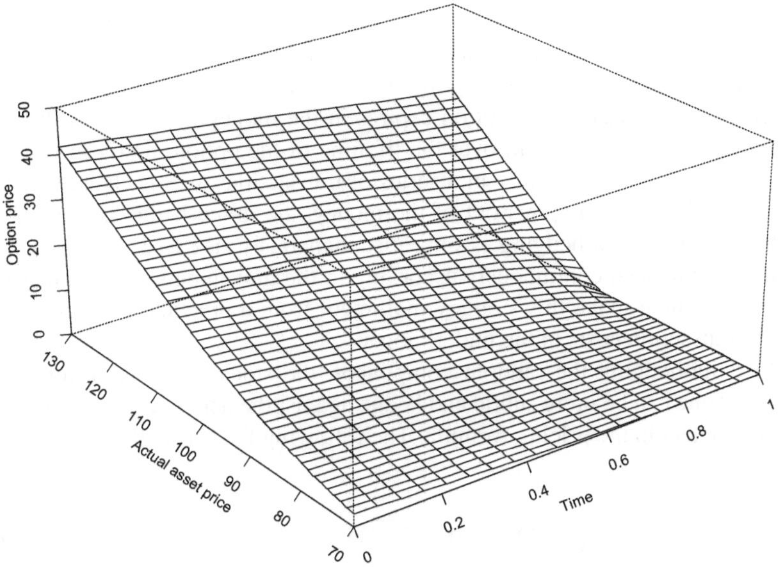

Figure 9.2: The price of a European call option with the Black–Scholes model with the following parameters: $\sigma = 0.1$, $T = 1$, $K = 100$ and $r = 0.1$.

price. Notice furthermore that the price as a function of the actual stock price converges towards the payoff function $\max(S(T) - K, 0)$ as the time to expiry $T - t$ decreases.

9.2.2 *Hedging strategies*

In the derivation of the partial differential equation for the Black–Scholes model, we constructed a relative portfolio (u^1, u^2) in the stock and the call option, which eliminated the stochastic part of the SDE for the price process of the call option. This trading strategy is called *Delta-hedging* in the financial literature. Hedging means reduction of the sensitivity of a portfolio to the movements of the underlying asset by taking opposite positions in different financial instruments. The delta is defined as $\Delta = \frac{\partial F(t,S(t))}{\partial S(t)}$. The idea behind Delta-hedging is that the writer of a call option can eliminate the risk associated with the call option by taking a position in the underlying asset (the stock). If we look at the absolute portfolios h^1, h^2 instead of the relative ones we immediately get from (9.26)

$$h^1 = S(t)F_s(t,S(t)) = S(t)\Phi(h + \sigma\sqrt{T-t}) \quad (9.47)$$

$$h^2 = -F(t,S(t)) = -(S\Phi(h + \sigma\sqrt{T-t}) - e^{-r(T-t)}K\Phi(h)) \quad (9.48)$$

where $F(t,S(t))$ denotes the price of the call option. By holding this portfolio the writer of the call option will automatically hold the correct amount (one or zero units) of the stock at expiry. This should be expected since delta-hedging is a risk-free strategy. If the option expires in-the-money $(S(T) > K)$, the required asset has been bought over the lifetime of the option, firstly in setting the initial hedge and secondly in a series of transactions as S(t) change. Conversely, if the option expires out-of-the-money, the initial hedge is gradually sold. Since the delta-hedging is only instantaneously risk-free, the portfolio must be rebalanced continuously according to the movements of the underlying stock, which make this strategy inefficient from a practical point of view due to transaction costs in the underlying stock.

In delta-hedging the random component, the stock price, is eliminated. However one can be more subtle and hedge against the dependency of some of the parameters in the pricing formula. The following list is usually considered.

$$\Delta = \frac{\partial F}{\partial S} = \Phi(d+\sigma\sqrt{T-t}), \tag{9.49}$$

$$\Gamma = \frac{\partial^2 F}{\partial S^2} = \frac{1}{\sigma S\sqrt{T-t}}\Phi'(d+\sigma\sqrt{T-t}), \tag{9.50}$$

$$\Theta = \frac{\partial F}{\partial t} = \frac{S\Phi'(d+\sigma\sqrt{T-t})\sigma}{2\sqrt{T-t}} - rKe^{-r(T-t)}\Phi(d), \tag{9.51}$$

$$\rho = \frac{\partial F}{\partial r} = K(T-t)e^{-r(T-t)}\Phi(d), \tag{9.52}$$

$$\nu = \frac{\partial F}{\partial \sigma} = S\Phi'(d+\sigma\sqrt{T-t})\sqrt{T-t}. \tag{9.53}$$

These are for obvious reasons called the *Greeks*. Hedging against any of these dependencies requires the use of other options as well as the call option and the stock. It is beyond the scope of this book to go any further into the subject of hedging.

9.2.2.1 *Quadratic hedging*

Hedging based on the Greeks (e.g., Δ or $\Delta - \Gamma$ strategies) may be accurate enough as long as then rebalancing is frequent and the asset paths are continuous. An alternative that is more appropriate for advanced models in general and jump processes in particular is to minimize the quadratic hedge error

$$\{h_1,h_2\} = \arg\min \mathbf{E}\left[(V(t+\Delta t) - h_1B(t+\Delta t) + h_2S(t+\Delta t))^2 \,|\mathscr{F}(t)\right] \tag{9.54}$$

where we are deliberately vague regarding the probability measure; see Cont and Tankov [2004] for a discussion on using the $\mathbb{P}$ measure or the $\mathbb{Q}$ measure.

It turns out that quadratic hedging and adaptive calibration can be done simultaneously, as shown by Lindström and Guo [2013], Wiktorsson and Lindström [2014]. This makes it computationally comparable to using Greeks, while in general providing better hedge strategies (especially when there are jumps in the asset dynamics).

9.3 Modern approach using martingale measures

In the following section we shall use some of the advanced techniques presented in Chapter 7 in order to derive a general pricing formula for contingent claims in the Black–Scholes model. In the derivation of the partial differential equation of Theorem 9.1, it was assumed that the price $P(t) = F(t,S(t))$ only depended on the time and the actual value of the underlying asset. By using a modern approach this assumption is not needed, which from a mathematical point of view is more satisfactory. However the primary object of deriving the pricing formula for contingent claims once again is that it demonstrates how the Girsanov measure transformation may be applied to a concrete financial model. Hopefully the reader will get a better understanding of the basic idea of measure transformations, which will be used in a subsequent chapter concerning the term structure of interest and bond pricing.

In the following the results are stated for the simple Black–Scholes model, although they are valid for a larger class of financial models. To begin with, the Black–Scholes model is restated. On the filtered probability space $(\Omega, \mathscr{F}, \mathbb{P}, \{\mathscr{F}(t)\}_{t\geq 0})$, we have the following two assets

$$
\begin{aligned}
\mathrm{d}B(t) &= rB(t)\mathrm{d}t, && (9.55)\\
\mathrm{d}S(t) &= \alpha S(t)\mathrm{d}t + \sigma S(t)\mathrm{d}\tilde{W}(t), && (9.56)
\end{aligned}
$$

where $\tilde{W}(t)$ is a Wiener process with respect to the probability measure $\mathbb{P}$, and B denotes a risk-free asset and S denotes a risky asset. As in discrete time we shall need the concept of martingale measures.

Definition 9.1 (Martingale measure). *We say that a probability measure $\mathbb{Q}$ is a martingale measure if*

1. *$\mathbb{Q} \sim \mathbb{P}$ i.e., the two measures are equivalent.*
2. *The discounted price process $Z(t) = S(t)/B(t)$ is a martingale under the measure $\mathbb{Q}$.*

The set of martingale measures is denoted by $\mathscr{P}$. The denominator $B(t)$ is called the numeraire.

In the Black–Scholes model it is easy to find the class of equivalent martingale measures. The stochastic differential equation of the discounted price process $Z(t) = \varphi(S(t), B(t)) = S(t)/B(t)$ is found by applying the multivariate

Itō formula stated in Theorem 8.5. The following derivatives are needed

$$\frac{\partial \varphi}{\partial t} = 0, \qquad \frac{\partial \varphi}{\partial S(t)} = \frac{1}{B(t)}, \qquad \frac{\partial^2 \varphi}{\partial S(t)^2} = 0$$

$$\frac{\partial \varphi}{\partial B(t)} = -\frac{S(t)}{B(t)^2}, \qquad \frac{\partial^2 \varphi}{\partial B(t)^2} = -2\frac{S(t)}{B(t)^3},$$

$$\frac{\partial^2 \varphi}{\partial S(t)\partial B(t)} = -\frac{1}{B(t)^2}$$

which gives

$$\begin{aligned} \mathrm{d}Z(t) &= \left[-\frac{S(t)}{B(t)^2} rB(t) + \frac{1}{B(t)}\alpha S(t)\right] \mathrm{d}t + \frac{1}{B(t)}\sigma S(t)\mathrm{d}\tilde{W}(t) \\ &= (\alpha - r)Z(t)\mathrm{d}t + \sigma Z(t)\mathrm{d}\tilde{W}(t). \end{aligned} \tag{9.57}$$

Thus the discounted price process is again a geometric Brownian motion, where the drift is $(\alpha - r)$. In order to find the class of equivalent martingale measures we perform an absolute continuous measure transformation by applying the Girsanov theorem (8.15). Define a new measure $\mathbb{Q}$ where

$$\mathrm{d}L(t) = g(t)L(t)\mathrm{d}W(t), \tag{9.58}$$

$$L(0) = 1. \tag{9.59}$$

According to the Girsanov theorem we have

$$\mathrm{d}\tilde{W}(t) = g(t)\mathrm{d}t + \mathrm{d}W(t) \tag{9.60}$$

where $W(t)$ is a Wiener process with respect to the probability measure $\mathbb{Q}$. By substituting $\mathrm{d}\tilde{W}(t)$ into (9.57) we get the following dynamics of the Z-process under the $\mathbb{Q}$-measure

$$\mathrm{d}Z(t) = (\alpha - r + \sigma g(t))Z(t)\mathrm{d}t + \sigma Z(t)\mathrm{d}W(t). \tag{9.61}$$

By choosing the Girsanov kernel $g(t)$ to be

$$g(t) = \frac{r - \alpha}{\sigma} \tag{9.62}$$

the drift term in the Z-process is removed; hence the process is a martingale under the measure $\mathbb{Q}$. Since $\mathbb{P}$ and $\mathbb{Q}$ are equivalent measures the $\mathbb{Q}$ measure is a martingale measure according to Definition 9.1.

Definition 9.2 (Wealth process). *For a given portfolio strategy* $\mathbf{h}$ *we define the wealth processes* $V(t,\mathbf{h})$ *and* $V^Z(t,\mathbf{h})$ *as*

$$V(t,\mathbf{h}) = h^1(t)B(t) + h^2(t)S(t), \tag{9.63}$$

$$V^Z(t,\mathbf{h}) = \frac{V(t,\mathbf{h})}{B(t)} = h^1(t) + h^2(t)Z(t). \tag{9.64}$$

Definition 9.3 (Self-financing portfolio strategy). *A portfolio strategy* **h** *is self-financing if*

$$V(t,\mathbf{h}) = V(0,\mathbf{h}) + \int_0^t h^1(u)\mathrm{d}B(u) + \int_0^t h^2(u)\mathrm{d}S(u). \tag{9.65}$$

The self-financing condition is intended to formalize the intuitive idea of a trading strategy with no exogenous infusion or withdrawals of money, i.e., a strategy where the purchase of a new asset is financed solely by the sale of assets already in the portfolio.

Lemma 9.1 (Self-financing portfolio strategy).

1. *A portfolio strategy* **h** *is self-financing if and only if*

$$\mathrm{d}V^Z(t,\mathbf{h}) = h^2(t)\mathrm{d}Z(t). \tag{9.66}$$

2. *If* **h** *is a self-financing portfolio, the wealth process* $V^Z(t,\mathbf{h})$ *is a* $\mathbb{Q}$-*martingale.*

Proof. Let **h** be a self-financing portfolio, then we want to prove (9.66). Since $V^Z(t,\mathbf{h}) = e^{-rt}V(t,\mathbf{h})$, we can apply the Itō formula and get

$$\begin{aligned}
\mathrm{d}V^Z(t,\mathbf{h}) &= \mathrm{d}[e^{-rt}V(t,\mathbf{h})] = -re^{-rt}V(t,\mathbf{h})\mathrm{d}t + e^{-rt}\mathrm{d}V(t,\mathbf{h}) \\
&= -re^{-rt}(h^1(t)B(t) + h^2(t)S(t))\mathrm{d}t \\
&+ e^{-rt}(h^1(t)\mathrm{d}B(t) + h^2(t)\mathrm{d}S(t)) \\
&= (\alpha - r)h^2(t)e^{-rt}S(t)\mathrm{d}t + h^2(t)\sigma e^{-rt}S(t)\mathrm{d}W(t) = h^2(t)\mathrm{d}Z(t).
\end{aligned}$$

The opposite implication is proved in a similar way.

By integration of (9.66) we get

$$\begin{aligned}
V^Z(t,\mathbf{h}) &= V^Z(0,\mathbf{h}) + \int_0^t h^2(u)\mathrm{d}Z(u) \\
&= V^Z(0,\mathbf{h}) + \int_0^t h^2(u)\sigma Z(u)\mathrm{d}\tilde{W}(u).
\end{aligned} \tag{9.67}$$

By taking conditional expectations under the measure $\mathbb{Q}$ on each side the stochastic integral cancels and we get

$$\mathbf{E}^{\mathbb{Q}}[V^Z(t,\mathbf{h})|\mathscr{F}(t)] = V^Z(0,\mathbf{h}) \tag{9.68}$$

which shows that $V^Z(t,\mathbf{h})$ is a $\mathbb{Q}$-martingale. □

Definition 9.4 (Contingent claims). *A contingent claim with expiry date T is a $\mathscr{F}(T)$-measurable random variable.*[2]

[2]This means that the value of the contingent claim, e.g., an option, is known at time T.

The set of contingent claims is called $\mathscr{X}$. Now define a subset $\mathscr{X}^+$ consisting of contingent claims $X \in \mathscr{X}$ such that

$$\mathbb{P}(X \geq 0) = 1, \quad \text{and} \quad \mathbb{P}(X > 0) > 0. \tag{9.69}$$

These two conditions ensure that X is non-negative and not all the probability mass is assigned to the event $X = 0$.

Definition 9.5 (Arbitrage strategies). *A trading strategy $h \in \mathscr{H}$ is an arbitrage strategy if*

$$V_0(h) = 0, \quad \textit{and} \quad V_T(h) \in \mathscr{X}^+. \tag{9.70}$$

The definition says that a trading strategy is an arbitrage strategy if the value of the portfolio initially is zero, and the value at time T is non-negative and with a positive probability greater than zero. We recognize that the definition is similar to the one stated in discrete time financial models (3.1). A model without any arbitrage strategies is free of arbitrage.

Theorem 9.3. *Assume that there exists a martingale measure $\mathbb{Q}$. Then the model is free of arbitrage in the sense that there exist no arbitrage portfolios.*

Proof. Assume that $\mathbf{h}$ is an arbitrage portfolio with $\mathbb{P}(V(T,\mathbf{h}) \geq 0) = 1$ and $\mathbb{P}(V(T,\mathbf{h}) > 0) > 0$. Then since $\mathbb{Q} \sim \mathbb{P}$ we also have $\mathbb{Q}(V^Z(T,\mathbf{h}) \geq 0) = 1$ and $\mathbb{Q}(V^Z(T,\mathbf{h}) > 0) > 0$ and consequently

$$V(0,\mathbf{h}) = V^Z(0,\mathbf{h}) = \mathbf{E}^{\mathbb{Q}}[V^Z(T,\mathbf{h})] > 0 \tag{9.71}$$

which contradicts the arbitrage condition $V(0) = 0$. □

Since we have found an equivalent martingale measure in the Black–Scholes model, it immediately follows that it is free of arbitrage.

We have seen that the existence of a martingale measure implies the absence of arbitrage, and a natural question is whether there is a converse to this statement, i.e., if the absence of arbitrage implies the existence of a martingale measure. For models in discrete time with a finite sample space, we have seen that this is indeed the case. In continuous time there is not complete equivalence between the existence of a martingale measure and absence of arbitrage. Although it is somewhat unsatisfactory, the general consensus seems to be that the existence of a martingale measure is (informally) considered to be more or less equivalent to the absence of arbitrage.

Definition 9.6 (Complete markets).

1. *A contingent claim X with expiry date T is said to be attainable if there exists a self-financing portfolio* $\mathbf{h}$, *such that the corresponding wealth process has the property that*

$$V(T,\mathbf{h}) = X, \qquad \mathbb{P}\text{-}a.s. \tag{9.72}$$

2. *The market is said to be complete if every claim is attainable.*

Theorem 9.4. *If the martingale measure Q is unique, then the market is complete in the sense that every claim X satisfying*

$$\frac{X}{S_0(T)} \in L^1(\Omega, \mathscr{F}(T), \mathbb{Q}) \tag{9.73}$$

is attainable, with $L^1(\Omega, \mathscr{F}_T, \mathbb{Q})$ being the class of stochastic variables with finite expected values under the measure $\mathbb{Q}$. The class $L^1(\Omega, \mathscr{F}(T), \mathbb{Q})$ is defined explicitly in Definition 8.3.

Proof. Omitted. See e.g. Duffie [2010]. □

Remark 9.2. *In the Black–Scholes model we found a unique martingale measure by Girsanov transformation of the objective probability measure $\mathbb{P}$; thus the model is complete.*

9.4 Pricing

We now turn to the problem of determining a "reasonable" price process $\Pi(t,X)$ for a contingent claim with a fixed date of expiry T. Assume that the market is free of arbitrage and the market is complete, i.e., a martingale measure exists and it is unique for the market consisting of the money market account B and the stock S. Then it seems reasonable to demand that the price process $\Pi(\cdot,X)$ should be chosen such that the extended market $[B,S,\Pi(\cdot,X)]$ is free of arbitrage possibilities. This can be obtained by requiring that the discounted price process $\Pi(t,X)/B(t)$ is a martingale under $\mathbb{Q}$, where $\mathbb{Q}$ is the martingale measure for the market $[B,S]$. Thus we have

$$\frac{\Pi(t,X(t))}{B(t)} = \mathbf{E}^{\mathbb{Q}}\left[\frac{\Pi(T,X(T))}{B(T)}\middle|\mathscr{F}(t)\right] = \mathbf{E}^{\mathbb{Q}}\left[\frac{X(T)}{B(T)}\middle|\mathscr{F}(t)\right] \tag{9.74}$$

and since $B(T)$ is deterministic we get the following pricing formula

$$\Pi(t,X(t)) = B(t)\mathbf{E}^{\mathbb{Q}}\left[\frac{X(T)}{B(T)}\middle|\mathscr{F}(t)\right] = e^{-r(T-t)}\mathbf{E}^{\mathbb{Q}}\left[X(T)\middle|\mathscr{F}(t)\right]. \tag{9.75}$$

Notice that this is the same pricing formula as (9.33) where the classical approach to arbitrage-free pricing was taken.

Example 9.1 (Binary option). *A so-called binary option (or digital option) is a claim which pays a fixed amount if the stock at certain dates lies within some prespecified interval. Otherwise nothing will be paid out. Consider a binary option which pays K \$ to the holder at date T if the stock price at time T lies in the interval $[\alpha,\beta]$, i.e., the contingent claim $X = 1_{[\alpha,\beta]}(S(T))K$ where $1_{[\cdot,\cdot]}$ is the indicator function. The arbitrage-free price of the option is determined by the pricing formula above. We get*

$$\Pi(t,X) = \exp^{-r(T-t)}\mathbf{E}^{\mathbb{Q}}[1_{[\alpha,\beta]}(S(T))K|\mathscr{F}(t)]. \tag{9.76}$$

Since the solution $S(T)$ under the equivalent martingale measure $\mathbb{Q}$ is given by

$$S(T) = S(t)\exp\left((r-\frac{1}{2}\sigma^2)(T-t)+\sigma(W(T)-W(t))\right) \tag{9.77}$$

we notice that the exponent $(r-\frac{1}{2})(T-t)+\sigma(W(T)-W(t))$ is normally distributed with mean $m_z = (r-\frac{1}{2}\sigma^2)(T-t)$ and variance $\sigma_z^2 = \sigma^2(T-t)$

$$S(T) = S(t)\exp(m_z+\sigma_z z). \tag{9.78}$$

It is easily found that the option pays K \$ if $m_z+\sigma_z z \in [\log(\alpha/S(t)), \log(\beta/S(t))]$. Thus we have

$$\begin{aligned}\Pi(t,X) &= e^{-r(T-t)}\int_0^{\infty} 1_{[\alpha,\beta]}(S(T))K\mathrm{d}\mathbb{Q}(S(T))\\ &= e^{-r(T-t)}K\int_{\log\left(\frac{\alpha}{S(t)}\right)}^{\log\left(\frac{\beta}{S(t)}\right)} \mathrm{d}\mathbb{Q}(S(T))\\ &= e^{-r(T-t)}K\int_{\log\left(\frac{\alpha}{S(t)}\right)}^{\log\left(\frac{\beta}{S(t)}\right)} \frac{1}{\sqrt{2\pi}\sigma_z}e^{-\frac{(z-m_z)^2}{2\sigma_z}}\mathrm{d}z\\ &= e^{-r(T-t)}K\left[\Phi\left(\frac{\log\left(\frac{\beta}{S(t)}\right)-m_z}{\sigma_z}\right)-\Phi\left(\frac{\log\left(\frac{\alpha}{S(t)}\right)-m_z}{\sigma_z}\right)\right],\end{aligned} \tag{9.79}$$

where $\Phi(\cdot)$ is the cumulative normal distribution function.

The standard Black & Scholes framework reduces the statistical problem to a single parameter, the volatility parameter σ. This can be estimated from either historical price data (the $\mathbb{P}$ measure) or from options (which in general carries information about the $\mathbb{Q}$ measure) as the parameter coincides under both measures. Calibration in a more general context is discussed in Section 14.11.1.

It turns out, however, that the model fit is not perfect (it is still very good compared to most models in social science!), something that should be reasonable as few of the stylized facts reviewed in Chapter 1 were incorporated into the model. Model extensions (or rather classes of models) are briefly introduced in Section 9.5, but it is worth remembering that a good model is both able to capture the relevant empirical properties and is computationally convenient to work with (for pricing, hedging and calibration purposes). Efficient computational techniques are discussed in Section 9.6.

9.5 Model extensions

The risk-neutral framework is very general and applies for all extensions below. Modern pricing theory has developed in several overlapping directions; cf. Section 7.5.

- Stochastic volatility (Hull and White [1987], Heston [1993]). Adding an extra process means that the market becomes incomplete, but the completeness of the market can be recovered by introducing a liquid vanilla option. Some models, like the SABR model, even admit closed form expressions for the price (Hagana et al. [2002], Larsson [2012]).
- Jump models (Merton [1976], Kou [2002]) introduce random jumps to capture the small, but non-zero risk of large price movements that are hard to hedge. Cont and Tankov [2004] is a good starting point for further studies. Mathematics needed for jump processes was developed in Section 7.5.
- Local volatility models define the volatility as a complex function of time and the underlying asset (Derman and Kani [1994]) so that the market is complete, and still provides perfect fit to the market. The approach is similar to fitting splines the observations, as the fit to data (in sample) is perfect but there is a real risk for overfitting the data (Orosi [2010]). The overfitting may lead to models that provides good fit in sample, but also introduces arbitrage. Lindholm [2014] introduces a regularizaton through optimal control that forces the recovered local volatilty model to be free from arbitrage.
- Uncertain volatility models (Cont [2006], Lindström [2010], Lindström and Strålfors [2012], Lindstrom and Wu [2014]) tries to account to the imperfect-facing investors. Small, but consistent, improvements are found correcting for uncertainty.

Some models, like the class of affine jump diffusions (Duffie et al. [2003]), include both stochastic volatility and jumps, but still allow for computationally efficient methods for pricing (Fourier methods, see Carr and Madan [1999], Lindström et al. [2008], Hirsa [2013]).

9.6 Computational methods

There is a need to be able to compute prices, at least numerically, if we are going to use option prices in a statistical model. There are roughly speaking four main techniques used today

- **Trees**, typically binomial or trinomial tree (Cox et al. [1979]). Trees were initially introduced as an easy alternative to the continuous-time derivation of the Black & Scholes model, but have also found useful applications when considering path dependent options, or local volatility models.
- **Monte Carlo** methods are very general, and therefore well suited for computing expectations as convergence is ensured by the law of large numbers. The method is very easy to implement for European type contracts, but can also be used for path dependent contracts (least squares Monte Carlo) (see Longstaff and Schwartz [2001]). Monte Carlo methods are often the only feasible method for high-dimensional problems.

- **PDEs or PIDEs** (for jump processes) are the equivalent formulation due to the Feynman–Kac representation. Numerical methods for PDEs/PIDEs, such as finite difference or finite element methods, are generally more efficient than Monte Carlo or binomial/trinomial trees for low-dimensional problems (one or two dimensions), but they also work well for some multi-asset options (Lötstedt et al. [2007]). The methodology can also handle path-dependent problems well; see Hirsa [2013] for many schemes.
- **Fourier methods** that use the characteristic function of the log-price process to obtain nearly analytical expressions. These approximations are magnitudes more accurate and faster to compute than any of the others listed here.

9.6.1 Fourier methods

The title of the section may be misleading as there are several similar methods, using different transform methods, including several standard (Lindström et al. [2008]), and Fast Fourier methods (Carr and Madan [1999]), fractional Fourier methods (Hirsa [2013]) and cosine methods (Fang and Oosterlee [2008]); see Hirsa [2013] for a general overview.

However, we will review some of the basic steps of the Fourier method below. Assume that the characteristic function (cf. Section 7.5) of the log price $s(T) = \log S(T)$ is known

$$\psi(u) = \mathbf{E}\left[e^{ius(T)}\right] = \int e^{ius} \mathrm{d}\mathbb{Q}(s). \tag{9.80}$$

The risk-neutral measure is absolutely continuous with respect to the Lebesgue measure in virtually every model we consider in this book, and we will therefore assume that we can use the density instead, $\mathrm{d}\mathbb{Q}(s) = q(s)\mathrm{d}s$.

It is known from Section 9.4 that the price of a European call option is given by

$$C(k) = \int_k^\infty e^{-rT}(e^s - e^k)q(s)\mathrm{d}s \tag{9.81}$$

where $k = \log(K)$ is the log strike price. The option price is not a square integrable (which is required by the Parseval's theorem), but a modified version of the price is

$$c(k) = e^{\alpha k} C(k) \tag{9.82}$$

where α is some positive number. It is then possible to compute the Fourier transform of modified price $c(k)$ as

$$\phi(v) = \int e^{ivk} c(k)\mathrm{d}k. \tag{9.83}$$

This expression can be extend further accordingly

$$\phi(v) = \int e^{ivk} c(k) \mathrm{d}k \tag{9.84}$$

$$= \int e^{ivk} e^{\alpha k} \int_k^\infty e^{-rT} (e^s - e^k) q(s) \mathrm{d}s \mathrm{d}k \tag{9.85}$$

$$= \frac{e^{-rT} \psi(v - (\alpha+1)i)}{\alpha^2 + \alpha - v^2 + i(2\alpha+1)v}. \tag{9.86}$$

It is also possible to compute the option price by applying the inverse Fourier transform to (9.83)

$$C(k) = \frac{e^{-\alpha k}}{2\pi} \int e^{-ivk} \phi(v) \mathrm{d}v = \frac{e^{-\alpha k}}{\pi} \int_0^\infty e^{-ivk} \phi(v) \mathrm{d}v. \tag{9.87}$$

where the second equality holds as $C(k)$ is real. Hence, call prices are given by inserting Equation (9.86) into (9.87) arriving at

$$C(k) = \frac{e^{-\alpha k}}{\pi} \cdot \int_0^\infty e^{-ivk} \frac{e^{-rT} \psi(v - (\alpha+1)i)}{\alpha^2 + \alpha - v^2 + i(2\alpha+1)v} \mathrm{d}v. \tag{9.88}$$

The integral can be computed using either Fast Fourier Transform (FFT) or related fast transforms (Hirsa [2013]) or Gauss-Laguerre quadrature methods (Lindström et al. [2008]) as both types of methods provide very accurate approximations with very limited computational efforts.

The modification, here parametrized by α, is needed due to Parseval, but it can also be seen that choosing $\alpha = 0$ would introduce a singularity in (9.88). It can also be shown that the α parameter can dampen numerical oscillations in the integrand, leading to better numerical approximations (Lee [2004], Lindström et al. [2008]) for further details.

9.7 Problems

Problem 9.1

Consider a standard Black–Scholes model with the usual dynamics

$$\mathrm{d}S(t) = \alpha S(t)\mathrm{d}t + \sigma S(t)\mathrm{d}W(t), \tag{9.89}$$

$$\mathrm{d}B(t) = rB(t)\mathrm{d}t \tag{9.90}$$

and T_2 with $0 < T_1 < T_2$, and consider the contingent claim $X = S(T_2)/S(T_1)$. The claim is to be paid out at T_2.

1. Compute the arbitrage-free price.
2. Try to construct the replicating portfolio.

Problem 9.2
Consider a standard Black–Scholes model with the usual dynamics

$$\begin{aligned} dS(t) &= \alpha S(t)dt + \sigma S(t)dW(t), && (9.91)\\ dB(t) &= rB(t)dt. && (9.92) \end{aligned}$$

1. Determine the arbitrage-free price of a put option $X = \max[K - S(T), 0]$, where K is the strike price and T is the time of expiry.
2. Express the value of a put option in terms of a call option, the underlying stock and the money market account.
Remark. This formula is called the put-call parity.

Problem 9.3
Consider the standard Black–Scholes model. Fix the time of maturity T and consider a so-called *butterfly* defined by

$$X = \begin{cases} K - S(T) & \text{if } 0 < S(T) \leq K, \\ S(T) - K & \text{if } K < S(T). \end{cases} \qquad (9.93)$$

This contract can be replicated using a portfolio, consisting solely of bonds, stock and European call options, which are constant over time.
1. Determine this portfolio.
2. Determine the arbitrage-free price of the contract.

Chapter 10

Stochastic interest rate models

In this chapter, we shall provide a catalogue of a number of well-known models of interest rates as it is important to be familiar with these often referenced models and, in particular, their properties. The main focus is on univariate stochastic differential equations or *one-factor models* as they are called in the financial literature because only one state variable (or factor), $r(t)$, is used to describe variations in the interest rate.

Conceptually $r(t)$ is the continuously compounded interest rate of risk-free financial securities, which was introduced in Section 2.3. Thus $r(t)$ denotes the instantaneous interest rate or the *spot rate* obtained by investing in a riskless security in the time interval $[t, t+dt]$.

Application of univariate SDEs is based on the assumption that the spot rate contains all relevant information about the financial market, the expectations of the market participants (agents), etc. For some time interest rates were assumed to follow a random walk, which implies that the mean and variance structures are independent of time and the current level of interest rate, i.e., there are no *level effects*. The analysis of interest rates in the problems and exercises has shown that this is clearly not the case.

Empirical studies have shown that at least 3–4 state variables are required to explain the variations in observed interest rates (e.g. Braes and Larsen [1989], Nielsen [1995], Piazzesi [2010]). The former reference uses multivariate statistics (principal component analysis, etc.) and the latter uses the concept of the fractal dimension of an attractor in state space and other methods from deterministic chaos theory. The first component will typically capture parallel shifts in the interest rate, the second difference between short and long term interest rates, while the third will capture how intermediate rates will move contrary to the movements of the short and long term rates.

In Section 2.3, we assumed that the interest rates were deterministic, but our discussion of e.g., the CIBOR time series in Section 2.4 showed that interest rates are indeed stochastic.

As we shall see interest rates models are inherently important for pricing and hedging financial derivatives which should be clear from the definition of a money market account (Definition 2.2). Recall that this is used to discount future payments of some contingent claim to determine its present value. In particular for *fixed income securities*, i.e., securities whose future payoffs are contingent on future interest rates, it is important to model interest rates. As we have argued previously, interest rates are obtained from bond prices, and we will briefly discuss this relation in order to view interest rate models in their context. The bond pricing framework and a detailed study of the so-called term structure of interest rates shall be postponed to later.

This chapter is organized as follows: Section 10.1 describes models that give rise to normally distributed interest rates. Section 10.2 extends these models to non-Gaussian interest rates. Section 10.3 extends the last section by allowing the drift and diffusion parameters to be time-dependent functions. Section 10.4 provides a brief introduction to a very broad class of multivariate SDEs or *multifactor models*, where additional variables are used to model the interest rate. It also considers *stochastic volatility models*, where one aims at modelling the volatility by considering a function of the volatility as a state variable.

10.1 Gaussian one-factor models

We fix a standard Wiener process $W(t)$ restricted to some finite time interval $[0,T]$ on a given probability space $(\Omega, \mathscr{F}, \mathbb{P})$ augmented by the natural filtration $\{\mathscr{F}(t)\}_{t\geq 0}$. This establishes the structure of information in the considered models. We assume that $r(t)$ is $\mathscr{F}(t)$-adapted and that it does not explode.

10.1.1 Merton model

The simplest, non-trivial model for spot interest rates was suggested by one of the pioneers in continuous-time finance, Robert Merton (Merton [1993]) for an overview of his work. The *Merton model* is a Wiener process with a constant drift, i.e.,

$$\mathrm{d}r(t) = \theta \mathrm{d}t + \sigma \mathrm{d}W(t) \tag{10.1}$$

where θ and σ are some constants and $r(0)$ is a deterministic initial value. The model is sometimes called the *arithmetic Brownian motion*.

This model was considered in Example 8.2, where we found that

$$\mathbf{E}[r(t)] = r(0) + \theta t \tag{10.2}$$

$$\mathbf{Var}[r(t)] = \sigma^2 t. \tag{10.3}$$

We see that there is a drift in the mean and that the variance grows with time. The solution to (10.1) is given by

$$r_r = r(0) + \theta t + \sigma W(t). \tag{10.4}$$

As the Wiener process generates normally distributed stochastic variables, it is clear that r_t is also normally distributed with the parameters given in (10.2). Thus the Merton model (10.1) does not exclude negative interest rates, which renders the model unapplicable for empirical work. It is also unclear why the interest rate should have a constant drift at all times.

10.1.2 Vasicek model

The constant drift and unlimited variance of the Merton model (10.1) is not found in the classical model attributable to Vasicek[1] (Vasicek [1977]).

The *Vasicek model* is given by

$$\mathrm{d}r_t = (\theta + \eta r(t))\mathrm{d}t + \sigma \mathrm{d}W(t) \tag{10.5}$$

where $\eta < 0$, θ and σ are some constants, r_0 is a deterministic initial value and W_t is a standard Wiener process.

The Vasicek model belongs to the class of linear SDEs in the narrow sense considered in Section 8.2.1. Thus the solution is readily found from Theorem (8.6), i.e.,

$$r(t) = \left(r(0) + \frac{\theta}{\eta}\right)e^{\eta t} - \frac{\theta}{\eta} + \sigma e^{\eta t}\int_0^t e^{-\eta s}\mathrm{d}W(s). \tag{10.6}$$

This stochastic process is also called the *Ornstein-Uhlenbeck process.*

The mean and variance are

$$\mathbf{E}[r_t] = \left(r(0) + \frac{\theta}{\eta}\right)e^{\eta t} - \frac{\theta}{\eta}, \tag{10.7}$$

$$\mathbf{Var}[r_t] = \frac{\sigma^2}{2\eta}\left(e^{2\eta t} - 1\right). \tag{10.8}$$

It is seen that the process tends to the long term mean value $-\theta/\eta$, and that the variance is finite for $\eta < 0$.

Remark 10.1. *A reparametrization of the Vasicek model, which is often seen in the literature, makes the interpretation of the parameters more clear,*

$$\mathrm{d}r(t) = \alpha(\beta - r(t))\mathrm{d}t + \sigma \mathrm{d}W(t). \tag{10.9}$$

With this parametrization the long term mean is β and the process is said to mean-revert around this mean with the speed of adjustment α.

The Vasicek model is sometimes called an elastic Brownian motion, because the diffusion term is a Brownian motion, but the mean reverting drift term pulls the process towards a long term mean if the short term rate is either above or below the long term mean.

The mean-revertion property of the Vasicek model (10.5) is a very important property of interest rate models, although it may be difficult to estimate the two parameters in the drift term from financial time series.

Clearly the solution to (10.5) is also normally distributed and hence negative interest rates cannot be excluded. The probability of negative interest rates

[1]The original paper Vasicek [1977] is highly recommended reading.

depends on the actual parameter values. This means that if there is a fast speed of adjustment to a relatively high long term mean and a low level of volatility in the market then negative interest rates are clearly highly unlikely, but still negative interest rates can not be excluded.[2] Thus the model is not considered as a reasonable model for observed interest rates, but it is nonetheless often used for theoretical work.

Thus we turn our attention to non-Gaussian models in the hope that negative interest rates may be excluded in some of these models. A more important objective is to be able to model the state dependent diffusion, which is, perhaps, *the* most important property of any interest rate model.

10.2 A general class of one-factor models

In this section, we consider a fairly general one-factor model class, which is attributable to Chan et al. [1992]. With reference to the authors of this article this model is typically called the *CKLS* model or the *generalized Cox–Ingersoll–Ross (CIR)* model.[3] The CKLS models has also been used to model mean reverting commodities such as electricity (Regland and Lindström [2012]).

The CKLS model class is as follows

$$dr(t) = (\theta + \eta r(t))dt + \sigma r(t)^{\gamma} dW(t) \tag{10.10}$$

where σ denotes a proportional rate of volatility and γ denotes the elasticity of the volatility with respect to spot interest rate changes, and the specification of the drift term is as in the Vasicek model (10.5).

Although this general model specification pertains to the important properties of a mean-reverting drift and a state dependent diffusion term, it is not possible to solve it unless some parameter restrictions are imposed in (10.10). An overview of the important models that belong to this model class is depicted in Figure 10.1. The hierachical structure is well suited for statistical inference. The models obtained by these parameter restrictions are listed in Table 10.1.

Theorem 10.1 (Existence and uniqueness for the CKLS model). *A sufficient condition for the existence and uniqueness of the solution to* (10.10) *is that the parameters* $\theta = (\theta, \eta, \gamma)$ *fulfil one of the conditions*

1. $\gamma = \frac{1}{2}$, $\theta > \frac{1}{2}\sigma^2$, $\eta < 0$,
2. $\gamma \in (\frac{1}{2}, 1)$, $\theta > 0$, $\eta \leq 0$,
3. $\gamma = 1$, $\theta = 0$, $\eta = \frac{1}{2}\sigma^2$, *or*
4. $\gamma = 1$, $(\theta, \eta, \sigma) \in \mathbb{R}_+ \times \mathbb{R} \times \mathbb{R}_+$.

Proof. The conditions are obtained using the scale function (8.8) and Theorem 8.3. See Honoré [1996] for further details. □

[2] Nevertheless the normal distribution is often applied as a reasonable model of the height, weight, etc., of a population even though a negative height or weight is impossible.

[3] The reason for the latter will be clear later.

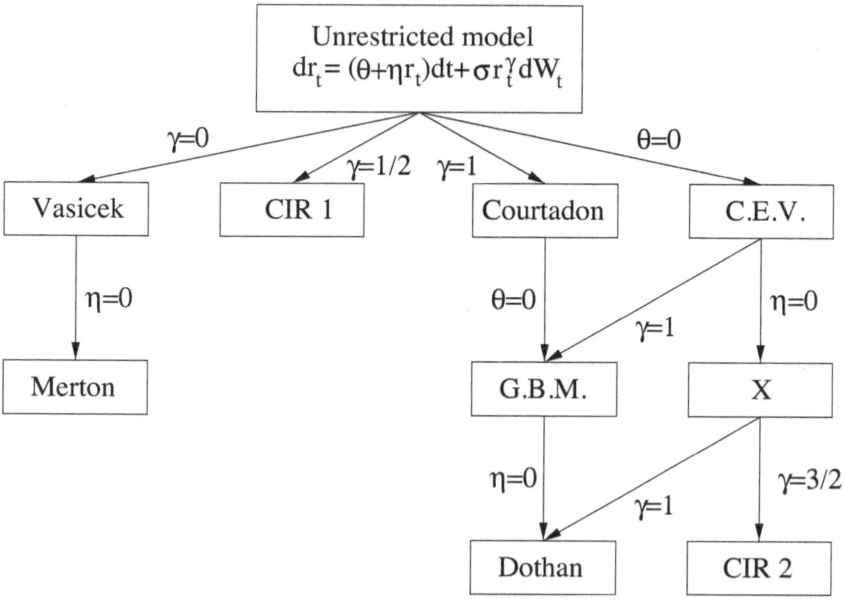

Figure 10.1: The nested models of the CKLS model class.

Remark 10.2. *It is duly noted that the case $\gamma > 1$ is not covered by the theorem. This will have some implications when estimating parameters in the model. Figure 10.2 presents the US 3 month T-bill between 1983–1995. It can be seen that the variance increases with increasing interest rates.*

This empirical property will have some consequences.... The γ parameter will typically be less than one if the interest rate is less than one and greater than one when the interest rate is greater than one. A linear scaling (i.e., using $r = 0.05$ or $r = 5$) will often change the estimates!

In the following some comments will be made to each of these models. The Merton and Vasicek models have already been discussed, and they are also members of the CKLS model class.

The *Cox–Ingersoll–Ross* model (Cox et al. [1985]), is possibly the most popular one-factor model:

$$dr(t) = (\theta + \eta r(t))dt + \sigma\sqrt{r(t)}dW(t). \tag{10.11}$$

It also has the mean-revertion property and it allows the interest rate level to proportionally influence the variance of the process. Depending on the parameters the process will have a *reflecting* or an *absorbing* barrier at zero with the appealing and obvious implication that interest rates will never become negative. The model is for obvious reasons also called the *square root process.* The CIR model does not belong to the class of linear SDEs in the strong sense

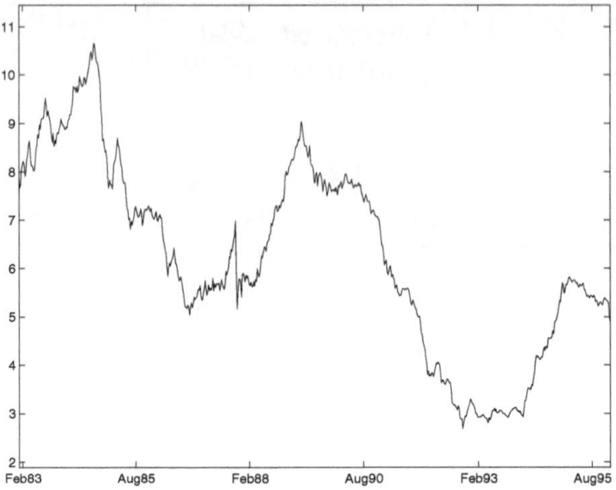

Figure 10.2: US 3 month T-bill between 1983–1995.

Author	θ	η	γ	Model
Merton		0	0	$\mathrm{d}r(t) = \theta\mathrm{d}t + \sigma\mathrm{d}W(t)$
Vasicek			0	$\mathrm{d}r(t) = (\theta + \eta r(t))\mathrm{d}t + \sigma\mathrm{d}W(t)$
CIR 1			$\frac{1}{2}$	$\mathrm{d}r(t) = (\theta + \eta r(t))\mathrm{d}t + \sigma\sqrt{r(t)}\mathrm{d}W(t)$
Dothan	0	0	1	$\mathrm{d}r(t) = \sigma r(t)\mathrm{d}W(t)$
Marsh & Rosenfeld	0		1	$\mathrm{d}r(t) = \eta r(t)\mathrm{d}t + \sigma r_t\mathrm{d}W(t)$
Courtadon			1	$\mathrm{d}r(t) = (\theta + \eta r(t))\mathrm{d}t + \sigma r(t)\mathrm{d}W(t)$
CIR 2	0	0	$\frac{3}{2}$	$\mathrm{d}r(t) = \sigma r(t)^{3/2}\mathrm{d}W(t)$
Cox (& Ross)	0			$\mathrm{d}r(t) = \eta r(t)\mathrm{d}t + \sigma r(t)^{\gamma}\mathrm{d}W(t)$

Table 10.1: By imposing restrictions on the parameters in (10.10) a large number of known models are obtained.

considered in Section 8.2, but it may nevertheless be solved in the sense that the marginal distribution of the solution r_t is known to be a gamma-distribution (the conditional density is a non-central χ^2-distribution).

The *Marsh & Rosenfeld* model is the well-known geometric Brownian motion (GBM) that has been applied as a model of stock prices in the Black & Scholes model. However, it is highly questionable whether this model conforms to the characteristics that economic intuition would normally lead one to expect from an interest rate model, as the interest would either grow towards infinity or converge towards zero (at least under the $\mathbb{P}$ measure).

The *Courtadon* model is a combination of the Vasicek and Dothan model, and it belongs to the class of linear SDEs in the strong sense considered in Section 8.2.

The *Cox (& Ross)* model is also called the *constant elasticity of variance (CEV)* model, and it allows for a very general modelling of the volatility. However, the drift term does not seem reasonable.

An empirical comparison of these models shall be made in the following chapters on parameter estimation in stochastic differential equations.

10.3 Time-dependent models

In this section, we introduce time-dependent counterparts to some of the models from the last section. The financial reasons for allowing the parameters in, e.g., (10.10) to be time-dependent will be discussed later. It is, however, rather obvious that a better fit to observed time series may be obtained by allowing the parameters to be time-dependent.

10.3.1 Ho–Lee

The *Ho–Lee* model is simply obtained by allowing the drift term in the Merton model (10.1) to be time-dependent, i.e.,

$$\mathrm{d}r(t) = \theta(t)\mathrm{d}t + \sigma \mathrm{d}W(t). \tag{10.12}$$

It can be shown that $\theta(t)$ can be chosen such that a perfect fit to all zero-coupon prices can be obtained (Section 11.3.2).

10.3.2 Black–Derman–Toy

The *Black–Derman–Toy* model is obtained by allowing the parameters in the Marsh & Rosenfeld model to be time-dependent, i.e.,

$$\mathrm{d}r(t) = \eta(t)r(t)\mathrm{d}t + \sigma(t)r(t)\mathrm{d}W(t) \tag{10.13}$$

where both the drift $\theta(t)$ and the diffusion $\sigma(t)$ are allowed to be time-dependent. This will make the model more flexible, but also more prone to overfitting. The BDT model is often implemented in a trinomial tree.

10.3.3 Hull–White

The *Hull–White* model exists in two versions, namely as extensions of either the Vasicek model (10.5) or the Cox–Ingersoll–Ross model. For brevity, we will only list the latter, i.e.,

$$\mathrm{d}r(t) = (\theta(t) + \eta(t)r(t))\mathrm{d}t + \sigma(t)\sqrt{r(t)}\mathrm{d}W(t). \tag{10.14}$$

This makes the model prone to overfitting as three functions are used to fit a finite number of observations, but the model is still not able to account for the dynamics of the term structure; cf. HJM models (Section 11.4).

10.3.3.1 CIR++ model

A rather clever special case of the Hull–White model is the so-called CIR++ model (Brigo and Mercurio [2001, 2006] for a detailed analysis). The idea is to introduce a time varying function such that a simple model (here a CIR process) plus that time varying function provides perfect fit to the term structure.

Consider the model where the interest rate is a combination of a diffusion process $x(t)$ and a deterministic function of time $\phi(t)$

$$r(t) = x(t) + \phi(t). \tag{10.15}$$

We focus on the case when $x(t)$ satisfies a CIR process. It is then clear that all we need to know in order to obtain a perfect fit to the current term structure is knowledge about the model implied term structure of $x(t)$. The time varying function $\phi(t)$ can then be chosen such that perfect fit to the term structure is obtained (Brigo and Mercurio [2006] for details on theory and implementation).

10.4 Multifactor and stochastic volatility models

An alternative approach to obtain more flexibility than in the constant parameter univariate case is to introduce additional state variables, such as the price level, the inflation level, the money supply, etc.

One way to introduce the so-called *multifactor models* is to assume that the spot interest rate is given by a function $r(t) = R(t, \mathbf{X}(t))$, where the n-dimensional state variable $\mathbf{X}(t)$ is described by the multivariate Itō stochastic differential equation

$$\mathrm{d}\mathbf{X}(t) = \mu(t, \mathbf{X}(t))\mathrm{d}t + \sigma(t, \mathbf{X}(t))\mathrm{d}\mathbf{W}(t) \tag{10.16}$$

where $R\colon [0,\infty) \times \mathbb{R}^n \to \mathbb{R}$, $\mu\colon [0,\infty) \times \mathbb{R}^n \to \mathbb{R}$, $\sigma\colon [0,\infty) \times \mathbb{R}^n \to \mathbb{R}^{n\times n}$ are sufficiently well-behaved functions such that existence and uniqueness of the solutions are guaranteed, and $\mathbf{W}(t)$ is a n-dimensional Wiener process.

We shall provide a few examples of multifactor models as the theoretical analysis of such models is outside the scope of this book.

First, we extend the CIR model (10.11), which we choose to parametrize slightly different in this case

$$\mathrm{d}r(t) = \alpha(\mu - r(t))\mathrm{d}t + \sigma\sqrt{r(t)}\mathrm{d}W(t) \tag{10.17}$$

where α is the speed of adjustment and μ is the long term. Although this model contains the level effects discussed previously, it is unreasonable to assume that the long term mean μ should be a constant. Thus we may model the long term mean μ as another CIR model, i.e.,

$$\mathrm{d}r(t) = \alpha(\mu(t) - r(t))\mathrm{d}t + \sigma\sqrt{r(t)}\mathrm{d}W^{(1)}(t) \tag{10.18}$$

$$\mathrm{d}\mu(t) = \beta(\theta - \mu(t))\mathrm{d}t + \delta\sqrt{\mu(t)}\mathrm{d}W^{(2)}(t) \tag{10.19}$$

where β, θ and δ are constants, and $W^{(1)}(t)$ and $W^{(2)}(t)$ are two mutually independent standard Wiener processes. A problem with this model specification is that the long term mean process $\mu(t)$ is unobservable. Conversely, that also means that bond prices no longer will be perfectly correlated, an empirical fact that is often observed.

Alternatively, we may choose to introduce additional explanatory variables. As an example we consider the model proposed by Pearson and Tong-Schen [1994], i.e.,

$$\mathrm{d}r(t) = \kappa_1(\theta_1 - r(t))\mathrm{d}t + \sigma_1\sqrt{r(t)}\mathrm{d}W^{(1)}(t) \tag{10.20}$$
$$\mathrm{d}p(t) = y(t)p(t)\mathrm{d}t + \sigma_p p(t)\sqrt{y(t)}\mathrm{d}W^{(2)}(t) \tag{10.21}$$
$$\mathrm{d}y(t) = \kappa_2(\theta_2 - y(t))\mathrm{d}t + \sigma_2\sqrt{y(t)}\mathrm{d}W^{(3)}(t) \tag{10.22}$$

where κ_1, κ_2, θ_1, θ_2, σ_1, σ_2 and σ_p (< 1) are positive constants; $W^{(2)}(t)$ and $W^{(3)}(t)$ are correlated Wiener processes but both are independent of $W^{(1)}(t)$. We see that the model is essentially two CIR models supplemented by a process that couples $y(t)$ and $p(t)$. The interesting part is that the state variables have an economical interpretation and may be observed on the market. The state variable $r(t)$ denotes the real interest rate, $p(t)$ denotes the price level and $y(t)$ the inflation rate. This particular model specification has the advantage that it is possible to solve the bond pricing equation as we shall see later.

Empirical studies have shown the interest rate *and* the volatility of the former are two of the most important factors in the financial markets. If we denote the volatility by $V(t)$, we may, e.g., consider the model proposed by Longstaff and Schartz [1992], i.e.,

$$\mathrm{d}r(t) = \left(\alpha\gamma + \beta\eta - \frac{\beta\delta - \gamma\zeta}{\beta - \alpha}r(t) - \frac{\zeta - \delta}{\beta - \alpha}V(t)\right)\mathrm{d}t + \alpha\sqrt{\frac{\beta r(t) - V(t)}{\alpha(\beta - \alpha)}}\mathrm{d}W^{(1)}(t) + \beta\sqrt{\frac{V(t) - \alpha r(t)}{\beta(\beta - \alpha)}}\mathrm{d}W^{(2)}(t) \tag{10.23}$$

$$\mathrm{d}V(t) = \left(\alpha^2\gamma + \beta^2\eta - \frac{\alpha\beta(\delta - \zeta)}{\beta - \alpha}r(t) - \frac{\beta\zeta - \alpha\delta}{\beta - \alpha}V(t)\right)\mathrm{d}t + \alpha^2\sqrt{\frac{\beta r(t) - V(t)}{\alpha(\beta - \alpha)}}\mathrm{d}W^{(1)}(t) + \beta^2\sqrt{\frac{V(t) - \alpha r(t)}{\beta(\beta - \alpha)}}\mathrm{d}W^{(2)}(t) \tag{10.24}$$

where the parameters α, β, γ, δ, η and ζ are assumed to be constant.[4] Again this particular model parametrization has been chosen because it is possible to

[4]We have chosen to use the parametrization from the original paper.

solve the bond pricing equation. Furthermore, it may be shown that

$$\mathbf{E}[r(t)] = \frac{\alpha\gamma}{\delta} + \frac{\beta\eta}{\zeta} \tag{10.25}$$

$$\mathbf{Var}[r(t)] = \frac{\alpha^2\gamma}{2\delta^2} + \frac{\beta^2\eta}{2\zeta^2} \tag{10.26}$$

$$\mathbf{E}[V(t)] = \frac{\alpha^2\gamma}{\delta} + \frac{\beta^2\eta}{2\zeta^2} \tag{10.27}$$

$$\mathbf{Var}[V(t)] = \frac{\alpha^4\gamma}{2\delta^2} + \frac{\beta^4\eta}{2\zeta^2}. \tag{10.28}$$

It should be evident that an *infinite number* of multifactor models may be proposed. So far the criterion in the financial literature has been that it should be possible to determine closed form solutions to the bond pricing equation. However, this may also be done by Monte Carlo simulation or another numerical method such that this criterion is no longer valid. Instead the model that provides the best fit (in some sense) to observed time series should be chosen, but this is clearly a very difficult problem.

10.4.1 Stochastic volatility models

A stochastic volatility model is obtained by using a function of the time-dependent volatility σ_t as a state variable. These models may be considered as a continuous-time extension of the ARCH models considered in Section 5.5.2, but we shall not go into the mathematical details here.

Empirical studies have shown that $\log \sigma_t^2$ is an important state variable. As a very general example consider the model

$$dr(t) = \alpha_1(\mu(t) - r(t))dt + \sigma(t)r(t)^{\gamma}dW^{(1)}(t) \tag{10.29}$$

$$d(\log \sigma^2(t)) = \alpha_2(\beta - \log \sigma^2(t))dt + \xi_1\sqrt{r(t)}dW^{(2)}(t) \tag{10.30}$$

$$d\mu(t) = \alpha_3(\theta - \mu(t))dt + \xi_2\sqrt{\mu(t)}dW^{(3)}(t). \tag{10.31}$$

We recognize (10.29) as the CKLS model (10.10), where the long term mean μ_t and the volatility σ_t are now assumed to be time-dependent. The time dependency of μ_t is simply modelled by (10.31), namely a Cox–Ingersoll–Ross model (10.11). The interesting part compared to multifactor models is (10.30), where the log volatility $\log \sigma_t^2$ is modelled with the mean-reversion and state dependent diffusion term that we have come to expect. In particular note that the short term interest rate r_t enters the diffusion term in (10.30). Although a clear-cut definition of stochastic volatility models is hard to find, it is (at least) required that (a function of) the volatility is modelled and that the short term interest rate enters this model as in (10.30). Clearly, it is very difficult to determine the parameter restrictions that must be imposed on (10.29)–(10.31) to ensure existence and uniqueness of solutions.

It is an unresolved question whether stochastic volatility models are superior to general multifactor models. The latter aims at modelling the drift by including additional (un)observable variables, whereas the former tends to disregard the drift (except mean-reversion) and focuses on the diffusion. As stochastic differential equations consist of both a drift term and a diffusion term, it is hardly surprising that (at least two) different schools have emerged in the financial community. The reader is encouraged to consider the fundamental difference between these two schools.

10.4.2 Affine Term Structure models

Computational considerations has caused much focus on models that are simple enough to admit a (semi-)closed form expression, and still be flexible enough to capture stylized facts. Here we consider models given by a multivariate jump diffusion

$$\mathrm{d}\mathbf{X}(t) = \mu(t, \mathbf{X}(t-))\mathrm{d}t + \sigma(t, \mathbf{X}(t-))\mathrm{d}W(t) + \mathrm{d}J(t) \tag{10.32}$$

where $J(t)$ is a compound Poisson process with jump distribution independent of $X(t-)$ having intensity $\lambda(\mathbf{X}(t))$; cf Section 7.5.

The class of *Affine Term Structure models* (Piazzesi [2010] for an extensive overview) requires the drift, squared diffusion and jump intensity to satisfy certain conditions under the risk-neutral measure $\mathbb{Q}$:

- The drift $\mu(t, \mathbf{X}(t))$ is affine in $\mathbf{X}(t)$.
- The squared diffusion $\sigma(t, \mathbf{X}(t))\sigma^T(t, \mathbf{X}(t))$ is affine in $\mathbf{X}(t)$.
- The jump intensity $\lambda(\mathbf{X}(t))$ is affine in $\mathbf{X}(t)$.

It is then possible to show that the price of a zero-coupon bond, formally computed as

$$p(t,T) = \mathbf{E}^{\mathbb{Q}}\left[e^{\int_t^T -r(s)\mathrm{d}s}|\mathscr{F}(t)\right], \tag{10.33}$$

can be expressed even when the model includes stochastic volatility and stochastic long term mean, etc., as

$$p(t,T) = e^{A(T-t)+B(T-t)^T X(t)} \tag{10.34}$$

where $A(\cdot)$ and $B(\cdot)$ are solutions to some differential equations (Piazzesi [2010] for examples). The solution here resembles the Fourier methods in Section 9.6.1, explaining the computational advantages.

The class of Affine Jump Diffusions is very general, including the Vasicek model and the Cox–Ingersoll–Ross model, as well as certain stochastic long term interest rates and stochastic volatility models.

10.5 Notes

Survey articles on interest rate models appear regularly in the financial literature, but we only list a couple, namely Chan et al. [1992] and Strickland [1996]. The first reference introduces an estimation method and compares univariate SDE models empirically. We shall in later chapters discuss and extend their work. The last reference is highly recommendable reading.

A theoretical analysis of interest models (or SDEs in general) may be found in Karatzas and Shreve [1996], Ikeda and Watanabe [1989], but very few results are available on multifactor models.

An excellent discussion of stochastic volatility (SV) models may be found in Musiela and Rutkowski [1997] and Andersen and Lund [1997]. The first reference gives an overview of continuous time models whereas the latter discusses the relation between (G)ARCH models and SV models in detail, and uses the Efficient Method of Moments for parameter estimation (Gallant and Tauchen [1996]).

10.6 Problems

Problem 10.1
Show (10.4).

Problem 10.2
One-factor stochastic interest rate models are very popular for theoretical analysis and thus a huge range of models have been proposed in the financial literature through the years. We have considered the CKLS model class previously. In this problem, we consider a slightly simpler model class (actually a subclass of the CKLS model class) attributable to *Courtadon*, which gives rise to linear models in the narrow sense. Thus the model may be solved and the first moments may be computed using the methods of Chapter 8.

Consider the one-factor stochastic interest rate model

$$dr(t) = (\theta + \eta r(t))dt + \rho r(t)dW(t) \quad r(0) = r_0 \tag{10.35}$$

where θ, η and ρ are constants, and $W(t)$ is a standard Wiener process.

1. Solve (10.35).
2. Determine the mean $\mathbf{E}[r(t)]$. In particular determine $\lim_{t\to\infty} \mathbf{E}[r(t)]$.
3. Determine the variance $\mathbf{Var}[r(t)]$. In particular determine $\lim_{t\to\infty} \mathbf{Var}[r(t)]$.

Problem 10.3
For $\theta = 0$ in (10.35), we get the geometric Brownian motion

$$dr(t) = \eta r(t)dt + \sigma r(t)dW(t) \tag{10.36}$$

which, according to Example 8.10, has the solution

$$r(t) = r(0)\exp((\eta - \sigma^2/2) + \sigma W(t)). \tag{10.37}$$

It appears that the deterministic growth rate in (10.37) is $(\eta - \sigma^2/2)$ as opposed to the growth rate η in (10.36).
1. Determine $\mathbf{E}[e^{\sigma W(t)}]$.
2. Use this result to show that there is no discrepancy between the expected growth rates in (10.36) and (10.37).

Problem 10.4
Show (10.25) and (10.27).

Problem 10.5
An even more general model of interest rates than (10.10) is considered in Duffie [2010]. It takes the form

$$\mathrm{d}r(t) = (\alpha_{1t} + \alpha_{2t}r(t) + \alpha_{3t}r(t)\log r(t))\mathrm{d}t + (\beta_{1t} + \beta_{2t}r(t))^{\nu}\mathrm{d}W(t) \tag{10.38}$$

where α_{1t}, α_{2t}, α_{3t}, β_{1t} and β_{2t} are time-dependent functions, ν is a constant and $W(t)$ is a standard Wiener process. The reader is encouraged to make a table of the parameter restrictions that must be imposed on (10.38) in order to obtain the models discussed in this chapter.

Assuming that the functions α_{1t}, α_{2t}, α_{3t}, β_{1t} and β_{2t} are constants, we shall now shed some light on the reasonability of the $\log r(t)$ term in (10.38).

It might be useful (e.g., for numerical reasons or in order to obtain some kind of variance homogeneity) to consider the process $l(t) = \log r(t)$, where l_t is described by a Vasicek model

$$\mathrm{d}l(t) = (a + bl(t))\mathrm{d}t + \sigma \mathrm{d}W(t).$$

Use the Itō formula (8.10) to determine the SDE for $r(t)$ and compare the result with (10.38).

Chapter 11

Term structure of interest rates

In this chapter the concept of no-arbitrage will be discussed in the interest rate markets, which we also refer to as the *bond market*. Just to motivate the discussion, it should be noted that trading in various types of bonds grossly exceeds trading in the financial derivatives considered so far.

In Chapter 3, we considered pricing in complete (and incomplete) markets in discrete time and showed that the existence of a state price vector resulted in an arbitrage-free market. In Chapter 9, we presented a similar theory in continuous time and the tremendously important result was the correspondence between the existence and uniqueness of an equivalent martingale measure and arbitrage-free prices.

In the Black & Scholes model it is possible to determine the arbitrage-free price of a large class of financial derivatives. This result stems from the fact that it was possible to trade in the underlying asset (the stock) and thus generate replicating portfolios. However, this important result does not hold in the interest rate (or bond) markets as it is not possible to trade directly in the underlying asset, namely the interest rate itself. Nevertheless, a large number of interest rate derivative products exist as discussed in Section 2.4.

It could be said that the concept of arbitrage in the Black–Scholes model was based on a *vertical* argument across the underlying asset and the financial derivative. In the bond markets, the concept of arbitrage is considered *horizontally* through time.

In Chapter 2, we considered deterministic interest rates and introduced the money market account in Definition 2.2 for continuously compounded interest rates. In Chapters 7–8, we introduced stochastic calculus and stochastic differential equations. These techniques were used in Chapter 9 to determine the arbitrage-free price of any financial derivative under the basic assumption that the interest rate was deterministic.

The objective of this chapter is to extend the theory to cover stochastic interest rates. In particular, we wish to discuss various types of interest rates such that we may determine the discounting factor in, e.g., (9.75) for stochastic interest rates. Basically, we wish to answer the following questions:

Q1: *How can one determine the interest rate at a future date when it is stochastic, i.e., described by a stochastic differential equation?*

Q2: *How can one discount future payments (i.e., the payoff of a financial derivative) when the discounting factor is stochastic?*

This chapter is organized as follows: Section 11.1 introduces a number of important concepts. Section 11.2 derives the term structure of interest rates using the classical approach. In Section 11.3 specific models of the term structure of interest rates are considered based on the interest rate models from Chapter 10. Section 11.4 briefly considers the socalled Heath–Jarrow–Morton framework for modelling the forward rates. As usual the chapter concludes with some notes and problems.

It should be stressed that this exposition does neither go into institutional details nor into the finer differences between the wide range of fixed income securities such as corporate bonds, mortgage backed securities and collateralized mortgage obligations (CMO). Some references will be given in the Notes.

11.1 Basic concepts

A *bond* is a contract, paid for up-front, that yields a known amount on a known date in the future, called the *maturity date*, $t = T$. The main purpose of a bond issue is to raise capital, and the up-front premium can be considered as a loan to the government or the company. In Denmark, bonds are issued by the government (i.e., The National Bank), all the major banks and a few trade-specific mutual funds.

A cash flow may be associated with the bond such that a cash dividend (or *coupon*) is paid out to the holder of the contract at fixed times during the lifetime of the contract. If there are no coupons the bond is known as a *zero-coupon bond* or just a *zero-bond.*

Definition 11.1 (A zero-coupon bond)**.** *A (zero-coupon) bond with maturity date T is a contract that gives the holder of the contract C units of account (e.g., DKK) at time T. The price at time t of a T-bond is denoted by $P(t,T)$.*

Example 11.1 (Zero-coupon bonds)**.** *On the Danish market, there will typically be three zero-coupon bonds in circulation. These are called skatkammerbeviser and have been issued by the Ministry of Finance since 1st April 1990. They have a relatively short lifetime of 3, 6 and 9 months, and the face value C is 1 000 000 DKK. These zero-bonds are traded under circumstances that differ from other bonds, e.g., the price is determined through an auction.*

11.1.1 Known interest rates

We now derive an equation for the value of the bond $P(t,T)$ at time t prior to the maturity date T. We assume that the interest rate $r(t)$ and the coupon payments $K(t)$ are known functions of time. Thus we assume that cash coupon payments may also be made continuously in time. Such payments are often called *dividends*. The change in the value of one bond $P(t,T)$ in the time interval $[t, t+dt[$ is

$$\frac{\mathrm{d}P}{\mathrm{d}t}\mathrm{d}t.$$

If we have received a coupon payment $K(t)$ during the time period dt, our holdings (including the cash) change by the amount

$$\left(\frac{\mathrm{d}P}{\mathrm{d}t} + K(t)\right)\mathrm{d}t.$$

Alternatively, we may also choose to deposit our capital in a savings account with the known interest rate $r(t)$ and the value $V(t)$. In order to exclude arbitrage possibilities, we must have

$$\frac{\mathrm{d}P}{\mathrm{d}t} + K(t) = r(t)V(t) = r(t)P(t,T). \tag{11.1}$$

Otherwise a riskless profit may be made by moving our holdings from the savings account to the bond (>) or vice versa. With the final condition $P(T,T) = C$, this ordinary differential equation may be shown to have the solution

$$P(t,T) = \exp\left(-\int_t^T r(s)\mathrm{d}s\right)\left(C + \int_t^T K(u)\exp\left(-\int_u^T r(s)\mathrm{d}s\right)\mathrm{d}u\right). \tag{11.2}$$

Assuming that there are no coupon payments $K(t) = 0$, we get

$$P(t,T) = C\exp\left(-\int_t^T r(s)\mathrm{d}s\right) \tag{11.3}$$

from (11.2). If the bond prices $P(t,T)$ are quoted today at time t for all values of the maturity date T, then we know the left-hand side of (11.3) for all T. Thus we may compute

$$-\int_t^T r(s)\mathrm{d}s = \log[P(t,T)], \tag{11.4}$$

where we have assumed that $C = 1$. This is a standard convention which states that the bond pays out 1 unit of account at time T. This unit of account may be 1 000 000 DKK (e.g., skatkammerbeviser) or some other appropriate value. It is merely a question of choosing a normalizing factor such that the mathematical computations may be slightly simplified, i.e., we may exclude the log C term because $\log 1 = 0$.

Assuming that $P(t,T)$ is differentiable with respect to T, we get

$$r(T) = -\frac{1}{P(t,T)}\frac{\partial P}{\partial T}(t,T). \tag{11.5}$$

Thus assuming that the prices of zero-coupon bonds genuinely reflect a known interest rate we may compute that interest rate at future dates $T > t$ from the bond prices.

Since interest rates $r(t)$ are inherently positive, we must have

$$\frac{\partial P}{\partial T}(t,T) < 0 \tag{11.6}$$

which shows that the longer a bond has to live, the less it is now worth. In other words, the longer you have to wait to get the payment of C DKK the less this amount is worth to you today.

11.1.2 Discrete dividends

So far we have assumed that coupon payments were made continuously in time. However, in practice, coupon payments are only made at discrete time instants $\mathbf{t} = (t_1, \ldots, t_N)'$, i.e., every three, six or twelve months or so. With respect to (11.1) this may be modelled using the Dirac delta "function"

$$\frac{\mathrm{d}P}{\mathrm{d}t} + K_c\delta(t - t_c) = r(t)V(t) = r(t)P(t,T) \tag{11.7}$$

where we have assumed that only one coupon payment K_c is made at time t_c for simplicity. The solution is

$$P(t,T) = \exp\left(-\int_t^T r(s)\mathrm{d}s\right)\left(C + K_c\mathscr{H}(t_c - t)\exp\left(\int_{t_c}^T r(s)\mathrm{d}s\right)\right) \tag{11.8}$$

where the *Heaviside function* is given by

$$\mathscr{H}(x) = \int_{-\infty}^x \delta(s)\mathrm{d}s = \begin{cases} 0 & \text{for } x < 0 \\ 1 & \text{for } x \geq 0 \end{cases}$$

or in other words

$$\mathscr{H}'(x) = \delta(x).$$

Let us consider the effect of a discrete coupon payment K_c at time t_c on the price of the coupon bond. Prior to time t_c, the bond has the value $P(t_c^-, T)$ and immediately after, at time t_c^+, the value of the coupon bond is decreased by the coupon payment K_c:

$$P(t_c^+, T) = P(t_c^-, T) - K_c. \tag{11.9}$$

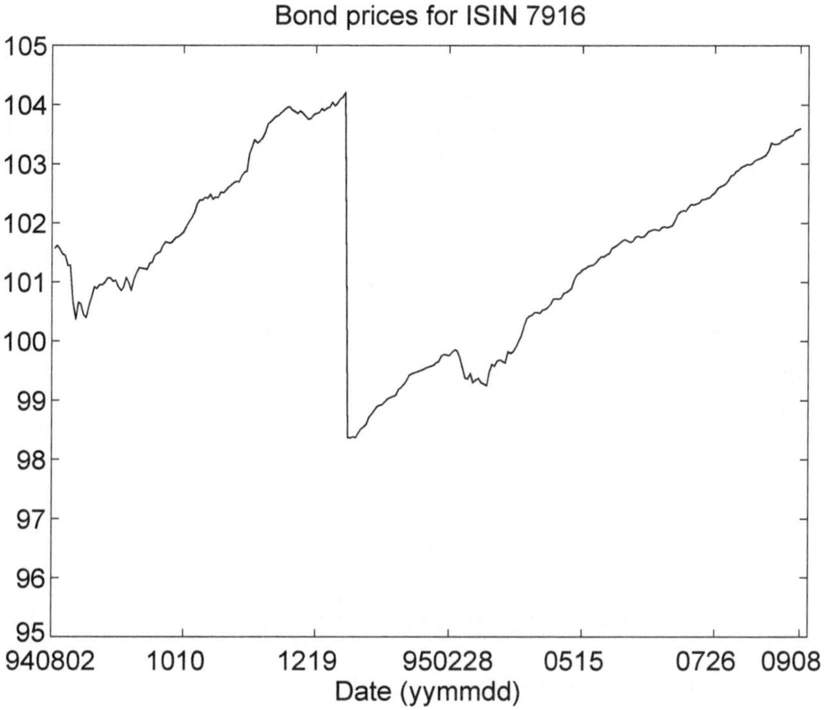

Figure 11.1: The graph shows the prices of a bond with the international code ISIN 7916 (to be precise DK000997916) from the period 2/8 1994 until 8/9 1995 with a coupon payment of 6 DKK. The bond is a 6% Danish Government bond (stående lån) that matured 10/2 1996 at which time the holder of the bond obtained 106 DKK. The jump in the bond price given by (11.9) is clear. It is also clear that the bond prices show random variations.

This will be called the *jump condition*, and it will still apply when we move on to consider stochastic interest rates. The coupon payment also implies that the bond price is not continuous. In turn this implies that the derivation of (11.5) is not valid. The jump condition is illustrated in Figure 11.1 for real market data.

Remark 11.1 (Notation). *As the maturity date T is a parameter, we occasionally use the notation*

$$P^T(t) = P(t,T).$$

Clearly we have

$$P^t(t) = P(t,t) = 1, \quad \textit{for all } t \geq 0 \tag{11.10}$$

which states the price of a bond at time t that matures at time t is 1.

11.1.3 Yield curve

If we consider stochastic interest rates, $P(t,T)$ becomes a stochastic process for every fixed T. Thus as a function of the time parameter t the trajectories of $P(t,T)$ become highly irregular (Figure 11.1). For a fixed t (and a fixed trajectory ω) the price process $P(t,T)$ is typically a smooth function and in particular differentiable with respect to T. Thus we introduce the notation

$$P_T(t,T) = \frac{\partial P(t,T)}{\partial T}.$$

The objective is now to determine the price process $P(t,T)$.

Definition 11.2 (Forward rates). *For $t \le S \le T$ the forward rate for the time period $[S,T]$ at time t is defined as*

$$R(t,S,T) = -\frac{\log[P(t,T)] - \log[P(t,S)]}{T-S}. \tag{11.11}$$

The instantaneous forward rate at time T seen from time t is defined as

$$f(t,T) = \lim_{S \to T} R(t,S,T) = -\frac{\partial \log[P(t,T)]}{\partial T}. \tag{11.12}$$

We consider a special case of (11.11) in the following definition.

Definition 11.3 (The yield curve). *The forward rate for the period $[t,T]$ is defined as*

$$Y(t,T) = R(t,t,T) = -\frac{\log[P(t,T)]}{T-t}. \tag{11.13}$$

A plot of $Y(t,T)$ against $T-t$ is called the yield curve.

In the following definition, we introduce the most important concept in this chapter, namely the *term structure of interest rates*.

Definition 11.4 (The term structure of interest rates). *The dependence of the yield curve on the time to maturity $T-t$ is called the term structure of interest rates.*

Remark 11.2. *The terms "the yield curve," "the term structure of interest rates" and bond prices are used interchangeably in the financial literature due to the following relationship.*

From (11.13), we immediately get

$$P(t,T) = \exp[-Y(t,T)(T-t)] \tag{11.14}$$

which shows that $Y(t,T)$ is the implied average interest rate for the time period $[t,T]$. The yield curve is another measure of future values of interest rates than (11.5). The yield curve has a couple of advantages which are important for empirical work, namely

- The bond prices $P(t,T)$ need not be differentiable, and
- a continuous distribution of bonds with all maturities is not required.

Example 11.2 (The yield curve). *Consider three zero-coupon bonds (skatkammerbeviser (SKBV)) with maturities $T_1 < T_2 < T_3$ and a face value C of DKK 1 000 000. From* (11.14)*, it follows that*

$$P(t,T_1) = \exp\left(-\int_t^{T_1} r(s)\mathrm{d}s\right) = \exp(-R_1(T_1-t)) \tag{11.15}$$

$$P(t,T_2) = \exp\left(-\int_t^{T_2} r(s)\mathrm{d}s\right) = \exp(-R_2(T_2-t)) \tag{11.16}$$

$$P(t,T_3) = \exp\left(-\int_t^{T_3} r(s)\mathrm{d}s\right) = \exp(-R_3(T_3-t)) \tag{11.17}$$

where the yield is denoted by R_i, $i = 1,2,3$, after the continuous convention used in Denmark.

In practice the yield is the interesting quantity when discussing zero-coupon bonds rather than the integral over continuously compounded interest rates as the latter cannot be observed in the market. A selection of real prices and yields is presented in Table 11.1.

An interesting and important observation from Table 11.1 is that the yield is not constant. The yield varies with the maturity of the bonds. This should come as no surprise, since this is exactly the same situation as in the bank where a savings account pays a higher interest than a check account. In other words, the longer your investment horizon the higher the return. This observation, that the interest rate depends on the investment horizon, is expressed by the zero-coupon term structure of interest rates (or, in short, the term structure). It is clear that only a limited number of points on the term structure is available, and our problem is basically to determine a reasonable interpolation method. We also note that the prices and the maturities confirm (11.6)*, namely that the price and the yield move in adverse directions.*

Zero-coupon bond	Price (DKK)	Maturity (years)	Yield
SKBV 97/III	991218	0.2417	0.0365
SKBV 97/IV	981640	0.4917	0.0377
SKBV 98/I	968117	0.7417	0.0437

Table 11.1: Skatkammerbeviser quoted at the Copenhagen Stock Exchange April 3, 1997.

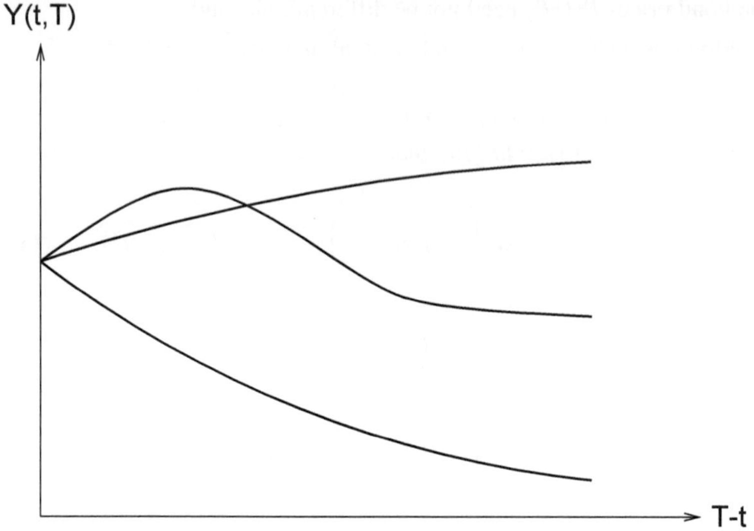

Figure 11.2: Typical yield curves.

From empirical market data it is observed that yield curves typically come in three distinct shapes (as illustrated in Figure 11.2), each associated with different economic conditions:

- *Increasing*: this is the most common form for the yield curve as it shows that future interest rates are higher than the short interest rate, since it should be more rewarding to tie money up for a long time than for a short time. E.g., the interest rate of a savings account is typically larger than for a check account.
- *decreasing*: this is typical of periods when the short rate is high but expected to fall.
- *humped*: again the short rate is expected to fall, although in a more complicated manner.

Now the last type of interest rates to be considered in these notes is defined.

Definition 11.5 (The spot interest rate). *The instantaneous (spot) interest rate at time t is defined by*

$$r(t) = f(t,t) \tag{11.18}$$

where $f(t,t)$ is given by (11.12).

Note that the spot interest rate (for which a number of SDE models were proposed in Chapter 10) is connected to the forward rate. The spot interest rate $r(t)$ is simply the forward rate obtained by investing our money in a bond in the time interval $[t, t+dt]$. For obvious reasons the spot rate is also called *the*

Figure 11.3: A graphical interpretion of the interest rate concepts in Definitions 11.2, 11.3 and 11.5. The eye should indicate that all the interest rates are evaluated as they are seen at time t regardless of the time (interval) for which the interest rates apply.

instantaneous rate of interest or *the short rate*. The process of continuously investing our holdings at the spot rate $r(t)$ is referred to as *rolling over the money* (see the discussion later on page 220).

All of the considered interest rate concepts are illustrated in Figure 11.3.

11.1.4 Stochastic interest rates

In the following we assume that the spot rate, the bond price and the forward rate may be described by the univariate Itō SDEs

$$\mathrm{d}r(t) = \mu(t)\mathrm{d}t + \sigma(t)\mathrm{d}W(t) \tag{11.19}$$

$$\mathrm{d}P(t,T) = m(t,T)P(t,T)\mathrm{d}t + v(t,T)P(t,T)\mathrm{d}W(t) \tag{11.20}$$

$$\mathrm{d}f(t,T) = \alpha(t,T)\mathrm{d}t + \sigma(t,T)\mathrm{d}W(t) \tag{11.21}$$

where $W(t)$ is a standard Wiener process defined on the usual filtered probability space $(\Omega, \mathscr{F}, \mathbb{P})$.

The functions $\mu(t)$ and $\sigma(t)$ may depend on $r(t)$, while $m(t,T)$ and $v(t,T)$ may depend on $P(t,T)$ and so forth; we use this slightly more sloppy notation for convenience. The functions μ and σ are adapted processes, defined for all $t \geq 0$. For every fixed T, the functions $m(\cdot,T)$, $v(\cdot,T)$, $\alpha(\cdot,T)$ and $\sigma(\cdot,T)$ are adapted processes defined for $0 \leq t \leq T$.

Assumption 11.1. *In situations where some of the SDEs* (11.19)–(11.21) *are given, we assume that the involved processes are continuous functions of t and twice differentiable continuous functions of the parameter T. Furthermore we* *assume that*

$$\nu(T,T) = 0, \quad \textit{for all } T \geq 0. \tag{11.22}$$

Remark 11.3. *The assumption* (11.22) *is a necessary condition for* (11.20) *to satisfy the boundary condition* (11.10)*. It may be shown that this boundary condition also implies that the drift term* $m(t,T)P(t,T)$ *in* (11.20) *should be finite with probability 1.*

From the definitions of the bond prices, spot rates and forward rates, it is clear that the infinitesimal characteristics in (11.19)–(11.21) are related to one another.

Lemma 11.1 (From $P(t,T)$ to $f(t,T)$)**.** *Let* $P(t,T)$ *for every fixed* T *be described by* (11.20)*. Then* $f(t,T)$ *for every fixed* T *is described by* (11.21) *where*

$$\begin{aligned} \alpha(t,T) &= \nu(t,T)\nu_T(t,T) - m_T(t,T) & (11.23) \\ \sigma(t,T) &= -\nu_T(t,T) & (11.24) \end{aligned}$$

where $\nu_T(t,T) = \partial\nu/\partial T(t,T)$*, etc.*

Proof. First, we write (11.20) in stochastic integral form

$$P(t,T) = P(0,T) + \int_0^t m(s,T)P(s,T)\mathrm{d}s + \int_0^t \nu(s,T)P(s,T)\mathrm{d}W(s). \tag{11.25}$$

Taking derivatives with respect to T yields

$$\begin{aligned} P_T(t,T) = P_T(0,T) &+ \int_0^t \{m_T(s,T)P(s,T) + m(s,T)P_T(s,T)\}\,\mathrm{d}s \\ &+ \int_0^t \{\nu_T(s,T)P(s,T) + \nu(s,T)P_T(s,T)\}\,\mathrm{d}W(s) \end{aligned} \tag{11.26}$$

or in SDE form

$$\begin{aligned} \mathrm{d}P_T(t,T) = \{m_T(t,T)P(t,T) + m(t,T)P_T(t,T)\}\,\mathrm{d}t \\ + \{\nu_T(t,T)P(t,T) + \nu(t,T)P_T(t,T)\}\,\mathrm{d}W(t). \end{aligned} \tag{11.27}$$

From (11.12), it follows that

$$f(t,T) = -\frac{P_T(t,T)}{P(t,T)} = \varphi(P_T(t,T), P(t,T)) \tag{11.28}$$

where the function $\varphi(\cdot,\cdot)$ has been introduced.

In order to apply the multidimensional Itō formula (8.18) to this function, we need

$$\frac{\partial \varphi}{\partial t}=0,\quad \frac{\partial \varphi}{\partial P}=\frac{P_T}{P^2},\quad \frac{\partial \varphi}{\partial P_T}=-\frac{1}{P},\quad \frac{\partial^2 \varphi}{\partial P \partial P_T}=\frac{1}{P^2},$$

$$\frac{\partial^2 \varphi}{\partial P^2}=-2\frac{P_T}{P^3},\quad \frac{\partial^2 \varphi}{\partial P_T^2}=0,\quad \frac{\partial^2 \varphi}{\partial P_T \partial P}=\frac{1}{P^2}.$$

Now (8.18) yields

$$\begin{aligned} \mathrm{d}\varphi = 0\cdot \mathrm{d}t + \frac{P_T}{P^2}\mathrm{d}P - \frac{1}{P}\mathrm{d}P_T + \frac{1}{2}\frac{1}{P^2}\mathrm{d}P\mathrm{d}P_T + \frac{1}{2}(-2)\frac{P_T}{P^3}(\mathrm{d}P)^2 \\ + \frac{1}{2}\frac{1}{P^2}\mathrm{d}P_T\mathrm{d}P + \frac{1}{2}\cdot 0(\mathrm{d}P_T)^2 \end{aligned} \quad (11.29)$$

where the shorthand notation should be clear.

By inserting (11.20) for $\mathrm{d}P$ and (11.27) for $\mathrm{d}P_T$ herein, we get, after some trivial computations,

$$\begin{aligned} \mathrm{d}\varphi = \left[m\frac{P_T}{P} - m_T - m\frac{P_T}{P} + \nu\nu^T + \nu^2\frac{P_T}{P} - \nu^2\frac{P_T}{P}\right]\mathrm{d}t \\ + \left[\nu\frac{P_T}{P} - \nu_t - \nu\frac{P_T}{P}\right]\mathrm{d}W(t). \end{aligned} \quad (11.30)$$

Now the results in (11.23) readily follow.

The reader is encouraged to perform all the computations in this proof in detail. The results in Remark 8.6 on page 150 may be helpful. □

Lemma 11.2 (From $f(t,T)$ to $r(t)$). *Assume that $f(t,T)$ for every fixed T is described by the SDE in* (11.21). *Then $r(t)$ may be described by* (11.19) *where*

$$\mu(t) = f_T(0,T)+\alpha(t,t)+\int_0^t \alpha_T(s,t)\mathrm{d}s+\int_0^t \sigma_T(s,t)\mathrm{d}W(s) \quad (11.31)$$

$$\sigma(t) = \sigma(t,t). \quad (11.32)$$

Proof. This proof is omitted as it is of purely technical nature and quite hard. See Björk [2009]. □

Lemma 11.3 (From $f(t,T)$ to $P(t,T)$). *Let $f(\cdot,T)$ be described by* (11.21) *for every fixed T. Then $P(t,T)$ may be described by the SDE*

$$\mathrm{d}P(t,T) = (r(t)+b(t,T))P(t,T)\mathrm{d}t + a(t,T)P(t,T)\mathrm{d}W(t) \quad (11.33)$$

where the functions $a(t,T)$ and $b(t,T)$ are given by

$$a(t,T) = -\int_t^T \sigma(t,s)\mathrm{d}s \tag{11.34}$$

$$b(t,T) = -\int_t^T \alpha(t,s)\mathrm{d}s + \frac{1}{2}a^2(t,T). \tag{11.35}$$

In relation to (11.20)*, we have*

$$m(t,T) = r(t) + b(t,T) \tag{11.36}$$

$$v(t,T) = a(t,T). \tag{11.37}$$

Proof. Omitted. See Björk [2009]. □

The forward rate $R(t,S,T)$ is the return over the time period $[S,T]$, $t \le S \le T$, of a bond purchased at time t, and $f(t,T)$ is the instantaneous return at time T of a bond purchased at time t (see Figure 11.3).

From (11.18), we get that $r(t) = f(t,t)$, which shows that we may interpret the spot rate $r(t)$ as the instantaneous return of a bond with expiry $t + \mathrm{d}t$ purchased at time t. Thus the spot rate is the return of the following trading strategy: At every time instant t, we invest our entire wealth in a bond that is just about to mature. Such a strategy is called a *roll-over strategy*. Formally the value process $V(t)$ of the roll-over strategy is

$$\mathrm{d}V(t) = V(t)u(t)\frac{\mathrm{d}P(t,t)}{P(t,t)}$$

where $u(t)$ denotes the fraction of our wealth invested in the bond at time t. A roll-over strategy is thus defined by $u(t) = 1$ for all t. From (11.33), we get

$$\frac{\mathrm{d}P(t,T)}{P(t,T)} = \{r(t) + b(t,T)\}\mathrm{d}t + a(t,T)\mathrm{d}W(t).$$

It follows immediately from (11.125) that $a(t,t) = b(t,t) = 0$ such that we get

$$\mathrm{d}V(t) = V(t)r(t)\mathrm{d}t. \tag{11.38}$$

Thus the possibility of using a roll-over strategy on the bond markets implies the existence of a locally riskless paper with the stochastic interest rate $r(t)$. Note that the paper is riskless although the interest rate is a stochastic process, because the interest rate process $r(t)$ is adapted, which means that $r(t)$ is known at time t (recall that the pricing formulas for financial derivatives are conditioned on $\mathcal{F}(t)$). To be precise, it should be said that *future* interest rates are stochastic.

So far we have considered the internal relations between bond prices and various types of interest rates. We have yet to determine the fair price of a bond.

Thus we wish to answer the following questions:

Q3: *Assume that the dynamics of the short rate $r(t)$ is known. Which bond prices will be consistent with this particular choice of $r(t)$ and is it possible to determine unique bond prices from $r(t)$ and the no-arbitrage requirement?*

Q4: *Which restrictions must be imposed on $P(t,T)$, $0 \le t \le T$, in order to obtain an arbitrage-free money market?*

Q5: *Which restrictions must be imposed on $f(t,T)$, $0 \le t \le T$, in order to obtain an arbitrage-free money market?*

Q6: *What can we say about the prices of financial derivatives in an arbitrage-free money market? Is it, e.g., possible to determine the arbitrage-free price of a European call option on a bond?*

11.2 Classical approach

Let us now model the short rate of interest $r(t)$ by the univariate Itō stochastic differential equation

$$\mathrm{d}r(t) = \mu(t,r(t))\mathrm{d}t + \sigma(t,r(t))\mathrm{d}W(t) \tag{11.39}$$

where μ and σ are adapted processes, and $W(t)$ is a standard Wiener process defined on the usual probability space $(\Omega, \mathcal{F}, \mathbb{P})$.

The only possibility of investing our capital a priori is to invest it in the bank using a roll-over strategy. As argued above this implies that our capital evolves according to the ordinary differential equation

$$\mathrm{d}B(t) = r(t)B(t)\mathrm{d}t. \tag{11.40}$$

We have considered this money market account repeatedly before, but we should now take into account that the interest rate is stochastic. As argued previously the possibility of using a roll-over strategy implies the existence of a paper with the price process given by (11.40). Now we formalize this as an assumption.

Assumption 11.2 (Price process $B(t)$)**.** *On the capital market, there exists a financial security, $B(t)$, with a price process given by* (11.40), *where the interest rate dynamics of $r(t)$ is given by* (11.39).

The value of a bond clearly depends on the (expected value of the) future evolution of the short rate of interest $r(t)$, so we may consider a bond as *an interest rate derivative*.

Our primary interest is now to discuss what can be said about the structure of the prices of bonds $P(t,T)$ with different maturity dates (Q3). We are faced with the difficulty that it is not possible to trade in the underlying asset, namely the interest rate.

Recall that the arbitrage-free price of a financial derivate in the Black–Scholes model was determined by Δ-hedging a portfolio consisting of a bond and a stock (the underlying asset). In particular, we could trade in both the bond and the stock, and thus generate a replicating portfolio. With respect to bond pricing, there is no underlying asset to trade in, thus we must make the arbitrage argument using at least two bonds with different maturity dates T_1 and T_2.

Before we formalize this approach, let us consider if we can expect to obtain a complete market and if we can determine unique, arbitrage-free prices in this market.

Let us for a moment consider a financial market with M securities (bonds, options, etc.) and N independent sources of noise (Wiener processes). For instance in the Black–Scholes model, we have $M = 2$ and $N = 1$ and we recall that this market is complete and arbitrage-free. We see that $M = 2$ and $N = 1$ satisfies the relation $M = N + 1$ and we may wonder if this relation is generic or if it is merely a coincidence. What happens if $M \leq N + 1$ or $M \geq N + 1$?

The first important observation is that the concepts of no-arbitrage and completeness introduce diametrically opposite restrictions on M versus N. If for instance we fix the number of random sources, N, then each new security yields arbitrage possibilities, which imply that the number of papers should be small compared to the number of random sources, which means that $M \leq N + 1$. On the other hand, each new paper allows us to replicate a given financial derivative X using a replicating portfolio. Thus completeness requires a large number of securities compared to the number of random sources, i.e., at least $M \geq N + 1$.

We state these results in a metatheorem, which does not have a precise mathematical meaning. In each particular case, we should rephrase the metatheorem as a genuine theorem.

Theorem 11.1 (No-arbitrage and completeness metatheorem). *Let M denote the number of a priori given securities (including the risk-free paper, if any). Let N denote the number of independent random sources. Then we have*

- *The market is arbitrage-free if and only if $M \leq N + 1$.*
- *The market is complete if and only if $M \geq N + 1$.*
- *The market if arbitrage-free and complete if and only if $M = N + 1$.*

Proof. The proof is far from trivial in the general case (Delbaen and Schachermayer [1994, 1998] for details). However, the arguments presented above should make it plausible that this holds for diffusion processes. □

Remark 11.4 (Geometrical interpretation). *Let M' denote the number of securities excluding the riskless paper $B(t)$, i.e., $M' = M - 1$. Then we should have*

$M' = N$ in order to obtain an arbitrage-free and complete market. Interpret a realization of the N random sources at time t as a point in the N-dimensional Euclidean space. If $M' = N$ then we have a sufficient number of papers to reach this point (to eliminate the randomness, so to speak).

For the financial market described by (11.39) and (11.40), it follows that there is one security $M = 1$ and one random source $N = 1$. Thus the market is arbitrage-free, but it is not complete. Thus it should be expected that we cannot price a bond uniquely in terms of the riskless paper $B(t)$. The number of securities is simply too limited to enable us to construct a replicating portfolio. However, this does not imply that the fair price of a bond can be an arbitrary value. On the contrary, the point is that in order to obtain arbitrage-free prices, bonds with different maturity dates must satisfy some internal consistency conditions.

In other words, if we assume that the fair price of *one* bond with a *fixed* maturity date T is given, then *all other* bonds may be priced uniquely in *terms of this bond* (and the short rate of interest).

This statement is in complete accordance with (Meta)theorem 11.1 because the market consists of the riskless paper $B(t)$, the short rate of interest model and the bond yields $N = 1$ and $M = 2$. The particular bond given above is called the *benchmark* and it is very important to note that the price of all other bonds are given conditioned on the price of the benchmark bond. In practice, it is, by no means, a trivial task to determine the benchmark.

In order to make the arbitrage argument, we replace the previous assumption by the following.

Assumption 11.3. *Assume that there exists a financial market consisting of the riskless paper $B(t)$ described by* (11.40) *and bonds for every choice of maturity date $T \geq 0$. In addition, assume that the market is arbitrage-free and that the price of a T-bond may be written on the form*

$$P(t,T) = F(r(t),t,T) \tag{11.41}$$

where F is only a function of three real valued variables, and $r(t)$ is given by (11.39).

As T is a parameter, we may also write $F^T(r,t) = F(r,t,T)$. It follows immediately from (11.10) that

$$F(r,T,T) = 1 \text{ for all } r. \tag{11.42}$$

Given this boundary condition, we will now determine the properties of the function F, see (Q4). In the following derivation, we write μ for $\mu(t,r(t))$, and F^T for $F(r(t),t,T)$, etc., for simplicity.

In order to obtain portfolios consisting of bonds with different maturity dates, we need to determine the dynamics of each T-bond. By applying the

Itō formula (8.10) to (11.41) and (11.39), we get

$$dF^T = \left(F_t^T + \mu F_r^T + \frac{1}{2}\sigma^2 F_{rr}^T\right) dt + \sigma F_r^T dW(t) \tag{11.43}$$

where $F_t^T = \partial F^T/\partial t$, etc.

By introducing the following in (11.43)

$$\alpha_T = \frac{F_t^T + \mu F_r^T + \frac{1}{2}\sigma^2 F_{rr}^T}{F^T} \tag{11.44}$$

$$\sigma_T = \frac{\sigma F_r^T}{F^T}, \tag{11.45}$$

we get

$$dF^T = F^T \alpha_T dt + F^T \sigma_T dW(t). \tag{11.46}$$

Note that α_T does not mean the partial derivative of α with respect to T.

Next we consider a self-financing portfolio (u^S, u^T), where u^S denotes the fraction of bonds with maturity date S, and u^T denotes the fraction of bonds with a different maturity date T in the portfolio. The associated value process $V(t)$ is given by

$$dV = V\left(u^T \frac{dF^T}{F^T} + u^S \frac{dF^S}{F^S}\right). \tag{11.47}$$

By inserting (11.46) for F^T and a similar formula for F^S, we get

$$dV = V(u^T \alpha_T + u^S \alpha_S)dt + V(u^T \sigma_T + u^S \sigma_S)dW(t). \tag{11.48}$$

If the portfolio is constructed such that

$$u^T \sigma_T + u^S \sigma_S = 0,$$

then the stochastic part of (11.48) drops out. Under the natural assumption that $u^S + u^T = 1$, we get (after some tedious calculations)

$$dV = V\left(\frac{\alpha_s \sigma_T - \alpha_T \sigma_S}{\sigma_T - \sigma_S}\right) dt. \tag{11.49}$$

Now we have constructed a portfolio without a stochastic element and for the market to be arbitrage-free we must have that the relative growth in $V(t)$ equals the short rate of interest $r(t)$, i.e.,

$$\frac{\alpha_s \sigma_T - \alpha_T \sigma_S}{\sigma_T - \sigma_S} = r(t) \text{ for all } t \tag{11.50}$$

or equivalently

$$\frac{\alpha_S(t) - r(t)}{\sigma_S(t)} = \frac{\alpha_T(t) - r(t)}{\sigma_T(t)}. \tag{11.51}$$

Note that the left hand side of (11.51) does not depend on T and the right hand side does not depend on S. Thus we have obtained a property that does not depend on the particular choices of S and T. We restate this important result in a theorem.

Theorem 11.2 (The market price of risk). *Assume that the bond market is arbitrage-free. Then there exists a process $\lambda(t)$ such that*

$$\frac{\alpha_T(t) - r(t)}{\sigma_T(t)} = \lambda(t) \tag{11.52}$$

for every choice of maturity date $T \geq 0$.

Proof. Follows from the preceding discussion. □

Although the term *the market price of risk* should not be taken too literally, it plays an important role in the following. By inserting (11.52) into (11.46), we get

$$\mathrm{d}F^T = F^T(r + \lambda\sigma_T)\mathrm{d}t + F^T\sigma_T\mathrm{d}W(t). \tag{11.53}$$

We see that the return (the relative growth in F^T) of a T-bond differs from the return of the riskless paper $B(t)$ by the term $\lambda\sigma_T$. This term is called the *risk premium* as it is required to exclude arbitrage opportunities. The risk premium is simply the additional return that the holder of the bond should have in order to take on the risk associated with σ_T diffusion, which is not present in the price process (11.40) for the riskless paper $B(t)$. As σ_T denotes the volatility, λ is also called the *risk premium per unit of volatility*.

It is important to note that $\lambda(t)$ does not depend on T, which implies that all bonds have the same risk premium per unit of volatility (regardless of the maturity date T).

Eq. (11.52) also gives rise to the most important equation in this theory.

Theorem 11.3 (The term structure equation). *In an arbitrage-free market $P^T = P(t,T) = F(r(t),t,T)$ satisfies the term structure equation*

$$\frac{\partial P^T}{\partial t} + (\mu - \lambda\sigma)\frac{\partial P^T}{\partial r} + \frac{1}{2}\sigma^2\frac{\partial^2 P^T}{\partial r^2} - rP^T = 0 \tag{11.54}$$

$$P(T,T) = 1. \tag{11.55}$$

Proof. The boundary condition follows immediately from (11.42). From (11.52), we get

$$\lambda(t)\sigma_T(t) = \alpha_T(t) - r(t).$$

Inserting (11.44) herein yields

$$F_t^T + \mu F_r^T + \frac{1}{2}\sigma^2 F_{rr}^T - r(t)F = \lambda(t)\sigma F_r^T$$

which completes the proof using the fact that $P(t,T) = F(r(t),t,T)$. □

Two important concepts are related to the solution of the term structure equation (11.54).

Definition 11.6 (The duration). *The duration of a security with the price $P(t,T)$ is defined as*

$$\tilde{D}(t,T) = \tilde{D}^T = \frac{\partial P(t,T)}{\partial r} \tag{11.56}$$

and the modified duration is

$$D(t,T) = D^T = \frac{\partial P(t,T)}{\partial r} \Big/ P(t,T). \tag{11.57}$$

Definition 11.7 (The convexity). *The convexity of a security with the price $P(t,T)$ is defined as*

$$\tilde{C}(t,T) = \tilde{C}^T = \frac{\partial^2 P(t,T)}{\partial r^2} \tag{11.58}$$

and the modified convexity is

$$C(t,T) = C^T = \frac{\partial^2 P(t,T)}{\partial r^2} \Big/ P(t,T). \tag{11.59}$$

Rewriting (11.54) we get

$$P^T = \left(\frac{\partial P^T}{\partial t} + (\mu - \lambda\sigma)\frac{\partial P^T}{\partial r} + \frac{1}{2}\sigma^2 \frac{\partial^2 P^T}{\partial r^2} \right) \Big/ r \tag{11.60}$$

or

$$r = \theta + (\mu - \lambda\sigma)D(t,T) + \frac{1}{2}\sigma^2 C(t,T) \tag{11.61}$$

where we have introduced $\theta = \frac{\partial P^T}{\partial t}/P^T$, the durations and the convexity.

Thus it is possible to give each term in (11.61) an economic interpretation: The first term accounts for the time-dependency of the price. The second term accounts for the interest rate dependency of the price, and we call this term the modified duration. The last term accounts for the interest rate dependency of the duration and we call this term the modified convexity.

Remark 11.5 (Approximating the bond price). *If we consider two zero-coupon bonds with different maturity dates T_1 and T_2 with the prices P^1 and P^2, then it is possible to obtain a fairly accurate price by using the associated durations and convexities as opposed to solving* (11.54). *If we assume that the bonds have the same duration D then Equation* (11.61) *yields*

$$r = \theta^1 + (\mu - \lambda\sigma)D(t,T) + \sigma^2 C^1(t,T), \tag{11.62}$$

$$r = \theta^2 + (\mu - \lambda\sigma)D(t,T) + \sigma^2 C^2(t,T). \tag{11.63}$$

Arbitrage possibilities may be excluded by equating (11.62) *with* (11.63), *from which*

$$\sigma^2(C^1 - C^2) = \theta^2 - \theta^1. \tag{11.64}$$

Notice the inverse relations between the convexities and time dependencies.

Whereas durations are available from the Copenhagen Stock Exchange (Københavns Fondsbørs), this is not the case for the convexities. Thus in order to use this simple approximation, one must compute the convexities (e.g., using a finite-difference approximation based on the duration). The approximation is fairly accurate provided that the interest rate changes are small.

11.2.1 Exogenous specification of the market price of risk

The term structure equation is clearly related to the Black–Scholes equation, but it is more complicated to solve due to the presence of the market price of risk, $\lambda(t)$. From (11.52), it follows that λ is a function of both t and $r(t)$, which implies that (11.54) is a partial differential equation in the usual sense. The problem is that $\lambda(t,r)$ is not specified within the modelling framework. It must be specified exogenously and this is an important observation.

It is possible to obtain a Feynman–Kac representation theorem for a closed form solution of the term structure equation (11.54) by studying the process

$$\exp\left(-\int_0^t r(s)\mathrm{d}s\right)\cdot F(r(t),t,T). \tag{11.65}$$

Applying the Itō formula (8.10) to this process and using that $F(r(t),t,T)$ satisfies (11.54) the following theorem may be proved.

Theorem 11.4 (The bond pricing equation)**.** *The bond price $P(t,T)$ is given by the formula*

$$P(t,T) = F(r(t),t,T) = \mathbf{E}^{\mathbb{Q}}\left[\exp\left(-\int_t^T r(s)\mathrm{d}s\right)|\mathscr{F}(t)\right] \tag{11.66}$$

where the martingale measure $\mathbb{Q}$ implies that the expectation should be taken with respect to a martingale measure conditional on $\mathscr{F}(t)$ and that the short rate of interest $r(t)$ has the dynamics

$$\mathrm{d}r(s) = (\mu(s,r(s)) - \lambda(s,r(s))\sigma(s,r(s)))\,\mathrm{d}s + \sigma(s,r(s)\mathrm{d}W(s) \tag{11.67}$$

$$r(0) = r_0. \tag{11.68}$$

Proof. The proof is sketched prior to the theorem, and the (purely technical) details are omitted. □

Equation (11.66) has a very natural interpretation, which becomes clear if it is written as

$$F(r(t),t,T) = \mathbf{E}^{\mathbb{Q}}\left[\exp\left(-\int_t^T r(s)\mathrm{d}s\right)\cdot 1|\mathscr{F}(t)\right].$$

We see that the bond price is simply the expected value of the payoff $X = 1$ at time T discounted until today. The expectation should not be taken with respect to the objective probability measure $\mathbb{P}$. Instead the socalled *risk-adjusted* martingale measure $\mathbb{Q}$ should be used. Recall from the Black–Scholes model

$$\mathrm{d}S(t) = \alpha S(t)\mathrm{d}t + \sigma S(t)\mathrm{d}W(t)$$

that the absolute continuous measure transformation from $\mathbb{P}$ to $\mathbb{Q}$ was obtained by replacing the drift term α by the short rate of interest r. The elimination of arbitrage opportunities is connected to transformations of the drift term, i.e., the drift term should be equal to the short rate of interest $r(t)$. From (11.66)–(11.67) it readily follows that a new martingale measure $\mathbb{Q}$ is associated with each particular choice of $\lambda(t, r(t))$, that is, the martingale measure $\mathbb{Q}$ is not uniquely determined. Thus the model is not complete, and the bond price may not be uniquely determined from the short rate of interest $r(t)$. As previously discussed the market price of risk should be specified exogenously. In other words, there exists a multitude of arbitrage-free bond prices that are consistent with the interest rate $r(t)$. The particular market price of risk (or martingale measure $\mathbb{Q}$) is determined by supply and demand in the bond market. Thus the market participants select the appropriate market price of risk and the associated martingale measure $\mathbb{Q}$ (although they are probably not and need not be aware of it).

In conclusion: the market participants select a market price of risk by trading a particular T-bond (the benchmark bond mentioned before). Thereby they select the martingale measure $\mathbb{Q}$ and the arbitrage-free prices of all other bonds may then be determined uniquely from (11.66)–(11.67). The point is that the other bond prices are given in terms of the benchmark.

11.2.2 Illustrative example

Now we shall apply the presented techniques to a very simple model of the term structure. It is assumed throughout that the spot interest rate $r(t)$ follows the univariate Itō stochastic differential equation (or the single-factor model using the terminology from Chapter 10)

$$\mathrm{d}r(t) = \mu \mathrm{d}t + \sigma \mathrm{d}W(t); \quad r(0) = r_0 \tag{11.69}$$

where μ and σ are constants and $W(t)$ is a standard Wiener process. This model is called the arithmetic random walk or the Merton model. It was considered in Section 10.1.1 (with different parameters), where it was shown that the solution is

$$r(t) = r_0 + \mu t + \sigma W(t) \tag{11.70}$$

and the mean and variance readily follow

$$\mathbf{E}[r(t)] = r_0 + \mu t, \tag{11.71}$$

$$\mathbf{Var}[r(t)] = \sigma^2 t. \tag{11.72}$$

It is seen that there is a drift in the mean, the variance grows with time and negative interest rates cannot be excluded. This model is merely chosen here for its simplicity.

We further assume that the market price of risk is a constant $\lambda(t, r(t)) = \lambda$. These assumptions lead to the following term structure equation

$$\frac{\partial P^T}{\partial t} + (\mu - \lambda\sigma)\frac{\partial P^T}{\partial r} + \frac{1}{2}\sigma^2\frac{\partial^2 P^T}{\partial r^2} - rP^T = 0 \tag{11.73}$$

$$P(T,T) = 1 \tag{11.74}$$

where μ, σ and λ are constants compared to (11.54). It is duly noted that the introduction of the market price of risk implies that the riskless spot interest rate is described by

$$\mathrm{d}r(t) = (\mu - \lambda\sigma)\mathrm{d}t + \sigma \mathrm{d}W(t) \tag{11.75}$$

which follows from (11.73) using the connection between parabolic PDEs and SDEs provided by the Feynman–Kac representation theorems (discussed in Section 8.3). To be precise, the factor in front of the $\partial P^T/\partial r$ term in (11.73) is the drift term in the associated SDE. Similarly the (squared) diffusion term is written in front of the $\partial P^T/\partial r$ term.

In order to determine $P(t,T)$, we assume that it takes the following form

$$P(t,T) = \exp[A(\tau) + B(\tau)r(t)], \qquad \tau = T - t \tag{11.76}$$

where $A(\tau)$ and $B(\tau)$ are functions that only depend on the constants μ, σ and λ and the time-to-maturity $\tau = T - t$. Next, we compute the derivatives given in (11.73)

$$\frac{\partial P}{\partial r} = B(\tau)P(t,T) \tag{11.77}$$

$$\frac{\partial^2 P}{\partial r^2} = B^2(\tau)P(t,T) \tag{11.78}$$

$$\frac{\partial P}{\partial t} = -\frac{\partial P}{\partial \tau} = -(A_\tau(\tau) + B_\tau(\tau)r(t))P(t,T) \tag{11.79}$$

where $A_\tau(\tau)$ denotes the derivative of the function $A(\tau)$ with respect to τ. Inserting these in (11.73) we get

$$\left[-(A_\tau(\tau) + B_\tau(\tau)r(t)) + (\mu - \lambda\sigma)B(\tau) + \frac{1}{2}\sigma^2 B^2(\tau) - r(t)\right] \cdot P(t,T) = 0 \tag{11.80}$$

or

$$-(B_\tau(\tau) + 1)r(t) + \frac{1}{2}\sigma^2 B^2(\tau) + B(\tau)(\mu - \lambda\sigma) - A_\tau(\tau) = 0 \tag{11.81}$$

which shows that (11.76) is indeed a solution to (11.73). If this equation is to be satisfied for all $r(t)$ the following two ordinary differential equations must clearly be satisfied

$$\begin{aligned} -B_\tau(\tau) - 1 &= 0 \qquad (11.82)\\ \frac{1}{2}\sigma^2 B^2(\tau) + B(\tau)(\mu - \lambda\sigma) - A_\tau(\tau) &= 0. \qquad (11.83) \end{aligned}$$

The initial conditions $A(0) = 0$ and $B(0) = 0$ follow immediately from (11.76) as the initial condition $P(T,T) = 1$ should hold for all $r(t)$. By simple integration of (11.82), we get

$$B(\tau) = -\tau \qquad (11.84)$$

which is then substituted into (11.83). As $A(0) = 0$, the solution to (11.83) is easily obtained

$$A(\tau) = \int_0^\tau \left(-(\mu - \lambda\sigma)s + \frac{1}{2}\sigma^2 s^2 \right) ds = -\frac{1}{2}(\mu - \lambda\sigma)\tau^2 + \frac{1}{6}\sigma^2\tau^3. \qquad (11.85)$$

This implies that the bond price $P(t,T)$ is given by

$$P(t,T) = \exp\left(-(T-t)r(t) - \frac{1}{2}(\mu - \lambda\sigma)(T-t)^2 + \frac{1}{6}\sigma^2 (T-t)^3 \right). \qquad (11.86)$$

From (11.13), we get the adjacent term structure of interest rates

$$\begin{aligned} Y(t,T) &= -\frac{\log P(t,T)}{T-t} \\ &= r(t) + \frac{1}{2}(\mu - \lambda\sigma)(T-t) - \frac{1}{6}\sigma^2(T-t)^2. \qquad (11.87) \end{aligned}$$

This expression illustrates a flaw in single-factor spot interest rate models, namely that the entire term structure is shifted if $r(t)$ shifts. Thus if $r(t)$ increases, the entire term structure is shifted upwards. This implies that longer interest rates should rise with the same order of magnitude as the short rate of interest, which is clearly at odds with empirical findings. The long interest rate should clearly be less sensitive to changes in the short rate, i.e., the dynamics of the long interest rates should be slower.

From Definitions 11.6–11.7, we get

$$\begin{aligned} D(t,T) &= -\tau = -(T-t), \qquad (11.88)\\ C(t,T) &= \tau^2 = (T-t)^2. \qquad (11.89) \end{aligned}$$

The shape of the term structure is generally determined by a mixture of (i) future adjustment of the short rate and (ii) the *volatility effects*. Thus it is possible to give each term in (11.87) an economic interpretation as follows:

The future adjustment effect stems from the fact that the larger the drift μ, the more upward sloping is the yield curve. The interest rate volatility exerts two influences on the term structure. First, there is the drift adjustment $-\lambda\sigma$, whose effect is similar to the (pure) adjustment effect discussed above. As empirical studies show that the market price of risk λ is generally negative, the first volatility effect tends to increase the drift $\mu - \lambda\sigma$, which causes lower bond prices (and higher interest rates).

The second volatility effect is the term proportional to σ^2 in (11.87), but its influence is more complicated than the adjustment effect.

If the risk adjusted drift $\mu - \lambda\sigma = 0$, it seems natural to assume a flat term structure, but from (11.87) it is seen that the term structure is uniformly downward sloping which is caused by the socalled second volatility effect. The intuitive argument is that the price reaction to interest rate changes is asymmetrical. The percentage increase from a drop in the short rate (and hence $Y(t,T)$) is greater than the drop in $P(t,T)$ followed by a similar increase in interest rates, and the difference is again positively related to the variance of interest rates. The mathematical reason for the second volatility effect is that the bond price is a convex function of future spot interest rates, and if $f(x)$ is a convex function of x then $\mathbf{E}[f(X)]$ is greater than $f(\mathbf{E}[X])$ (this follows from Jensen's inequality). This phenomenon is called the *convexity of the bond*. Therefore the present bond prices are higher, the higher the interest rate volatility, because they are *potentially* higher in the future.

Generally, the first and second volatility effects have opposite signs, but it is not possible to say which one dominates the other. In (11.87), the second effect clearly dominates as $P(t,T) \to \infty$ as $T \to \infty$. In this model the bond price is not bounded from above by 1 (as it should be), but 0 is still a lower bound for the bond price. As the interest rate can become arbitrarily negative for long periods of time, the bond price may tend to infinity due to the convex relation between short rates and bond prices. Whereas the convexity and the two volatility effects apply in general, the last remarks about the (un)boundedness of the bond price only apply for this (too) simple model.

11.2.3 Modern approach

The results in this section may be derived using the modern approach (basically the Girsanov theorem) along the same lines as in Section 9.3, where a general pricing formula for a large class of financial derivatives was presented. We do not choose so, because it is merely an academic exercise that does not reveal anything new. The main result is, of course, the same as in this section. In particular, the Girsanov kernel turns out to be equal to (minus) the market price of risk, which clearly illustrates the close relation between the market price of risk and the martingale measure $\mathbb{Q}$. See the Notes for references.

Author	Model
Merton	$dr(t) = \theta dt + \sigma dW(t)$
Vasicek	$dr(t) = (\theta + \eta r(t))dt + \sigma dW(t)$
CIR 1	$dr(t) = (\theta + \eta r(t))dt + \sigma\sqrt{r(t)}dW(t)$
Dothan	$dr(t) = \sigma r(t)dW(t)$
Courtadon	$dr(t) = (\theta + \eta r(t))dt + \sigma r(t)dW(t)$
CIR 2	$dr(t) = \sigma r(t)^{3/2}dW(t)$
Cox (& Ross)	$dr(t) = \eta r(t)dt + \sigma r(t)^{\gamma}dW(t)$
Ho–Lee	$dr(t) = \theta(t)dt + \sigma dW(t)$
Black–Derman-Toy	$dr(t) = \eta(t)r(t)dt + \sigma(t)dW(t)$
Hull & White	$dr(t) = (\theta(t) + \eta(t)r(t))dt + \sigma(t)\sqrt{r(t)}dW(t)$

Table 11.2: An overview of one-factor spot interest rate models. Not all of these gives rise to an affine term structure.

11.3 Term structure for specific models

In this section we consider an immediate generalization of the example given above, which gives rise to the socalled *affine term structure models*. This general model class is not empirically founded. It is merely used because it is possible to determine solutions in a closed form of the term structure equation (11.54), which enables us to discuss its properties. We shall provide the general framework and use the Vasicek, Ho–Lee and CIR models as examples. Other examples will be given in the Problems. For an easy reference, the one-factor models considered in Chapter 10 are repeated in Table 11.2.

As argued in Section 11.2.3, the introduction of the market price of risk $\lambda(t, r(t))$ is equivalent to an absolutely continuous measure transformation from the objective probability measure $\mathbb{P}$ to a martingale measure $\mathbb{Q}$. According to the bond pricing equation (11.66), the bond price may be expressed as an expectation under $\mathbb{Q}$. This implies that we could consider a model of the spot interest rate $r(t)$ under $\mathbb{Q}$. In order to limit the amount of tedious calculations, we will simply assume that the models in Table 11.2 *are formulated under* $\mathbb{Q}$, which thus accounts for the market price of risk. Should we wish to specify the spot interest rate model under $\mathbb{P}$, the market price of risk must be inserted explicitly.[1] Please note that the actual interest rates $r(t)$ under $\mathbb{Q}$ have no economic interpretation. They are a mathematical abstraction (at least for $\lambda \neq 0$).

Now we define the affine term structure of interest rates.

[1] In order to remember this we have chosen to use the notation $r(t)$ as opposed to r_t in Chapter 10.

Definition 11.8 (Affine term structure). *If the term structure of interest rates $P(t,T)$ takes the form*

$$P(t,T) = F(r(t),t,T) \tag{11.90}$$

where the function F has the property

$$\log F(r(t),t,T) = A(t,T) - B(t,T)r(t) \tag{11.91}$$

then the term structure is said to be affine in $r(t)$.

Remark 11.6. *Note that the example in Section 11.2.2 gave rise to an affine term structure. We choose to parametrize the functions $A(t,T)$ and $B(t,T)$ in t,T in this more general discussion. The sign in front of $B(t,T)$ is also changed. This notation is the most often applied in the literature. However, the previous notation may also be found.*

The class of affine term structure models is associated with a number of nice properties. It is, e.g., possible to determine simple formulae for the duration and convexity, so it is important to determine the particular infinitesimal characteristics μ and σ in the spot interest rate model

$$\mathrm{d}r(t) = \mu(t,r(t))\mathrm{d}t + \sigma(t,r(t))\mathrm{d}W(t) \tag{11.92}$$

which gives an affine term structure. On the other hand, if $A(t,T)$ and $B(t,T)$ are given a priori then it is an interesting question whether there exist uniquely defined infinitesimal characteristics μ and σ which give rise to this particular term structure. In short, we need to determine the relations between (A,B) and (μ,σ).

First, we consider the restrictions that need to be imposed on μ and σ in order to obtain an affine term structure. Assume that the term structure is of the form (11.91) such that

$$F(x,t,T) = \exp(A(t,T) - B(t,T)x). \tag{11.93}$$

As F should satisfy the term structure equation (11.54), we get

$$A_t(t,T) - \{1 + B_t(t,T)\}x - \mu(t,x)B(t,T) + \frac{1}{2}\sigma^2(t,x)B^2(t,T) = 0 \tag{11.94}$$

where the boundary condition $P(T,T) = 1$ implies that

$$A(T,T) = 0, \quad B(T,T) = 0. \tag{11.95}$$

Assuming that (μ,σ) are given a priori then (11.94) provides a differential equation for the determination of (A,B) and vice versa. We state an important result as a lemma.

Lemma 11.4 (Unique $\mu(t,x)$). *Given a particular set of functions $\sigma(t,x)$, $A(\cdot,T)$ and $B(\cdot,T)$ for every $T \geq 0$, then there exists a unique choice of $\mu(t,x)$ such that μ and σ yield the term structure described by A and B.*

Proof. Follows immediately by solving (11.94) with respect to $\mu(t,x)$. □

If μ and σ are affine functions in x then (11.94) is separable with respect to A and B. Thus we obtain two ordinary differential equations which might be solved as in Section 11.2.2.

Lemma 11.5. *Assume that A, B, μ and σ satisfy* (11.94)*. Then μ is affine in x if and only if σ^2 is affine in x.*

Proof. Trivial. □

Assume that both μ and σ^2 are affine in x, i.e.,

$$\mu(t,x) = a(t)x + b(t), \quad \sigma(t,x) = \sqrt{c(t)x + d(t)}, \tag{11.96}$$

where $a(t)$, $b(t)$, $c(t)$ and $d(t)$ are sufficiently well-behaved functions.

Then (11.94) takes the form

$$A_t(t,T) - b(t)B(t,T) + \frac{1}{2}d(t)B^2(t,T) \\ - \{1 + B_t(t,T) + a(t)B(t,T) - \frac{1}{2}c(t)B^2(t,T)\}x = 0. \tag{11.97}$$

As this equation should be valid for all t and x, it may be separated and written as a system of two ODEs

$$B_t(t,T) = -a(t)B(t,T) + \frac{1}{2}c(t)B^2(t,T) - 1, \tag{11.98}$$

$$A_t(t,T) = b(t)B(t,T) - \frac{1}{2}d(t)B^2(t,T), \tag{11.99}$$

which should be solved subject to the boundary conditions $A(T,T) = 0$ and $B(T,T) = 0$.

Equation (11.98) is called a *Riccati equation.* This is used extensively in control and filtering theory. Once $B(t,T)$ has been determined $A(t,T)$ may be determined by integration of (11.99).

Remark 11.7 (An important trick)**.** *In order to solve* (11.99) *by direct integration it is necessary to reverse the signs on the two terms in* (11.99)*, because the time-derivative of $A_t(t,T) = \partial A(t,T)/\partial t$ is computed with respect to the lower integration limit t. This also implies that the initial condition $A(T,T) = 0$ is automatically fulfilled and we need not introduce (and determine) additional integration constants.*

Lemma 11.6. *Assume that μ and σ are given by* (11.96)*. If the equations* (11.98)–(11.99) *are solvable for $0 \le t \le T$ for every $T \le 0$, then the model has an affine term structure of the form* (11.93) *with the coefficients given by* (11.98)–(11.99).

Proof. Follows from the preceding discussion. □

An interesting question is whether it is only affine functions μ and σ^2 that yield an affine term structure. In general this is *not* the case. However, if we assume that μ and σ are independent of time, then it may be shown that affine functions μ and σ^2 are necessary conditions for an affine term structure. (See the Problems for a proof.)

One of the advantages of affine models (from a mathematical point of view) is that the dynamics of the bond prices (11.20) and the forward rates (11.21) becomes very simple.

Theorem 11.5. *Assume that the model is affine. Then the following holds under the martingale measure* $\mathbb{Q}$.

$$\begin{aligned} \mathrm{d}P(t,T) &= r(t)P(t,T)\mathrm{d}t - \sigma(t,r(t))B(t,T)P(t,T)\mathrm{d}W(t) \qquad (11.100)\\ \mathrm{d}f(t,T) &= \sigma^2(t,r(t))B(t,T)B_T(t,T)\mathrm{d}t + \sigma(t,r(t))B_T(t,T)\mathrm{d}W(t) \end{aligned}$$

where $B_T(t,T) = \partial B/\partial T(t,T)$.

Proof. Omitted. See Björk [2009]. □

In the next four sections, we give examples of the theory described above.

11.3.1 Example 1: The Vasicek model

We wish to determine the term structure for the Vasicek model, which we choose to parametrize under the measure $\mathbb{Q}$ as

$$\mathrm{d}r(t) = \alpha(\beta - r(t))\mathrm{d}t + \sigma \mathrm{d}W(t). \qquad (11.101)$$

Compared to (11.96), we have $a(t) = -\alpha$, $b(t) = \alpha\beta$, $c(t) = 0$ and $d(t) = \sigma^2$.

Eq. (11.98) takes the form

$$B_t(t,T) = \alpha B(t,T) - 1; \quad B(T,T) = 0$$

which has the solution

$$B(t,T) = \frac{1}{\alpha}\left(1 - \exp\left(-\alpha(T-t)\right)\right).$$

Eq. (11.99) takes the form

$$A_t(t,T) = \alpha\beta B(t,T) - \frac{1}{2}\sigma^2 B^2(t,T); \quad A(T,T) = 0$$

which has the solution (using the trick in Remark 11.7)

$$
\begin{aligned}
A(t,T) &= -\alpha\beta \int_t^T B(s,T)ds + \frac{\sigma^2}{2}\int_t^T B^2(s,T)ds \\
&= \left(\frac{\sigma^2}{2\alpha^2} - \beta\right)(T-t) + \frac{1}{\alpha}(1-\exp(-\alpha(T-t)))\left(\beta - \frac{\sigma^2}{\alpha^2}\right) \\
&\quad + \frac{\sigma^2}{4\alpha^3}(1-\exp(-2\alpha(T-t)))
\end{aligned}
$$

where we have left out a number of tedious calculations. Thus the term structure is

$$
\begin{aligned}
Y(t,T) &= -\frac{\log P(t,T)}{T-t} \\
&= \left(\beta - \frac{\sigma^2}{2\alpha^2}\right) + \frac{1}{\alpha(T-t)}\left(1-e^{-\alpha(T-t)}\right)\left(r + \frac{\sigma^2}{\alpha^2} - \beta\right) \\
&\quad - \frac{\sigma^2}{4\alpha^3(T-t)}(1-\exp(-2\alpha(T-t))).
\end{aligned}
$$

It is easily seen that the term structure tends to

$$Y(\infty) = \lim_{T\to\infty} Y(t,T) = \beta - \frac{\sigma^2}{2\alpha^2}.$$

It may be shown that the yield curve is monotonically increasing for $r(t)$ and smaller than or equal to

$$Y(\infty) - \frac{\sigma^2}{4\alpha^2}.$$

For values of $r(t)$ larger than that but below

$$Y(\infty) + \frac{\sigma^2}{2\alpha^2}$$

it is a humped curve. When $r(t)$ is equal to or exceeds this last value, the yield curves are monotonically decreasing; see Figure 11.2 for a sketch.

Note that these results are given under the arbitrage-free martingale measure $\mathbb{Q}$. In order to obtain the results under the objective probability measure $\mathbb{P}$, we should introduce the market price of the risk λ, which we assume is a constant (for simplicity). Recall from the previous discussion that the drift term μ in the spot interest rate model under $\mathbb{P}$ is replaced by $\mu - \lambda\sigma$ under $\mathbb{Q}$. Now we go from $\mathbb{Q}$ to $\mathbb{P}$, which implies that we should add $\lambda\sigma$ to the drift term. Due to the specific parametrization of the Vasicek model in this example, we could substitute β for $\tilde{\beta} + \lambda\sigma/\alpha$, where $\tilde{\beta}$ is the long term mean of the spot interest rate $r(t)$ under the measure $\mathbb{P}$. The reader is encouraged to make this substitution such that the results above are available under $\mathbb{P}$ for future reference.

11.3.2 Example 2: The Ho–Lee model

We now will consider the slightly more complicated Ho–Lee model, which has the $\mathbb{Q}$-dynamics

$$\mathrm{d}r(t) = \phi(t)\mathrm{d}t + \sigma \mathrm{d}W(t) \tag{11.102}$$

where the drift term $\phi(t)$ is allowed to be a deterministic function of time t and σ is a constant. A typical application of this model is to estimate σ from historical data of the spot interest rate, whereas the function $\phi(t)$ is chosen such that the theoretical term structure fits the observed yield curve.

Although the model (11.102) is specified under the measure $\mathbb{Q}$ and the spot interest rates are observed under the objective probability measure $\mathbb{P}$, it is actually reasonable to estimate σ directly from historical data, because the diffusion term is not affected by a measure transformation from $\mathbb{Q}$ to $\mathbb{P}$ and vice versa.

The Ho–Lee model gives rise to an affine term structure, where $B(t,T)$ and $A(t,T)$ should satisfy

$$\begin{aligned} B_t(t,T) &= -1, \qquad B(T,T) = 0 \\ A_t(t,T) &= \phi(t)B(t,T) - \frac{1}{2}\sigma^2 B^2(t,T), \qquad A(T,T) = 0. \end{aligned}$$

It is easy to show the solutions of these ODEs are

$$B(t,T) = T - t, \tag{11.103}$$

$$A(t,T) = \int_0^T \phi(s)(s-T)\mathrm{d}s + \frac{\sigma^2}{2}\frac{(T-t)^3}{3}. \tag{11.104}$$

Thus we have determined the theoretical term structure which we wish to fit to the observed initial yield curve, i.e., the observed bond prices at time $t = 0$. Now we are going to discuss estimation of $\phi(t)$. We denote observed entities by a $*$ such that the observed bond prices at time $t = 0$ are denoted by $P^*(0,T)$ and the associated forward rates by $f^*(0,T)$.

It is easy to show that the forward rates are given by

$$f(0,T) = r(0) + \int_0^T \phi(s)\mathrm{d}s - \frac{\sigma^2}{2}T^2. \tag{11.105}$$

Derivation with respect to T yields

$$f_T(0,T) = \phi(T) - \sigma^2 T. \tag{11.106}$$

As σ^2 is estimated from historical data, and $f_T(0,T)$ may be observed in the market at time $t = 0$, we have that the deterministic function $\phi(t)$ may be determined from

$$\phi(t) = f_T^*(0,t) + \sigma^2 t. \tag{11.107}$$

Thus we have estimated both σ and $\phi(t)$ from market data and we may compute the estimated theoretical term structure by inserting (11.103) into (11.93). However, this is computationally rather demanding. However, it turns out that it is easier to proceed using the forward rates. From Theorem 11.5, we get

$$\mathrm{d}f(t,T) = \sigma^2(t,r(t))B(t,T)B_T(t,T)\mathrm{d}t + \sigma(t,r(t))B_T(t,T)\mathrm{d}W(t).$$

As $B(t,T) = T - t$, this SDE is readily solved and we get

$$f(t,T) = f(0,T) + \sigma^2 t(T - t/2) + \sigma W(t). \tag{11.108}$$

From (11.12), it follows that

$$P(t,T) = \exp\left(-\int_t^T f(t,s)\mathrm{d}s\right). \tag{11.109}$$

Inserting (11.108) herein we get

$$P(t,T) = \exp\left(-\int_t^T f(0,s)\mathrm{d}s - \frac{\sigma^2 Tt}{2}(T-t) - \sigma(T-t)W(t)\right). \tag{11.110}$$

By computing $P(0,T)$ and $P(0,t)$ from this expression and using (11.109), we obtain

$$P(t,T) = \frac{P(0,T)}{P(0,t)}\exp\left(-\frac{\sigma^2 Tt}{2}(T_t) - \sigma(T-t)W(t)\right). \tag{11.111}$$

In order to remove the Wiener process from this result we use a little trick. From Definition 11.5 it follows that

$$r(t) = f(t,t) = f(0,t) + \frac{\sigma^2 t^2}{2} + \sigma W(t). \tag{11.112}$$

Isolating $W(t)$ herein and inserting the result in (11.111) we get the final result

$$P(t,T) = \frac{P^*(0,T)}{P^*(0,t)} \times \exp\left((T-t)f^*(0,t) - \frac{\sigma^2}{2}t(T-t)^2 - (T-t)r(t)\right).$$

Although this result does not look very handy, it is important. As $P^*(0,T)$, $P^*(0,t)$, $f^*(0,t)$ and σ are determined from market data, this result allows us to determine the price of any T-bond.

11.3.3 Example 3: The Cox–Ingersoll–Ross model

In this example, the famous Cox–Ingersoll–Ross model is considered with respect to bond pricing. The spot interest rate model is

$$\mathrm{d}r(t) = \kappa(\theta - r(t))\mathrm{d}t + \sigma\sqrt{r(t)}\mathrm{d}W(t) \tag{11.113}$$

where $\kappa, \theta > 0$ and $\sigma > 0$. It is clear that the drift $\mu(t, r(t)) = \kappa(\theta - r(t))$ and the squared diffusion $\sigma^2(t, r(t)) = \sigma^2 r(t)$ are affine in $r(t)$. Let us repeat the properties of the CIR model. Negative interest rates are ruled out because, loosely speaking, the drift will force the interest rates to rise when it is very small. The line $r(t) = 0$ as a function of t is called a *barrier*.[2] The drift term is mean reverting, meaning that the interest rate reverts around the long term mean θ.

This model also gives rise to an affine term structure and it may be shown that

$$A(t,T) = \frac{2\kappa\theta}{\sigma^2} \ln\left[2\gamma e^{(\kappa-\gamma)(T-t)/2}/g(t,T)\right], \tag{11.114}$$

$$B(t,T) = 2(e^{-\gamma(T-t)} - 1)/g(t,T), \tag{11.115}$$

$$\gamma = \sqrt{\kappa^2 + 2\sigma^2}, \tag{11.116}$$

$$g(t,T) = 2\gamma - (\kappa - \gamma)(e^{-\gamma(T-t)} - 1). \tag{11.117}$$

The forward rate is

$$f(t,T) = r(t) + \kappa(r - \theta)B(t,T) - \frac{1}{2}\sigma^2 r(t) B^2(t,T). \tag{11.118}$$

It may be shown that the long term yield is

$$Y(\infty) = \lim_{T\to\infty} Y(t,T) = \frac{2\kappa\theta}{\kappa + \gamma}. \tag{11.119}$$

This steady-state value implies that the interest rate volatility decreases as a function of T.

For different sets of parameter values, it is possible to obtain yield curves as sketched in Figure 11.2 for the CIR model.

So far we have only considered the yield curve $Y(t,T)$ as a function of $T - t$ (or T), which gave rise to the term structure of interest rates. This is also referred to as the *zero-coupon term structure* because it is based on the yield of zero-coupon bonds. The forward rate $f(t,T)$ as a function of T gives rise to another term structure, namely the *forward rate term structure*.

11.3.4 Multifactor models

In this section, we have only considered one-factor models of the term structure and we have stated that they have a number of flaws. As an example of multifactor models, we briefly discuss the term structure implied by the two-factor model proposed by Longstaff and Schartz [1992], which was discussed

[2]The precise behavior at the barrier depends on the relation between the drift and diffusion parameters (Feller [1951]).

in Section 10.4. Another example is the class of affine term structure models discussed in Section 10.4.2. Despite the nice properties of multifactor models, we do not pursue the topic any further in this book (see the Notes for references). We shall now move on to an alternative framework, where the spot interest rate model may be considered as infinite-dimensional.

11.4 Heath–Jarrow–Morton framework

Our discussion of the bond pricing framework in Section 11.2 was essentially based on a specification of a univariate SDE model of the short rate of interest $r(t)$. Although multifactor models may also be considered, only a limited number of parameters are available. This makes it impossible to make a perfect fit of the term structure, because a parsimonious parametrization imposes some restrictions on the shape of the term structure. The Ho–Lee model, which was considered in Section 11.3.3, contained an infinite number of parameters as the drift term was allowed to be time-dependent. It turned out that it was more tractable to obtain important results using the forward rates. It should also be clear that this approach will be very difficult to complete for more complicated spot interest rate models.

We will now provide an introduction to a formal analysis based on the forward rates, which has been suggested by Heath et al. [1992]. It is therefore often referred to as the *HJM-framework.*

We commence by repeating some important results.

Assumption 11.4. *For every fixed $T \geq 0$, we assume that the forward rates $f(t,T)$ are described by the Itō SDE*

$$\mathrm{d}f(t,T) = \alpha(t,T)\mathrm{d}t + \sigma(t,T)\mathrm{d}W(t) \tag{11.120}$$

where $\alpha(\cdot,T)$ and $\sigma(\cdot,T)$ are adapted processes. The initial forward curve $\{f(0,T);\ T \geq 0\}$ is assumed to be given a priori.

Once the infinitesimal characteristics α and σ, and the initial forward curve $\{f(0,T);\ T \geq 0\}$, have been specified, the entire forward structure $f(t,T)$ is given. Due to the relation

$$P(t,T) = \exp\left(-\int_t^T f(t,s)\mathrm{d}s\right) \tag{11.121}$$

the entire term structure is also given.

The problem is now to determine the infinitesimal characteristics α and σ such that (11.120) and (11.121) give rise to a financial market that generates arbitrage-free bond prices.

As usual, we assume that we have access to a money market account or a riskless paper with the dynamics

$$\mathrm{d}B(t) = r(t)B(t)\mathrm{d}t, \quad B(0) = 1 \tag{11.122}$$

where the short rate is defined by $r(t) = f(t,t)$.

In order to obtain an arbitrage-free market, we wish to establish conditions that guarantee the existence of a measure $\mathbb{Q}$ under which all processes $Z(t,T)$ on the following form become martingales

$$Z(t,T) = \frac{P(t,T)}{B(t)}. \tag{11.123}$$

Remark 11.8. *As the solution to* (11.122) *is*

$$B(t) = \exp\left(\int_t^T r(s)\mathrm{d}s\right),$$

we may refer to the $Z(t,T)$-process as the discounted bond price process.

Lemma 11.3 states that the forward dynamics (11.120) implies that the bond prices have the dynamics

$$\mathrm{d}P(t,T) = (r(t) + b(t,T))\,P(t,T)\mathrm{d}t + a(t,T)P(t,T)\mathrm{d}W(t) \tag{11.124}$$

where the functions $a(t,T)$ and $b(t,T)$ are given by

$$a(t,T) \quad = \quad -\int_t^T \sigma(t,s)\mathrm{d}s, \tag{11.125}$$

$$b(t,T) \quad = \quad -\int_t^T \alpha(t,s)\mathrm{d}s + \frac{1}{2}a^2(t,T). \tag{11.126}$$

It follows from (11.123) that $Z(t,T)$ has the dynamics

$$\mathrm{d}Z(t,T) = b(t,T)Z(t,T)\mathrm{d}t + a(t,T)Z(t,T)\mathrm{d}W(t). \tag{11.127}$$

Thus the question of the existence of a martingale measure $\mathbb{Q}$ is reduced to determining whether there exists a Girsanov transformation $g(t)$ such that the drift term in (11.127) may be eliminated for all T simultaneously.

We fix T and choose a Girsanov kernel g. As discussed in Section 8.4, we may exchange measure from $\mathbb{P}$ to $\mathbb{Q}$ using

$$\mathrm{d}\mathbb{P} = L(T)\mathrm{d}\mathbb{Q} \quad \text{on } \mathscr{F}_T \tag{11.128}$$

where the likelihood process $L(t)$ is given by

$$\mathrm{d}L(t) = g(t)L(t)\mathrm{d}W(t); \quad L(0) = 1. \tag{11.129}$$

This transformation implies that

$$\mathrm{d}W(t) = g(t)\mathrm{d}t + \mathrm{d}V(t), \tag{11.130}$$

where $V(t)$ is a $\mathbb{Q}$-Wiener process.

Inserting (11.130) into (11.127) yields

$$dZ(t,T) = \{b(t,T) + g(t)a(t,T)\}Z(t,T)dt + a(t,T)Z(t,T)dV(t). \quad (11.131)$$

It is readily seen that if $Z(t,T)$ should be a $\mathbb{Q}$-martingale (i.e., the drift term should drop out) we must choose the Girsanov kernel $g(t)$ such that

$$g(t,T) = -\frac{b(t,T)}{a(t,T)} \quad (11.132)$$

where we have stressed that the choice of $g(t,T)$ depends on the fixed T.

Thus, if we fix T, then we may choose the Girsanov kernel given by (11.132), which generates a measure Q_T under which $Z(t,T)$ is a martingale. As both the Girsanov kernel and the measure depend on T, we have no guarantee that a process $Z(t,S)$, $S \neq T$, becomes a $\mathbb{Q}_T$-martingal. However, we wanted to determine a Girsanov transformation that generated a measure under which $Z(t,T)$ would become a martingale for all $T \geq 0$. This implies that the Girsanov kernel may *not* depend on the choice of T.

We state this result as a theorem.

Theorem 11.6. *The following conditions are equivalent:*

(i) *There exists a measure $\mathbb{Q}$ under which every $Z(t,T)$-process becomes a martingale.*

(ii) *For every choice of T and S, we have*

$$\frac{b(t,T)}{a(t,T)} = \frac{b(t,S)}{a(t,S)}, \quad \mathbb{P}\text{-almost surely} \quad (11.133)$$

for all $t \leq \min(T,S)$.

(iii) *The process $g(\cdot,T)$ does not depend on the choice of T.*

(iv) *For every choice of S and T, we have*

$$\alpha(t,T) = -\sigma(t,T)\left(g(t,S) - \int_t^T \sigma(t,s)ds\right). \quad (11.134)$$

Proof. Omitted. □

We state an important result in the following theorem.

Theorem 11.7. *Assume that one of the conditions in Theorem 11.6 is fulfilled. Then the market is arbitrage-free.*

Proof. See Björk [2009]. □

As stated earlier the Girsanov kernel is sometimes referred to as the *market price of risk for T-bonds*. It follows immediately from condition (iii) in Theorem 11.6 that the market price of risk does not depend on T.

Assume that one of the sufficient conditions in Theorem 11.6 is fulfilled. Then we may define a measure $\mathbb{Q}$ under which all discounted bond price processes are martingales. The implications of this statement on the relations between the infinitesimal characteristics $\alpha(t,T)$ and $\sigma(t,T)$ are remarkably simple and are stated in the following important theorem.

Theorem 11.8 (Unique drift term). *Let the forward dynamics under $\mathbb{P}$ be given by*

$$\mathrm{d}f(t,T) = \alpha(t,T)\mathrm{d}t + \sigma(t,T)\mathrm{d}W(t) \tag{11.135}$$

and assume that one of the conditions in Theorem 11.6 is fulfilled. Then the dynamics of the forward rates $f(t,T)$ under the martingale measure $\mathbb{Q}$ is given by

$$\mathrm{d}f(t,T) = \bar{\alpha}(t,T)\mathrm{d}t + \sigma(t,T)\mathrm{d}V(t) \tag{11.136}$$

where the process $\bar{\alpha}(t,T)$ is given by

$$\bar{\alpha}(t,T) = \sigma(t,T)\int_t^T \sigma(t,s)\mathrm{d}s. \tag{11.137}$$

Proof. After the Girsanov transformation the $\mathbb{Q}$-dynamics of (11.135) is

$$\mathrm{d}f(t,T) = \{\alpha(t,T) + g(t)\sigma(t,T)\}\,\mathrm{d}t + \sigma(t,T)\mathrm{d}W(t) \tag{11.138}$$

and then (11.137)–(11.138) follows from (11.134). □

Let us illustrate this setup in a simple example.

Example 11.3 (The Heath–Jarrow–Morton framework). *Consider the simple process*

$$\sigma(t,T) = \sigma > 0.$$

From (11.137), *it follows that*

$$\bar{\alpha}(t,T) = \sigma^2(T-t)$$

such that forward rate process is

$$\begin{aligned}
f(t,T) &= f^*(0,T) + \int_0^t \bar{\alpha}(s,T)\mathrm{d}s + \int_0^t \sigma(s,T)\mathrm{d}V(s) \\
&= f^*(0,T) + \int_0^t \sigma^2(T-s)\,ds + \int_0^t \sigma^2\mathrm{d}V(s) \\
&= f^*(0,T) + \sigma^2 t(T-t/2) + \sigma V(t).
\end{aligned}$$

We see that this solution is equal to the solution of the Ho–Lee model in (11.108)*, and we may proceed as we did in Section 11.3.3.*

Remark 11.9 (Comparison with the classical approach)**.** *We note that the HJM-framework is based upon a specification of the initial forward curve* $f(0,T)$*, which may be determined from market data at time 0. This initial forward curve corresponds to the determination of the market price of risk from a benchmark bond in the classical approach. In addition, we should just specify the diffusion term. Theorem 11.8 states that the drift term is uniquely specified in order to obtain an arbitrage-free market.*

If one wishes to use a more complicated volatility structure than in the previous example, then it is rather straightforward to assume that the volatility depends on the forward rate, i.e.,

$$\sigma(t,T,f(t,T)) : \mathbb{R}^3 \to \mathbb{R}.$$

Given such a function, we must solve

$$\begin{aligned} \mathrm{d}f(t,T) &= \alpha(t,T)\mathrm{d}t + \sigma(t,T,f(t,T))\mathrm{d}V(t), && (11.139)\\ f(0,T) &= f^*(0,T), && (11.140) \end{aligned}$$

where

$$\alpha(t,T) = \sigma(t,T,f(t,T)) \int_0^t \sigma(t,s,f(t,s))\mathrm{d}s. \tag{11.141}$$

The question is now which restrictions must we impose on $\sigma(t,T,f(t,T))$ in order to obtain a solution that does not explode. Such restrictions exist and they are given in the following theorem for completeness.

Theorem 11.9. *Let* $\sigma(t,T,f(t,T)) : \mathbb{R}^3 \to \mathbb{R}$ *be a given function with the properties that*

(i) σ *is Lipschitz-continuous in the third variable.*

(ii) σ *is uniformly bounded.*

(iii) σ *is positive.*

Then there exists a solution of (11.139) *for every choice of the initial forward curve* $f(0,T)$.

Proof. Omitted. □

It is clear that the solution of (11.139) is a difficult problem, which may, in general, only be solved numerically. We shall not go into such methods of solution in this book.

11.5 Credit models

Most models is this book implicitly assume that there is no counterparty risk. However, there is counterparty risk in most over the counter (OTC) trades.

Counterparty risk is the risk that the other party in a derivatives trade is unable to fully pay its debt. It is common that the defaulting party will pay a small fraction ("the recovery") of the debt, but the size of the recovery is typically not known beforehand and will vary from time to time.

Regulatory institutions are currently requiring banks to include this type of risk in the overall risk management; cf. the Basel II and Basel III framework.[3]

This section will introduce counterparty risk in a risk-neutral framework, which can be used to price the basic credit derivative, the *Credit Default Swap*, but can equally well be used to value hybrid derivatives combining credit and market risks. Specifically, we will focus on so-called *reduced form* models, also known as *intensity models*, as these share some nice features with interest rate models.

11.5.1 Intensity models

Default is a binary process (default/no default). Hence, we introduce the default time τ as the stochastic time when a company no longer will be able to pay its debt.

The default time can be thought of as the time when a Poisson process increases from 0 to 1. Poisson processes can have deterministic or stochastic (Cox process) intensity.

A Poisson process is a stochastic process with stationary and independent increments, increasing in unit steps. The risk-neutral probability for default (i.e., the probability for the time inhomogeneous Poisson process to jump) within a (to be infinitesimally) small time interval δt, conditional that the process has not defaulted, is

$$\mathbb{Q}(\tau \in [t, t+\delta t) | \tau > t) = \lambda(t)\delta t. \tag{11.142}$$

Integrating this quantity is known as the Hazard function

$$\Lambda(t) = \int_0^t \lambda(u) \mathrm{d}u. \tag{11.143}$$

It is well known that the jump time, transformed with the Hazard function, is a standard exponential random variable η

$$\Lambda(\tau) \overset{d}{=} \eta \sim Exp(1). \tag{11.144}$$

Hence, we find that

$$\mathbb{Q}(\tau > t) = \mathbb{Q}(\Lambda(\tau) > \Lambda(t) = \mathbb{Q}(\Lambda(\tau) > \eta) = e^{-\int_0^t \lambda(u) \mathrm{d}u}. \tag{11.145}$$

[3] `http://www.bis.org`.

This can be extended to stochastic intensities, arriving at

$$\mathbb{Q}(\tau > t) = \mathbf{E}^{\mathbb{Q}}\left[e^{-\int_0^t \lambda(u)\mathrm{d}u}\right]. \tag{11.146}$$

The similarity with short rate interest models is remarkable!

We can use this framework for defaultable bonds, which will be denoted by $\bar{P}(t,T)$. It follows that

$$\mathbf{1}_{\{\tau>t\}}\bar{P}(t,T) = \mathbf{E}^{\mathbb{Q}}\left[D(t,T)\mathbf{1}_{\{\tau>T\}}|\mathscr{F}(t)\right] \tag{11.147}$$

where $D(t,T) = \exp(-\int_t^T r(s)\mathrm{d}s)$ is a stochastic discount factor. It is rather common that some value is recovered during the default; this is modelled through the recovery rate RR. The value of the bond, when assuming that the recovery is paid out at time T, would then be

$$\mathbf{1}_{\{\tau>t\}}\bar{P}(t,T) = \mathbf{E}^{\mathbb{Q}}\left[D(t,T)\mathbf{1}_{\{\tau>T\}} + RR\cdot D(t,T)\mathbf{1}_{\{\tau\leq T\}}|\mathscr{F}(t)\right] \tag{11.148}$$

$$= \mathbf{E}^{\mathbb{Q}}\left[D(t,T)(1-\mathbf{1}_{\{\tau\leq T\}}) + RR\cdot D(t,T)\mathbf{1}_{\{\tau\leq T\}}|\mathscr{F}(t)\right] \tag{11.149}$$

$$= \mathbf{E}^{\mathbb{Q}}\left[D(t,T)(1-\mathbf{1}_{\{\tau\leq T\}}(1-RR))|\mathscr{F}(t)\right] \tag{11.150}$$

$$= P(t,T)(1-PD\cdot LGD) \tag{11.151}$$

where we used that *probability of default* is given by $PD = \mathbf{E}^{\mathbb{Q}}\left[\mathbf{1}_{\{\tau\leq T\}}|\mathscr{F}(t)\right]$ and *Loss Given Default* is given by $LGD = 1 - RR$.

11.6 Estimation of the term structure — curve-fitting

Clearly the term structure of interest rates plays an important role in our attempts to model financial markets. So far we have discussed it from a theoretical point of view and deduced some properties that pertain to a term structure model.

It should be clear from the material in this chapter that it is by no means a simple task to estimate the term structure, especially not if one wishes to gain some understanding of the properties of the term structure with minimal effort. The estimation methods to be presented differ mainly by their application of a priori knowledge about the term structure of interest rates.

In this section, we describe a number of methods for estimating the term structure from empirical market data. In the financial literature this is sometimes referred to as *calibration*, *the inverse problem* or *inversion of the yield curve*. Here the statistical term *estimation of the term structure* will be used throughout.

In Section 14.11.3, the Extended Kalman filtering technique from Chapter 14 will be used, where the spot interest rate model describes the underlying process and the solution of the bond pricing equation is the measurement equation. Thus the method enables us to estimate both parameters and implied interest rates directly from observed bond prices.

11.6.1 Polynomial methods

In practice it is fairly common to assume that the yield curve may be approximated by a polynomial in T of order s, i.e.,

$$Y(T) = \alpha - 1 + \alpha_1 T + \alpha_2 T^2 + \ldots + \alpha_s T^s. \qquad (11.152)$$

This is a reasonably general formulation. A number of estimation methods exist and have been implemented in statistical packages, which we shall not discuss here.

A program package called RIO, which is based on *cubic splines*, has been developed at the Aarhus School of Business. This package is also used today in a number of financial institutions, because it allows the modeller to split the term structure into a number of segments. The package can also calculate other types of information.

11.6.2 Decay functions

Decay functions are very useful for term structure estimation if the term structure should converge to a constant interest rate for $T \to \infty$. The simplest possible decay function is

$$Y(T) = \alpha_0 + \alpha_1 \exp(-\alpha_2 T). \qquad (11.153)$$

In the next section, we discuss in some detail an extension of this model.

11.6.3 Nelson–Siegel method

The relation between the price of a zero-coupon bond, $P(t,T)$, and the instantaneous forward rate, $F(t,T)$, is given by (11.109), i.e.,

$$P(t,T) = \exp\left(-\int_t^T f(t,s)\mathrm{d}s \right). \qquad (11.154)$$

The yield curve follows from (11.13), i.e.,

$$Y(t,T) = -\frac{\log[P(t,T)]}{T-t} = \frac{1}{T-t}\int_t^T f(t,s)\mathrm{d}s. \qquad (11.155)$$

Today, at $t = 0$, we may observe the yield of a number of bonds with different maturities. In accordance with Nelson and Siegel [1987], we define

$$Y(T) = Y(0,T) = \frac{1}{T}\int_0^T f(0,s)\mathrm{d}s. \qquad (11.156)$$

We assume that the instantaneous forward rate at time is given by

$$f(0,T) = \beta_0 + \beta_1 \exp(-T/\tau) + \beta_2 (T/\tau) \exp(-T/\tau)) \tag{11.157}$$

where β_0, β_1, β_2 and τ are constants. Note that τ is not related to the time-to-maturity $T-t$. By direct integration of (11.157) in (11.156), we get

$$Y(T) = \beta_0 + \beta_1 \frac{1-\exp(-T/\tau)}{T/\tau} + \beta_2 \left(\frac{1-\exp(-T/\tau)}{T/\tau} - \exp(-T/\tau) \right). \tag{11.158}$$

The three components of this equation represent the level, scope and curvature of the yield curve. Assuming that a number of yields for bonds with different maturities are given, the parameters in (11.158) may be estimated by a nonlinear least squares method.

For $\tau = 1$, $\beta_0 = 0$ and $\beta_1 = -1$, we get

$$Y(T) = 1 - (1-\beta_2)(1-\exp(-T))/T - \beta_2 \exp(-T). \tag{11.159}$$

For $\beta_2 \in [-6, 12]$ and T up to 10 years, the yield curves in Figure 11.4 are obtained. It is seen that the Nelson–Siegel model is able to fit a large variety of yield curves, increasing, decreasing and humped yield curves.

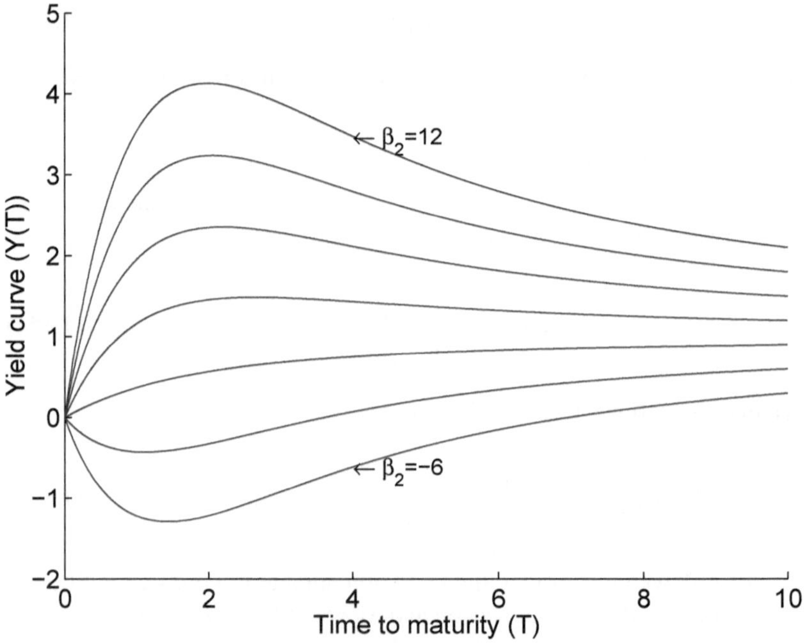

Figure 11.4: A variety of the term structures encompassed by the Nelson–Siegel model.

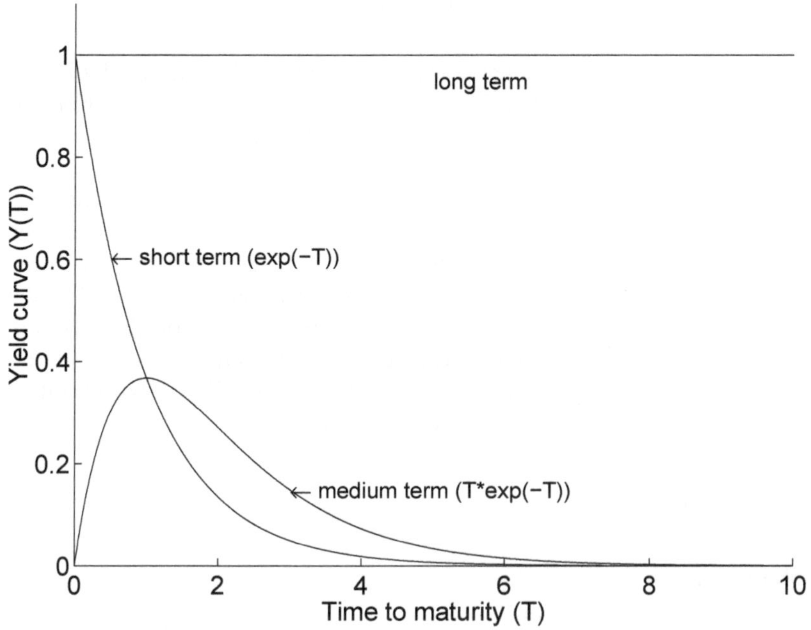

Figure 11.5: An illustration of the short, medium and long term components of the Nelson–Siegel model.

Another way to see the shape of the attainable yield curves is to interpret the terms in (11.159) as measuring the strength of the short, medium and long-term components (or segments) of the yield curve. The contribution of the long term component is β_0, that of the short term components is β_1 and β_2 indicates the contribution of the medium term component. This is depicted in Figure 11.5. Thus estimation of the yield curve is merely a question of obtaining parameter estimates that weigh these three contributions simultaneously.

It can be shown that the Nelson–Siegel model does not give rise to arbitrage-free prices, but there are arbitrage free extensions (Christensen et al. [2011]). Nevertheless the Nelson–Siegel method is used today in a number of financial institutions.

11.7 Notes

For an introduction to the large variety of bonds on the Danish market (Jensen et al. [1994] and Christensen [1995]). In these notes, we have only considered univariate models for the short rate of interest and the forward rates. Extensions to multivariate SDEs may be found in Strickland [1996], Jørgensen [1994],

Duffie [1996], Brennan and Schwartz [1979], Longstaff and Schartz [1992], Chen [1996] or the original paper by Heath et al. [1992] with respect to forward rates.

Multivariate affine models are considered in an excellent article by Duffie and Kan [1996]. See Björk [2009] for the derivation of the term structure equation using the modern approach. A more thorough analysis of the CIR model from a PDE point of view is given by Feller [1951].

Whether one chooses to build the bond pricing framework on the short rate of interest or the forward rate, the pricing equations turn out to be parametrized in (t,T) with T being the fundamental parameter in spite of the fact that the initial discussion showed that a more natural choice would be the time-to-maturity $T-t$. The latter approach is taken in the socalled *Musiela parametrization* (Björk [1996] for further details and references). See Wilmott et al. [1995] and Brigo and Mercurio [2006] for two different but excellent overviews of interest rate and credit derivative products.

11.8 Problems

Problem 11.1

Consider a coupon bond with N payments $\mathbf{c}=(c_1,\ldots,c_N)'$ at discrete time instants $\mathbf{T}=(T_1,\ldots,T_N)'$ and maturity date $T=T_N$.

1. Show that the price of a coupon bond is given by

$$P(t,\mathbf{c},\mathbf{T})=\sum_{i=1}^{n} c_i P(t,T_i) \tag{11.160}$$

by direct application of (11.2).

Problem 11.2

1. Show that the following applies for $t\le s\le T$

$$P(t,T)=P(t,s)\exp\left(-\int_s^T f(t,u)\mathrm{d}u\right) \tag{11.161}$$

and in particular

$$P(t,T)=\exp\left(-\int_t^T f(t,u)\mathrm{d}u\right). \tag{11.162}$$

Problem 11.3

Show that the zero-coupon bond and forward rate term structures are equal for the time-to-maturity τ^*, where the zero-coupon term structure reaches its highest value in the following special cases:

1. The Merton model.
2. The Vasicek model.
3. The Cox–Ingersoll–Ross model.
Can you give an intuitive or financial explanation of this property?

Problem 11.4
Consider an affine term structure.
1. Show that the duration $D(t,T)$ is $-B(t,T)$.
2. Show that the convexity $C(t,T)$ is $B^2(t,T)$.

Problem 11.5
Consider the CIR model

$$\mathrm{d}r(t) = \kappa(\theta - r(t))\mathrm{d}t + \sigma\sqrt{r(t)}\mathrm{d}W(t). \tag{11.163}$$

Assume that the term structure is affine, i.e.,

$$P(t,T) = e^{A(\tau)+B(\tau)r(t)}. \tag{11.164}$$

1. Determine $A(\tau)$ and $B(\tau)$.

Problem 11.6
Consider the Ho–Lee model

$$\mathrm{d}r(t) = \theta(t)\mathrm{d}t + \sigma\mathrm{d}W(t), \tag{11.165}$$

which gives rise to an affine term structure

$$P(t,T) = e^{A(t,T)-B(t,T)r(t)}. \tag{11.166}$$

1. Determine $A(t,T)$ and $B(t,T)$.
2. Determine the forward rates $f(0,T)$.
3. Determine the forward rates $f(t,T)$.
4. Use the relation

$$P(t,T) = \exp\left\{-\int_t^T f(t,u)\mathrm{d}u\right\} \tag{11.167}$$

to show that

$$P(t,T) = \frac{P(0,T)}{P(0,t)}\exp\left\{-\frac{\sigma^2 Tt}{2}(T-t) - \sigma(T-t)W(t)\right\}. \tag{11.168}$$

5. Determine the spot interest rate $r(t)$ from $f(t,\cdot)$.
6. Use this result to eliminate the Wiener process in (11.168).

Problem 11.7

Consider the Nelson–Siegel model described in Section 11.6.3.

1. Show (11.158).

2. Determine $\lim_{T\to\infty} Y(T)$ and $\lim_{T\to 0} Y(T)$. Use these limits to explain why it is reasonable to impose the constraints $\beta_0 > 0$ and $\beta_0 + \beta_1 > 0$.

3. Plot (11.156) and (11.157) as a function of T.

4. Show that the curvature component of (11.158) reaches its maximum for $T = \tau$.

In Svensson [1994], an additional term, $\beta_3 (T/\tau_2) \exp(-T/\tau_2)$, $\tau_2 > 0$, is added to (11.157) to add flexibility to the model and to allow for better fits to real data. The resulting model is called the *Nelson–Siegel-Svensson* model.

5. Compute ($Y(T)$, defined by (11.156), for the Nelson–Siegel-Svensson model.

6. Determine $\lim_{T\to\infty} Y(T)$ and $\lim_{T\to 0} Y(T)$ for the Nelson–Siegel-Svensson model.

In Gilli et al. [2010] and Annaert et al. [2013] some of the problems related to estimating the parameters in the Nelson–Siegel and Nelson–Siegel-Svensson models are discussed.

Chapter 12

Discrete time approximations

In this chapter we introduce some basic issues concerning discrete time approximations of stochastic differential equations, which are used in a later chapter to estimate the parameters in SDEs using the Generalized Method of Moments (GMM). Furthermore the methods are used to simulate discrete observations from a continuous time system, which, for example, can be used to determine the price of a financial derivative in cases where no closed form solution of the pricing formula exist.

12.1 Stochastic Taylor expansion

The stochastic Taylor expansion is a stochastic counterpart of the Taylor expansion in a deterministic framework, and it is essential for the discrete time approximation of stochastic differential equations to be described later in this chapter. The stochastic Taylor expansion is based on an iterated application of the Itō formula. Due to the high complexity of the multi dimensional case we shall only consider one-dimensional stochastic differential equations (Kloeden and Platen [1995]).

Consider the integral form

$$X(t) = X(t_0) + \int_{t_0}^{t} \mu(X(s))\mathrm{d}s + \int_{t_0}^{t} \sigma(X(s))\mathrm{d}W(s) \tag{12.1}$$

for $t \in [t_0, T]$, where it is assumed that the functions μ and σ are "sufficiently" smooth in the neighbourhood of $X(t_0)$. If we apply the Itō formula to the functions μ and σ, and assume that the functions are time homogeneous, we obtain the following

$$X(t) = X_{t_0} + \mu(X(t_0)) \int_{t_0}^{t} \mathrm{d}s + \sigma(X(t_0)) \int_{t_0}^{t} \mathrm{d}W(s) + R \tag{12.2}$$

$$\begin{aligned} R = {} & \int_{t_0}^{t}\int_{t_0}^{s} \mathscr{L}^0 \mu(X(z))\mathrm{d}z\mathrm{d}s + \int_{t_0}^{t}\int_{t_0}^{s} \mathscr{L}^1 \mu(X(z))\mathrm{d}W(z)\mathrm{d}s \\ & + \int_{t_0}^{t}\int_{t_0}^{s} \mathscr{L}^0 \sigma(X(z))\mathrm{d}z\mathrm{d}W(s) \\ & + \int_{t_0}^{t}\int_{t_0}^{s} \mathscr{L}^1 \sigma(X(z))\mathrm{d}W(z)\mathrm{d}W(s) \end{aligned} \tag{12.3}$$

where the operators $\mathscr{L}^0$ and $\mathscr{L}^1$ are defined as

$$\mathscr{L}^0 = \mu \frac{\partial}{\partial X} + \frac{1}{2}\sigma^2 \frac{\partial^2}{\partial X^2}, \tag{12.4}$$

$$\mathscr{L}^1 = \sigma \frac{\partial}{\partial X}. \tag{12.5}$$

This is the most simple Taylor expansion, where Itō's formula is only used once. The deterministic integral in the Taylor expansion (12.2) is equal to the length of the discretization interval $t - t_0$, and the stochastic integral is Gaussian with distribution $N(0, t - t_0)$.

By continuously expanding the integrands of the multiple integrals in the remainder R, multiple integrals with constant integrands will appear. For example if we use the Itō formula on the integrand $\mathscr{L}^1\sigma(X(z))$ in (12.2) we get the following

$$\begin{aligned} X(t) = {} & X(t_0) + \mu(X(t_0)) \int_{t_0}^{t} \mathrm{d}s + \sigma(X(t_0)) \int_{t_0}^{t} \mathrm{d}W(s) \\ & + \mathscr{L}^1 \sigma(X(t_0)) \int_{t_0}^{t} \int_{t_0}^{s} \mathrm{d}W(z)\mathrm{d}W(s) + \bar{R} \end{aligned} \tag{12.6}$$

where the remainder $\bar{R}$ is a sum of multiple integrals with non-constant integrands.

In Section 12.3 the Itō-Taylor expansion is used to obtain discrete time approximations with different degrees of accuracy. In the same manner, we can obtain more accurate Taylor approximations by including more multiple stochastic integrals in the Taylor expansion, because these integrals contain additional information about the sample path of the stochastic process.

12.2 Convergence

In order to get a measure of the amount of error introduced in the discrete time approximation, two definitions of convergence are stated in the following. The distinction between the two definitions refers to whether the continuous-time discretized stochastic process approximates the sample paths of (12.1) pathwise for all t, or if it just approximates the moments or some probabilistic properties of (12.1).

To measure the magnitude of the approximation error introduced by the pathwise approximation $\{Y^\delta(t)\}$, with maximum step size δ, of an Itō process $\{X(t)\}$, consider the absolute error criterion

$$\varepsilon = \mathbf{E}[|X(T) - Y^\delta(T)|] \tag{12.7}$$

where the error is expressed as the expectation of the absolute value of the difference between the Itō process and the approximation at a finite terminal time T.

Definition 12.1 (Strong convergence). *A general time discrete approximation $Y^\delta(t)$ with maximum step size δ* converges strongly *to X at time T if*

$$\lim_{\delta \to 0} \mathbf{E}[|X(T) - Y^\delta(T)|] = 0, \tag{12.8}$$

and if there exists a positive constant C, which does not depend on δ, and a finite $\delta_0 > 0$ such that

$$\varepsilon(\delta) = \mathbf{E}[|X(T) - Y^\delta(T)|] \le C\delta^\alpha \tag{12.9}$$

for each $\delta \in (0, \delta_0)$, then Y^δ is said to converge strongly of order $\alpha > 0$.

In many practical situations we do not need such a strong convergence as the pathwise approximation considered above. For instance, we may only be interested in the computation of moments, probabilities or other functionals of the Itō process. Since the requirements for such a simulation are not as demanding as for the pathwise approximations, it is natural and convenient to classify these approximations separately. For that purpose we define the concept of weak convergence.

Definition 12.2 (Weak convergence). *A general time discrete approximation Y^δ with maximum step size δ* converges weakly *to X, at time T as $\delta \downarrow 0$, with respect to a class C of polynomials $g : \mathbb{R}^d \to \mathbb{R}$ if we have*

$$\lim_{\delta \to 0} \left| \mathbf{E}[g(X(T))] - \mathbf{E}[g(Y^\delta(T))] \right| = 0, \tag{12.10}$$

and if there exists a positive constant D, which does not depend on δ, and a finite $\delta_0 > 0$ such that

$$\varepsilon(\delta) = \left| \mathbf{E}[g(X(T))] - \mathbf{E}[g(Y^\delta(T))] \right| \le D\delta^\beta \tag{12.11}$$

for each $\delta \in (0, \delta_0)$, then Y^δ is said to converge weakly of order $\beta > 0$.

In Kloeden and Platen [1995] it is shown that the strong and weak convergence criteria lead to the development of different discretization schemes. As we shall see in the following a given dicretization scheme usually has different orders of convergence with respect to the two criteria.

12.3 Discretization schemes

12.3.1 Strong Taylor approximations

12.3.1.1 Explicit Euler scheme

The simplest strong Taylor approximation is the Euler scheme, also called the Euler-Maryama scheme. It utilizes only the first two terms in the simple Taylor expansion (12.2), and it attains the order of strong convergence $\gamma = 0.5$. In the one-dimensional case the *Euler scheme* has the form

$$Y_{n+1} = Y_n + \mu(Y_n)\Delta + \sigma(Y_n)\Delta W \tag{12.12}$$

where

$$\Delta = \tau_{n+1} - \tau_n \tag{12.13}$$

is the length of the time discretization interval, and

$$\Delta W = W_{\tau_{n+1}} - W_{\tau_n} \tag{12.14}$$

is the $N(0,\Delta)$ increment of the Wiener process W.

12.3.1.2 Milstein scheme

If we add one additional term to the Euler scheme, we obtain a scheme proposed by Milstein [1974], which is of order 1.0 strong convergence.

$$Y_{n+1} = Y_n + \mu(Y_n)\Delta + \sigma(Y_n)\Delta W + \frac{1}{2}\sigma(Y_n)\sigma^{'}(Y_n)[(\Delta W)^2 - \Delta] \tag{12.15}$$

where the prime denotes the derivative with respect to the state variable. It is readily seen that the Euler scheme and the Milstein scheme coincide if the diffusion term σ is independent of the state variable, because then the last term in (12.15) drops out. Due to the fact that the multiple integral can be expressed as

$$\int_{t_0}^{t}\int_{t_0}^{s} \mathrm{d}W(z)\mathrm{d}W(s) = \frac{1}{2}[(\Delta W)^2 - \Delta] \tag{12.16}$$

the Milstein scheme appears to correspond with the stochastic Taylor expansion (12.6) — refer to Kloeden and Platen [1995] for details.

12.3.1.3 The order 1.5 strong Taylor scheme

The order 1.5 strong Taylor scheme is given by

$$\begin{aligned} Y_{n+1} \quad = \quad & Y_n + \mu\Delta + \sigma\Delta W + \frac{1}{2}\sigma\sigma^{'}[(\Delta W)^2 - \Delta] \\ & +\mu^{'}\sigma\Delta Z + \frac{1}{2}(\mu\mu^{'} + \frac{1}{2}\sigma^2\mu^{''})\Delta^2 \\ & +(\mu\sigma^{'} + \frac{1}{2}\sigma^2\sigma^{''})[\Delta W\Delta - \Delta Z] \\ & +\frac{1}{2}\sigma(\sigma\sigma^{''} + (\sigma^{'})^2)[\frac{1}{3}(\Delta W)^2 - \Delta]\Delta W \end{aligned} \tag{12.17}$$

where μ and σ are evaluated at Y_n and ΔZ is a random variable representing the double stochastic integral

$$\Delta Z = \int_{\tau_n}^{\tau_{n+1}}\int_{\tau_n}^{s} \mathrm{d}W(s)\mathrm{d}s. \tag{12.18}$$

In Kloeden and Platen [1995] it is shown that ΔZ is normally distributed with zero mean and variance equal to $\frac{1}{3}\Delta^3$. The covariance between ΔW and ΔZ is $\frac{1}{2}\Delta^2$.

12.3.2 Weak Taylor approximations

As with the strong approximations, the desired order of convergence determines where the Taylor expansion must be truncated. However, the weak convergence criterion only concerns probabilistic aspects of the sample path and not the sample path itself. Therefore, for a certain degree of convergence, the required number of terms of the expansion is less for the case of weak convergence than for the case of strong convergence if a certain degree of convergence is desired.

For example it can be shown that the Euler approximation attains the order of weak convergence $\beta = 1.0$, whereas it only attains the order $\alpha = 0.5$ of strong convergence.

12.3.2.1 The order 2.0 weak Taylor scheme

The order 2.0 weak Taylor scheme is given by

$$\begin{aligned} Y_{n+1} &= Y_n + \mu\Delta + \sigma\Delta W + \frac{1}{2}\sigma\sigma'[(\Delta W)^2 - \Delta] + \\ &\quad \mu'\sigma\Delta Z + \frac{1}{2}(\mu\mu' + \frac{1}{2}\sigma^2\mu'')\Delta^2 + \\ &\quad (\mu\sigma' + \frac{1}{2}\sigma^2\sigma'')[\Delta W\Delta - \Delta Z]. \end{aligned} \tag{12.19}$$

Compared with the order 1.5 strong Taylor scheme the order 2.0 weak Taylor scheme is simpler, even though the degree of convergence is higher.

12.3.3 Exponential approximation

Some attention has recently been given to so-called exponential schemes (Mora [2005]) as these are generally better for stiff systems. The methodology does only apply to models where the diffusion is independent of the state, reducing the applicability somewhat.

The idea is to approximate the diffusion by an Ornstein-Uhlenbeck process, rather than an arithmetic Brownian motion (cf. the explicit Euler scheme). This idea is far from new, as it was used in Madsen and Melgaard [1991], Kristensen and Madsen [2003]. The advantage of approximating using an Ornstein-Uhlenbeck process is increased stability and, for some schemes, increased rate of convergence. Here, we present the Euler-exponential scheme

$$Y_{n+1} = e^{J(\mu)\delta}(Y_n + (\mu - J(\mu)Y_n)\Delta + \sigma\Delta W) \tag{12.20}$$

where $J(\mu)$ is the Jacobian of μ. This is a first-order scheme, but a similar, second order version can be found in Mora [2005].

12.4 Multilevel Monte Carlo

Consider the standard problem of approximating an expectation, $\mathbf{E}[\Phi(S(T))]$, with some numerical scheme, say the Euler-Maruyama scheme, $\{S_t^\delta\}_{t\in[0,T]}$, with $\delta = T/M$. The error between the numerical approximation and the exact value is then given by

$$\varepsilon = \frac{1}{N}\sum_{n=1}^{N}\Phi(S^\delta(T)) - \mathbf{E}[\Phi(S(T))]. \tag{12.21}$$

This error can be decomposed into

$$\varepsilon = \underbrace{\left(\frac{1}{N}\sum_{n=1}^{N}\Phi(S^\delta(T)) - \frac{1}{N}\sum_{n=1}^{N}\Phi(S(T))\right)}_{\text{Discretization bias}} + \underbrace{\left(\frac{1}{N}\sum_{n=1}^{N}\Phi(S(T)) - \mathbf{E}[\Phi(S(T))]\right)}_{\text{Variance}} \tag{12.22}$$

where the bias from the first term is $\mathcal{O}(\delta)$ and the variance from the second term is $\mathcal{O}(1/N)$, leading to a mean squared error (MSE) of

$$MSE = c_1\delta^2 + \frac{c_2}{N}. \tag{12.23}$$

Balancing these terms means that $\delta^2 \propto 1/N$. If the MSE equals ε^2, the $\delta^2 = \mathcal{O}(\varepsilon^2)$ and $1/N = \mathcal{O}(\varepsilon^2)$ which means that the complexity needed for a root mean squared error of size ε is

$$\text{Complexity} = M_\varepsilon N_\varepsilon = \mathcal{O}(\varepsilon^{-1})\mathcal{O}(\varepsilon^{-2}) = \mathcal{O}(\varepsilon^{-3}). \tag{12.24}$$

It turns out that this complexity can be reduced substantially to $\mathcal{O}(\varepsilon^{-2}(\log(\varepsilon))^2)$ by organizing the computations in a clever way (Giles [2008]), called MultiLevel Monte Carlo (MLMC).

Consider a simple approximation computed at the crudest possible scale, $\delta_0 = T$, computed using N_0 samples. That approximation, called P_0, will be severely biased but the complexity is low as only a single step is taken. The idea behind multilevel Monte Carlo is to compute a series of corrections with $\delta_l = M^{-1}T$ (M being an integer) to this crude level. Denote the Monte Carlo approximation at level l using N_l samples by P_l. It then follows that the expected value of the sequence of approximations is

$$\mathbf{E}\left[P_0 + \sum_{l=1}^{L}(P_l - P_{l-1})\right] = \mathbf{E}[P_L] \tag{12.25}$$

which is the accuracy of the finest level of approximations. The question is if the sequence of approximations can be computed in a less expensive way. This can in fact be done, provided that ideas related to so-called control variates are used.

The correction term, $Y_l = P_l - P_{l_1}$, is computed from two different levels of discretization using the same Brownian path, as this will introduce a strong coupling between these approximations. The paths should be independent of the other levels of approximation. Straightforward calculations (Giles [2008] for details), show that the variance of the sequence of corrections $\sum_{l=1}^{L} Y_l$ is given by

$$\mathbf{Var}[Y_l] = \sum_{l=1}^{L} N_l^{-1} V_l \tag{12.26}$$

where V_l is the variance computed for a single Brownian path while the computational cost is given by

$$\text{Cost} = \sum_{l=1}^{L} N_l \delta_l^{-1}. \tag{12.27}$$

It can be shown that the variance is minimized for a fixed computational cost when $N_l \propto \sqrt{V_l \delta_l}$, and that $V_l = \mathcal{O}(\delta_l)$.

The number of samples N_l needed to obtain an overall variance of ε^2 is $N_l = \mathcal{O}(L\delta_l \varepsilon^{-2})$ while the corresponding bias, provided that an Euler-Maruyama scheme is used, is $\mathcal{O}(\delta_L)$. Hence, we can compute the number of levels needed as

$$\mathcal{O}(M^{-L}T) = \varepsilon \tag{12.28}$$

leading to $L = \log(\varepsilon^{-1}))/\log(M) + \mathcal{O}(1)$. The total computational cost for achieving a MSE of at most $2\varepsilon^2$ would then be

$$\text{Cost} = \sum_{l=1}^{L} N_l \delta_l^{-1} = \sum_{l=1}^{L} \mathcal{O}(L\delta_l \varepsilon^{-2})\delta_l^{-1} = \mathcal{O}(\varepsilon^{-2}L^2) = \mathcal{O}(\varepsilon^{-2}(\log(\varepsilon))^2). \tag{12.29}$$

This is a remarkable result as the cost for a perfect algorithm without bias would be $\mathcal{O}(\varepsilon^{-2})$. Variations of the multilevel Monte Carlo method have been applied to, e.g., American options (Belomestny et al. [2013]). For simulation of exit times, see Higham et al. [2013].

12.5 Simulation of SDEs

Since explicit solutions of stochastic differential equations do only exist in a limited number of cases, numerical solution methods must be used. Different numerical approaches have been proposed, such as Markov chain approximations where both the state and the time variables are discretized. However for simulation purposes we shall use discrete time approximations because they have been presented in this chapter. By choosing a sufficiently small length of the subinterval Δ, the discretization schemes above can be used to generate discrete observations of a continuous-time system.

To illustrate some aspects of the simulation of a time discrete approximation of an Itō process we shall examine a simple example.

Example 12.1. *Consider the geometric Brownian motion*

$$dX(t) = \mu X(t)dt + \sigma X(t)dW(t), \qquad X(0) = x_0 > 0. \tag{12.30}$$

We know from Example 8.10 that the solution of (12.30) *is given by*

$$X(t) = x_0 \exp\left(\left(\mu - \frac{1}{2}\sigma^2\right)t + \sigma W(t)\right). \tag{12.31}$$

The knowledge of the explicit solution gives us the possibility of comparing the discretization schemes with the exact solution and to calculate the error. To simulate a trajectory of the Euler approximation of the geometric Brownian motion we simply start from the initial value $Y(0) = X(0)$ and proceed recursively to generate the next value from

$$Y_{n+1} = Y_n + \mu Y_n \Delta + \sigma Y_n \Delta W_n \tag{12.32}$$

where ΔW_n is the $N(0,\Delta)$ increment of the Wiener process in the interval with length $\Delta = \tau_n - \tau_{n-1}$, which we assume constant. The Milstein approximation of the Geometric Brownian Motion is given by

$$Y_{n+1} = Y_n + \mu Y_n \Delta + \sigma Y_n \Delta W_n + \frac{1}{2}\sigma^2 Y_n((\Delta W_n)^2 - \Delta). \tag{12.33}$$

For comparison, we can use (12.31) *to determine the corresponding values of the exact solution for the same sample path of the Wiener process, obtaining*

$$X_{\tau_n} = x_0 \exp\left(\left(\mu - \frac{1}{2}\sigma^2\right)\tau_n + \sigma \sum_{i=1}^{n} \Delta W_{i-1}\right). \tag{12.34}$$

In Figure 12.1 the exact process as well as the Euler and Milstein approximation are plotted for different values of the interval length Δ. It is readily seen that the approximations become better as the number of subintervals increases. Furthermore it is seen, as expected, that the Milstein scheme provides a better approximation than the Euler scheme.

Example 12.2. *Valuation of European call options in the Black & Scholes universe was covered in Chapter 9. Here, we have valuation options using Monte Carlo. The model we consider is given by*

$$dS(t) = rS(t)dt + \sigma S(t)dW(t) \tag{12.35}$$

with $S_0 = 100$, $r = 0.4$ and $\sigma = 0.3$. The time to maturity was $T = 0.5$, while the strike was varied between 80 and 120 in steps of 10. We consider four different cases:

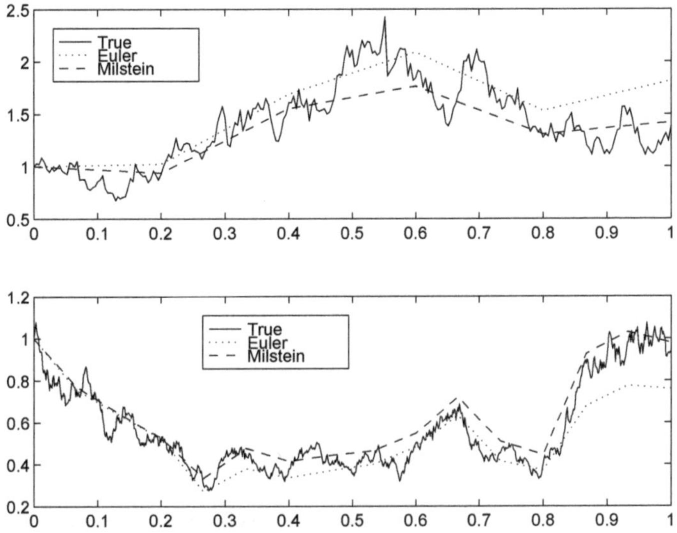

Figure 12.1: Euler and Milstein approximation and the exact solution to (12.31) with initial value $X(0) = 1$, drift parameter $\mu = 1$ and diffusion parameter $\sigma = 1$ for $\Delta = \frac{1}{5}$ (upper plot) and $\Delta = \frac{1}{15}$ (lower plot).

- *Exact value, computed using Equation* (9.45) *and* (9.46).
- *Crude Monte Carlo, using Euler-Maruyama without subsampling.*
- *Monte Carlo simulation using exact simulation, i.e., using the solution to the geometric Brownian motion.*
- *Multilevel Monte Carlo, using* $M = 4$.

All Monte Carlo algorithms used the same number of random samples (in all $N = 21\,760$ *samples) in order to make the results comparable.*

The resulting call prices are presented in Figure 12.2. It can be seen that the exact Monte Carlo is unbiased, the multilevel Monte Carlo is virtually unbiased, while the crude Monte Carlo is clearly biased (but the sign of the bias depends on the contract). The variance is roughly the same for all methods.

The convergence of the multilevel Monte Carlo for different levels of refinement is shown in Figure 12.3. It can be seen that just a few correction terms are usually enough to obtain nearly unbiased results.

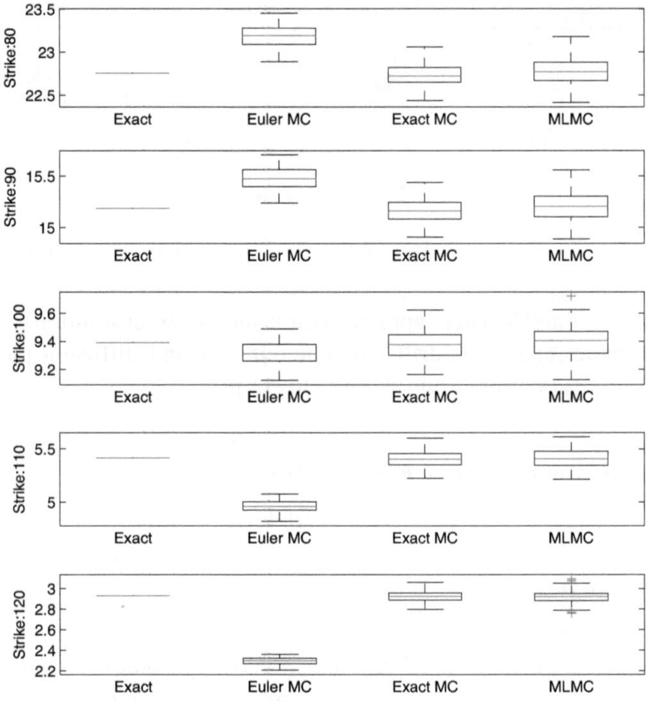

Figure 12.2: Prices for a European call option computed using the exact formula, an Euler-Maruyama scheme without subsampling, exact Monte Carlo and multilevel Monte Carlo.

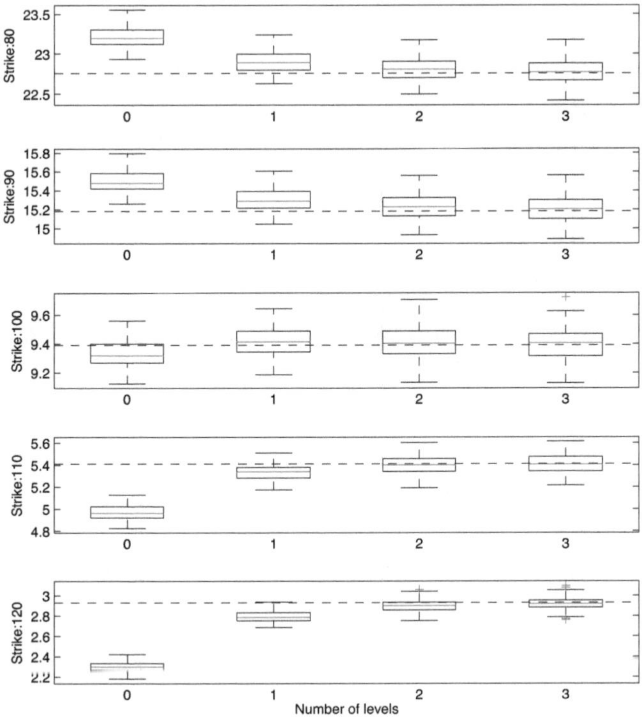

Figure 12.3: Convergence of multilevel Monte Carlo to the exact price (dashed line) as a function of the number of correction terms used.

Chapter 13

Parameter estimation in discretely observed SDEs

13.1 Introduction

This chapter describes methods for estimating parameters in stochastic differential equations (SDEs). A brief introduction to the GMM method is given, but a major part of the presentation is devoted to a class of maximum likelihood methods which can be used for estimation parameters in both linear and non-linear SDEs.

It is clear that a method for estimating parameters of non-linear stochastic differential equations can also be used for estimating the parameters of a linear stochastic differential equation. If a linear model is considered, it is, however, advantageous to take the linearity into account at the estimation procedure. Likewise it is beneficial to simplify the method if it is known that the model is time invariant.

In this section we shall briefly introduce the various types of models which will be considered in the subsequent sections.

There are several reasons why it is advantageous to consider the continuous-discrete time state space approach:

- If any physical knowledge is available it is easily included in the model, since the system equation is described in continuous time.
- The estimated parameters are readily interpreted by experts in the field.
- Multivariate models are easily considered.
- Time varying models can be handled.
- Missing observations, as well as time varying sampling times, can be handled.
- It is often the case that less parameters are needed for the continuous time formulation than for the traditional discrete time formulation.
- The solution of the Itō equation is a Markov process.

The main limitation is the difficulty to derive estimators, or, rather, deriving the Maximum Likelihood estimator in closed form. Instead, we have to rely on approximations of the Maximum Likelihood estimator.

There are some perhaps unexpected results[1] regarding asymptotic properties of the estimators that are useful to know.

Example 13.1 (Estimating parameters in the drift and diffusion). *Consider the arithmetic Brownian motion*

$$\mathrm{d}X(t) = \mu \mathrm{d}t + \sigma \mathrm{d}W(t). \tag{13.1}$$

The solution is well known, $X(t_{n+1}) - X(t_n) = \mu(t_{n+1} - t_n) + \sigma(W(t_{n+1}) - W(t_n))$, implying that each difference of observations is an independent Gaussian random variable. All that is needed is to compute the mean and covariance! The drift is estimated by computing the mean, and compensating for the sampling $\delta = t_{n+1} - t_n$

$$\hat{\mu} = \frac{1}{\delta N} \sum_{n=0}^{N-1} X(t_{n+1}) - X(t_n). \tag{13.2}$$

Expanding this expression reveals that the MLE for μ is given by

$$\hat{\mu} = \frac{X(t_N) - X(t_0)}{t_N - t_0}. \tag{13.3}$$

The only thing that matters is the lengths of the observation window; recording measurements inside the sample is of no use whatsoever for the drift parameter.

The situation is different for the diffusion (σ) parameter, as the MLE is given by

$$\hat{\sigma}^2 = \frac{1}{\delta(N-1)} \sum_{n=0}^{N-1} (X(t_{n+1}) - X(t_n) - \hat{\mu}\delta)^2 \overset{d}{\to} \sigma^2 \frac{\chi^2(N-1)}{N-1} \tag{13.4}$$

which converges to the correct quantity. The σ parameter can be well estimated by either having a short sampling interval and sampling frequently, or by having a fixed sampling frequency and sampling for a very long time.

13.2 High frequency methods

It should be clear from Example 13.1 that the variance term can be estimated using high frequency data. In fact, that variance estimator is closely linked to the convergence of the stochastic integral and the Itō formula. Here we assume that the process we study is a compound Poission Jump Diffusion

$$\mathrm{d}X(t) = \mu(t, X(t))\mathrm{d}t + \sigma(t, X(t))\mathrm{d}W(t) + \mathrm{d}Z(t) \tag{13.5}$$

with $Z(t) = \sum_{n=1}^{N(t)} J_n$ where J are the stochastic jumps and $N(t)$ is the Poisson process.

---

[1] Similar results exist in the theory on discrete time series analysis.

Let $\pi_N = [0 = \tau_0 < \tau_1 < \ldots \tau_N = T]$ be a partition of the interval $[0,T]$, where $\sup|\tau_{m+1} - \tau_m| \to 0$, and define

$$RV = \sum_{n=1}^{N} (X(\tau_n) - X(\tau_{n-1}))^2. \tag{13.6}$$

Then it follows the statistic RV, called the *Realized Variance* estimator, converges to the Quadratic Variation (QV) of the process, cf. Section 13.7.

$$RV \xrightarrow{p} \int \sigma(s,X(s))^2 \mathrm{d}s + \sum_{n=1}^{N(t)} J_n^2 = QV \tag{13.7}$$

while a small modification called the *bipower* estimator defined as

$$BPV = \frac{\pi}{2} \sum_{n=1}^{N} |X(\tau_{n+1}) - X(\tau_n)|\,|X(\tau_n) - X(\tau_{n-1})| \tag{13.8}$$

converges to the continuous component

$$BPV \xrightarrow{p} \int \sigma(s,X(s))^2 \mathrm{d}s. \tag{13.9}$$

Shifting the computations a single step will eliminate jumps as the jumps only contribute to one of the terms, while the other term will be very small when the partitioning gets finer and finer.

The implication of these methods (Barndorff-Nielsen [2002], Barndorff-Nielsen and Shephard [2004]) is that high frequency data can be used to estimate the variance and jump parts with very good accuracy. However, market microstructure (Hansen and Lunde [2006], Zhang et al. [2005]), generally prevents us from going to the limit, and there seems to be a consensus that sampling too often will contaminate the data more than the additional variance reduction obtained due to the larger data set.

We illustrate the realized volatility by computing it on simulated data from a geometric Brownian motion; see Figure 13.1. The constant volatility of the log returns implies that the integrated squared volatility grows linearly.

Computing the realized variance and bipower variation on index returns on the Swedish OMXS30, as shown in top graph in Figure 13.2, reveals that the variance is not constant; cf. Section 5.5.2 and 5.5.3.

These statistics can also be used to investigate whether there are jumps as the difference $RV - BPV$ should equal to the sum of the squared jumps

$$RV - BPV \xrightarrow{p} \sum_{n=1}^{N(t)} J_n. \tag{13.10}$$

This difference is computed in the lower graph in Figure 13.2, where some

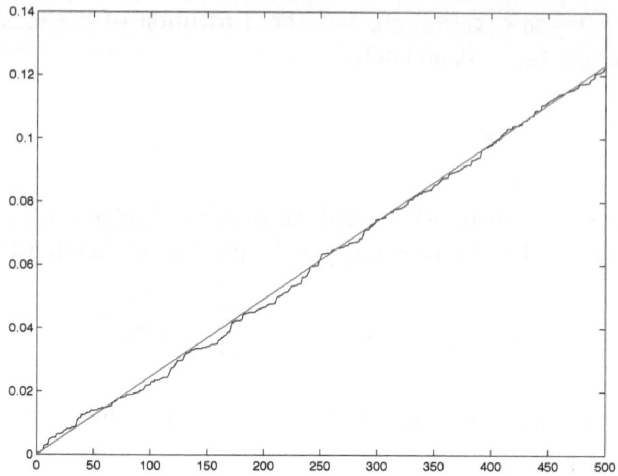

Figure 13.1: Realized variance computed on simulated log returns from a geometric Brownian motion

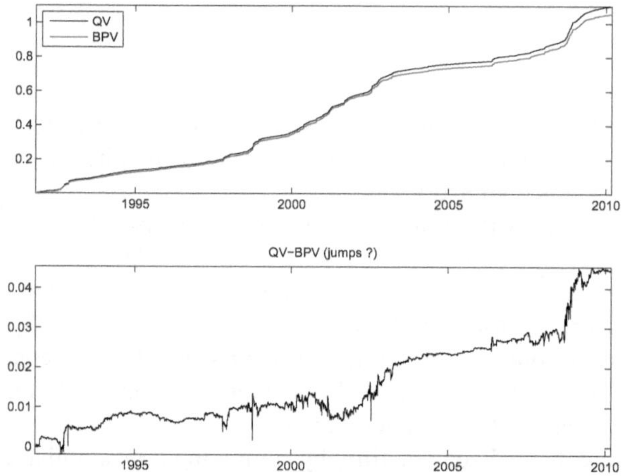

Figure 13.2: Realized variance and bipower variation computed on log returns on the OMXS30 index (top graph) and the difference between the bipower variation and realized variance (bottom graph).

evidence for jumps is presented. Notice that most jumps are rather modest in size, and also that the jumps often seem to cluster to periods of high variance.

Realized volatility was used in Phillips and Yu [2009] to derive Maximum Likelihood estimators for some diffusion processes by first estimating the integrated volatility and then using methods like those in Section 8.4.4.

13.3 Approximate methods for linear and non-linear models

The complexity estimating parameters in discretely observed diffusions, i.e., estimating parameters when the full state vector is observed as discrete time points, depends on a number of factors, most important being the dynamics of the process and the sampling frequency.

Many data sets are sampled at high frequency, compared to the dominant dynamics of the stochastic system, making the bias due to discretization of the SDEs using any of the schemes in Chapter 12 acceptable.

The simplest discretization, the explicit Euler method, would for the stochastic differential equation

$$dX(t) = \mu(t, X(t))dt + \sigma(t, X(t))dW(t) \tag{13.11}$$

correspond to the *Discretized Maximum Likelihood* (DML) estimator given by

$$\hat{\theta}_{DML} = \underset{\theta \in \Theta}{\operatorname{argmax}} \sum_{n=1}^{N-1} \log \phi\left(X(t_{n+1}), X(t_n) + \mu(t_n, X(t_n))\Delta, \Sigma(t_n, X(t_n))\Delta\right) \tag{13.12}$$

where $\phi(x, m, P)$ is the density for a multivariate normal distribution with argument x, mean m and covariance P and

$$\Sigma(t, X(t)) = \sigma(t, X(t))\sigma(t, X(t))^T, \tag{13.13}$$

and $\Delta = t_{n+1} - t_n$ is the time between two consecutive observations.

Note that the Euler scheme and the Milstein scheme coincide when the diffusion term is independent of the state vector. Similarly, it was shown in Chapter 12 that higher order method can readily be derived when the diffusion term is independent of the state vector, which indicates that transformations to get rid of state dependence are generally a good idea.

13.4 State dependent diffusion term

If the SDE contains a state dependent diffusion term then the methods described in the previous section cannot be used directly. Frequently it is, however, possible to transform the SDE into an equivalent SDE where the diffusion term is independent of the state vector. The equivalent SDE contains the same parameters and describes a relation between the same input and output variables.

13.4.1 A transformation approach

We shall only consider the scalar case here. The transformation approach is based on the Itō formula which we restate here for convenience.

Theorem 13.1 (The Itō formula). *Let $X(t)$ be a solution to*

$$\mathrm{d}X(t) = \mu(t,X(t))\mathrm{d}t + \sigma(t,X(t))\mathrm{d}W(t) \tag{13.14}$$

and $\varphi\colon \mathbb{R}^2 \mapsto \mathbb{R}$ be a $C^{1,2}(\mathbb{R}^2)$-function applied to $X(t)$

$$Y(t) = \varphi(t,X(t)). \tag{13.15}$$

Then it holds that

$$\mathrm{d}Y(t) = \left[\frac{\partial \varphi}{\partial t} + \mu \frac{\partial \varphi}{\partial X(t)} + \frac{1}{2}\sigma^2 \frac{\partial^2 \varphi}{\partial X(t)^2}\right] \mathrm{d}t + g\frac{\partial \varphi}{\partial X(t)}\mathrm{d}W(t). \tag{13.16}$$

Proof. See page 147. □

Notice that the diffusion term in the new Itō process $\mathrm{d}Y(t)$ is equal to the product of g and $\partial\varphi/\partial x$. This leads us to the following lemma.

Lemma 13.1. *Let $X(t)$ and φ be defined as above, then by choosing the transformation*

$$\varphi(x_t,t) = \int \frac{1}{\sigma(t,X(t))}\,\mathrm{d}X(t) \tag{13.17}$$

the new process $Z(t) = \varphi(X(t),t)$ will be an Itō process with a constant diffusion term.

The procedure is easily generalized to the multivariate case where the matrix $\mathbf{g}(\mathbf{X}(t),t)$ only contains non-zero values on the diagonal, but is far more complicated in the general case (cf. Aït-Sahalia [2008]).

Example 13.2 (Transformation of the CKLS-model). *Consider the CKLS-model (Chan et al. [1992]):*

$$\mathrm{d}X(t) = \alpha(\theta - X(t))\mathrm{d}t + \sigma X(t)^{\gamma}\mathrm{d}W(t) \tag{13.18}$$

where $X(t)$ is the short term interest rate, and α and θ are parameters related to the drift term and δ and γ are related to the diffusion term.

The drift term represents a tendency to pull the process back towards its long-term mean θ with the rate of adjustment determined by α. The diffusion term describes that the variability (the volatility) is increasing with x if $\gamma > 0$.

Some important models used in the field of finance are obtained as a special case of the CKLS-model:

$$\begin{aligned} \gamma &= 0 \text{ we get the Vasicek model (Vasicek [1977])} \\ \gamma &= \frac{1}{2} \text{ we get the Cox–Ingersoll–Ross model (Cox et al. [1985])} \end{aligned}$$

By applying the lemma, the following transformation is suggested in order to obtain a constant diffusion term in a new process which contains the same parameters and relates the same input and output.

$$Z(t) = \varphi(x_t, t) = \int \frac{1}{X(t)^\gamma} \,\mathrm{d}X(t) = \frac{1}{1-\gamma} X(t)^{1-\gamma}. \tag{13.19}$$

The SDE for $Z(t)$ is found by using the Itō formula. Hence we need

$$\frac{\partial \varphi}{\partial t} = 0\,, \; \frac{\partial \varphi}{\partial x} = X(t)^{-\gamma}\,, \; \frac{\partial^2 \varphi}{\partial x^2} = -\gamma X(t)^{-\gamma-1}. \tag{13.20}$$

Insertion into the Itō formula leads to the following SDE for $Z(t)$

$$\mathrm{d}Z(t) = \left[\alpha\theta \left((1-\gamma)Z(t)\right)^{\frac{\gamma}{\gamma-1}} - \alpha(1-\gamma)Z(t) - \frac{\gamma\sigma^2}{2(1-\gamma)Z(t)} \right] \mathrm{d}t \tag{13.21}$$

$$+\sigma \mathrm{d}W(t). \tag{13.22}$$

13.5 MLE for non-linear diffusions

It is rarely possible to do full maximum likelihood estimation for non-linear diffusions, but the likelihood function can often be approximated arbitrarily well. Some technical difficulties are avoided if the class of models is restricted to discretely observable models.

There are at least three types of competing algorithms that are computationally efficient. The most general, and also the computationally least efficient class of algorithms, are the Monte Carlo simulation based estimators. The Fokker-Planck based estimators are computationally more efficient (at least in low dimensions). Finally, the series expansion approach is the computationally most efficient algorithm but it is also the most restrictive estimator. Common for all estimators is that their computational efficiency is usually improved if the diffusion term is independent of the states of the process; cf. Section 13.4.

13.5.1 Simulation-based estimators

The class of simulation based estimators can be applied to virtually any continuous time Markov process, for which a numerical scheme has been derived. The basic idea is to calculate the unknown transition probability density $p(x_t|x_s)$ by successive approximations. Assume that $s < \tau_1 < \tau_i < \tau_{N-1} < t$. The transition probability density is then (due to the law of total probability and the Markov property) given by

$$p(x_t|x_s) = \int p(x_t|x_{\tau_i}) p(x_{\tau_i}|x_s) dx_{\tau_i}.$$

This can be iterated N times, and the following expression is derived

$$p(x_t|x_s) = \int p(x_t|x_{\tau_N}) \int \dots \int p(x_{\tau_1}|x_s) dx_{\tau_1} \dots dx_{\tau_N}.$$

The $N \times d_X$ dimensional integral ($d_X = \dim(X(t))$) is easily calculated using Monte Carlo methods (e.g. Pedersen [1995]). An implementation of this algorithm is actually quite easy as the numerical representation of the integral

$$p(x_t|x_s) = \int p(x_t|x_\tau)p(x_\tau|x_s)\mathrm{d}x_{\tau_i}$$

is given by

$$p_K(x_t|x_s) = \frac{1}{K}\sum_{k=1}^{K} p(x_t|x_\tau^k)$$

where x_τ^k was generated from $p(x_\tau|x_s)$, see Chapter 12 for numerical schemes. However, the simple Monte Carlo approximation is usually too inaccurate to be useful (e.g. Durham and Gallant [2002]), and variance reduction is regularly applied. An efficient version was introduced in Durham and Gallant [2002], and uses a combination of antithetic variables, moment matching and importance sampling (so-called Brownian bridge sampler, see Problem 8.9). Lindström [2012a] improves that Brownian bridge sampler further by introducing a regularization term that improves the performance for sparsely sampled models.

The simulation based estimators converge as $1/\sqrt{K}$ regardless of dimension. This leads to relatively slow convergence in low dimensions but is very competitive in higher dimensions.

13.5.1.1 Jump diffusions

Similar methods have been developed for jump diffusions and Lévy driven SDEs (e.g. Hellquist et al. [2010], Lindström [2012b]). A computationally attractive alternative to direct maximization of the likelihood function is to use the EM algorithm (e.g. Sundberg [1974], Dempster et al. [1977]).

The EM algorithm finds the Maximum Likelihood estimate by iteratively alternating between computing the Expectation of the *intermediate quantity*

$$Q(\theta, \theta') = \mathbf{E}\left[\log p_\theta(X,Y)|Y,\theta'\right] \tag{13.23}$$

where X are some latent variable and Y the observations, and maximizing that quantity

$$\theta_{m+1} = \operatorname{argmax} Q(\theta, \theta_m). \tag{13.24}$$

Computing the posterior distribution is similar to the simulated maximum likelihood methods. Define Y as the observations ($Y = Y_{t_1}, \ldots, Y_{t_N}$) and $X = (X_{\tau_1}, \ldots, X_{\tau_{N-1}})$ as latent values of the process in between the observation ($t_1 < \tau_1 < \ldots < \tau_{N-1} < t_N$). The posterior is then given by

$$p(X_{\tau_n}|Y_{t_n}, Y_{t_{n+1}}) \propto p(Y_{t_{n+1}}|X_{\tau_n})p(X_{\tau_n}|Y_{t_n}). \tag{13.25}$$

It is therefore possible (this is very similar to what is done in the bootstrap filter, see Section 14.10) to use resampling of particles generated from the naive dynamics to compute a sample from the posterior distribution (Lindström [2012b]).

The intermediate quantity will typically be easy to maximize as the transition density for a short time interval is well approximate using even simple discretization schemes (cf. Chapter 12), typically leading to a sum of logarithms of Gaussian densities.

13.5.2 Numerical methods for the Fokker–Planck equation

The Fokker-Planck based estimators apply deterministic numerical schemes to the Fokker-Planck equation, a parabolic partial differential equation governing the evoluation of the transition probability density.

The Crank-Nicholson scheme was applied in Lo [1988] while Lindström [2007] used higher order schemes as well. It is usually computationally efficient to use higher order finite difference schemes. The Fokker-Planck equation is typically solved by defining a grid in the domain of the process and approximating the derivatives in the domain with central differences on the grid. This reduces the partial differential equation

$$\frac{\partial p}{\partial t}(x,t) = -\frac{\partial}{\partial x}\left(\mu(x_t)p(x,t)\right) + \frac{1}{2}\frac{\partial^2}{\partial x^2}\left(\sigma^2(x_t)p(x,t)\right)$$

to a system of linear differential equations

$$\frac{\mathrm{d}\mathbf{p}}{\mathrm{d}t}(t) = \mathbf{A}\mathbf{p}(t) + \mathbf{b}$$

which has a closed form solution. It was shown in Lindström [2007] that the rate of convergence of the Fokker-Planck based estimators is significantly faster than, i.e., simulation based estimators, but it is known the rate deteriorates as the dimension increases.

The partial differential equation approach can also be used to compute moments or eigenfunctions, which could lead to substantial computational savings as fewer PDEs need to be solved numerically. These can be used to derive GMM or Quasi-likelihood estimators (see Höök and Lindström [2014] for details).

13.5.3 Series expansion

The Aït-Sahilia estimator (Aït-Sahalia [2002, 2003]) derives a closed form expression of the transition probability density. This is achieved by approximating the true transition probability density by a standard Gaussian random variable and correcting for the deviations using Hermite polynomials (Hermite polynomials are orthogonal polynomials associated to the standard Gaussian density). Unfortunately the correction only does converge if the true density is similar to the standard Gaussian density.

The solution in Aït-Sahalia [2002] is to transform the process $\mathrm{d}X(t) = \mu_X(X(t))\mathrm{d}t + \sigma_X(X(t))\mathrm{d}W(t)$ to a new representation where the diffusion term is independent of $X(t)$; cf. Section 13.4. This can be achieved by introducing

$$Y(t) = \gamma(X(t)) = \int^{X(t)} \frac{\mathrm{d}u}{\sigma_X(u)}$$

resulting in

$$\mathrm{d}Y(t) = \left(\frac{\mu_X(\gamma^{-1}(Y(t)))}{\sigma_X(\gamma^{-1}(Y(t)))} - \frac{1}{2}\frac{\partial \sigma_X}{\partial x}(\gamma^{-1}(Y(t))) \right) \mathrm{d}t + \mathrm{d}W(t).$$

The second step is to normalize $Y(t)$ by its approximative standard deviation

$$Z(t) = \frac{Y(t) - Y(s)}{\sqrt{t-s}}.$$

The density for $Z(t)$ is then expanded in Hermite polynomials (orthogonal polynomials with respect to the Gaussian density) as

$$p_Z(z|y_s) = \phi(z)\left(1 + \sum_{j=1}^{\infty} \eta_Z^{(j)}(t-s, y_s; \theta) H_j(z)\right),$$

where the formula to calculate $\eta_Z^{(j)} = 1/(j!)E_Z[H_j(Z)]$ is given in Aït-Sahalia [2003], $H_j(z)$ are Hermite polynomials and $\phi(z)$ is the density of a standard Gaussian random variable. The closed form expression for $p_Z(z|y_s)$ is then used to calculate $p_X(x_t|x_s)$. It is not guaranteed that the Hermite expansion will generate a pdf (i.e., a density that $\geq$ for all function values and integrates to one). Another approach is then to work with log densities ($\log p$) rather than densities (p) (Aït-Sahalia [2002]). That would eliminate the risk for negative densities, but the approximation will still not integrate to one, unless infinitely many terms are included in the expansion.

The estimator is very efficient from a computational point of view when $t-s$ is small. A multivariate version of the algorithm was presented in Aït-Sahalia [2008], but the generalization is not as smooth as one could hope; the expansion is only valid for so-called *reducible diffusions*, which excludes many models in financial economics such as stochastic volatility models.

13.6 Generalized method of moments

The *Generalized Method of Moments* is a method attributable to Hansen [1982] which can be used for estimating parameters in stochastic differential equations. Similar ideas (called estimation function) can be found in Bibby and Sørensen [1995]; see Sørensen [2012] for a recent overview.

For the GMM method no explicit assumption about the distribution of the observations is made, but the method can include such assumptions. In fact, it is possible to derive the ML estimator as a special case of the GMM estimator.

The standard version of the GMM method requires that all the state variables are observed directly. This is clearly a drawback of the method, since it dramatically limits the complexity of the models which can be considered. In the modeling of spot interest rates, this is a severe restriction, due to the fact that the spot interest rate is not observed directly, but only implicitly via the bond prices. Furthermore, the estimation does not take place directly in the continuous-time model; the stochastic differential equations must be discretized (see Chapter 12), before using the GMM method, and the sampling time must be constant. The best reference to discretization techniques so far is Kloeden and Platen [1995] and Platen and Bruti-Liberati [2010]; see also Chapter 12.

13.6.1 GMM and moment restrictions

We shall introduce the moment restrictions by first considering an example which is of great interest in statistical finance.

Example 13.3 (GMM estimates of the CKLS model). *Consider the following stochastic differential equation*

$$dr(t) = (\theta + \eta r(t))dt + \sigma r(t)^{\gamma} dW(t) \tag{13.26}$$

where $W(t)$ is a standard Wiener process. This model, which is called the CKLS model (Chan et al. [1992]), is often used to model the short term risk-less interest rate. The structure of the CKLS model implies that the conditional mean and variance of the short term rate depend on the level of $r(t)$.

The observations are in general given in discrete time. Hence the model (13.26) has to be formulated in discrete time before setting up any moment restrictions which can be evaluated using the discrete time data.

In financial and economical applications the Euler approximation method (see Chapter 12) is most often used to formulate the discrete time equivalent of the continuous time model. Using the Euler approximation of model (13.26) we obtain the following discrete time model

$$r_{k+1} = r_k + (\theta + \eta r_k)\Delta + \varepsilon_{k+1} \tag{13.27}$$

where

$$\mathbf{E}[\varepsilon_{k+1}|B_k] = 0 \tag{13.28}$$

$$\mathbf{E}[\varepsilon_{k+1}^2|\mathscr{F}_k] = \sigma^2 r_k^{2\gamma}\Delta \tag{13.29}$$

and where $\mathscr{F}_k$ denotes the information set at time t_k.

Under the assumption that the restrictions implied by the model, i.e., by (13.27), (13.28) *and* (13.29) *are true, the following moment restrictions follow*

$$\mathbf{E}[\varepsilon_{t+1} - \mathbf{E}[\varepsilon_{t+1}|\mathscr{F}_t]] = 0, \tag{13.30}$$

$$\mathbf{E}[\varepsilon_{t+1}^2 - \mathbf{E}[\varepsilon_{t+1}^2|\mathscr{F}_t]] = 0. \tag{13.31}$$

The GMM procedure consists of replacing the expectation $\mathbf{E}[\cdot]$ *with its sample counterpart, using the N observations available* $\{r(k)\ ;\ k = 1, \cdots, N\}$.

Now we are ready to formulate the GMM method more formally. Assume that the observations are given as the following sequence of random vectors:

$$\{\mathbf{x}_t\ ;\ t = 1, \cdots, N\}$$

and let θ denote the unknown parameters ($\dim(\theta) = p$).

Let $\mathbf{f}(\mathbf{x}_t, \theta)$ be a $q \geq p$-dimensional zero mean function, which is chosen as some *moment restrictions* implied by the discretized model of $\mathbf{x}_t$.

The GMM estimates are found by minimizing

$$J_N(\theta) = \left(\frac{1}{N}\sum_{t=1}^{N}\mathbf{f}(\mathbf{x}_t, \theta)\right)^T \mathbf{W}_N \left(\frac{1}{N}\sum_{t=1}^{N}\mathbf{f}(\mathbf{x}_t, \theta)\right) \tag{13.32}$$

where $\mathbf{W}_N \in \mathbb{R}^{q\times q}$ is a positive semidefinite *weight matrix*, which defines a metric subject to which the quadratic form has to be minimized. The key observation is that any remaining bias in the moment conditions (e.g., (13.30) or (13.31)) is going to increase the J_N function.

Example 13.4 (GMM estimates of the CKLS model (cont.)). *Consider again the CKLS model given in Eq. (13.26), and the Euler approximative discrete time equivalent model given by* (13.28)–(13.29). *The unknown parameters are* $\theta = (\theta, \eta, \gamma, \sigma)^T$.

In order to use the GMM method we may use the moment restrictions given by

$$\mathbf{f}(r_k, \theta) = \begin{pmatrix} \varepsilon_{k+1} - \mathbf{E}[\varepsilon_{k+1}|\mathscr{F}_k] \\ (\varepsilon_{k+1} - \mathbf{E}[\varepsilon_{k+1}|\mathscr{F}_k])\, r_k \\ \varepsilon_{k+1}^2 - \mathbf{E}[\varepsilon_{k+1}^2|\mathscr{F}_k] \\ (\varepsilon_{k+1}^2 - \mathbf{E}[\varepsilon_{k+1}^2|\mathscr{F}_k])\, r_k \end{pmatrix} = \begin{pmatrix} \varepsilon_{k+1} \\ \varepsilon_{k+1} r_k \\ \varepsilon_{k+1}^2 - \sigma^2 r_k^{2\gamma}\Delta \\ (\varepsilon_{k+1}^2 - \sigma^2 r_k^{2\gamma}\Delta) r_k \end{pmatrix}. \tag{13.33}$$

Note that in the second and fourth equation the variable r_k *is used as an instrumental variable. Those equations are justified by the fact that* r_k *is independent of the entities* $(\varepsilon_{k+1} - \mathbf{E}[\varepsilon_{k+1}|\mathscr{F}_k])$ *and* $(\varepsilon_{t+1}^2 - \mathbf{E}[\varepsilon_{k+1}^2|\mathscr{F}_k])$.

Some extensions of the GMM for diffusions include *Simulated GMM* often called Simulated Method of Moments (SMM) (McFadden [1989]). Monte Carlo simulations can be used to compute arbitrarily accurate approximations of moments, thereby eliminating the bias caused by the discretization scheme. Solving PDEs is a computationally attractive alternative in many cases (Höök and Lindström [2014]).

The characteristic function is known for a fairly large class of processes, as presented in Section 7.5. These can be used to construct suitable moments without having to use any discretization scheme (Singleton [2001] and Chacko and Viceira [2003]). It can be useful to add many moment conditions (Carrasco et al. [2007]), who showed that Maximum Likelihood efficiency is achieved when a continuum of moments is employed in the estimation, although there is a practical upper limit when employing the method on real data (for example, the number of conditions has to be smaller than the number of observations).

Another approach suitable for diffusion (or Markov processes in general) is to use eigenfunctions of the generator as moments (Kessler and Sørensen [1999]). The downside is that these can be tricky to compute, and other methods may be preferred (i.e., maximum likelihood methods) for simple models where eigenfunctions are computable in closed form.

13.7 Model validation for discretely observed SDEs

Model validation for linear, discrete time models is a well known subject. Not only do we know how to estimate the parameters in most models, but there is also a large variety of suggestions on how we can validate the models.

Continuous-time models based on stochastic differential equations are harder to validate except for linear models, where validation techniques developed for discrete time models can be applied. Instead, we are often restricted to techniques telling us whether one model is better than another using e.g. LR and Wald tests, which is based on general theory on likelihood functions, not the models per se.

13.7.1 Generalized Gaussian residuals

Discrete time residuals are usually defined as standardized martingale increments, i.e.,

$$\varepsilon_k = \frac{X_k - \mathbf{E}[X_k|\mathscr{F}_{k-1}}{\sigma(X_k|\mathscr{F}_{k-1})}$$

where $\{\varepsilon_k\}_{k\geq 0}$ is assumed to be a sequence of *iid* random variables. This definition is only valid for discrete time models, and using this definition on data generated by a diffusion process will not (in general) generate an *iid* sequence.

The difficulties encountered when working with validation of diffusion processes can be attributed to the (unknown) transition probability density, $p(x_s, s; x_t, t)$, implying that $\{\varepsilon_k\}_{k\geq 0}$ is not an *iid* sequence.

Let us, however, assume that we know (or can calculate) the transition probability density. We could then transform all innovations to a sequence of identically distributed random variables with a known distribution, making the validation problem easier.

This is done by calculating the conditional distribution function for all pairs of observation, $F_{X_k|X_{k-1}}(x) = \mathbb{P}(X_k \le x_k|X_{k-1}) = \int_{-\infty}^{x_k} p(x_{t_{k-1}}, t_{k-1}; x, t_k)\mathrm{d}x$. Having calculated the distribution function, we use the fact that the distribution function applied to the stochastic variable is a uniformly distributed random variable

$$U_k = F_{X_{t_k}|X_{t_{k-1}}}(X_{t_k};\theta).$$

It can also be shown that the sequence $\{U_k\}_{k\ge 0}$ is pairwise independent (e.g. Lindström [2004, 2003]). Note that we have not assumed stationarity of the process, i.e., time variations, non-linearities and non-equidistantly sampled data are allowed. Stationarity will, however, often simplify the calculations of the cumulative transition probability density. The sequence can be used to obtain generalized Gaussian residuals by transforming the sequence once more:

$$Y_k = \Phi^{-1}(U_k).$$

The sequence $\{Y_k\}_{k\ge 0}$ will inherit the nice properties of $\{U_k\}_{k\ge 0}$ but the Gaussian residuals offer many advantages to uniform residuals. Most important is the property that uncorrelated Gaussian random variables are independent random variables, but it may also be argued that there are other advantages of using Gaussian residuals for validation (e.g. distributional tests and outlier detection).

The Gaussian residuals may be difficult to calculate as the inversion of the standard Gaussian distribution function is numerically sensitive. It is thus important that the transition probability density can be calculated accurately for all pairs of observations. It is recommended to approach this problem by solving the Fokker-Planck equation (see Section 13.5.2) numerically to calculate the transition probability density. Simulation could also be used but importance sampling would be needed to preserve the accuracy in the tails.

13.7.1.1 Case study

The first set of data used is simulated data from the Cox–Ingersoll–Ross model (Cox et al. [1985]). The model is widely used in the finance community as a model for short interest rates, but it has also been used as a model for volatility. The model is specified by the stochastic differential equation

$$\mathrm{d}X_t = \alpha(\beta - X(t))\mathrm{d}t + \sigma\sqrt{X(t)}\mathrm{d}W(t).$$

The data were simulated using a Milstein scheme using equidistant observations. The distance between the observations is $\Delta t = 1$ and the parameters used were chosen as $\alpha = 0.17$, $\beta = 0.05$ and $\sigma = 0.07$. The simulation produced

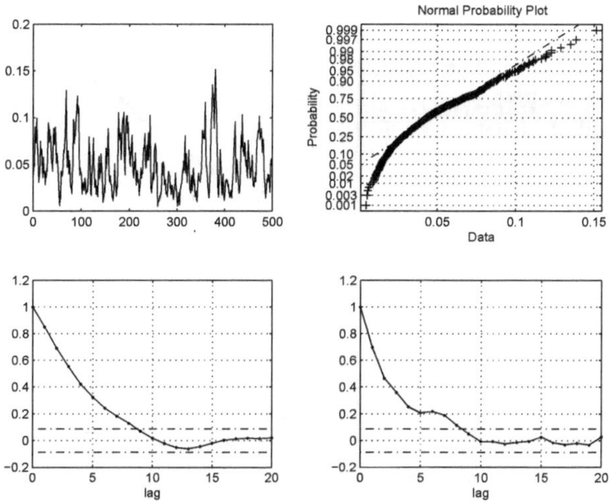

Figure 13.3: Simulated Cox–Ingersoll–Ross process (left) and corresponding normal probability plot.

500 observations, where 100 intermediate steps between each observation have been simulated to decrease the bias (Figure 13.3).

The sample autocorrelation and QQ plot for the generalized Gaussian residuals are presented in Figure 13.4. These are uncorrelated and Gaussian (and thus independent) which is not surprising since the data were simulated using the correct model.

The benchmark for stocks is the geometric Brownian motion, $\mathrm{d}S(t) = \mu S(t)\mathrm{d}t + \sigma S(t)\mathrm{d}W(t)$. Let $\Delta_k = t_k - t_{k-1}$ be the sampling interval and let $\Delta W_i = W_{t_k} - W_{t_{k-1}}, \tilde{\mu} = (\mu - \sigma^2/2)$. The solution to the stochastic differential equation is given by $S_{t_k} = S_{t_{k-1}} e^{\tilde{\mu}\Delta_k + \sigma\Delta W_k}$. We obtain U_k by applying the distribution function. Thc conditional distribution of S_{t_k} is given by

$$\mathbb{P}(S_{t_{k-1}} e^{\tilde{\mu}\Delta_k + \sigma\Delta W_k} \leq s_k | S_{t_{k-1}}) = \Phi\left(\frac{\log\left(s_k/S_{t_{k-1}}\right) - \tilde{\mu}\Delta_k}{\sigma\sqrt{\Delta_k}}\right).$$

By applying the inverse of the distribution function of the standard Gaussian random variable, we find that

$$Y_k = \Phi^{-1}(U_k) = \frac{\log\left(s_k/S_{t_{k-1}}\right) - \tilde{\mu}\Delta_k}{\sigma\sqrt{\Delta_k}}.$$

The generalized Gaussian residuals are consistent with the ordinary standardized residuals (for linear diffusions) but the technique is also able to handle non-linear models. We have calculated the generalized Gaussian residuals

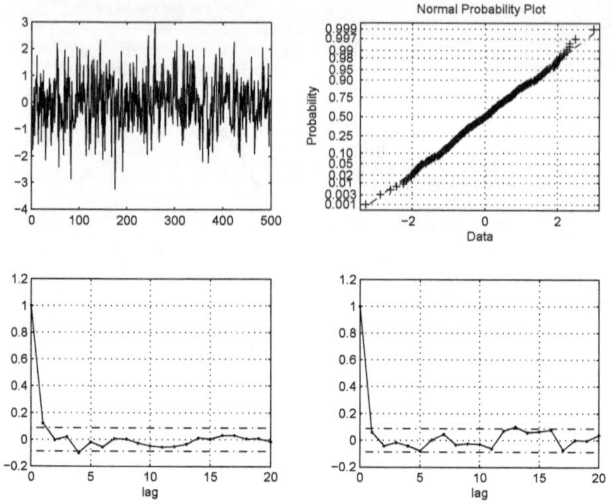

Figure 13.4: Sample autocorrelation and QQ plot for the generalized Gaussian residuals computed for the Cox–Ingersoll–Ross process.

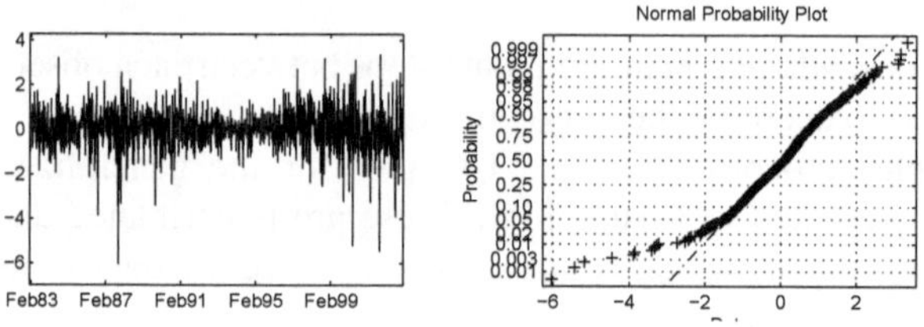

Figure 13.5: Generalized Gaussian residuals (left) and QQ plot (right) for continuously compounded returns on the S & P 500.

for the S & P 500 using weekly data from 1983–2002. The residuals are presented in Figure 13.5. It can be seen that the residuals are non-Gaussian and heteroscedastic, reaffirming the well-known fact that the S & P 500 is not generated by a geometric Brownian motion.

13.8 Problems

Problem 13.1

Consider the stochastic variable $X \in N(\mu, \sigma^2)$.

1. Specify two moment conditions that can be used for estimating the parameters μ and σ^2.

2. Specify an additional moment condition.

3. Simulate 100 observations of X. Estimate the parameters and their covariances based on these observations using the two moment conditions. Estimate the parameters and their covariances based on these observations using the three moment conditions. Comment on the results.

Problem 13.2 Consider the *GARCH* model (5.67) for $p = 1$ and $q = 1$, i.e., the *GARCH(1,1)* model.

1. Write down suitable moment conditions for estimating the parameters. Illustrate the choice of moment conditions!

Hint: Use (5.69).

Problem 13.3 Consider the CKLS model

$$dX(t) = \kappa(\theta - X(t))dt + \sigma X(t)^{\gamma} dW(t).$$

1. Calculate the simple estimation functions obtained from choosing $h(x) = x,\ x^2, x^3,\ x^4$.

2. Do an Euler approximation of the CKLS model with timestep Δ. Use this to derive suitable moment conditions for a GMM estimation of the parameters.

Chapter 14

Inference in partially observed processes

14.1 Introduction

This section concentrates on filtering (state estimation) and prediction theory related to state space models. There are several reasons for considering state space models. The primary reason is probably that the process described by the system equation of the state space model is a (first-order) Markov process (assuming that the Itō interpretation is used). Furthermore, the state space formulation contains a measurement equation which allows for a rather flexible structure of the observations (aggregation of the state variables, missing measurements, etc.).

More specifically we shall assume that the system is described by the *continuous-discrete state space model*, which will be introduced in the next section. The evolution of the state vector of the model will be described by a vector Itō stochastic differential equation, which is the system equation of the state space model. The observations are taken at discrete time instants, and the measurement equation of the state space model describes how the observations are obtained as a function of the states plus some measurement noise.

In many references on filtering for SDE (as for instance Øksendal [2010]) a continuous-continuous time setup is used. The continuous-discrete-time setup is, however, the most relevant setup in practice, since the changes of the system most often take place in continuous time, whereas the observations are obtained at discrete time instants.

Assume that we want to estimate the state of the system at time t based on measurements until time t_k. Then this chapter describes some estimation methods which might be useful:

- State interpolation ($t < t_k$)
- State filtering (estimation) ($t = t_k$)
- State prediction ($t > t_k$)

In particular the methods are needed for estimating parameters in the stochastic differential equations.

14.2 Model

In the most general case we shall assume that the system equation is the *vector Itō stochastic differential equation*

$$\mathrm{d}\mathbf{X}(t) = \mu(\mathbf{X}(t), \mathbf{U}(t), t)\mathrm{d}t + \sigma(\mathbf{X}(t), t)\mathrm{d}\mathbf{W}(t) \tag{14.1}$$

with $\{\mathbf{W}(t)\}$ being a vector Wiener process with incremental covariance $\mathbf{Q}(t)$, and $\mathbf{U}(t)$ some input vector valued function. The observations $\mathbf{y}_k$ are taken at discrete time instants, t_k, as described by the measurement equation:

$$\mathbf{y}_k = \mathbf{h}(\mathbf{x}_k, \mathbf{u}_k, \theta, t_k) + \mathbf{e}_k \tag{14.2}$$

where $\{\mathbf{e}_k\}$ is a vector Gaussian white noise process independent of $\mathbf{W}(t)$, for all t, k, and $\mathbf{e}_k \sim N(\mathbf{0}, \mathbf{S}_k)$. (The super- or subscript k is a shorthand notation for t_k.)

However, occasionally a scalar version of the above model will be considered. From the deterministic settings it is well known that a solution to a differential equation $\partial\mathbf{X}(t)/\partial t = \mu(t, \mathbf{X}(t))$ with initial condition $\mathbf{X}(0)$ exists and $\mu(t, \mathbf{X}(t))$ is unique if $\mu(\mathbf{X}(t), t)$ satisfies the Lipschitz conditions in $\mathbf{X}(t)$, and is bounded with respect to t for every $\mathbf{X}(t)$. Similar conditions are relevant for the SDE in Equation (14.1).

Condition 14.1 (Lipschitz and growth conditions)**.** *Suppose the real functions μ and σ, and initial condition $\mathbf{X}(0)$, satisfy the following conditions. The functions μ and σ satisfy the uniform Lipschitz conditions in $\mathbf{x}$:*

$$\|\mu(\mathbf{x}_2, t) - \mu(\mathbf{x}_1, t)\| \le K\|\mathbf{x}_2 - \mathbf{x}_1\|,$$
$$\|\sigma(\mathbf{x}_2, t) - \sigma(\mathbf{x}_1, t)\| \le K\|\mathbf{x}_2 - \mathbf{x}_1\|.$$

The functions μ and σ satisfy Lipschitz conditions in t on $[t_0, T]$:

$$\|\mu(\mathbf{x}, t_2) - \mu(\mathbf{x}, t_1)\| \le K|t_2 - t_1|,$$
$$\|\sigma(\mathbf{x}, t_2) - \sigma(\mathbf{x}, t_1)\| \le K|t_2 - t_1|.$$

Furthermore, assume that the drift and diffusion term satisfies

$$\|\mu(\mathbf{x}, t)\|^2 + \|\sigma(\mathbf{x}, t)\|^2 \le K(1 + \|\mathbf{x}\|^2). \tag{14.3}$$

The initial condition $\mathbf{X}(0)$ is a random variable with $\mathbf{E}[\|\mathbf{X}(0)\|^2] < \infty$, independent of $\{\mathbf{W}(t), t \in [t_0, T]\}$.

If condition 14.1 is satisfied then $\{\mathbf{X}(t)\}$ is a Markov process, and, in the mean square sense, is uniquely determined by the initial condition $\mathbf{X}(0)$ (Jazwinski [1970], Øksendal [2010]).

The Lipschitz condition in $\mathbf{x}$ guarantees that the equation has a unique solution, while the Lipschitz condition in t guarantees that the solution does not explode, i.e., it is a restriction on the growth of the functions. The latter is illustrated in the following example.

Example 14.1 (Growth restriction on μ). *Consider the deterministic differential equation*

$$\frac{\mathrm{d}x(t)}{\mathrm{d}t} = x(t)^2. \tag{14.4}$$

The general solution is

$$x(t) = \frac{1}{C-t}, \tag{14.5}$$

where C is an arbitrary constant. For the initial condition $x_0 = 1$ the solution is

$$x(t) = \frac{1}{1-t} \tag{14.6}$$

which is defined only for $0 \leq t < 1$.

Given this initial condition no solutions exists for $t \geq 1$, and we see that the solution explodes for $t \uparrow 1$.

14.3 Exact filtering

In the general case exact filtering requires that the whole distribution is used.

14.3.1 Prediction

We start by analysing the Scalar case to build some intuition, before proceeding to the multivariate case.

14.3.1.1 Scalar case

Let us first consider the scalar SDE

$$\mathrm{d}X(t) = \mu(X(t),t)\mathrm{d}t + \sigma(X(t),t)\mathrm{d}W(t). \tag{14.7}$$

From a previous chapter it is well known that (given the Itō interpretation, which will be adapted in the following) $X(t)$ *is a Markov process*. Being Markov, the process is then characterized by the density $p(x,t)$ and the *transition probability* $p(x(t)|x(s))$ $(s < t)$, and the key issue is to find out how this transition probability propagates in time. Note that we use the shorthand notation $p(x(t)|x(s))$ instead of the more correct notation $p(x(t),t|x(s),s)$.

Let us consider the process at times $s < t < t + \delta t$. For a Markov process we have the *Chapman–Kolmogorov equation*

$$p\left(x(t+\delta t)|x(s)\right) = \int_{-\infty}^{\infty} p\left(x(t+\delta t)|x(t)\right) p\left(x(t)|x(s)\right) \mathrm{d}x(t) \tag{14.8}$$

where it is used that $p\left(x(t+\delta t)|x(t),x(s)\right) = p\left(x(t+\delta t)|x(t)\right)$ because of the Markov property.

Using the Chapman–Kolmogorov in a Taylor expansion of $p(x(t)|x(\tau)$ (see Maybeck [1982a] p. 192–196) we get the *Fokker–Planck equation* (F-P) (or the *forward Kolmogorov equation*)

$$\frac{\partial p(x(t)|x(\tau))}{\partial t} = -\frac{\partial p(x(t)|x(\tau))\mu(x,t)}{\partial x} + \frac{1}{2}\frac{\partial^2 p(x(t)|x(\tau))\sigma^2(x,t)}{\partial x^2} \tag{14.9}$$

for the Scalar case (14.7).

Example 14.2 (Einstein's 1905 paper on Brownian motion)**.** *As an example of the F-P equation and its solution we might consider the 1905 paper of Einstein where he treated the Brownian motion. Take* $\mu = 0$ *and* $\sigma = 2D$ *in Equation 14.7. Then Einstein proved that the density p conditioned on a known initial state* x_0 *satisfies*

$$\frac{\partial p(x(t)|x(\tau))}{\partial t} = D\frac{\partial^2 p(x(t)|x(\tau))}{\partial x^2}. \tag{14.10}$$

This is the heat diffusion equation with diffusion coefficient D. Notice that this equation is a special case of the F-P Equation 14.9.

It is well known and easy to check that the solution is

$$p(x(t)|x(0) = 0) = \frac{1}{\sqrt{2\pi 2Dt}}\exp\left(-\frac{x^2(t)}{2(2Dt)}\right) \tag{14.11}$$

which is the Gaussian density with mean zero and variance 2Dt.

14.3.1.2 General case

For the general state space model (14.1)–(14.2) the evolution of the probability density $p(\mathbf{X}(t)|\mathscr{F}_k)$, $t \in [t_k, t_{k+1}[$ is described by *Kolmogorov's forward equation* or the *Fokker–Planck* (F-P) equation:

$$\mathrm{d}p(\mathbf{x}(t)|\mathscr{F}(0) = L(p)\,\mathrm{d}t \tag{14.12}$$

where

$$L(\cdot) = -\sum_{i=1}^{n}\frac{\partial(\cdot\,\mu_i)}{\partial x_i} + \frac{1}{2}\sum_{i,j=1}^{n}\frac{\partial^2(\cdot\,(\sigma\mathbf{Q}\sigma^T)_{ij})}{\partial x_i x_j} \tag{14.13}$$

is the forward diffusion operator (Jazwinski [1970], Maybeck [1982b]). This is the evolution *between* observations. The *initial condition*, at t_k, is $p(\mathbf{x}_k|\mathscr{F}(0))$. We assume this density exists and is once continuously differentiable with respect to t and twice with respect to $\mathbf{x}$.

Example 14.3 (The F-P equation used on a linear system)**.** *Consider the linear system*

$$\mathrm{d}\mathbf{X}(t) = \mathbf{A}(t)\mathbf{X}(t)\,\mathrm{d}t + \sigma_t\,d\mathbf{W}(t) \tag{14.14}$$

where $\mathbf{W}(t)$ *is a Wiener process with incremental covariance* $\mathbf{Q}(t)$*.*

If we assume that the initial density is Gaussian, then the density for $\mathbf{X}(t)$ *will be Gaussian. Hence also the conditional densities will be Gaussian. The Fokker–Planck equation gives the following equation for the conditional density*

$$\frac{\partial p}{\partial t} = -p\text{tr}\left(\mathbf{A}(t)\right) - \frac{\partial p}{\partial x}^T \mathbf{A}(t)\mathbf{x} + \frac{1}{2}\text{tr}\left(\sigma \mathbf{Q} \sigma^T \frac{\partial^2 p}{\partial x^2}\right). \tag{14.15}$$

Since it is known that the solution is the Gaussian density, the (conditional) characteristic function for the solution can be written as

$$\phi(\mathbf{u},t) = \int_{-\infty}^{\infty} \exp(i\mathbf{u}^T\mathbf{x})p(\mathbf{x})\mathrm{d}\mathbf{x} \tag{14.16}$$

$$= \exp(i\mathbf{u}^T\mathbf{m}_t - \frac{1}{2}\mathbf{u}^T\mathbf{P}_t\mathbf{u}) \tag{14.17}$$

where $\mathbf{m}_t$ *and* $\mathbf{P}_t$ *are the conditional mean and covariance, respectively.*

Using a similar Fourier transformation of the Fokker–Planck equations and comparing the terms with the terms in (14.16) we get (after some calculations — see McGarty [1974]):

$$\frac{\mathrm{d}\mathbf{m}(t)}{dt} = \mathbf{A}(t)\mathbf{m}(t), \tag{14.18}$$

$$\frac{\mathrm{d}\mathbf{P}(t)}{dt} = \mathbf{A}(t)\mathbf{P}(t) + \mathbf{P}(t)\mathbf{A}(t)^T + \sigma(t)\mathbf{Q}(t)\sigma(t)^T. \tag{14.19}$$

This gives the exact solution for linear systems driven by a Wiener process, but for non-linear systems it is not sufficient to consider only the conditional mean and covariance. However, some approximative solutions involving only the first and second moment will be considered in some subsequent sections.

14.3.2 Updating

Now, we also assume that the observation mapping $\mathbf{h}$, given in (14.2), is continuous in $\mathbf{x}$ and in t, and bounded for each t_k with probability 1.

An integrating of the Kolmogorov's equation yields $p(\mathbf{x}_{k+1}|\mathcal{F}(t_k))$. When a new measurement is available at t_{k+1}, the distribution can be updated through Bayes' rule yielding $p(\mathbf{x}_{k+1}|\mathcal{F}(t_{k+1}))$. This is used in turn as the new initial condition for Kolmogorov's equation.

The updating equation is therefore

$$p(\mathbf{x}_k|\mathcal{F}(t_k)) = \frac{p(\mathbf{y}_k|\mathbf{x}_k)p(\mathbf{x}_k|\mathcal{F}(t_{k-1}))}{\int_{[\mathbf{x}_k]} p(\mathbf{y}_k|\xi)p(\xi|\mathcal{F}(t_{k-1}))\,\mathrm{d}\xi}. \tag{14.20}$$

Note that the denominator is simply $p(\mathbf{y}_k|\mathcal{F}(t_{k-1}))$. Conceptually, we now have the analytical tool to solve the state filtering problem, but in practice the tool is in general not feasible. Therefore some approximations or truncated expansions are often used. One possibility is to concentrate on only the first moments of the entire distribution. This will be considered in the next section.

14.4 Conditional moment estimators

What we have achieved so far is that by defining a suitable integral (Itō integral), we presented a solution to the transition (prediction) distribution of the state (Kolmogorov's equation). Then we used the observation equation and the Bayes' rule to update the distribution after each measurement. Thus, we have the whole posterior probability distribution of the state. We often like to reduce the distribution to some numbers that are much easier to work with.

A very common approach is to look only upon the first and second moments of the posterior distribution. In fact, it can be shown that choosing the posterior mean of the state as an estimate for the value of the state, we have minimized a Bayesian risk. More precisely, we have the following theorem:

Theorem 14.1 (Optimal state estimation). *The estimate that minimizes* $\mathbf{E}[(\mathbf{X}(t)-\hat{\mathbf{x}}_t)^T\mathbf{W}(\mathbf{X}(t)-\hat{\mathbf{x}}_t)]$*, is the conditional mean. Here* $\mathbf{W}$ *is some positive definite weight matrix and* $\hat{\mathbf{x}}_t$ *a functional on* $\mathscr{F}(t_k)$ *for* $t \geq t_k$*.*

Proof. See Jazwinski [1970]. □

14.4.1 Prediction and updating

Let $\mathbf{E}^k[\cdot]$ denote the conditional mean of $[\cdot]$ given $\mathscr{F}(t_k)$. Also, let $\hat{\mathbf{x}}_{t|k}$ and $\mathbf{P}_{t|k}$ denote the conditional first and second (central) moments given $\mathscr{F}(t_k)$, respectively.

The time propagation (prediction) and the update of the conditional mean and covariance are described by the following theorem:

Theorem 14.2 (Conditional moment estimators). *Assume the conditions required for the derivation of the conditional density in (14.12) and (14.20).*

Prediction: Between observations, the conditional mean and covariance satisfy

$$\frac{\mathrm{d}\hat{\mathbf{x}}_{t|k}}{\mathrm{d}t} = \hat{\mu}(\mathbf{X}(t),t) \tag{14.21}$$

$$\frac{\mathrm{d}\mathbf{P}_{t|k}}{\mathrm{d}t} = \widehat{\mathbf{x}_t\mu^T} - \hat{\mathbf{x}}_{t|k}\hat{\mu}^T + \widehat{\mu\,\mathbf{x}_t^T} - \hat{\mu}\,\hat{\mathbf{x}}_{t|k}^T + \widehat{\sigma\mathbf{Q}\sigma^T} \tag{14.22}$$

for $t \in [t_k, t_{k+1}[$*, where* $\widehat{[\cdot]} = \mathbf{E}[\cdot|\mathscr{F}(t_k)]$*, i.e., the conditional mean with respect to* $\mathscr{F}(t_k)$*.*

Updating: When a new observation arrives at t_k *we have*

$$\hat{\mathbf{x}}_{k|k} = \frac{\mathbf{E}\left[\mathbf{x}_k p(\mathbf{y}_k|\mathbf{x}_k)|\mathscr{F}(t_k)\right]}{\mathbf{E}\left[p(\mathbf{y}_k|\mathbf{x}_k))|\mathscr{F}(t_k)\right]}, \tag{14.23}$$

$$\mathbf{P}_{k|k} = \frac{\mathbf{E}\left[\mathbf{x}_k\mathbf{x}_k^T p(\mathbf{y}_k|\mathbf{x}_k)|\mathscr{F}(t_k)\right]}{\mathbf{E}\left[p(\mathbf{y}_k|\mathbf{x}_k)|\mathscr{F}(t_k)\right]} - \hat{\mathbf{x}}_{k|k}\hat{\mathbf{x}}_{k|k}^T. \tag{14.24}$$

Predictions $\hat{\mathbf{x}}_{t|k}$ *and* $\mathbf{P}_{t|k}$*, with* $t > t_k$*, based on* $\mathscr{F}_k$*, also satisfy (14.21) and (14.22).*

Proof. Is found, e.g., in Maybeck [1982b]. □

The theorem provides the complete solution to the state filtering problem, but an evaluation of the conditional expectations requires knowledge of the entire conditional density. In order to obtain a computationally realizable filter, some approximations must be made. First, we restrict our attention to a special, though at the same time, very important class of models, namely, linear models.

14.5 Kalman filter

The exact solution of the state filtering problem for *linear dynamic models*, i.e., models described by stochastic differential equations of the form

$$\begin{aligned} d\mathbf{X}(t) &= \mathbf{A}(\mathbf{U}(t),t)\mathbf{X}(t)\,dt + \mathbf{B}(\mathbf{U}(t),t)\,dt + \sigma(t)\,d\mathbf{W}(t) \\ \mathbf{y}_k &= \mathbf{C}(\mathbf{u}_k,t_k)\,\mathbf{x}_k + \mathbf{D}(\mathbf{u}_k,t_k)\,\mathbf{u}_k + \mathbf{e}_k \end{aligned}$$

where $\mathbf{W}(t)$ is a Wiener process with incremental covariance $\mathbf{Q}(t)$, and $\mathbf{e}_k$ is the Gaussian white noise, given by the Kalman Filter.

Theorem 14.3 (Continuous-discrete Kalman filter). *The Kalman filter (KF) consists of recursive equations for updating and prediction. In the following the dependencies of time and external input of the matrices in the Kalman filter equations have been suppressed for convenience.*

The formulas for predicting the mean and covariance of the state-vector and observations are given by,

$$\frac{d\hat{\mathbf{x}}_{t|k}}{dt} = \mathbf{A}\,\hat{\mathbf{x}}_{t|k} + \mathbf{B}\,\mathbf{u}_t, \tag{14.25}$$

$$\frac{d\mathbf{P}_{t|k}}{dt} = \mathbf{A}\,\mathbf{P}_{t|k} + \mathbf{P}_{t|k}\mathbf{A}^T + \sigma\mathbf{Q}\sigma^T, \; t \in [t_k, t_{k+1}[. \tag{14.26}$$

The initial conditions are $\hat{\mathbf{x}}_{1|0} = \mu_0$ *and* $\mathbf{P}_{1|0} = \mathbf{V}_0$.

Having the moments for predicting the state vector, the mean and covariance of the next observation are readily found:

$$\hat{\mathbf{y}}_{k+1|k} = \mathbf{C}\,\hat{\mathbf{x}}_{k+1|k} + \mathbf{D}\,\mathbf{u}_{k+1}, \tag{14.27}$$

$$\mathbf{R}_{k+1|k} = \mathbf{C}\,\mathbf{P}_{k+1|k}\mathbf{C}^T + \mathbf{S}. \tag{14.28}$$

The formulas for updating the mean and the covariance are given by the following equations:

$$\hat{\mathbf{x}}_{k|k} = \hat{\mathbf{x}}_{k|k-1} + \mathbf{K}_k(\mathbf{y}_k - \hat{\mathbf{y}}_{k|k-1}), \tag{14.29}$$

$$\mathbf{P}_{k|k} = \mathbf{P}_{k|k-1} - \mathbf{K}_k\mathbf{R}_{k|k-1}\mathbf{K}_k^T, \tag{14.30}$$

$$\mathbf{K}_k = \mathbf{P}_{k|k-1}\mathbf{C}^T\mathbf{R}_{k|k-1}^{-1}. \tag{14.31}$$

Proof. See e.g., Maybeck [1982b]. □

14.6 Approximate filters

The derivation of the standard Kalman filter is done under the assumption of linearity and Gaussian distributions. However, it can be shown using Hilbert space formalism, (Appendix A) that these predictions and updates are the optimal linear updates, even when the distributions are non-Gaussian.

14.6.1 Truncated second order filter

Let us for simplicity first consider the scalar SDE

$$dX(t) = \mu(X(t),t)dt + \sigma(X(t),t)dW(t). \tag{14.32}$$

Furthermore, let $\phi(\cdot)$ be some function of $x(t)$. It is well known that $\mathbf{E}[\phi(X)] = \int_{-\infty}^{\infty} \phi(x)p(x,t)dx$. Hence

$$\begin{aligned}\frac{d}{dt}\mathbf{E}[\phi(X)] &= \int_{-\infty}^{\infty} \phi(x)\frac{\partial p}{\partial t}dx \\ &= -\int_{-\infty}^{\infty} \phi(x)\frac{\partial}{\partial x}(p\mu)dx + \frac{1}{2}\int_{-\infty}^{\infty} \phi(x)\frac{\partial^2}{\partial x^2}(p\sigma^2)dx \\ &= \mathbf{E}[\frac{d\phi(x)}{dx}\mu(X(t),t)] + \frac{1}{2}\mathbf{E}[\frac{\partial^2\phi(x)}{\partial x^2}\sigma^2(X(t),t)] \end{aligned} \tag{14.33}$$

where the first equality follows from the F-P equations for (14.32), whereas the second one follows by using partial integration.

Equation (14.33) is fundamental for finding the truncated second order filter. Choosing $\phi(x) = x$, then (14.33) implies that $m(t) = \mathbf{E}[X(t)]$ and

$$\frac{dm(t)}{dt} = \mathbf{E}[\mu(X(t),t)] \approx \mu(m(t),t) \tag{14.34}$$

which describes the time propagation of the conditional mean, or the conditional first moment when the process $X(t)$ and the conditional mean $m(t)$ are similar. Note that the time propagation depends on the entire distribution for x.

Now, by taking $\phi(x) = x^2$ and again using (14.33) we get

$$\frac{d}{dt}\mathbf{E}[x^2](t) = \mathbf{E}[2X(t)\mu(X(t),t)] + \mathbf{E}[\sigma^2(X(t),t)]. \tag{14.35}$$

A first-order approximation of this expression is given by

$$\frac{d}{dt}\mathbf{E}[x^2](t) \approx 2m(t)\mu(m(t),t) + 2P_t\frac{\partial\mu(m_t,t)}{\partial x}. \tag{14.36}$$

Since $d(m_t^2) = 2m_t\frac{dm(t)}{dt}dt \approx 2m(t)\mu(m(t),t)dt$ we finally get the prediction equation for the conditional variance

$$\frac{d}{dt}P_t = 2(\mathbf{E}[X(t)\mu(X(t),t)] - m_t\mu(m(t),t)) + \mathbf{E}[\sigma^2(X(t),t)] \tag{14.37}$$

$$\approx 2P_t\frac{\partial\mu(m_t,t)}{\partial x} + \sigma^2(m_t,t) \tag{14.38}$$

where the second line is the first-order linearized dynamics.

These equations for the conditional (on $\mathscr{F}(t_k)$) mean and variance are valid for times $t > t_k$. These prediction equations are generalized to the vector case in (14.21)–(14.22).

The prediction equations of the *truncated second order filter* are now obtained by approximating the various expectations above by using a Taylor series representation, truncating to second order and taking conditional expectations for the resulting terms:

$$\frac{\mathrm{d}m_t}{\mathrm{d}t} = \mu(m_t,t) + \frac{1}{2}P_t\frac{\partial^2\mu(m_t,t)}{\partial x^2} \tag{14.39}$$

$$\begin{aligned}\frac{\mathrm{d}P_t}{\mathrm{d}t} &= 2P_t\frac{\partial\mu(m_t,t)}{\partial x} \\ &\quad + \left(\sigma^2(m_t,t) + P_t\left(\frac{\partial}{\partial x}\sigma(m_t,t)\right)^2 + P_t\sigma(m_t,t)\frac{\partial^2}{\partial x^2}\sigma(m_t,t)\right)\end{aligned} \tag{14.40}$$

which clearly is a system of non-linear differential equations.

14.6.2 Linearized Kalman filter

In the general non-linear case, a very common approach is based on linearization of the functions around a nominal trajectory. Thus, we can use the Kalman filter derived for the linear model. The matrices are calculated by $\mathbf{A}(\mathbf{W}(t),\theta,t) = \partial\mu/\partial\mathbf{x}\big|_{\mathbf{x}=\mathbf{x}^*}$, $\mathbf{B}(\mathbf{W}(t),\theta,t) = \partial\mu/\partial\mathbf{u}\big|_{\mathbf{x}=\mathbf{x}^*}$, etc., where $\mathbf{x}^*$ is some reference signal.

There are different ways to calculate the reference trajectory. One way is integrating the state equation after setting the noise equal to zero. This method, called the *linearized Kalman filter*, will only converge if the noise levels are sufficiently small.

14.6.3 Extended Kalman filter

Consider now the slightly simplified, vector-valued, non-linear state space model

$$\mathrm{d}\mathbf{X}(t) = \mu(\mathbf{X}(t),t)\mathrm{d}t + \sigma(t)\mathrm{d}\mathbf{W}(t) \tag{14.41}$$

with $\{\mathbf{W}(t)\}$ being a Wiener process with incremental covariance $\mathbf{Q}(t)$. The observations $\mathbf{y}_k$ are taken at discrete time instants, t_k,

$$\mathbf{y}_k = \mathbf{h}(\mathbf{x}_k,t_k) + \mathbf{e}_k \tag{14.42}$$

where $\{\mathbf{e}_k\}$ is a Gaussian white noise process independent of $\mathbf{W}(t)$, for all t,k and $\mathbf{e}_k \sim N(\mathbf{0},\mathbf{S}_k)$.

Compared to the state space model (14.1)–(14.2) the simplification is mainly obtained by assuming that the diffusion term is independent of the state vector.

The extended Kalman filter (EKF) is a better choice for the linearization trajectory. The EKF uses the current estimate of the state in the linearization and applies then a Kalman filter to the resulting linearized model.

Theorem 14.4 (Continuous-discrete extended Kalman filter). *For the continuous-discrete state space model (14.41)–(14.41) the (linearized) prediction equations are*

$$\frac{d\mathbf{m}_t}{dt} = \mu(\mathbf{m}_t, t), \tag{14.43}$$

$$\frac{d\mathbf{P}_{t|k}}{dt} = \mathbf{F}(\mathbf{m}_t, t)\mathbf{P}_{t|k} + \mathbf{P}_{t|k}\mathbf{F}^T(\mathbf{m}_t, t) + \sigma\mathbf{Q}\sigma^T, \tag{14.44}$$

$$\mathbf{F}(\mathbf{m}_t, t) = \left.\frac{\partial \mu}{\partial \mathbf{x}}\right|_{\mathbf{x}=\mathbf{m}_t}, \tag{14.45}$$

for $t > t_k$. Remember that $\mathbf{m}_t = \hat{\mathbf{x}}_{t|k}$ denotes the conditional mean.

The update at time t_k is given by

$$\mathbf{K}_k = \mathbf{P}_{k|k-1}\mathbf{H}_k^T[\mathbf{H}_k\mathbf{P}_{k|k-1}\mathbf{H}_k^T + \mathbf{S}]^{-1}, \tag{14.46}$$

$$\hat{\mathbf{x}}_{k|k} = \hat{\mathbf{x}}_{k|k-1} + \mathbf{K}_k(\mathbf{y}_k - \hat{\mathbf{h}}), \tag{14.47}$$

$$\mathbf{P}_{k|k} = \mathbf{P}_{k|k-1} - \mathbf{K}_k\mathbf{H}_k\mathbf{P}_{k|k-1}, \tag{14.48}$$

$$\mathbf{H}_k = \left.\frac{\partial \mathbf{h}}{\partial \mathbf{x}}\right|_{\mathbf{x}=\hat{\mathbf{x}}_{k|k-1}}. \tag{14.49}$$

The conditional expectations are calculated as if $\mathbf{x}_k$ were Gaussian with mean $\hat{\mathbf{x}}_{k|k-1}$ and covariance $\mathbf{P}_{k|k-1}$.

Proof. See Jazwinski [1970]. It is seen that, e.g., the prediction equations are obtained as a simplification of the truncated second order filter. □

Performance improvement for the extended Kalman filter may be obtained by local iterations (over a single sample period) on nominal trajectory redefinition and subsequent re-linearization.

The algorithm called the *iterated extended Kalman filter (IEKF)* is obtained by iterating the equations for the measurement update, where we replace Equation (14.29) with the following iterator

$$\eta_i = \hat{\mathbf{x}}_{k|k-1} + \mathbf{K}_k(\mathbf{y}_k - \mathbf{h}(\eta_{i-1}, t_k) - \mathbf{C}(\hat{\mathbf{x}}_{k|k-1} - \eta_{i-1})) \tag{14.50}$$

with $\mathbf{C} = (\partial\mathbf{h}/\partial\mathbf{x})\big|_{\mathbf{x}=\eta_{i-1}}$, and $\mathbf{K}_k = \mathbf{K}_k(\eta_{i-1})$, iterated for $i = 1, \cdots, l$, starting

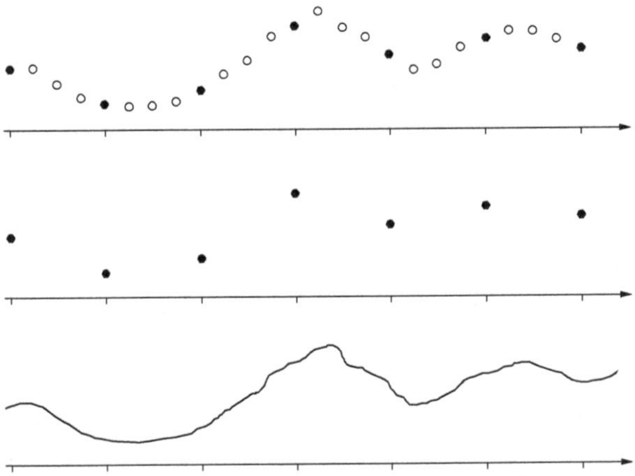

Figure 14.1: The continuous-time and discrete time scales considered for the iterated extended Kalman filter.

with $\eta_0 = \hat{\mathbf{x}}_{k|k-1}$, and terminating with the result $\hat{\mathbf{x}}_{k|k} = \eta_l$. The algorithm is illustrated on Figure 14.1. Linearizing often leads to significant improvements when the observations are informative; cf. Lindström et al. [2008].

14.6.4 Statistically linearized filter

In this approach, we approximate $\mu(\mathbf{X}(t),t)$ by a linear approximation of the form

$$\mu(\mathbf{X}(t),t) = \mu_0(t) + \mathbf{F}(t)\mathbf{X}(t) + \varepsilon_t \tag{14.51}$$

which has the minimum mean square error

$$J = \mathbf{E}[\varepsilon_t^T \mathbf{W} \varepsilon_t | \mathscr{F}_{k-1}] \tag{14.52}$$

for all $t \in [t_{k-1}, t_k[$, where $\mathbf{W}$ is a positive definite weight matrix. Calculating the partial derivatives of (14.52), with respect to $\mu_0(t)$ and $\mathbf{F}(t)$ and setting them to zero, we get by using the notation of Theorem 14.2

$$\begin{aligned} \mu_0(t) &= \hat{\mu} - \mathbf{F}(t)\hat{\mathbf{x}}_t \qquad (14.53) \\ \mathbf{F}(t) &= (\widehat{\mu \mathbf{X}(t)^T} - \hat{\mu}\hat{\mathbf{x}}_t^T)\mathbf{P}_{t|t}^{-1} \qquad (14.54) \end{aligned}$$

where $\widehat{\mu \mathbf{X}(t)^T}$ notation indicated that the quantity is an approximation of $\mathbf{E}[\mu(\mathbf{X}(t),t)\mathbf{X}(t)^T]$, with $\mathbf{P}_{t|t}$ being the conditional covariance of $\mathbf{X}(t)$.

Similarly for the measurement equation:

$$\mathbf{h}(\mathbf{x}_k, t_k) \cong \mathbf{h}_0(t_k) + \mathbf{H}(t_k)\mathbf{x}_k \tag{14.55}$$

with the coefficients statistically optimized to get

$$\mathbf{h}_0(t_k) = \hat{h} - \mathbf{H}(t_k)\,\hat{\mathbf{x}}_{k-1} \tag{14.56}$$

$$\mathbf{H}(t_k) = (\widehat{\mathbf{h}\mathbf{x}_k^T} - \hat{\mathbf{h}}\hat{\mathbf{x}}_{k-1}^T)\,\mathbf{P}_{k|k-1}^{-1}. \tag{14.57}$$

The issue now is the computation of $\hat{\mu}$, $\hat{\mathbf{h}}$, $\mathbf{F}(t)$ and $\mathbf{H}(t_k)$. They all depend upon the conditional probability density function of $\mathbf{x}$, which in general is not available. We therefore assume that the density is Gaussian.

We obtain the *statistically linearized filter*, with the following equations for the time propagation

$$\frac{\mathrm{d}\hat{\mathbf{x}}_{t|k}}{\mathrm{d}t} = \hat{\mu}(\mathbf{x}_{t|k}, t) \tag{14.58}$$

$$\frac{\mathrm{d}\mathbf{P}_{t|k}}{\mathrm{d}t} = \mathbf{F}(t)\mathbf{P}_{t|k} + \mathbf{P}_{t|k}\mathbf{F}^T(t) + \sigma\mathbf{Q}\sigma^T, \quad t \in [t_k, t_{k+1}[\tag{14.59}$$

with $\mathbf{F}(t)$ given by (14.54), and the conditional expectations involved calculated under the assumption that $\mathbf{x}_t$ is Gaussian with mean $\hat{\mathbf{x}}_{t|k}$ and covariance $\mathbf{P}_{t|k}$. The measurement update at time t_k is given by

$$\mathbf{K}_k = \mathbf{P}_{k|k-1}\mathbf{H}^T(t_k)[\mathbf{H}(t_k)\mathbf{P}_{k|k-1}\mathbf{H}^T(t_k) + \mathbf{S}]^{-1} \tag{14.60}$$

$$\hat{\mathbf{x}}_{k|k} = \hat{\mathbf{x}}_{k|k-1} + \mathbf{K}_k(\mathbf{y}_k - \hat{\mathbf{h}}) \tag{14.61}$$

$$\mathbf{P}_{k|k} = \mathbf{P}_{k|k-1} - \mathbf{K}_k\mathbf{H}(t_k)\mathbf{P}_{k|k-1}. \tag{14.62}$$

The conditional expectations are calculated as if $\mathbf{x}_k$ were Gaussian with mean $\hat{\mathbf{x}}_{k|k-1}$ and covariance $\mathbf{P}_{k|k-1}$. The equations for the gain and covariance are the same as those for the EKF, with the changes $\mathbf{F}(t)$ replacing $(\partial\mu/\partial\mathbf{x})\big|_{\mathbf{x}=\hat{\mathbf{x}}_{t|k}}$ and $\mathbf{H}(t_k)$ replacing $(\partial\mathbf{h}/\partial\mathbf{x})\big|_{\mathbf{x}=\hat{\mathbf{x}}_{k|k-1}}$.

14.6.5 Non-linear models

Let us first introduce the most general class of models which will be considered, namely the *non-linear models* where the *system equation* is the Itō equation

$$\mathrm{d}\mathbf{X}(t) = \mu(\mathbf{X}(t), \mathbf{U}(t), \theta, t)\mathrm{d}t + \mathbf{G}(\mathbf{U}(t), \theta, t)\mathrm{d}\mathbf{W}(t), \tag{14.63}$$

where the state vector $\mathbf{x}$ is d-dimensional. The r-dimensional input $\mathbf{u}$ is assumed to be known. The functions μ and $\mathbf{G}$ are continuous and given up to the unknown parameter $\theta \in \Theta \subseteq \mathbb{R}^p$, and $\mathbf{W}_t$ is a standard Wiener process. The solution $\mathbf{X}(t)$ of the Itō equation is a Markov process. The initial state $\mathbf{X}(0)$ is assumed to be Gaussian with mean $\mathbf{m}_0$ and covariance $\mathbf{P}_0$.

The observations are taken at discrete time instants, t_k, as described by the *measurement equation*

$$\mathbf{y}_k = \mathbf{h}(\mathbf{x}_k, \mathbf{u}_k, \theta, t_k) + \mathbf{e}_k \tag{14.64}$$

where $\mathbf{y}$ is m-dimensional and $\mathbf{e}$ is a Gaussian white noise process independent of $\mathbf{w}$, and $\mathbf{e}_k \sim N_m(\mathbf{0}, \mathbf{S}_k(\theta))$. (The super- or subscript k is a shorthand notation for t_k.)

Note that the state dependence of the σ matrix is discarded, which makes the state filtering much simpler than described in Section 14.3. Furthermore, it will be shown that if the actual system contains a state dependent diffusion term, then a transformation approach might be used to transform the equations into an equivalent state space model where the diffusion term is independent of the state. It is equivalent in the sense that it contains the same parameters and relates the same input and output.

14.6.6 *Linear time-varying models*

If the model is linear in the state variable, then a considerable simplification is obtained in the estimation procedure. Hence, consider the linear time-varying stochastic differential equation

$$\mathrm{d}\mathbf{X}(t) = \mathbf{A}(\mathbf{U}(t), \theta, t)\,\mathbf{X}(t)\,\mathrm{d}t + \mathbf{B}(\mathbf{U}(t), \theta, t)\,\mathbf{U}(t)\,\mathrm{d}t + \sigma(\mathbf{U}(t), \theta, t)\,\mathrm{d}\mathbf{W}(t). \tag{14.65}$$

The measurement equation is

$$\mathbf{y}_k = \mathbf{C}(\mathbf{u}_k, \theta, t_k)\,\mathbf{x}_k + \mathbf{D}(\mathbf{u}_k, \theta, t_k)\,\mathbf{u}_k + \mathbf{e}_k. \tag{14.66}$$

The specifications of the noise terms are the same as for the non-linear models in the previous section.

There are different approaches leading to the model (14.65)–(14.66). The model may be formulated directly in this form. Alternatively the model may typically be formulated as a linear model, only with coefficients varying according to some known external signal. Yet another approach leading to this class of models is a linearization of the general Itō differential equation around some reference signal $\mathbf{x}^*$. In this case the matrices are calculated by $\mathbf{A}(\mathbf{W}(t), \theta, t) = \partial\mu/\partial\mathbf{x}\big|_{x=x^*}$, $\mathbf{B}(\mathbf{W}(t), \theta, t) = \partial\mu/\partial\mathbf{u}\big|_{x=x^*}$, etc.

14.6.7 *Linear time-invariant models*

A further simplification is obtained if the model is linear and time-invariant. Hence, the system equation is

$$\mathrm{d}\mathbf{X}(t) = \mathbf{A}(\theta)\,\mathbf{X}(t)\,\mathrm{d}t + \mathbf{B}(\theta)\,\mathbf{U}(t)\,\mathrm{d}t + \sigma(\theta)\,\mathrm{d}\mathbf{W}(t) \tag{14.67}$$

and the measurement equation is

$$\mathbf{y}_k = \mathbf{C}(\theta)\,\mathbf{x}_k + \mathbf{D}(\theta)\,\mathbf{u}_k + \mathbf{e}_k. \tag{14.68}$$

Note that the matrices in (14.67)–(14.68) are now constant, and thus independent of t and $\mathbf{W}(t)$.

14.6.8 *Case: Affine term structure models*

The price of a zero-coupon bond valued in the affine term structure framework, (Section 10.4.2), is given by an exponentially affine function of latent variables such as the infinitesimal interest rate $r(t)$, stochastic volatility $v(t)$, etc.

$$p(t,T) = \exp\left(A(t,T) + B(t,T)r(t) + C(t,T)v(t)\right). \tag{14.69}$$

This form makes it easy to estimate the latent factors within the Kalman filter framework by defining the measurement equation using log prices

$$y_k = \log p_k(t,T) = A(t,T) + B(t,T)r(t) + C(t,T)v(t) + e_k \tag{14.70}$$

while the latent processes are given by diffusion models for the short term interest rate and stochastic volatilty.

14.7 State filtering and prediction

In order to estimate the embedded parameters of the various continuous-discrete time state space models introduced in the previous section, we need the one-step prediction errors of the measurements and the associated covariance.

The one-step *prediction error* or *innovation* is

$$\varepsilon_k(\theta) \triangleq \mathbf{y}_k - \hat{\mathbf{y}}_{k|k-1} \tag{14.71}$$

$$\hat{\mathbf{y}}_{k|k-1} = \mathbf{h}(\hat{\mathbf{x}}_{k|k-1}, \mathbf{u}_k, \theta, t_k) \tag{14.72}$$

where the predictor, $\mathbf{g}(t_k, \theta, \mathbf{y}^{k-1}, \mathbf{u}^N)$ is a function of old outputs, the parameters and the inputs. In the following the input sequence $\mathbf{u}^N$ is skipped for convenience, but since we are considering off-line methods the inputs are assumed to be known.

The issue now is to formulate the predictor corresponding to the various models. For the *Gaussian maximum likelihood method*, which will be considered in subsequent sections, we also need the covariance of the predictions, for evaluation of the likelihood function. For *non-Gaussian maximum likelihood methods* higher order moments or even the whole distribution $p(\mathbf{y}_k|\mathscr{F}_{k-1}, \theta)$ is needed.

To solve these problems, we must establish the conditional density for $\mathbf{x}_k$ conditioned on the measurements $p(\mathbf{x}_k|\mathscr{F}_k)$ up to and including time t_k. If this objective can be accomplished, then various estimators can be defined, optimal with respect to some specified criterion, such as the conditional mean or the conditional mode.

Gaussian maximum likelihood methods will be used for parameter estimation. For linear models the Gaussianity follows directly from the Wiener and Gaussian noise assumption, whereas for non-linear models the Gaussian method is an approximation.

As indicated in Eq. (14.72) a prediction of the state vector is needed in order to predict the output. For the different state space models this prediction is provided by either an *ordinary* or an *extended Kalman filter*. Let us first consider the ordinary Kalman filter, which can be used for linear models.

14.7.1 Linear models

14.7.1.1 Linear time-varying models

It is known from Section 14.5 that for linear models the ordinary Kalman filter provides an exact solution of the filtering problem. Hence, for the linear models (14.65)–(14.66) and (14.67)–(14.68), the *updating formulas* are

$$\hat{\mathbf{x}}_{k|k} = \hat{\mathbf{x}}_{k|k-1} + \mathbf{K}_k \varepsilon_k \tag{14.73}$$

$$\mathbf{P}_{k|k} = \mathbf{P}_{k|k-1} - \mathbf{K}_k \mathbf{R}_{k|k-1} \mathbf{K}_k^T \tag{14.74}$$

$$\mathbf{K}_k = \mathbf{P}_{k|k-1} \mathbf{C}^T \mathbf{R}_{k|k-1}^{-1} \tag{14.75}$$

and the *prediction formulas* for the conditional mean and covariance of the state vector are

$$\frac{d\hat{\mathbf{x}}_{t|k}}{dt} = \mathbf{A}\hat{\mathbf{x}}_{t|k} + \mathbf{B}\mathbf{u}_t \quad t \in [t_k, t_{k+1}[, \tag{14.76}$$

$$\frac{d\mathbf{P}_{t|k}}{dt} = \mathbf{A}\mathbf{P}_{t|k} + \mathbf{P}_{t|k}\mathbf{A}^T + \sigma\sigma^T \quad t \in [t_k, t_{k+1}[. \tag{14.77}$$

Then the one-step prediction of $\mathbf{y}$ and the associated covariance are finally obtained

$$\hat{\mathbf{y}}_{k+1|k} = \mathbf{C}\hat{\mathbf{x}}_{k+1|k} + \mathbf{D}\mathbf{u}_{k+1}, \tag{14.78}$$

$$\mathbf{R}_{k+1|k} = \mathbf{C}\mathbf{P}_{k+1|k}\mathbf{C}^T + \mathbf{S}. \tag{14.79}$$

The dependencies of time and external input of the matrices in the Kalman filter equations have been suppressed for convenience. This implementation of the Kalman filter thus involves the solution of a set of ordinary differential equations between each sampling instant.

14.7.1.2 Linear time-invariant models

If the matrices in the system equation, i.e., $\mathbf{A}$, $\mathbf{B}$ and σ, are time invariant, then it is possible to find an explicit solution for (14.25) and (14.26), by integrating the equations over the time interval $[t_k, t_{k+1}[$ and assuming that $u_t = u_k$ in this interval, thus obtaining

$$\hat{\mathbf{x}}_{k+1|k} = \Phi\hat{\mathbf{x}}_{k|k} + \Gamma\mathbf{u}_k \tag{14.80}$$

$$\mathbf{P}_{k+1|k} = \Phi\mathbf{P}_{k|k}\Phi^T + \Lambda \tag{14.81}$$

where the matrices Φ, Γ and Λ are calculated as

$$\Phi(\tau) = e^{\mathbf{A}\tau} \tag{14.82}$$

$$\Gamma(\tau) = \int_0^\tau e^{\mathbf{A}s}\mathbf{B}\mathrm{d}s \tag{14.83}$$

$$\Lambda(\tau) = \int_0^\tau \Phi(s)\sigma\sigma^T\Phi(s)^T\mathrm{d}s \tag{14.84}$$

and $\tau = t_{k+1} - t_k$ is the sampling time. This implementation of the Kalman filter thus involves the calculation of the exponential of a matrix. In the time invariant case this is done only once for each set of parameters.

14.7.2 The system equation in discrete time

Let us first consider the linear and time invariant case.

Assuming that the sample interval is $[t_k, t_k+\tau[= [t_k, t_{k+1}[$ the discrete time model corresponding to the continuous-time model (14.67) is in the same way given as

$$\mathbf{x}_{k+1} = e^{\mathbf{A}\tau}\mathbf{x}_k + \int_{t_k}^{t_{k+1}} e^{\mathbf{A}(t_k+\tau-s)}\mathbf{B}\mathbf{u}(s)\mathrm{d}s + \int_{t_k}^{t_{k+1}} e^{\mathbf{A}(t_k+\tau-s)}\mathrm{d}\mathbf{W}(s). \tag{14.85}$$

Under the assumption that $\mathbf{W}(t)$ is constant in the sample interval the sampled version can be written as the following discrete time model in state space form

$$\mathbf{x}_{k+1} = \phi(\tau)\mathbf{x}_k + \Gamma(\tau)\mathbf{u}_k + \mathbf{v}_k(\tau) \tag{14.86}$$

where

$$\phi(\tau) = e^{\mathbf{A}\tau}, \quad \Gamma(\tau) = \int_0^\tau e^{\mathbf{A}s}\mathbf{B}\,\mathrm{d}s\,, \tag{14.87}$$

$$\mathbf{v}_k(\tau) = \int_{t_k}^{t_{k+1}} e^{\mathbf{A}(t_k+\tau-s)}\,\mathrm{d}\mathbf{W}(s). \tag{14.88}$$

On the assumption that $\mathbf{W}$ is a Wiener process, $\mathbf{v}_k(\tau)$ becomes Gaussian distributed white noise with zero mean and covariance

$$\mathbf{R}_1(\tau) = E\left[\mathbf{v}_k(\tau)\mathbf{v}_k(\tau)^T\right] = \int_0^\tau \phi(s)\mathbf{R}_1^c\phi(s)^T\mathrm{d}s \tag{14.89}$$

where $\mathbf{R}_1^c$ is the incremental covariance of the Brownian motion; cf. the Itō isometry. If the sampling time is constant (equally spaced observations), the stochastic difference equation can be written

$$\mathbf{x}_{k+1} = \phi\mathbf{x}_k + \Gamma\mathbf{u}_k + \mathbf{v}_k \tag{14.90}$$

where the time scale now is transformed such that the sampling time becomes equal to one time unit.

If the time dependence is slow compared to the dominating eigenvalues of the system, this implementation of the Kalman filter may also be used for time varying systems, by evaluating (14.88) for each sampling instant, assuming that **A**, **B** and σ are constant within a sampling time. This solution requires less computations and is more robust than integrating (14.25) and (14.26) (Moler and van Loan [1978], van Loan [1978]).

14.7.3 Non-linear models

Let us now consider the non-linear model defined by (14.63)–(14.64). In this case the *extended Kalman filter* is used as a first-order approximative filter. Being linearized about $\hat{\mathbf{x}}_t$ the state and covariance propagation equations have structures similar to the Kalman filter propagation equations for linear systems. Hence, we are able to reuse the numerical stable routines implemented for the Kalman filter.

The necessary modifications of the equations in the previous section are the following. The matrix **C** is the linearization of the measurement equation,

$$\mathbf{C}(\hat{\mathbf{x}}_{k|k-1}, \mathbf{u}_k, \theta, t_k) = \left.\frac{\partial \mathbf{h}}{\partial \mathbf{x}}\right|_{x=\hat{x}_{k|k-1}}, \tag{14.91}$$

and **A** is the linearization of the system equation,

$$\mathbf{A}(\hat{\mathbf{x}}(t), \mathbf{U}(t), \theta, t) = \left.\frac{\partial \mu}{\partial \mathbf{x}}\right|_{x=\hat{x}_t}, \tag{14.92}$$

and Φ is the discrete system matrix calculated as a transformation of **A**, (Equation (14.88)). The prediction of the output, Eq. (14.78), is replaced by

$$\hat{\mathbf{y}}_{k+1|k} = \mathbf{h}(\hat{\mathbf{x}}_{k+1|k}, \mathbf{u}_{k+1}, \theta, t_{k+1}). \tag{14.93}$$

The formulas for prediction of mean and covariance of the state-vector are normally given by

$$\frac{\mathrm{d}\hat{\mathbf{x}}_{t|k}}{\mathrm{d}t} = \mu(\hat{\mathbf{x}}_{t|k}, \mathbf{U}(t), \theta, t) \tag{14.94}$$

$$\begin{aligned}\frac{\mathrm{d}\mathbf{P}_{t|k}}{\mathrm{d}t} = {} & \mathbf{A}(\hat{\mathbf{x}}_{t|k}, \mathbf{U}(t), \theta, t)\,\mathbf{P}_{t|k} + \mathbf{P}_{t|k}\mathbf{A}^T(\hat{\mathbf{x}}_{t|k}, \mathbf{U}(t), \theta, t) \\ & + \sigma(\theta, t)\sigma^T(\theta, t)\end{aligned} \tag{14.95}$$

where **A** is given by (14.92) and $t \in [t_k, t_{k+1}[$. In order to make the integration of (14.94) and (14.95) computationally feasible and numerically stable for stiff systems, the time interval $[t_k, t_{k+1}[$ is subsampled and the equations are linearized about the state estimate at the given subsampling time. For the state propagation the equation becomes

$$\begin{aligned} \frac{d\hat{\mathbf{x}}_t}{dt} &= \mu(\hat{\mathbf{x}}_j) + \mathbf{A}(\hat{\mathbf{x}}_j)\{\hat{\mathbf{x}}_t - \hat{\mathbf{x}}_j\} \\ &= \mathbf{A}(\hat{\mathbf{x}}_j)\hat{\mathbf{x}}_t + \{\mu(\hat{\mathbf{x}}_j) - \mathbf{A}(\hat{\mathbf{x}}_j)\hat{\mathbf{x}}_j\} \ , \ t \in [t_j, t_{j+1}[\qquad (14.96) \end{aligned}$$

where $[t_j, t_{j+1}[$ is one of the subintervals of the sampling interval $[t_k, t_{k+1}[$, and we assume that the sampling interval has been divided in n_s subintervals. In these derivations only the state dependency is given for simplicity. Equation (14.96) is a linear ordinary differential equation which has the exact solution

$$\begin{aligned} \hat{\mathbf{x}}_{j+1} &= \hat{\mathbf{x}}_j + (e^{\mathbf{A}(\hat{\mathbf{x}}_j)\tau_s} - \mathbf{I})(\mathbf{A}(\hat{\mathbf{x}}_j)^{-1}\mu(\hat{\mathbf{x}}_j)) \qquad (14.97) \\ &= \hat{\mathbf{x}}_j + (\Phi_s(\hat{\mathbf{x}}_j) - \mathbf{I})(\mathbf{A}(\hat{\mathbf{x}}_j)^{-1}\mu(\hat{\mathbf{x}}_j)) \qquad (14.98) \end{aligned}$$

where $\tau_s = t_{j+1} - t_j = \tau/n_s$, and τ is the sampling time. Correspondingly the equation for the state covariance becomes

$$\mathbf{P}_{j+1} = \Phi_s(\hat{\mathbf{x}}_j)\mathbf{P}_j\Phi_s(\hat{\mathbf{x}}_j)^T + \Lambda_s(\hat{\mathbf{x}}_j) \ , \qquad (14.99)$$

which is similar to (14.81). The algorithm to solve (14.94) and (14.95) uses $\hat{\mathbf{x}}_{k|k}$ and $\hat{\mathbf{P}}_{k|k}$ as starting values for (14.98) and (14.99) and then performs n_s iterations of (14.98) and (14.99) simultaneously. This algorithm has the advantage of being numerically stable for stiff systems and still computationally efficient, since the fast and stable routines of the linear Kalman filter can be used.

14.8 Unscented Kalman Filter

The approximations in Section 14.6 can sometimes be a bit crude, and/or can be complicated to compute in practice. Specifically, the covariances can be poorly approximated, and may even become negative definite under certain circumstances which would lead to a diverging filter.

An alternative is to use the *unscented Kalman filter (UKF)* which computes second order (third if the density is Gaussian (Julier and Uhlmann [1997], Julier et al. [2000])) accurate approximation of the first and second central moments; see also Nørgaard et al. [2000] for a related idea called central difference Kalman filter.

The idea is to approximate the joint distribution of two random vectors X and Y when

$$\mathbf{X} \in N(m, P) \qquad (14.100)$$

$$\mathbf{Y} = g(\mathbf{X}) \qquad (14.101)$$

where $g : \mathbb{R}^n \mapsto \mathbb{R}^m$ is some non-linear function. This can of course be computed using standard quadrature methods, but the *unscented transform* is doing it in a computationally convenient way.

The unscented transform approximates the joint density of X and Y according to

$$\begin{pmatrix} \mathbf{X} \\ \mathbf{Y} \end{pmatrix} = N\left(\begin{pmatrix} m \\ \mu_U \end{pmatrix}, \begin{pmatrix} P & C_U \\ C_U^T & R_U \end{pmatrix} \right). \tag{14.102}$$

This is rather straightforward (perhaps a bit tedious though) to compute. Define the Cholesky factorization of the covariance matrix P as

$$P = LL^T. \tag{14.103}$$

This will be used to compute the *sigma point* and associated weights as

$$\mathbf{x}^{(0)} = m \tag{14.104}$$

$$\mathbf{x}^{(i)} = m + \left[\sqrt{(n+\lambda)L}\right], \; i = 1, \ldots, n \tag{14.105}$$

$$\mathbf{x}^{(i)} = m - \left[\sqrt{(n+\lambda)L}\right], \; i = n+1, \ldots, 2n \tag{14.106}$$

and

$$w_0^{(m)} = \frac{\lambda}{n+\lambda}, \tag{14.107}$$

$$w_0^{(c)} = \frac{\lambda}{n+\lambda} + (1 - \alpha^2 + \beta), \tag{14.108}$$

$$w_i^{(m)} = \frac{1}{2(n+\lambda)}, \; i = 1, \ldots, 2n \tag{14.109}$$

$$w_i^{(c)} = \frac{1}{2(n+\lambda)}, \; i = 1, \ldots, 2n \tag{14.110}$$

where $\lambda = \alpha^2(n+\kappa) - n$. These parameters can be used to tune the filter (α and κ control the spread of the sigma points while β is related to the distribution of $\mathbf{X}$), but a common choice is $\alpha = 10^{-3}$, $\kappa = 0$ and $\beta = 2$.

Each sigma point is propagated through the non-linear function g according to

$$\mathbf{y}^{(i)} = g(\mathbf{x}^{(i)}), \; i = 0, \ldots, 2n. \tag{14.111}$$

The parameters in Equation (14.102) are then computed as

$$\mu_U = \sum_{i=0}^{2n} w_i^{(m)} \mathbf{y}^{(i)}, \tag{14.112}$$

$$R_U = \sum_{i=0}^{2n} w_i^{(c)} \left(\mathbf{y}^{(i)} - \mu_U\right) \left(\mathbf{y}^{(i)} - \mu_U\right)^T, \tag{14.113}$$

$$C_U = \sum_{i=0}^{2n} w_i^{(c)} \left(\mathbf{x}^{(i)} - m\right) \left(\mathbf{y}^{(i)} - \mu_U\right)^T. \tag{14.114}$$

The unscented transform, taking a function g, a mean m and covariance P, will be denoted $UT(g,m,P)$ for the remainder of the text.

The resulting filter is then given by iterating the prediction and update steps. Assume that the discrete time model is given by

$$y_k = h(x_k) + e_k,\ e_k \in N(0,S), \tag{14.115}$$
$$x_k = f(x_{k-1}, u_{k-1}) + v_k,\ v_k \in N(0,Q). \tag{14.116}$$

Starting from a Gaussian density at time k, i.e., $x_k \in N(m_{k|k}, P_{k|k})$, the prediction step is then given by

$$[m_{k+1|k}, \tilde{P}_{k+1|k}] = UT(f, m_{k|k}, P_{k|k}) \tag{14.117}$$
$$P_{k+1|k} = \tilde{P}_{k+1|k} + Q \tag{14.118}$$

where the last line is needed to correct for the fact that the function f is ignoring the additive noise.

The update step is similar, computing predictions as

$$[\mu_U, \tilde{R}_U, C_U] = UT(h, m_{k+1|k}, P_{k+1|k}) \tag{14.119}$$
$$R_U = \tilde{R}_U + S \tag{14.120}$$

where the variance of the measurement noise S is added to the variance of y in the second line. No noise is added to the covariance, however, as the measurement noise is independent of the latent state x_k. Finally, the state is updated using the standard Kalman filter equations

$$K_{k+1} = C_U R_U^{-1}, \tag{14.121}$$
$$m_{k+1|k+1} = m_{k+1|k} + K_{k+1}\left(y_{k+1} - \mu_U\right), \tag{14.122}$$
$$P_{k+1|k+1} = P_{k+1|k} - K_{k+1} R_U K_{k+1}^T. \tag{14.123}$$

The near optimality (the equations are optimal in the class of linear updates) of these equations is proved using Hilbert space methods in Appendix A.

The unscented Kalman filter is generally seen as more robust than the extended Kalman filter (Van Der Merwe [2004], Lindström and Strålfors [2012], Wiktorsson and Lindström [2014]). The unscented Kalman filter has also been extended further to continuous-discrete models in Sarkka [2007].

14.9 A maximum likelihood method

This section describes how the embedded parameters of the linear and nonlinear continuous-discrete state space models can be estimated using a maximum likelihood method. We stress that much of these results presented in this Section carries over to the unscented Kalman filter, even though the results are presented for a simple class of processes.

First it is assumed that the evolution in time of the states of the system is described by the diffusion process

$$\mathrm{d}\mathbf{X}(t) = \mathbf{A}\mathbf{X}(t)\mathrm{d}t + \mathbf{B}\mathbf{W}(t)\mathrm{d}t + \sigma\mathrm{d}\mathbf{W}(t),\ t \geq 0 \tag{14.124}$$

where $\mathbf{X}$ is d dimensional, and the process $\mathbf{W}(t)$ is assumed to be a Wiener process with the incremental covariance $\mathbf{R}_1^c(t)$. Furthermore it is assumed that $\mathbf{X}(0)$ is $N_d(m_0, P_0)$.

As described in Section 14.7.2 the evolution of the states in discrete time is under some conditions exactly described by the following discrete time stochastic process

$$\mathbf{X}_k = \Phi_k\mathbf{X}_{k-1} + \Gamma_k\mathbf{U}_k + \mathbf{v}_k,\ k = 1,\ldots,N \tag{14.125}$$

where $\{\mathbf{X}_k\}_{k=0}^N$ are random $d \times 1$ vectors, and $\{\mathbf{U_k}\}_{k=0}^N$ are non-random $r \times 1$ input vectors, and $\mathbf{x}_0$ is $N_d(\mathbf{m}_0, \mathbf{P}_0)$ and $\mathbf{v}_k \sim N_d(0, \mathbf{P}_k^v), k = 1,\ldots,N$. The random vector x_0 and the system noise $\mathbf{v}_1,\ldots,\mathbf{v}_N$ are all assumed to be stochastic independent. Here, $\{\Phi_k\}$ and $\{\Gamma_k\}$ are non-random $d \times d$ and $d \times r$ matrices, respectively.

The relation between the continuous-time matrices and the discrete time matrices are described in Section 14.7.2.

If we assume that the functions $\mathbf{A}$, $\mathbf{B}$ and $\mathbf{R}_1^c(t)$ are continuous and given up to the unknown parameter $\theta \in \Theta \subseteq \mathbb{R}^p$, then we can write down the likelihood function for θ

$$\begin{aligned} L^x(\theta) &= p(\mathbf{x}_0, \mathbf{x}_1, \ldots, \mathbf{x}_N|\theta) \\ &= \left(\prod_{k=1}^N p_{k|k-1}^x(\mathbf{x}_k|\mathbf{x}_{k-1}, \theta)\right) p^x(\mathbf{x}_0|\theta) \end{aligned} \tag{14.126}$$

where $p_0^x(\cdot;\theta)$ is the density for the distribution of $\mathbf{x}_0$ and $p_{k|k-1}^x(\cdot|\cdot;\theta)$ the density for the conditional distribution of $\mathbf{x}_k$ given $\mathbf{x}_{k-1}$. Hence

$$\log L^x(\theta) = \log(p_0^x(\mathbf{x}_0|\theta)) + \sum_{k=1}^N \log(p_{k|k-1}^x(\mathbf{x}_k|\mathbf{x}_{k-1};\theta)). \tag{14.127}$$

However, often we do not observe the state vectors $\mathbf{x}_0, \mathbf{x}_1, \ldots, \mathbf{x}_N$ directly. We assume that the state vector is only partially observed and possibly with measurement errors. We assume that the measured quantities are given by the *measurement equation*

$$\mathbf{y}_k = \mathbf{C}_k\mathbf{x}_k + \mathbf{D}_k\mathbf{u}_k + \mathbf{e}_k, k = 0, 1, \ldots, N \tag{14.128}$$

where $\{\mathbf{C}_k\}$ and $\{\mathbf{D}_k\}$ are non-random matrices of dimensions $m \times d$ and $m \times r$ ($m \leq d$). For the measurement error we assume that $\mathbf{e}_k \sim N_m(0, S_k), k = 0,\ldots,N$. Finally, we assume that $\mathbf{x}_0, \mathbf{v}_1, \ldots, \mathbf{v}_N, \mathbf{e}_0, \mathbf{e}_1, \ldots, \mathbf{e}_N$ are stochastically independent.

In the following let all the non-random elements in (14.124) and (14.128) including m_0 and the unknown variance parameters be given up to some unknown parameter $\theta \in \Theta \subseteq \mathbb{R}^p$ where Θ is some compact set. Furthermore, recall that

$$\mathscr{F}_k = [\mathbf{y}_k, \mathbf{y}_{k-1}, \ldots, \mathbf{y}_1, \mathbf{y}_0]^T \tag{14.129}$$

is the information set containing all the observations up to and including time t_k.

The likelihood function is

$$\begin{aligned} L(\theta) &= p(\mathbf{y}_1, \ldots, \mathbf{y}_N | \theta) \\ &= \left(\prod_{k=1}^{N} p_{k|k-1}(\mathbf{y}_k | \mathscr{F}_{k-1}, \theta) \right) p_0(\mathbf{y}_0 | \theta) \end{aligned} \tag{14.130}$$

where $p_0(\mathbf{y}_0|\theta)$ is the density for the distribution of y_0 and $p_{k|k-1}(\mathbf{y}_k|\mathscr{F}_{k-1}, \theta)$ the density for the conditional distribution of y_k given $\mathscr{F}_{k-1}$. Hence

$$\log L(\theta) = \log(p_0(\mathbf{y}_0|\theta)) + \sum_{k=1}^{N} \log(p_{k|k-1}(\mathbf{y}_k|\mathscr{F}_{k-1}; \theta)). \tag{14.131}$$

Note that due to the incomplete observation of the state variable we now need to condition on all previous observations and not only the previous observation as in (14.127).

Furthermore, note that the unknown vector m_0 can be a part of θ. Even the conditional log-likelihood function (conditioned on $\mathbf{y}_0$) for θ

$$\log L(\theta|\mathbf{y}_0) = \sum_{k=1}^{N} \log(p_{k|k-1}(\mathbf{y}_k|\mathscr{F}_{k-1}; \theta)) \tag{14.132}$$

depends on m_0. This is also clear from the fact that m_0 is needed as an initial value for calculating $p_{k|k-1}(\mathbf{y}_k|\mathscr{F}_{k-1}; \theta)$ (see for instance the filtering approach described in Section 14.7.1). In the literature, however, the initial value is often chosen at random (Pedersen [1993]).

Since $\mathbf{v}_k$, $\mathbf{e}_k$ and $\mathbf{x}_0$ are all Gaussian distributed, the conditional density $p_{k|k-1}(\mathbf{y}_k|\mathscr{F}_{k-1}; \theta)$ is also Gaussian. The Gaussian distribution is completely characterized by the mean and covariance.

Hence, in order to parameterize the conditional distribution, we introduce the conditional mean and covariance as

$$\hat{\mathbf{y}}_{k|k-1} = \mathbf{E}[\mathbf{y}_k|\mathscr{F}_{k-1}, \theta], \tag{14.133}$$

$$\mathbf{R}_{k|k-1} = \mathbf{Var}[\mathbf{y}_k|\mathscr{F}_{k-1}, \theta], \tag{14.134}$$

respectively. It is noticed that (14.133) is the one-step prediction and (14.134) the associated covariance. Furthermore, it is convenient to introduce the one-step prediction error (or innovation)

$$\varepsilon_k = \mathbf{y}_k - \hat{\mathbf{y}}_{k|k-1}. \tag{14.135}$$

Using (14.132)–(14.135) the conditional log-likelihood function becomes

$$\log L(\theta|\mathbf{y}_0) = -\tfrac{1}{2}\sum_{k=1}^{N}\left(\log\det\mathbf{R}_{k|k-1} + \varepsilon_k^T\mathbf{R}_{k|k-1}^{-1}\varepsilon_k\right) + \text{const} \tag{14.136}$$

where m is the dimension of $\mathbf{y}$.

The conditional mean $\hat{\mathbf{y}}_{k|k-1}$ and covariance $\mathbf{R}_{k|k-1}$ are calculated recursively by using the state filtering techniques described previously in Section 14.7.1.

The maximum likelihood estimate (ML estimate) is the set $\hat{\theta}$, which maximizes the likelihood function. Since it is not, in general, possible explicitly to optimize the likelihood function, a numerical method has to be used.

An estimate of the uncertainty of the parameters is obtained by the fact that the ML estimator is asymptotically normally distributed with mean θ and covariance

$$\mathbf{D} = \mathbf{H}^{-1} \tag{14.137}$$

where the matrix $\mathbf{H}$ is given by

$$\{h_{lk}\} = -\mathbf{E}\left[\frac{\partial^2}{\partial\theta_l\partial\theta_k}\log L(\theta|\mathbf{y}_0)\right]. \tag{14.138}$$

However, this is not necessarily true if the filter is not exact. Then Quasi-Maximum likelihood asymptotics should be used instead of this approximation.

An estimate of $\mathbf{D}$ is obtained by equating the observed value with its expectation and applying

$$\{h_{lk}\} \approx -\left(\frac{\partial^2}{\partial\theta_l\partial\theta_k}\log L(\theta|\mathbf{y}_0)\right)\bigg|_{\theta=\hat{\theta}}. \tag{14.139}$$

The above equation can be used for estimating the variance of the parameter estimates. The variance also serves as a basis for calculating t-test values for test under the hypothesis that the parameter is equal to zero. The correlation between the estimates is readily found based on the covariance matrix.

The maximum likelihood method described in this section is implemented in a software tool called CTSM (Kristensen et al. [2004]).

14.10 Sequential Monte Carlo filters

Recent advances in computational resources have made Monte Carlo methods viable. Sequential Monte Carlo methods (or particle filters) approximate the filter problems by Monte Carlo sampling and resampling; see Lopes and Tsay [2011], Creal [2012], for an overview.

14.10.1 *Optimal filtering*

The optimal filtering problem for general state space models is non-trivial, as we will see soon. Let us consider a model where the latent system equation is a Markov process, and hence is defined by the transition kernel

$$p_\theta\left(x_{n+1} | x_n\right). \tag{14.140}$$

We remind the reader that this is not a severe restriction as, for example, an AR(p) model (which is non-Markovian) can be rewritten as an VAR(1) model with dimension p which is a Markovian model. Other models, like fractional AR processes, can also be approximated by Markovian models.

Observations are thought of as noisy and/or incomplete readings of the latent state vector, formally expressed through the measurement kernel

$$p_\theta\left(y_n | x_n\right). \tag{14.141}$$

The observations are assumed to be independent, when conditioning on the latent state vector. We are now ready to compute (at least theoretically) the log-likelihood for the observations

$$\ell(\theta) = \sum_{n=1}^{N} \log p_\theta(y_n | y_{1:n-1}), \tag{14.142}$$

where $y_{1:n-1}$ is used as shorthand notation for $y_1, \ldots, y_{n-1}$.

The likelihood for observation y_n conditional on the history can be expressed as

$$p_\theta(y_n | y_{1:n-1}) = \int p_\theta\left(y_n | x_n\right) p_\theta\left(x_n | y_{1:n-1}\right) \mathrm{d}x_n \tag{14.143}$$

where we used the law of total probability and the conditional independence of the observations. The likelihood for observation can be seen as the measurement kernel, weighted by the prediction of the latent state $p_\theta\left(x_n | y_{1:n-1}\right)$.

The prediction can in turn be computed using the law of total probability and the Markov property, according to

$$\begin{aligned} p_\theta\left(x_n | y_{1:n-1}\right) &= \int p_\theta\left(x_n, x_{n-1} | y_{1:n-1}\right) \mathrm{d}x_{n-1} && (14.144)\\ &= \int p_\theta\left(x_n | x_{n-1}\right) p_\theta\left(x_{n-1} | y_{1:n-1}\right) \mathrm{d}x_{n-1}, && (14.145) \end{aligned}$$

where we see that the prediction is derived from the transition kernel and the *filter density*, $p_\theta\left(x_{n-1} | y_{1:n-1}\right)$. What remains is to compute the filter density, which is found by using Bayes' formula, arriving at

$$\begin{aligned} p_\theta\left(x_{n-1} | y_{1:n-1}\right) &= \frac{p_\theta\left(y_{n-1} | x_{n-1}\right) p_\theta(x_{n-1} | y_{1:n-2})}{p_\theta(y_{n-1} | y_{1:n-2})} && (14.146)\\ &= \frac{p_\theta\left(y_{n-1} | x_{n-1}\right) p_\theta(x_{n-1} | y_{1:n-2})}{\int p_\theta\left(y_{n-1} | x_{n-1}\right) p_\theta(x_{n-1} | y_{1:n-2}) \mathrm{d}x_{n-1}}. && (14.147) \end{aligned}$$

This closes the recursion if we also know the initial distribution for the latent Markov process, $p_\theta(x_0)$, as shown in Algorithm 1. The algorithm is similar to the Kalman filter, but this should not to surprise anyone as the Kalman filter is a very well-known special case of the general optimal filtering equations.

Algorithm 1 Optimal filtering recursion

Require: $p(X_0), p(X_n|X_{n-1}), p(Y_n|X_n)$
  for $n = 1 : N$ **do**
    Compute prediction using Equation (14.145)
    Update using Equation (14.147)
  end for

14.10.2 Bootstrap filter

The main problem with Equation (14.145) and (14.147) is the difficulties to solve them in practice. There are two well-known cases where we can solve them: the linear Gaussian case (leading to the Kalman filter) and the Hidden Markov model with a discrete and finite state space (as all integrals will be finite sums).

The main idea behind the bootstrap filter is to approximate the general state space model with a Hidden Markov model. This allows for very general results concerning stability and convergence of the approximate filters (Künsch [2005]).

Replacing a measure $p(x)$ with a Monte Carlo sample from that measure $p_K(x) = \sum_{k=1}^{K} \frac{\tilde{\omega}_k}{\sum_{l=1}^{K} \tilde{\omega}_l} \delta(x - x^{(k)}) = \sum_{k=1}^{K} \omega_k \delta(x - x^{(k)})$ (sometimes referred to as the empirical measure, cf. theoretical statistics) will introduce some unwanted variability, but it will also make computations easier. It is worth noticing that the empirical measure can be written, using the law of total probability as

$$p(x) = \sum_k p(x,k) = \sum_k p(x|k)p(k) \tag{14.148}$$

where $p(x|k) = \delta(x - x^{(k)})$ and $p(k) = \omega_k$.

Computing the expectation (assuming that the expectation is finite)

$$\mathbf{E}[f(X)] = \int f(x)p(x)\mathrm{d}x \tag{14.149}$$

is potentially very difficult whereas the Monte Carlo approximation

$$\widehat{\mathbf{E}[f(X)]} = \int f(x)p_K(x)\mathrm{d}x = \sum_{k=1}^{K} \omega_k f(x^{(k)}) \tag{14.150}$$

is a trivial to computation. The law of large numbers ensures that the approximation converges (a.s.) as $K \to \infty$. The convergence is more complicated when the samples are dependent, but the results still hold under rather general conditions (Douc and Moulines [2008]).

It is possible, given some minor modifications, to solve the optimal filtering problem (cf. Section 14.10.1) for arbitrary distributions when they are replaced with empirical samples. It should not be a problem (direct sampling, accept-reject, etc.) to sample from the initial distribution, generating $p_K(x_0) = \sum_{k=1}^{K} \omega_k \delta(x_0 - x_0^{(k)})$.

What remains in Algorithm 1 is to alternate between prediction and updating. Predicting is simple as

$$\begin{aligned} p_K(x_{n+1}|y_{1:n}) &= \int p(x_{n+1}|x_n) p_K(x_n|y_{1:N}) \mathrm{d}x_n \\ &= \int p(x_{n+1}|x_n) \sum_{k=1}^{K} \omega_k \delta(x_n - x_n^{(k)}) \mathrm{d}x_n \\ &= \sum_{k=1}^{K} \omega_k \int p(x_{n+1}|x_n^{(k)}). \end{aligned} \tag{14.151}$$

A common choice is simply to sample $x_{n+1}^{(k)}$ from $p(x_{n+1}|x_n^{(k)})$ leading to the empirical measure

$$p_K(x_{n+1}|y_{1:n}) = \sum_{k=1}^{K} \omega_k \delta(x_{n+1} - x_{n+1}^{(k)}). \tag{14.152}$$

Updating is less trivial, as the empirical filter measure is given by

$$\begin{aligned} p_K(x_{n+1}|y_{1:n+1}) &= \frac{p(y_{n+1}|x_{n+1}) p_K(x_{n+1}|y_{1:n})}{\int p(y_{n+1}|x_{n+1}) p_K(x_{n+1}|y_{1:n}) \mathrm{d}x_{n+1}} \\ &= \frac{p(y_{n+1}|x_{n+1}) p_K(x_{n+1}|y_{1:n})}{\sum_l \omega_l p(y_{n+1}|x_{n+1}^{(l)})}. \end{aligned} \tag{14.153}$$

It should be clear to the reader that this new empirical measure only takes values where there is a Dirac measure, meaning that the expression can be simplified as follows

$$\begin{aligned} p_K(x_{n+1}|y_{1:n+1}) &= \frac{\sum_k \omega_k p(y_{n+1}|x_{n+1}^{(k)}) \delta(x_{n+1} - x_{n+1}^{(k)})}{\sum_l \omega_l p(y_{n+1}|x_{n+1}^{(l)})} \\ &= \sum \lambda_k \delta(x_{n+1} - x_{n+1}^{(k)} \end{aligned} \tag{14.154}$$

where

$$\lambda_k = \frac{\omega_k p(y_{n+1}|x_{n+1}^{(k)})}{\sum_l \omega_l p(y_{n+1}|x_{n+1}^{(l)})} \tag{14.155}$$

which ensures that the weights sum to unity.

A practical problem, which can be shown theoretically, but is more easily seen in a "trial and error" Monte Carlo simulation, is that the weights tend to become unevenly distributed after only a few iterations, i.e., the largest weight will be close to one and the rest close to zero. This is called particle degeneracy, as the original K particles act as there is only one particle.

However, this is solved by resampling, thus creating a new empirical measure with equal weights. That prevents serious particle degeneracy as there will be plenty of particles with non-zero weight even if the weights are updated unequally.

The Sequential Importance Sampling with Resampling (SISR) algorithm (also known as the bootstrap filter) is presented in Algorithm 2, where we also consider using an importance sampler in order to improve the performance of the Monte Carlo approximations.

Algorithm 2 Sequential Importance Sample with Resampling

Require: $p(x_0), p(x_n|x_{n-1}), p(y_n|x_n)$

At time n=0, draw $x_0^{(k)} \sim q_0(x_0)$ and set $\omega_0^{(k)} = \frac{p(x_0^{(k)})}{q_0(x_0^{(k)})}$

for $n = 1 : N$ **do**

Draw $x_n^{(k)} \sim q_n(x_n|x_{n-1}^{(k)}, y_n)$ and compute $\tilde{\omega}_n^{(k)} = \omega_{n-1}^{(k)} \frac{p(y_n|x_n^{(k)})p(x_n^{(k)}|x_{n-1}^{(k)})}{q_n(x_n^{(k)}|x_{n-1}^{(k)}, y_n)}$

Normalize the importance weights to get $\omega_n^{(k)} = \frac{\tilde{\omega}_n^{(k)}}{\sum_{l=1}^{K} \tilde{\omega}_n^{(k)}}$

Draw (with replacement) K indices $I_n^{(k)} \sim \omega_n^{(k)}$ to get a new equally weight empirical measure with particle $x_n^{(I_n^{(k)})}$.

end for

14.10.3 Parameter estimation

A major problem with particle filters is that the straightforward approximation of the log-likelihood is only a pointwise approximation. It can also be shown that the approximation is discontinuous in the parameter space, due to the resampling of the particles (Figure 14.2). That graph shows the log-likelihood function for the model

$$y_k = x_k + e_k \tag{14.156}$$

$$x_k = ax_{k-1} + v_k \tag{14.157}$$

where e_k and v_k are standard Gaussian random variables, and $a = 0.6$ in the example. The simulation is based on $N = 500$ observations and $K = 1\,000$ particles. Still, the Monte Carlo approximation is sharing the same global features of the exact log-likelihood, and the Monte Carlo error can be controlled by using sufficiently many particles.

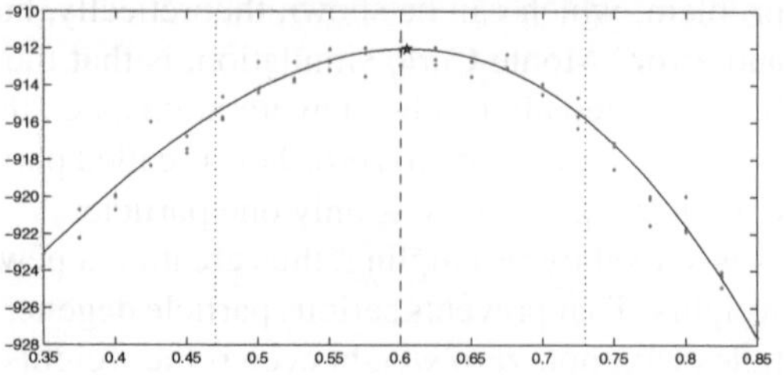

Figure 14.2: Log-likelihood function for a partially observed AR(1) model ($N = 500$ observations) with true parameter $a = 0.6$. The maximum likelihood estimate is shown with a pentagon, and 95% confidence intervals are shown with the dotted line. The solid line is the log-likelihood function computed using a Kalman filter, and the dots are 3 independent estimates of the log-likelihood function using a particle filter, each using $K = 1\,000$ particles.

It is argued in Spall [2005] that derivative-free optimization methods, such at the Nelder-Mead simplex (e.g., `fminsearch` in MATLAB®), often are quite capable of optimizing a noisy function, often reaching a point close to the true optima of the function.

Other methods include Expectation-Maximization methods (Cappé et al. [2005] and references therein), but this requires the smoothing distribution (as opposed to the filter distribution). Simple (typically slightly biased) approximations include fix lag smoothers (Olsson et al. [2008]) while Briers et al. [2010], Fearnhead et al. [2010], Douc et al. [2011] present computationally efficient algorithms for asymptotically unbiased approximations of smoothing distribution. The EM algorithm will have to be replaced by either a Monte Carlo EM (MCEM) algorithm (Cappé et al. [2005]) or a Stochastic Approximation EM algorithm (Ditlevsen and Samson [2014] for an example).

An alternative is to augment the state space with the parameters. This is in general not a consistent estimation technique, but Ionides et al. [2006, 2011] derived a version where consistency is proved. Their algorithm was later refined in Lindström et al. [2012] and fine-tuned in Lindström [2013b].

14.11 Application of non-linear filters

14.11.1 Sequential calibration of options

Non-linear Kalman filters have successfully been used to calibrate vanilla S & P 500 index options in Lindström et al. [2008]. The most common method for calibrating options to market data today is some non-linear weighted least squares estimator

$$\theta = \arg\min \sum_i \lambda_i \left(c_t^{Market}(S_i, K_i, r_i, \tau_i) - c_t^{Model}(S_i, K_i, r_i, \tau_i; \theta) \right)^2 \tag{14.158}$$

where $c^{Market}(S_i, K_i, r_i, \tau_i)$ are the market price that depends on the underlying asset S_i, strike level K_i, interest rate r_i and time to maturity τ_i and λ_i are weights (it is statistically optimal to relate the weight of an observation to the inverse of the variance of the measurement error for that observation — i.e., observations that we trust are given more weight than the others).

There are two main (implicitly related) problems with this approach:

- The parameter estimates are noisy,
- Old data are typically discarded, as only the most recent data are used.

Old data are discarded as adaptivity is sought, but this comes at a price. If yesterday's data are of little use today, then today's data will be of little use tomorrow! Lindström et al. [2008] rewrites the calibration problems as a filtering problem, augmenting the latent states with the parameter vector

$$c_t^{Market}(S_n, K_i, r_i, \tau_i) = c_t^{Model}(S_n, K_i, r_i, \tau_i; \theta_n) + \eta_n, \tag{14.159}$$

$$\theta_n = \theta_{n-1} + e_n. \tag{14.160}$$

This decomposes the change of the option prices into changes in the underlying state variables (i.e., the index level), changes in the parameters (which is captured by the random walk dynamics) and pure noise due to the ask-bid spread.

It is sometimes worthwhile to include the underlying asset in the calibration as well. The algorithm was extended further in Lindström and Guo [2013] where it was shown that quadratic calibration strategies are found for free when using this algorithm. A computational refinement of the simultaneous calibration and hedging algorithm was presented in Wiktorsson and Lindström [2014]. The extended calibration mode is given by the measurement equations

$$c_t^{Market}(S_n, K_i, r_i, \tau_i) = c_t^{Model}(S_n, K_i, r_i, \tau_i; \theta_t) + \eta_n^{(c)}, \tag{14.161a}$$

$$S_n^{Market} = S_n + \eta_n^{(S)}, \tag{14.161b}$$

and the latent states

$$\theta_n = \theta_{n-1} + e_n, \tag{14.162a}$$

$$S_n = p(S_n | S_{n-1}). \tag{14.162b}$$

The performance of the non-linear filter, when changing some parameters, is evaluated in Figure 14.3 for the Heston model.

The non-linear filter is able to track the changing parameters (smooth variations are tracked well, jumps in the parameters are assimilated after a few

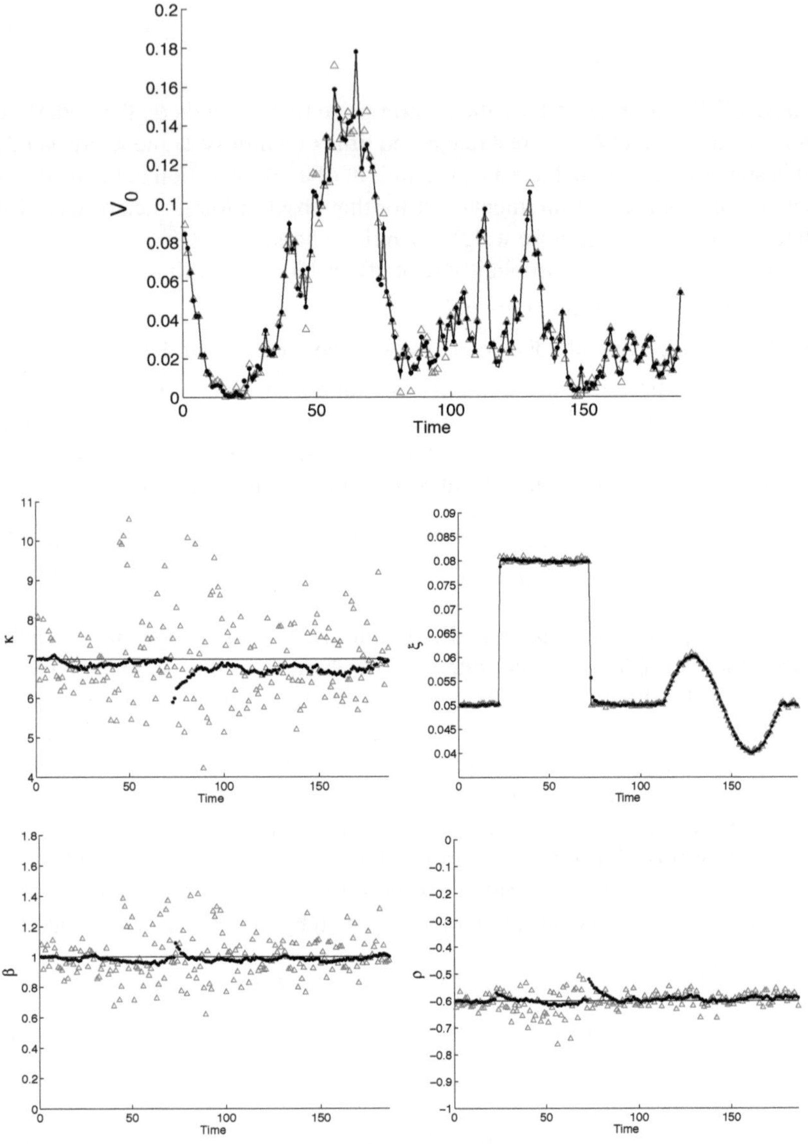

Figure 14.3: Adaptive calibration of the Heston model to simulated data, when parameters are changing. The true parameter value is the solid line, non-linear filter estimate is the dotted line and the triangles are daily non-linear least squares estimates.

consecutive observations), while the non-linear least squares using only the current observations are quite noisy but generally adapt somewhat quicker.

The performance of the sequential calibration algorithm, when calibrating a Heston model to S & P 500 data between late 2001 and 2003, is presented in Figure 14.4. The cloud of non-linear least squares estimates is again scattered around the filter estimates.

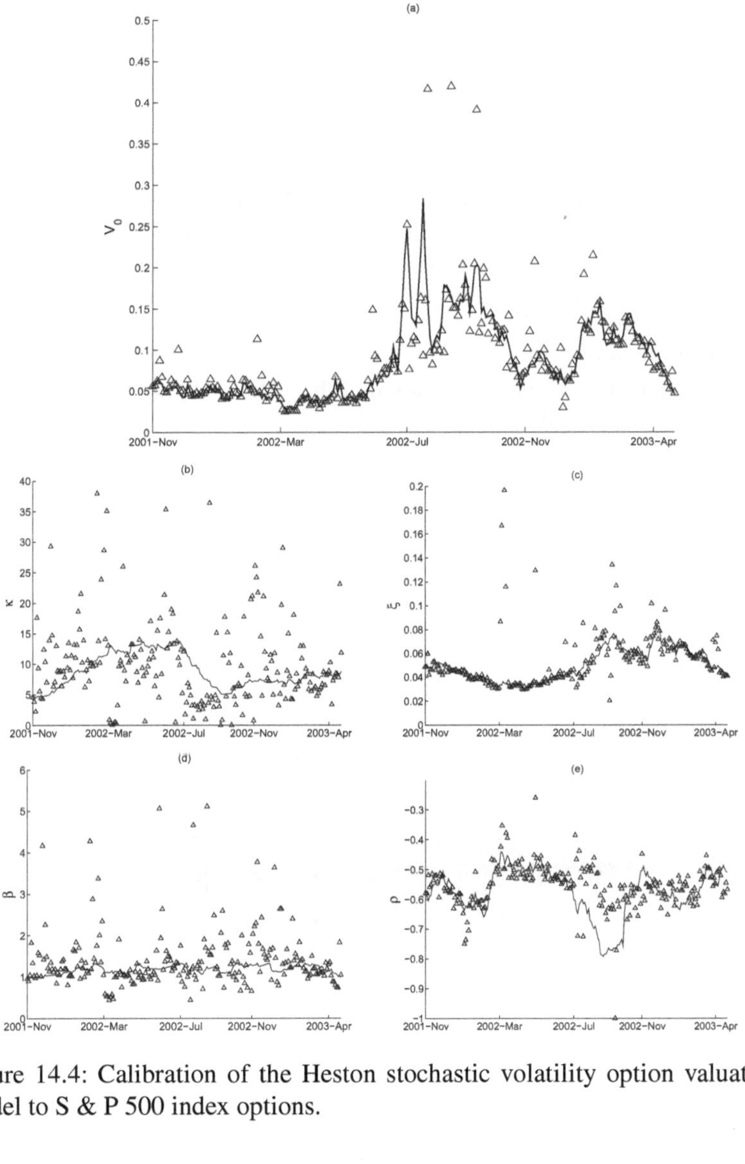

Figure 14.4: Calibration of the Heston stochastic volatility option valuation model to S & P 500 index options.

14.11.2 Computing Value at Risk in a stochastic volatility model

Value at risk is a popular measure of risk; cf. Embrechts et al. [2005], Hult et al. [2012]. It is well known that volatility varies over time (cf. Chapter 1), so some sort of stochastic volatility model is needed. The standard GARCH family of model (Section 5.5.2), is very popular, but is unable to cope with unexpected events as the volatility (according to the model) at time $n+1$ is perfectly known at time n. An alternative is the stochastic volatility model (Section 5.5.3),

$$y_n = \exp(V_n/2)z_n \tag{14.163}$$

$$V_n = a_0 + a_1 V_n + \sigma e_n \tag{14.164}$$

where z_n and e_n are independent standard Gaussian random variables.

A stochastic volatility model was fitted to OMXS30 (a Swedish stock index consisting of the 30 largest companies listed) with data from March 30th, 2005 to March 6th, 2009. The parameters were found by optimizing the likelihood using MATLAB'S `fminsearch` routine, which is a (derivative free) Nelder-Mead simplex method. The returns and estimated log-variance are presented in Figure 14.5 and 14.6.

More interesting is the computation of the Value at Risk (VaR) statistic. It is defined as the quantile

$$VaR_\alpha = \inf\{u \in \mathbb{R} : \int_{-\infty}^{u} p(y_n|y_{1:n-1})\mathrm{d}y_n = \alpha\}. \tag{14.165}$$

This is rather easy to compute as we know that the measurement kernel is

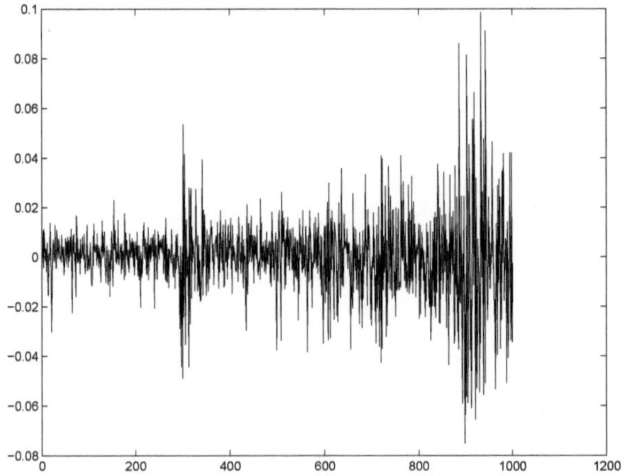

Figure 14.5: Returns on the OMXS30 from March 30th, 2005 to March 6th, 2009.

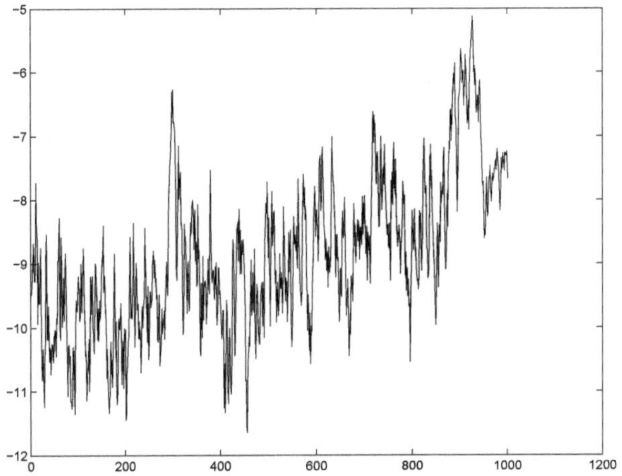

Figure 14.6: Estimated volatility on the OMXS30 from March 30th, 2005 to March 6th, 2009.

Gaussian and we have a particle representation for $p(x_n|y_{1:n-1})$. It follows that

$$\int_{-\infty}^{u} p(y_n|y_{1:n-1})\mathrm{d}y_n = \int_{-\infty}^{u} p(y_n|x_n)p(x_n|y_{1:n-1})\mathrm{d}y_n \tag{14.166}$$

$$\approx \int_{-\infty}^{u}\int_{\mathbb{R}^x} p(y_n|x_n)p_K(x_n|y_{1:n-1})\mathrm{d}y_n\mathrm{d}x_n \tag{14.167}$$

$$= \int_{-\infty}^{u} \sum \omega_n^{(k)} p(y_n|x_n^{(k)})\mathrm{d}y_n. \tag{14.168}$$

We know from the model specification that the measurement kernel is Gaussian with zero mean and variance v_n^2. Computing the VaR simply comes down to numerically solving Equation (14.165) with the measurement kernel plugged into Equation (14.168). The result in shown in Figure 14.7 where 61 returns were below the VaR level when computing VaR at the 5% level.

This deviation is not statistically significant as an approximate interval of the number of observations that is expected to end up below the VaR level is $(36, 64)$ observations.

14.11.3 Extended Kalman filtering applied to bonds

In this section, we utilize the modelling framework from Chapter 14 consisting of the state space model (14.1) and the measurement equation (14.2). In this particular case, the state space model will describe the spot interest rates and the measurement equation will be the solution of the bond pricing equation (11.66) (plus some additive white noise). This framework allows us to estimate both the parameters in the state space model and the *implied* interest

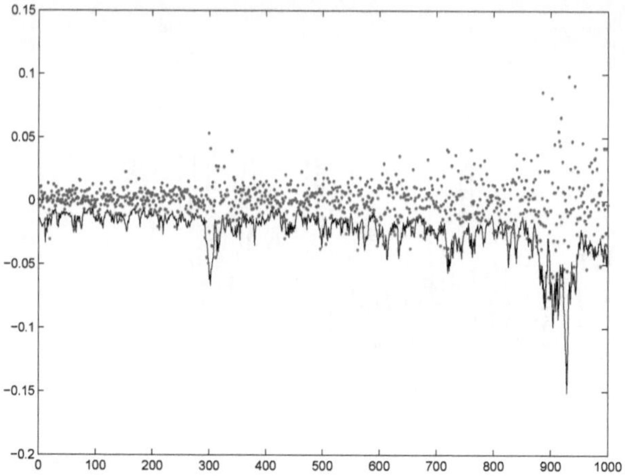

Figure 14.7: Value at Risk computed for the OMXS30 between March 30th, 2005 and March 6th, 2009. Approximately 5% of the returns are lower than the computed VaR at the 5% level.

rates. The term *implied* is used, because the estimated interest rates (obtained by utilizing the extended Kalman filter) are the interest rates implied by the bond prices and not the interest rates that are quoted in the financial markets.

It should be noted that this framework is only applicable for Gaussian interest rate models, although they may be multivariate. Thus it is not possible without some modification to use this method for, e.g., the Cox–Ingersoll–Ross model. This restriction may be overcome by introducing the transformation of the diffusion term with that was discussed in Section 13.4. In addition, it is a necessary requirement that an explicit solution to the bond pricing equation (11.66) is available.

For the large class of models, where this solution is not available, one has to resort to, e.g., Monte Carlo simulation. In this case, the measurement equation is estimated on the basis of a bond price which is obtained by a Monte Carlo simulation of the expectation in (11.66). Due to the Feynman–Kac representation theorem, the bond price may also be obtained by solving the PDE associated with (11.66) numerically. Although both methods are conceptually simple, they are extremely demanding from a computational point of view. We will not go into more details here, but a number of references are listed in the Notes.

Let us sketch the procedure that we wish to use:

- Given an interest rate model (or state space model),
- the bond pricing formula (11.66) is solved analytically. The solution constitutes a measurement equation.

ISIN	Bond	Maturity
DK0009915035	9% Danske Stat St. Laan	15/11 1996
DK0009915548	9% Danske Stat St. Laan	11/11 1998
DK0009916439	9% Danske Stat St. Laan	15/11 1995
DK0009917916	6% Danske Stat St. Laan	10/2 1996
DK0009918054	5.25% Danske Stat St. Laan	10/8 1996
DK0009918567	6.25% Danske Stat St. Laan	10/2 1997

Table 14.1: The considered Danish Government Bonds

- Input series are designed to model the payout of coupons and the time to maturity
- This is implemented in a program, and
- the model parameters are implemented using the conditional maximum likelihood method discussed in Chapter 14.9.

Data description

The method is applied to time series of daily observed prices for Danish Government Bonds[1] listed in Table 14.1 for the period 2/8-94 to 8/9-95. Each time series consists of 282 observations. These bonds pay out a coupon once a year and the size of the coupon c is constant throughout the lifetime of the bond. At maturity the bond pays out a coupon c and the amount C, where C = DKK 100 for Danish Government Bonds.

Certain conventions are associated with trading of Danish Government Bonds: A "bond year" consists of 12 months each containing 30 days. Therefore months with 31 days are cut one day short and February is extended by 2 days (or 1 day in leap years). This is not taken into account in this thesis. Furthermore the day of settlement is 3 days later than the day of agreement, but this is not deemed to be relevant as we are modelling the actual bond prices.

Bonds are not traded during weekends, so bond prices for weekend days are not available, but the model should take these "missing" prices into account as the underlying stochastic process that generates the spot interest rate evolves in continuous time. The extended Kalman filter is used to predict the missing prices using the dynamics of the interest rate model (rather than replacing bond prices for the weekends by some interpolation scheme). Hence each time series is expanded to cover a period of 402 days.

Should a bond be traded less than 30 "bond days" prior to the coupon being payed to the holder of the bond. Hence the bond price is reduced by the coupon value c 30 prior to the maturity date. Furthermore the time-to-maturity

[1]The ISIN number is an international coding used for bonds. Only the last four digits will be used in the following.

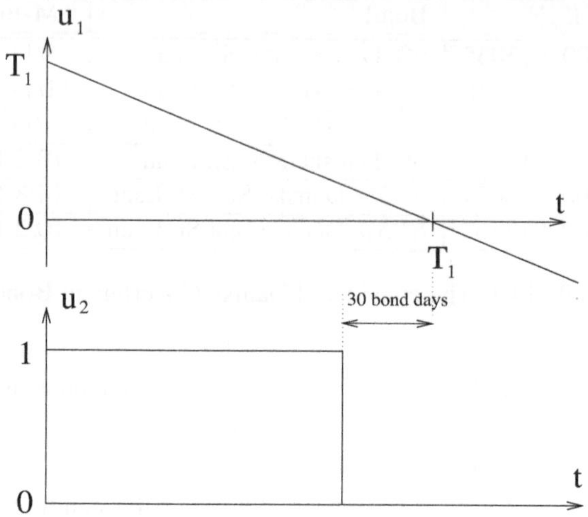

Figure 14.8: The designed input variables.

$T-t$ in the measurement equation has to be incorporated into the estimation procedure. These conventions have been implemented by incorporating two designed input variables $\mathbf{U} = [\mathbf{u}_1\, \mathbf{u}_2]$ in the measurement equation as illustrated in Figure 14.8, where $\mathbf{u}_1$ models the time to the first coming payout $T_1 - t$ and $\mathbf{u}_2$ models the payout of a coupon. If bond prices were available for a longer period of time spanning n coupon payouts, n similar input variables should be incorporated.

14.11.4 Case 1: A Wiener process

A simple Wiener process is considered initially

$$\mathrm{d}r(t) = \sigma \mathrm{d}W(t) \tag{14.169}$$

where $\sigma(r,t) = \sigma$ implies constant volatility. The solution to (14.169) is given by

$$r(t) = r(t_0) + \sigma W(t) \tag{14.170}$$

where $r(t_0)$ is the implied interest rate at time t_0.

Using this model, it may be shown that the price of a coupon bond should satisfy the equation

$$\begin{aligned} P(t, T_N, r(t)) = c \sum_{n=1}^{N} \exp\left(-(T_n - t)(r(t) - \frac{1}{6}\sigma^2(T_n - t)^2)\right) \\ + C \exp\left(-(T_N - t)(r(t) - \frac{1}{6}\sigma^2(T_N - t)^2)\right), \end{aligned} \tag{14.171}$$

or, by adding a noise term to account for measurements errors,

$$\begin{aligned} Y_k &= c\sum_{n=1}^{N} \exp\left(-(T_n - t_k)(r(t_k) - \frac{1}{6}\sigma^2(T_n - t_k)^2)\right) \\ &\quad + C\left(-(T_N - t_k)(r(t_k) - \frac{1}{6}\sigma^2(T_N - t_k)^2)\right) + e_k \end{aligned} \tag{14.172}$$

where $\{e_k\}$ is a white noise with zero mean and variance σ_2^2.

ISIN	$\hat{r}(t_0)$	$\hat{\sigma}^2$	$\hat{\sigma}_2^2$	$\hat{\sigma}_r$
DK0009916439	0.06562 (39.9924)	1.1941e-4 (12.3497)	0.1311e-8 (0.2282)	16.7%
DK0009917916	0.06649 (46.1670)	0.9004e-4 (14.8825)	0.1223e-8 (0.7197)	14.3%
DK0009918054	0.06748 (47.4841)	0.7502e-4 (13.5571)	0.1686e-8 (1.0042)	12.8%
DK0009918567	0.06927 (32.0052)	0.7801e-4 (12.4275)	0.4450e-8 (1.4287)	12.8%

Table 14.2: Estimation results for the Wiener process. The values given in parentheses are asymptotic t-test values for the hypothesis that the parameter is equal to zero. It is seen that $\hat{\sigma}_2^2$ does not differ significantly from zero, i.e., there are no measurement errors. Similar results are obtained by reestimation without the variance parameter σ_2^2.

14.11.5 Case 2: The Vasicek model

Again, we consider the Vasicek model

$$dr(t) = \alpha(\gamma - r(t))dt + \sigma dW(t) \tag{14.173}$$

where α, γ and σ are constants, and $W(t)$ is a standard Wiener process.

In the literature, it is reported that it is very difficult to estimate the adjustment parameter α, unless a long time series is available (i.e., at least several times longer than the half life of the process implied by α parameter). A long time series might give rise to other problems on its own, namely that the time series structural breaks, regime shifts or other nonlinear phenomena render the model 14.173 unappropriate. We had serious difficulties in obtaining reasonable and consistent estimates of the model parameters with the parameterisation of the original model suggested by Vasicek [1977].

In Jørgensen [1994], an alternative parameterisation of the model is suggested, but the bond pricing framework is not worked through with this new parameterisation:

$$\mathrm{d}r(t) = (\theta - \eta r(t))\mathrm{d}t + \sigma \mathrm{d}W(t). \tag{14.174}$$

The complete framework will be reported in this section. The bond pricing framework for this spot interest rate model is established by making the transformations

$$\alpha = \eta \tag{14.175}$$
$$\gamma = \theta/\alpha = \theta/\eta \tag{14.176}$$

in the framework introduced in Vasicek [1977].

This yields the bond pricing formula

$$P(t,T,r) = \exp\left\{ \left(\frac{1}{2}\left(\frac{\sigma}{\eta}\right)^2 - \frac{\theta}{\eta} \right)(T-t) + \frac{1}{\eta}\left(1 - e^{-\eta(T-t)}\right) \times \right.$$
$$\left. \left(\frac{\theta}{\eta} - r - \left(\frac{\sigma}{\eta}\right)^2 \right) + \frac{1}{4\eta}\left(\frac{\sigma}{\theta}\right)^2 \left(1 - e^{-2\eta(T-t)}\right) \right\}. \tag{14.177}$$

The conditional mean and variance of the interest rate is

$$\mathbf{E}[r(s)] = \frac{\theta}{\eta} + \left(r - \frac{\theta}{\eta}\right) e^{-\eta(T-t)}, \tag{14.178}$$

$$\mathbf{Var}[r(s)] = \frac{\sigma^2}{2\eta}\left(1 - e^{-2\eta(T-t)}\right). \tag{14.179}$$

Especially, in the limits, we get

$$\mathbf{E}[r(s)] = \begin{cases} r & \text{for } t = T \\ \frac{\theta}{\eta} & \text{for } T \to \infty \end{cases} \tag{14.180}$$

$$\mathbf{Var}[r(s)] = \begin{cases} 0 & \text{for } t = T \\ \frac{\sigma^2}{2\eta} & \text{for } T \to \infty \end{cases}. \tag{14.181}$$

It is seen from (14.181) that the variance is zero at maturity $t = T$, i.e., the instantaneous rate of return is exactly the spot interest rate r. This is in compliance with the deterministic nature of the partial differential equation that the individual bond prices must satisfy and the adjacent boundary condition $P(T,T,r) = 1$.

The results in Table 14.3 are obtained.[2] The estimates of θ are not shown as the obtained estimates did not differ significantly from zero. Therefore the estimation procedure was repeated for each time series with η fixed at zero. This also applies for the variance of the measurement noise.

[2] Unless stated otherwise, the values in parentheses are asymptotic t-test values for insignificant parameters.

	5548	8054	8567
$\hat{\eta}$	4.44167E-04 (13.7703)	5.70140E-04 (94.5229)	5.11133E-04 (1.5214)
$\hat{r}(t_0)$	0.0728404 (49.1246)	0.0675208 (43.9797)	0.0693201 (44.9230)
$\hat{\sigma}^2$	2.27742E-07 (12.8445)	2.06625E-07 (12.7473)	2.15661E-07 (13.1400)
$\hat{\sigma}_r$	12.4308%	12.7734%	12.7109%
χ^2 (α)	47.77 (44.1%)	59.06 (11.2%)	49.17 (38.6%)
ρ	$\begin{bmatrix} 1.00 & -.06 & .00 \\ -.06 & 1.00 & -.01 \\ .00 & -.01 & 1.00 \end{bmatrix}$	$\begin{bmatrix} 1.00 & .00 & .00 \\ .00 & 1.00 & -.02 \\ .00 & -.02 & 1.00 \end{bmatrix}$	$\begin{bmatrix} 1.00 & .02 & .00 \\ .02 & 1.00 & .02 \\ .00 & .02 & 1.00 \end{bmatrix}$

Table 14.3: Results for the Vasicek model

A first examination of the listed correlation matrices shows that the parameter estimates are uncorrelated, and, hence, each parameter may be interpreted independent of the others.

The estimates of η are very small, and similar across time series, but it should be kept in mind that η is a continuous-time parameter. The estimates of $r(t_0)$ seem reasonable and are well determined. Based on these estimates, the annual relative volatility σ_r is determined for each time series. As discussed previously, the σ_r should be within the range 10–20%, and this is indeed the case.

14.12 Problems

Problem 14.1

Let

$$\begin{pmatrix} X \\ Y \end{pmatrix} \in N\left(\begin{pmatrix} \mu_X \\ \mu_Y \end{pmatrix}, \begin{pmatrix} \Sigma_X & \Sigma_{XY} \\ \Sigma_{YX} & \Sigma_Y \end{pmatrix} \right)$$

be a vector of jointly multivariate Gaussian random variables.

1. Derive the distribution for $p(X|Y)$.

2. Show that

$$\mathbf{E}[X|Y=y] = \mu_X + \Sigma_{XY}\Sigma_Y^{-1}(y-\mu_Y),$$
$$\mathbf{Var}[X|Y=y] = \Sigma_X - \Sigma_{XY}\Sigma_Y^{-1}\Sigma_{YX}.$$

Problem 14.2

Let $y_t = m + \varepsilon_t$, where $\varepsilon_t \in N(0, \sigma_\varepsilon^2)$.

1. Derive the conditional distribution for $\hat{m}_t = p(m|y_{1:t})$ using a Kalman filter, assuming some Gaussian density for m_0, e.g., $p(m_0) = N(\mu_0, \Sigma_0)$.

Hint: Design a latent process such that the distribution of m_t can be found.

2. Relate the result to prior knowledge in statistics.

Appendix A

Projections in Hilbert spaces

A.1 Introduction

In many situations we want information about variables that are not directly measured, assuming that we have information about some variables which are correlated with the unmeasured variable. If this (cross)correlation is known or estimated, then it can be used for estimating the value of the unmeasured variables.

Consider for instance the interest rates. Short term interest rates are quoted on a daily basis in the money markets for maturities up to, say, one year; but longer term interest rates are traded only indirectly through the bond markets. Theoretically, options dependent on interest rates are priced according to a stochastic process describing the evolution in continuous time of the short term interest rate even though this process is not directly observable. The observed (or measured) variables, when modelling interest rate processes, are the bond prices.

The Wiener filter (see Madsen [2007]) is an example where the known cross-correlation is used together with the projection theorem to estimate an unmeasured time series based on a measured time series. The Kalman filter, which will be introduced in this appendix, is some sort of online version of the Wiener filter.

The main goal of this appendix is to present the *projection theorem*, and to illustrate the wide range of applications of this theorem. Finally the theorem is used to formulate the (ordinary) *Kalman filter*. The contents of this appendix is basically based on Madsen [1992] and Brockwell and Davis [1991], and more information about the theory and applications of the projection theorem can be found in those references.

One of the advantages by considering the projection theorem as it is formulated in this appendix is that many of the well-known concepts from two- and three-dimensional Euclidean geometry, such as orthogonality, carry over to the more general Hilbert spaces considered in the following.

By using the projection theorem it can be realized that a unified set of equations can be used in different contexts. Hence it can be shown that many of the methods used in time series analysis, such as prediction, filtering and estimation, are seen in a unified context.

A.2 Hilbert spaces

A Hilbert space is simply an inner-product space, i.e. a vector space supplied with an inner product, with an additional property of completeness. The inner product is a natural generalization of the inner (or scalar) product of two vectors in n-dimensional Euclidean space. Since many of the properties of Euclidean space carry over to the inner-product spaces, it will be helpful to keep Euclidean space in mind in all that follows.

Let us first consider a well-known inner-product space, namely the Euclidean space.

Example A.1 (Euclidean space). *The set of all column vectors*

$$x = (x_1, ..., x_k)^T \in \mathbb{R}^k \tag{A.1}$$

is a real inner-product space if we define

$$\langle x, y \rangle = \sum_{i=1}^{k} x_i y_i. \tag{A.2}$$

It is a simple matter to check that the conditions above are all satisfied.

Definition A.1 (Norm). *Let $\|x\| > 0$, if $x \neq 0$, then the norm of an element x of an inner-product space is defined to be*

$$\|x\| = \sqrt{\langle x, x \rangle}. \tag{A.3}$$

In the Euclidean space $\mathbb{R}^k$ the norm of the vector is simply its length.

Definition A.2 (The angle between elements). *The angle θ between two non-zero elements x and y belonging to any real inner-product space is defined as*

$$\theta = \arccos[\langle x, y \rangle / (\|x\| \|y\|)]. \tag{A.4}$$

In particular x and y are said to be orthogonal if and only if $\langle x, y \rangle = 0$.

Now let us define the Hilbert space:

Definition A.3 (Hilbert space). *A Hilbert space $\mathscr{H}$ is vector space, equipped with an inner product, in which every Cauchy sequence x_n converges in norm to some element in $x \in \mathscr{H}$. The inner-product space is then said to be complete.*

Example A.2 (Euclidean space). *The completeness of the inner-product space $\mathbb{R}^k$ can be verified. Thus $\mathbb{R}^k$ is a Hilbert space.*

Example A.3 (The space $L^2(\Omega, \mathscr{F}, \mathbb{P})$). *Consider a probability space $(\Omega, \mathscr{F}, \mathbb{P})$ and the collection C of all random variables X defined on Ω and satisfying the condition $\mathbf{E}[X^2] \leq \infty$. It is rather easy to show that C is a vector space.*

For any two elements $X, Y \in C$ we now define the inner product

$$\langle X, Y \rangle = \mathbf{E}[XY]. \tag{A.5}$$

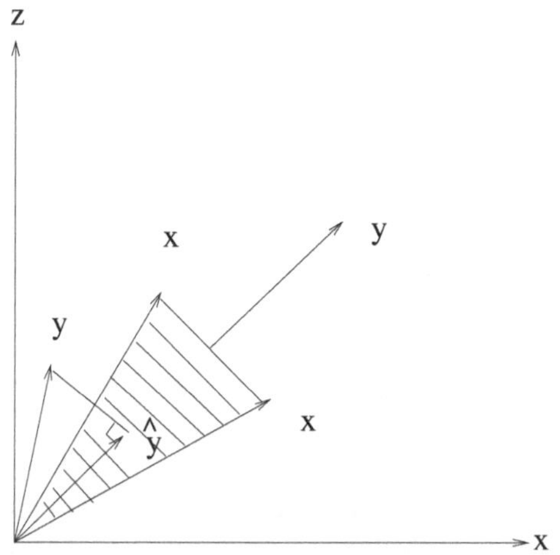

Figure A.1: Projection in $\mathbb{R}^3$.

Norm convergence of a sequence X_n of elements of L^2 to the limit X means

$$\|X_n - X\|^2 = \mathbf{E}[|X_n - X|^2] \to 0 \qquad \text{as } n \to \infty. \tag{A.6}$$

Norm convergence of X_n to X in an L^2 space is called mean-square convergence and is written as $X_n \overset{m.s.}{\to} X$.

To complete the proof that L^2 is a Hilbert space we need to establish completeness, i.e. that if $\|X_n - X\|^2 \to 0$ as $m, n \to \infty$, then there exists $X \in L^2$ such that $X_n \to X$ (see Brockwell and Davis [1991]).

A.3 The projection theorem

Let us start by considering two simple applications which illustrate the projection theorem in the two types of Hilbert spaces.

Example A.4 (Linear approximation in $\mathbb{R}^3$). *Suppose three vectors are given in $\mathbb{R}^3$.*

$$y = (1/4, 1/4, 1)^T, \tag{A.7}$$
$$x_1 = (1, 0, 1/4)^T, \tag{A.8}$$
$$x_2 = (0, 1, 1/4)^T. \tag{A.9}$$

Our problem is to find the linear combination $\hat{y} = \alpha_1 x_1 + \alpha_2 x_2$ which is closest to y in the sense that $S = \|y - \alpha_1 x_1 - \alpha_2 x_2\|^2$ is minimized.

One approach to this problem is to write S in the form $S = (1/4 - \alpha_1)^2 + (1/4 - \alpha_2)^2 + (1 - 1/4\alpha_1 - 1/4\alpha_2)^2$ and then to use calculus to minimize with respect to α_1 and α_2. In the alternative geometric approach we observe that *the required vector* $\hat{y} = \alpha_1 x_1 + \alpha_2 x_2$ *is the vector in the plane determined by* x_1 *and* x_2 *such that* $y - \alpha_1 x_1 - \alpha_2 x_2$ *is orthogonal to the plane of* x_1 *and* x_2 *(see the figure). The orthogonality condition may be stated as*

$$\langle y - \alpha_1 x_1 - \alpha_2 x_2, x_i \rangle = 0 \qquad i = 1,2 \tag{A.10}$$

or equivalently

$$\alpha_1 \langle x_1, x_1 \rangle + \alpha_2 \langle x_2, x_1 \rangle = \langle y, x_1 \rangle \tag{A.11}$$
$$\alpha_1 \langle x_1, x_2 \rangle + \alpha_2 \langle x_2, x_2 \rangle = \langle y, x_2 \rangle. \tag{A.12}$$

By solving these two equations for the particular values of x_1, x_2 *and* y *specified, it is seen that* $\alpha_1 = \alpha_2 = 4/9$, *and* $\hat{y} = (4/9, 4/9, 2/9)'$.

Example A.5 (Linear approximation in $L^2(\Omega, \mathscr{F}, P)$)**.** *Now suppose that* X_1, X_2 *and* Y *are random variables in* $L^2(\Omega, \mathscr{F}, P)$. *Only* X_1 *and* X_2 *are observed and we wish to estimate the value of* Y *by using the linear combination* $\hat{Y} = \alpha_1 X_1 + \alpha_2 X_2$ *which minimizes the mean square error,*

$$S = E|Y - \alpha_1 X_1 - \alpha_2 X_2|^2 = \|Y - \alpha_1 X_1 - \alpha_2 X_2\|^2. \tag{A.13}$$

As in the previous example there are at least two possible approaches to the problem. The first is to write

$$\begin{aligned} S = {} & \mathbf{E}[Y^2] + \alpha_1^2 \mathbf{E}[X_1^2] + \alpha_2^2 \mathbf{E}[X_2^2] - 2\alpha_1 \mathbf{E}[YX_1] - \\ & 2\alpha_2 \mathbf{E}[YX_2] + \alpha_1 \alpha_2 \mathbf{E}[X_1 X_2] \end{aligned} \tag{A.14}$$

and then to minimize with respect to α_1 *and* α_2.

The second method is to use the same geometric approach as in the previous example. Our aim is to find an element in $\hat{Y}$ *in the set*

$$\mathscr{M} = \{X \in L^2(\Omega, \mathscr{F}, P) : X = \alpha_1 X_1 + \alpha_2 X_2 (\alpha_1, \alpha_2 \in \mathbb{R})\} \tag{A.15}$$

which implies that the mean square error $\|Y - \hat{Y}\|^2$ *is as small as possible. By analogy with the previous example we might expect* $\hat{Y}$ *to have the property that* $Y - \hat{Y}$ *is orthogonal to all elements of* $\mathscr{M}$. *Applying it to our present problem, we can write*

$$\langle Y - \alpha_1 X_1 - \alpha_2 X_2, X \rangle = 0 \qquad \text{for all } X \in \mathscr{M} \tag{A.16}$$

or, equivalently, by the linearity of the inner product,

$$\langle Y - \alpha_1 X_1 - \alpha_2 X_2, X_i \rangle = 0, \; i = 1,2. \tag{A.17}$$

These are the same equations for α_1 *and* α_2 *as in the previous example, although the inner product is of course defined differently in (A.17). In terms of expectations we can rewrite (A.17) in the form*

$$\alpha_1 \mathbf{E}[X_1^2] + \alpha_2 \mathbf{E}[X_2 X_1] = \mathbf{E}[YX_1] \tag{A.18}$$
$$\alpha_1 \mathbf{E}[X_1 X_2] + \alpha_2 \mathbf{E}[X_2^2] = \mathbf{E}[YX_2] \tag{A.19}$$

from which α_1 *and* α_2 *are easily found.*

Before establishing the projection theorem for a general Hilbert space we need to introduce some new terminology.

Definition A.4 (Closed subspace). *A linear subspace $\mathscr{M}$ of a Hilbert space $\mathscr{H}$ is said to be a closed subspace of $\mathscr{H}$ if $\mathscr{M}$ contains all of its limit points (i.e. if $x_n \in \mathscr{M}$ and $\|x_n - x\| \to 0$ imply that $x \in \mathscr{M}$).*

Definition A.5 (Orthogonal complement). *The orthogonal complement of a subset $\mathscr{M}$ of $\mathscr{H}$ is defined to be the set $\mathscr{M}^\perp$ of all elements of $\mathscr{H}$ which are orthogonal to every element of $\mathscr{M}$. Thus*

$$x \in \mathscr{M}^\perp \quad \text{if and only if } \langle x, y\rangle = 0 \quad (\text{written } x \perp y) \tag{A.20}$$

for all $y \in \mathscr{M}$.

Theorem A.1. *If $\mathscr{M}$ is any subset of a Hilbert space $\mathscr{H}$ then $\mathscr{M}^\perp$ is a closed subspace of $\mathscr{H}$.*

Proof. Omitted. □

Theorem A.2 (The projection theorem). *If $\mathscr{M}$ is a closed subspace of the Hilbert space $\mathscr{H}$ and $x \in \mathscr{H}$, then*

1. *there is a unique element $\hat{x} \in \mathscr{M}$ such that*

$$\|x - \hat{x}\| = \inf_{y \in \mathscr{M}} \|x - y\| \tag{A.21}$$

and

2. *$\hat{x} \in \mathscr{M}$ and $\|x - \hat{x}\| = \inf_{y \in \mathscr{M}} \|x - y\|$ if and only if $\hat{x} \in \mathscr{M}$ and $(x - \hat{x}) \in \mathscr{M}^\perp$.*

The element $\hat{x}$ is called the (orthogonal) projection of x onto $\mathscr{M}$.

Proof. Omitted — see Brockwell and Davis [1991]. □

Theorem A.3 (The projection mapping of $\mathscr{H}$ onto $\mathscr{M}$). *If $\mathscr{M}$ is a closed subspace of the Hilbert space $\mathscr{H}$ and I is the identity mapping on $\mathscr{H}$, then there is a unique mapping $P_{\mathscr{M}}$ of $\mathscr{H}$ onto M such that $I - P_{\mathscr{M}}$ maps $\mathscr{H}$ onto $\mathscr{M}^\perp$. $P_{\mathscr{M}}$ is called the projection mapping of $\mathscr{H}$ onto $\mathscr{M}$.*

Proof. By the projection theorem, for each $x \in \mathscr{H}$ there is a unique $\hat{x} \in \mathscr{M}$ such that $x - \hat{x} \in \mathscr{M}^\perp$. The required mapping is therefore

$$P_{\mathscr{M}} x = \hat{x} \qquad x \in \mathscr{H}. \tag{A.22}$$

□

Theorem A.4 (Properties of projection mappings). *Let $\mathscr{H}$ be a Hilbert space and let $P_{\mathscr{M}}$ denote the projection mapping onto a closed subspace $\mathscr{M}$. Then*

1. *$P_{\mathscr{M}}(\alpha x + \beta y) = \alpha P_{\mathscr{M}} x + \beta P_{\mathscr{M}} y$.*
2. $\|x\|^2 = \|P_{\mathscr{M}} x\|^2 + \|(I - P_{\mathscr{M}})x\|^2$.

3. *each $x \in \mathscr{H}$ has a unique representation as a sum of an element of $\mathscr{M}$ and an element of $\mathscr{M}^{\perp}$, i.e.*

$$x = P_{\mathscr{M}}x + (I - P_{\mathscr{M}})x. \tag{A.23}$$

4. $P_{\mathscr{M}}x_n \to P_{\mathscr{M}}x$ *if* $\|x_n - x\| \to 0$.
5. $x \in \mathscr{M}$ *if and only if* $P_{\mathscr{M}}x = x$.
6. $x \in \mathscr{M}^{\perp}$ *if and only if* $P_{\mathscr{M}}x = 0$.
7. $\mathscr{M}_1 \subseteq \mathscr{M}_2$ *if and only if* $P_{\mathscr{M}_1}P_{\mathscr{M}_2}x = P_{\mathscr{M}_1}x$ *for all* $x \in \mathscr{H}$.

Proof. Omitted — but rather obvious from a geometrical point of view. □

A.3.1 Prediction equations

In the following a set of equations, the so-called prediction equations will be derived. The equations describe how to find the projection that gives the minimum mean square error (Minimum MSE).

Given a Hilbert space $\mathscr{H}$, a closed subspace $\mathscr{M}$ and an element $x \in \mathscr{H}$, then the projection theorem shows that the element of $\mathscr{M}$ closest to x is the unique element $\hat{x} \in \mathscr{M}$ such that

$$\langle x - \hat{x}, y \rangle = 0 \qquad \text{for all } y \in \mathscr{M}. \tag{A.24}$$

Compare the general equation above with the special cases in the examples prior to projection theorem.

The quantity, $\hat{x} = P_{\mathscr{M}}x$, is frequently called *the best predictor of x in the subspace $\mathscr{M}$*.

Remark A.1. *It is helpful to visualize the projection theorem in terms of Figure A.1, which depicts the special case in which $\mathscr{H} = \mathbb{R}^3$, and $\mathscr{M}$ is the plane containing x_1 and x_2, and $\hat{y} = P_{\mathscr{M}}y$. The prediction equation (A.24) is simply the statement that $y - \hat{y}$ must be orthogonal to $\mathscr{M}$. The projection theorem tells us that $\hat{y} = P_{\mathscr{M}}y$ is uniquely determined by this condition for any Hilbert space $\mathscr{H}$ and closed subspace $\mathscr{M}$.*

The projection theorem and the prediction equations play fundamental roles in time series analysis, especially for estimation, approximation, filtering and prediction. Examples will be given.

Example A.6 (Minimum MSE linear prediction).
Let $\{X_t, t = 0, \pm 1, ...\}$ be a stationary process on $(\Omega, \mathscr{F}, P)$ with mean zero and autocovariance function $\gamma(\cdot)$, and consider the problem of finding the best linear combination

$$\hat{X}_{n+1} = \sum_{j=1}^{n} \phi_{nj} X_{n+1-j} \tag{A.25}$$

which best approximates X_{n+1} in the sense that $\mathbf{E}[(X_{n+1} - \sum_{j=1}^{n} \phi_{nj} X_{n+1-j})^2]$

is minimum. This problem is easily solved with the aid of the projection theorem by taking $\mathscr{H} = L^2(\Omega, \mathscr{F}, \mathbb{P})$ *and* $\mathscr{M} = \{\sum_{j=1}^n \alpha_j X_{n+1-j} : \alpha_1, \dots, \alpha_n \in \mathbb{R}\}$*. Since minimization of* $\mathbf{E}[|X_{n+1} - \hat{X}_{n+1}|^2]$ *is identical to minimization of the squared norm* $\|X_{n+1} - \hat{X}_{n+1}\|^2$*, we see at once that* $\hat{X}_{n+1} = P_{\mathscr{M}} X_{n+1}$*. The prediction equations are*

$$\langle X_{n+1} - \sum_{j=1}^{n} \phi_{nj} X_{n+1-j}, Y \rangle = 0 \qquad \text{for all } Y \in \mathscr{M} \tag{A.26}$$

which, by the linearity of the inner product, are equal to the n equations

$$\langle X_{n+1} - \sum_{j=1}^{n} \phi_{nj} X_{n+1-j}, X_k \rangle = 0 \quad k = n, n-1, ..., 1. \tag{A.27}$$

Recalling the definition $\langle X, Y \rangle = \mathbf{E}[XY]$ *of the inner product in* $L^2(\Omega, \mathscr{F}, \mathbb{P})$*, we see that the prediction equations can be written in the form*

$$\Gamma_n \phi_n = \gamma_n \tag{A.28}$$

where $\phi_n = (\phi_{n1}, ..., \phi_{nn})'$*,* $\gamma_n = (\gamma(1), ..., \gamma(n))'$ *and* $\Gamma_n = [\gamma(i-j)]_{i,j=1}^n$*. The projection theorem guarantees that there is at least one solution* ϕ_n *to the problem. If* Γ_n *is singular then there are infinitely many solutions, but the projection theorem guarantees that every solution will give the same (uniquely defined) predictor.*

A.4 Conditional expectation and linear projections

It is well known that the conditional expectation plays a central role in time series analysis, as the optimal prediction (under some mild assumptions) is found using the conditional expectation.

Consider the random variables Y and X from L^2.

Definition A.6 (The conditional expectation)**.** *The conditional expectation of* X *given* $Y = y$ *is*

$$\mathbf{E}[X|Y = y] = \int_{-\infty}^{\infty} x f_{X|Y=y}(x)\, \mathrm{d}x \tag{A.29}$$

where $f_{X|Y=y}(x)$ *is the conditional density function for* X *given* $Y = y$*.*

Remember that $\mathbf{E}[X|Y = y]$ is a number, whereas $\mathbf{E}[X|Y]$ is a stochastic variable.

It can be shown that the operator $\mathbf{E}[X|Y]$ on L^2 has all the properties of a projection operator, in particular

$$\begin{aligned} \mathbf{E}[cX + dZ|Y] &= c\mathbf{E}[X|Y] + d\mathbf{E}[Z|Y], \\ \mathbf{E}[1|Y] &= 1. \end{aligned}$$

Theorem A.5 (Best mean square predictor). *The conditional expectation* $\mathbf{E}[X|Y]$ *is the best mean square predictor of* X *in* $\mathcal{M}_Y$*, i.e. the best function of* Y *for predicting* X.

Proof. Follows from the projection theorem. □

However, the determination of projections on $\mathcal{M}_Y$ is usually very difficult. On the other hand it is relatively easy instead to calculate the projection of X on $\text{span}\{1,Y\} \subseteq \mathcal{M}_Y$, i.e. *the linear projection*

$$\mathbf{E}[X|Y] = a + bY \tag{A.30}$$

which gives a subset of the best function of Y (in the mean square sense) for predicting X.

The linear projection (A.30) is a projection of X onto a subspace of $\mathcal{M}_Y$. Therefore it can never have a smaller mean square error than $\mathbf{E}[X|Y]$. However it is of great importance for the following reasons:

- The linear projection (A.30) is easier to calculate.
- It depends only on the first and second order moments, $\mathbf{E}[Y]$, $\mathbf{E}[X]$, $\mathbf{E}[Y^2]$, $\mathbf{E}[X^2]$ and $\mathbf{E}[XY]$, of the joint distribution of (Y,X).
- If $(Y,X)'$ has a multivariate normal distribution then the conditional expectation is linear, i.e.
$$\text{span}\{1,Y\} = \mathcal{M}_Y. \tag{A.31}$$

Let us now consider two multivariate stochastic variables X and Y and the corresponding second order representation (first and second order moments for $(X,Y)'$)

$$\mu_Y, \mu_X, \Sigma_{XX}, \Sigma_{XY}, \Sigma_{YY}. \tag{A.32}$$

Theorem A.6 (Linear projection in L^2). *Given the second order representation for* $(X,Y)'$ *the linear projection is given by*

$$\mathbf{E}[X|Y] = \mu_X + \Sigma_{XY}\Sigma_{YY}^{-1}(Y - \mu_y) \tag{A.33}$$

and the variance is

$$\mathbf{Var}[X - \mathbf{E}[X|Y]] = \Sigma_{XX} - \Sigma_{XY}\Sigma_{YY}^{-1}\Sigma_{YX}. \tag{A.34}$$

Furthermore

$$\text{Cov}[X - \mathbf{E}[X|Y], Y] = 0, \tag{A.35}$$

i.e. the error $X - \mathbf{E}[X|Y]$ *is uncorrelated with* Y.

Proof. From the prediction equations:

$$\begin{aligned}
\langle X - \mathbf{E}[X|Y], Y\rangle &= 0,\\
\langle X - \mathbf{E}[X|Y], 1\rangle &= 0,
\end{aligned}$$

or

$$\begin{aligned}\langle a+bY,Y\rangle &= \langle X,Y\rangle,\\ \langle a+bY,1\rangle &= \langle X,1\rangle.\end{aligned}$$

Using the fact that in the multivariate case the inner product in L^2 is $\langle X,Y\rangle = \mathbf{E}[XY^T]$ we get

$$\begin{aligned}a\mathbf{E}[Y]^T + b\mathbf{E}[YY^T] &= \mathbf{E}[XY^T],\\ a+b\mathbf{E}[Y] &= \mathbf{E}[X].\end{aligned}$$

By solving these equations and using the fact that $\Sigma_{XY} = \mathbf{E}[XY'] - \mathbf{E}[X]\mathbf{E}[Y]'$ we obtain

$$b = \Sigma_{XY}\Sigma_{YY}^{-1}, \tag{A.36}$$
$$a = \mu_X - \Sigma_{XY}\Sigma_{YY}^{-1}\mu_y. \tag{A.37}$$

Hence the linear projection is

$$\mathbf{E}[X|Y] = \mu_X - \Sigma_{XY}\Sigma_{YY}^{-1}(Y-\mu_Y). \tag{A.38}$$

The variance follows immediately

$$\begin{aligned}\mathbf{Var}[X-\mathbf{E}[X|Y]] &= \mathbf{Var}[X-a-bY]\\ &= \Sigma_{XX} + b\Sigma_{YY}b^T - b\Sigma_{YX} - \Sigma_{XY}b^T\\ &= \Sigma_{XX} - \Sigma_{XY}\Sigma_{YY}^{-1}\Sigma_{YX}.\end{aligned}$$

The orthogonality between the error $X-\mathbf{E}[X|Y]$ and Y follows directly from the projection theorem. □

Theorem A.7. *If $(X,Y)^T$ has a normal distribution then $X|Y$ is normal distributed with mean*

$$\mathbf{E}[X|Y] = \mu_X - \Sigma_{XY}\Sigma_{YY}^{-1}(Y-\mu_y) \tag{A.39}$$

and variance

$$\mathbf{Var}[X|Y] = \mathbf{Var}[X-\mathbf{E}[X|Y]] = \Sigma_{XX} - \Sigma_{XY}\Sigma_{YY}^{-1}\Sigma_{YX}. \tag{A.40}$$

The error $X-\mathbf{E}[X|Y]$ and Y are stochastic independent.

Proof. Omitted. □

Let us illustrate the importance of the equations above by a couple of examples.

Example A.7 (Regression). *Let us consider the regression in* L^2 *of* Y *on* X

$$\mathbf{E}[Y|X] = X\theta \tag{A.41}$$

and assume that $\mathbf{E}[X] = \mathbf{E}[Y] = 0$.

Note that — compared to the discussion above — we have interchanged X *and* Y. *And in order to compare the results directly with the ordinary LS estimator for the general linear model in* $\mathbb{R}^n$ *we have also interchanged* X *and* θ.

The best estimator is found by the prediction equations

$$\langle Y - \mathbf{E}[Y|X], X\rangle = 0 \tag{A.42}$$

or

$$\langle Y - X\theta, X\rangle = 0. \tag{A.43}$$

Then we get

$$\Sigma_{YX} - \theta^T \Sigma_{XX} = 0 \tag{A.44}$$

or

$$\hat{\theta} = \Sigma_{XX}^{-1} \Sigma_{XY}. \tag{A.45}$$

Compare this result with the well-known LS estimator in $\mathscr{R}^n$.

Next an example where the formulation of the linear projection above is used directly. As this example is very important it is embedded in a section.

A.5 Kalman filter

As mentioned in the introduction, the Kalman filter can be used for estimating some variables, which are not directly measured, by using some measured variables, which are correlated with the unmeasured variables. In the case of the Kalman filter the correlation between the unmeasured variables X and the measured variables Y is described by a linear state space model.

Consider the *linear stochastic state space model*

$$X_t = A_t X_{t-1} + B_t u_{t-1} + e_{1,t}, \tag{A.46}$$

$$Y_t = C_t X_t + e_{2,t}, \tag{A.47}$$

where X_t is a m-dimensional state vector, u_t is the input vector and Y_t is the measured output vector. The matrices A_t, B_t and C_t are known and have appropriate dimensions.

The two white noise sequences $\{e_{1,t}\}$ and $\{e_{2,t}\}$ are mutually uncorrelated with variance $\Sigma_{1,t}$ and $\Sigma_{2,t}$, respectively.

The matrices A_t, B_t, C_t, $\Sigma_{1,t}$ and $\Sigma_{2,t}$ might be time varying, as indicated by the notation. However, in the rest of this example we skip the index t although all the given results are valid in the time varying case.

Let us consider the problem of estimating X_{t+k} given the observations $\{Y_s; s = t, t-1, \ldots\}$ and input $\{u_s, s = t-1, \ldots\}$. In the case $k = 0$ the problem is called reconstruction or filtering. The solution to this problem is given by the linear projection theorem.

It is clear that the linear projection theorem also is valid for the conditioned stochastic variable $(YX)'|Z$. If the stochastic variables have a normal distribution we get

$$\mathbf{E}[X|Y,Z] = \mathbf{E}[X|Z] + \mathrm{Cov}[X,Y|Z]\mathbf{Var}^{-1}[Y|Z](Y - \mathbf{E}[Y|Z]), \tag{A.48}$$

$$\mathbf{Var}[X|Y,Z] = \mathbf{Var}[X|Z] - \mathrm{Cov}[X,Y|Z]\mathbf{Var}^{-1}[Y|Z]C^T[X,Y|Z]. \tag{A.49}$$

Let us now introduce

$$\mathcal{Y}_t = (Y_1, \cdots, Y_t), \tag{A.50}$$

which is a vector of all observations until time t. The input is assumed to be known.

Further introduce

$$\hat{X}_{t+k|t} = \mathbf{E}\left[X_{t+k}|\mathcal{Y}_t\right], \tag{A.51}$$

$$\hat{Y}_{t+k|t} = \mathbf{E}\left[Y_{t+k}|\mathcal{Y}_t\right], \tag{A.52}$$

and the variances

$$\Sigma^{xx}_{t+k|t} = \mathbf{Var}\left[X_{t+k}|\mathcal{Y}_t\right], \tag{A.53}$$

$$\Sigma^{yy}_{t+k|t} = \mathbf{Var}\left[Y_{t+k}|\mathcal{Y}_t\right], \tag{A.54}$$

$$\Sigma^{xy}_{t+k|t} = \mathrm{Cov}\left[X_{t+k}, Y_{t+k}|\mathcal{Y}_t\right], \tag{A.55}$$

then we have the Kalman filter

Theorem A.8 (Kalman filter — Optimal reconstruction). *The reconstruction $\hat{X}_{t|t}$ which has the smallest mean square error is given by*

$$\hat{X}_{t|t} = \hat{X}_{t|t-1} + \Sigma^{xy}_{t|t-1}\left(\Sigma^{yy}_{t|t-1}\right)^{-1}\left(Y_t - \hat{Y}_{t|t-1}\right) \tag{A.56}$$

and the variance of the reconstruction error is

$$\Sigma^{xx}_{t|t} = \Sigma^{xx}_{t|t-1} - \Sigma^{xy}_{t|t-1}\left(\Sigma^{yy}_{t|t-1}\right)^{-1}\left(\Sigma^{xy}_{t|t-1}\right)^T. \tag{A.57}$$

Further the construction error and the observations are orthogonal, i.e.

$$\mathrm{Cov}\left[X_{x+k} - \mathbf{E}\left[X_{t+k}|\mathcal{Y}_t\right], \mathcal{Y}_t\right] = 0. \tag{A.58}$$

Proof. Let $X = X_t$, $Y = Y_t$ and $Z = \mathcal{Y}_{t-1}$ and use the linear projection theorem. See e.g., Madsen [2007] for details.

Together with equations for making one-step predictions in the state space model the above equations give the *Kalman filter*. It is readily seen that *the prediction equations* are

$$\hat{X}_{t+1|t} = A\hat{X}_{t|t} + Bu_t, \tag{A.59}$$

$$\Sigma^{xx}_{t+1|t} = A\Sigma^{xx}_{t|t}A^T + \Sigma_1, \tag{A.60}$$

$$\Sigma^{yy}_{t+1|t} = C\Sigma^{xx}_{t+1|t}C^T + \Sigma_2 \tag{A.61}$$

with initial values

$$\hat{X}_{1|0} = \mathbf{E}[X_1] = \mu_0, \tag{A.62}$$

$$\Sigma^{xx}_{1|0} = \mathbf{Var}[X_1] = V_0. \tag{A.63}$$

□

We now leave the projections in L^2 and continue by considering projections in $\mathbb{R}^n$.

A.6 Projections in $\mathbb{R}^n$

Previously we showed that $\mathbb{R}^n$ is a Hilbert space with the inner product

$$\langle x, y \rangle = x^T y. \tag{A.64}$$

In many statistical applications it is convenient to consider the weighted inner product

$$\langle x, y \rangle_{\Sigma^{-1}} = x^T \Sigma^{-1} y \tag{A.65}$$

where Σ is a positive definite symmetric matrix.

For both definitions of the inner product we have the norm

$$||x|| = \sqrt{\langle x, x \rangle}. \tag{A.66}$$

Consider a closed subspace $\mathcal{M}$ of the Hilbert space $\mathbb{R}^n$. The following theorem enables us to compute $P_{\mathcal{M}}x$ directly from any specified set of vectors $\{x_1, \dots, x_m\}$ $(m < n)$ spanning $\mathcal{M}$.

Theorem A.9. *If $x_i \in \mathbb{R}^n, i = 1, \dots, m$, and $\mathcal{M} = span\{x_1, \dots, x_m\}$ then*

$$P_{\mathcal{M}}x = X\beta \tag{A.67}$$

where X is the $n \times m$ matrix whose j^{th} column is x_j and

$$X^T X\beta = X^T x. \tag{A.68}$$

Equation (A.68) has at least one solution for β but the prediction $X\beta$ is the same for all solutions. There is exactly one solution of (A.68) if and only if $X'X$ is non-singular and in this case

$$P_{\mathcal{M}}x = X(X^T X)^{-1} X^T x. \tag{A.69}$$

Proof. Since $P_{\mathscr{M}}x \in \mathscr{M}$, we can write

$$P_{\mathscr{M}}x = \sum_{i=1}^{m} \beta_i x_i = X\beta. \tag{A.70}$$

The prediction equations (A.24) are equivalent in this case to

$$\langle X\beta, x_j \rangle = \langle x, x_j \rangle, \qquad j = 1, \ldots, m \tag{A.71}$$

or in matrix form

$$X^T X\beta = X^T x. \tag{A.72}$$

The existence of at least one solution for β is guaranteed by the existence of the projection $P_{\mathscr{M}}x$. The fact that $X\beta$ is the same for all solutions is guaranteed by the uniqueness of $P_{\mathscr{M}}x$ — see the projection theorem. □

Remark A.2. *If $\{x_1, \ldots, x_m\}$ is a linearly independent set then there must be a unique vector β such that $P_{\mathscr{M}}x = X\beta$. This means that (A.68) must have a unique solution, which in turn implies that $X'X$ is non-singular and*

$$P_{\mathscr{M}}x = X(X^T X)^{-1}X^T x \qquad \text{for all } x \in \mathbb{R}^n. \tag{A.73}$$

The matrix $X(X^T X)^{-1}X^T$ must be the same for all linearly independent sets $\{x_1, \ldots, x_m\}$ spanning $\mathscr{M}$ since $P_{\mathscr{M}}$ is uniquely defined.

Remark A.3. *Given a real $n \times n$ matrix M, how can we tell whether or not there is a subspace $\mathscr{M}$ of $\mathbb{R}^n$ such that $Mx = P_{\mathscr{M}}x$ for all $x \in \mathbb{R}^n$? If there is such a subspace we say that M is a projection matrix. Such matrices are characterized by the next theorem.*

Theorem A.10. *The $n \times n$ matrix M is a projection matrix if and only if*

(a) $M^T = M$, and

(b) $M^2 = M$, i.e. the matrix M is idempotent.

Proof. Omitted — but it is easily verified that (a) and (b) are satisfied for the matrix $X(X^T X)^{-1}X^T$. □

Appendix B

Probability theory

In this appendix it is the intention to give a brief overview of probability theory. Some of the concepts introduced are widely used in the lecture notes. It is not necessary to understand all the technical details, but an intuitive understanding of the concepts introduced is important.

B.1 Measures and σ-algebras

Let Ω denote a finite sample space which contains all the elementary outcome ω_i for $i = 1,2,\dots,N$. In a two period binomial model the elementary outcome is the state of the world at time $t = 2$, which determines the stock price at that time.

Definition B.1 (σ-algebra)**.** *Let Ω be a set of points ω. A family $\mathscr{F}$ of subset of Ω is called a σ-algebra if*

1. $\varnothing \in \mathscr{F}$

2. $A \in \mathscr{F} \Rightarrow A^c \in \mathscr{F}$

3. $A_n \in \mathscr{F} \quad \text{for } n = 1,2,\dots \Rightarrow \bigcup_{n=1}^{\infty} A_n \in \mathscr{F}$.

The definition says that (1) the empty set is an element of $\mathscr{F}$. (2) If $A \in \mathscr{F}$, then the complement of A is in $\mathscr{F}$ as well. As an example the entire set $\Omega \in \mathscr{F}$ since the empty set is in $\mathscr{F}$. (3) Countable unions of elements of $\mathscr{F}$ are elements of $\mathscr{F}$ as well.

Example B.1. *The family of all subsets of Ω is an example of an σ-algebra, and it is denoted by 2^{Ω}. In the two period binomial model with $\Omega = (\omega_1,\omega_2,\omega_3,\omega_4)$ we have*

$$\begin{aligned} 2^{\Omega} = \; & \{\varnothing,\omega_1,\omega_2,\omega_3,\omega_4,\{\omega_1,\omega_2\},\{\omega_1,\omega_3\},\{\omega_1,\omega_4\},\{\omega_2,\omega_3\}, \\ & \{\omega_2,\omega_4\},\{\omega_3,\omega_4\},\{\omega_1,\omega_2,\omega_3\},\{\omega_1,\omega_2,\omega_4\}, \\ & \{\omega_1,\omega_3,\omega_4\},\{\omega_2,\omega_3,\omega_4\},\{\omega_1,\omega_2,\omega_3,\omega_4\},\Omega\}. \end{aligned} \tag{B.1}$$

Definition B.2 (Measurable space)**.** *A pair $(\Omega,\mathscr{F})$, where Ω is a set and $\mathscr{F}$ is a σ-algebra on Ω, is called a measurable space, and the subsets of Ω which are in $\mathscr{F}$ are called $\mathscr{F}$-measurable sets.*

Definition B.3. *A probability measure $\mathbb{P}$ on a measurable space $(\Omega,\mathscr{F})$ is a function $\mathbb{P} : \mathscr{F} \longrightarrow [0,1]$ such that*

1. $\mathbb{P}(\varnothing) = 0, \quad \mathbb{P}(\Omega) = 1.$

2. If $A_1, A_2, \ldots \in \mathscr{F}$ *and* $\{A_t\}_{i=1}^{\infty}$ *is disjoint (i.e.* $A_i \cap A_j = \varnothing$ *if* $i \neq j$*) then*

$$\mathbb{P}\left(\bigcup_{i=1}^{\infty} A_i\right) = \sum_{i=1}^{\infty} \mathbb{P}(A_i). \tag{B.2}$$

The triple $(\Omega, \mathscr{F}, \mathbb{P})$ is called a probability space.

B.2 Partitions and information

Definition B.4 (Partition). *A partition* $\mathscr{P}$ *of a set* Ω *is a finite family* $\{A_i, i = 1, 2, \ldots, K\}$ *of subsets of* Ω*, such that*

1. $\bigcup_{i=1}^{K} A_i = \Omega.$

2. $i \neq j \Rightarrow A_i \cap A_j = \varnothing.$

Consider a sample space Ω and a given partition $\mathscr{P} = \{A_i; i = 1, 2, \ldots, K\}$ of Ω. We can then interpret $\mathscr{P}$ intuitively in terms of "information" in the following way.

1. "Someone" chooses an outcome ω of the sample space Ω, which is unknown to us.

2. However, we are assumed to know which component of $\mathscr{P}$ that ω lies in.

With this interpretation of a partition the trivial partition $\mathscr{P} = \{\Omega\}$ corresponds to "no information." If we assume that the sample space $\Omega = \{\omega_1, \omega_2, \ldots, \omega_r\}$ is finite, and the partition $\mathscr{P} = \{\{\omega_1\}, \{\omega_2\}, \ldots, \{\omega_r\}\}$ then we have "full information," since we know exactly which ω is chosen.

Example B.2. *Let* $\Omega = \{\omega_1, \omega_2, \omega_3, \omega_4\}$ *denote the sample space, and define two partitions* $\mathscr{P}_1 = \{\{\omega_1, \omega_2\}, \{\omega_3, \omega_4\}\}$ *and* $\mathscr{P}_2 = \{\{\omega_1, \omega_2\}, \{\omega_3\}, \{\omega_4\}\}$*. Then intuitively speaking the partition* $\mathscr{P}_2$ *contains more information than partition* $\mathscr{P}_1$*, since one of the elements in* $\mathscr{P}_1$ $\{\omega_3, \omega_4\}$ *is partitioned into "smaller" elements in partition* $\mathscr{P}_2$*.*

This leads to the following definition:

Definition B.5. *A partition* $\mathscr{S}$ *is said to be "richer" than a partition* $\mathscr{P}$ *if* $\mathscr{S}$ *and* $\mathscr{P}$ *are partitions on the same sample space* Ω*, and each component of* $\mathscr{P}$ *is a union of components of* $\mathscr{S}$*.*

Although the more general concept of σ-algebras is used to denote the "information set," it might help to think of it as a partition. In the next section we need the following definition:

Definition B.6 (σ-algebra). *A* σ*-algebra* $\mathscr{G}$ *generated by a partition* $\mathscr{P}$ *is the smallest* σ*-algebra that includes* $\mathscr{P}$*, i.e.*

1. $\mathscr{P} \subseteq \mathscr{G}.$

2. $\mathscr{G}$ *is a* σ*-algebra.*

3. If $\mathscr{F}$ is a σ-algebra such that $\mathscr{P} \subseteq \mathscr{F}$ then $\mathscr{G} \subseteq \mathscr{F}$.

The generated σ-algebra is denoted $\mathscr{G} = \sigma\{\mathscr{P}\}$.

Example B.3. *Consider a sample space $\Omega = \{\omega_1, \omega_2, \omega_3, \omega_4\}$ and a partition $\mathscr{P} = \{\{\omega_1, \omega_2\}, \{\omega_3, \omega_4\}\}$. The σ-algebra generated by that partition is then given by*

$$\mathscr{G} = \{\varnothing, \{\omega_1, \omega_2\}, \{\omega_3, \omega_4\}, \Omega\}. \tag{B.3}$$

Example B.4. *Let the sample space Ω consist of the real numbers in the interval $[0,1]$. Define the partitions*

$$\mathscr{P}_1 = \{A_1, A_2, A_3, A_4\} \qquad \mathscr{P}_2 = \{B_1, B_2, B_3\}$$

where

$$A_1 = \left[0, \frac{1}{3}\right[, \quad A_2 = \left[\frac{1}{3}, \frac{1}{2}\right[, \quad A_3 = \left[\frac{1}{2}, \frac{3}{4}\right[, \quad A_4 = \left[\frac{3}{4}, 1\right]$$

$$B_1 = \left[0, \frac{1}{3}\right[, \quad B_2 = \left[\frac{1}{3}, \frac{3}{4}\right[, \quad B_3 = \left[\frac{3}{4}, 1\right].$$

It is intuitively appealing to state that $\mathscr{P}_1$ contains more information than $\mathscr{P}_2$, because $\mathscr{P}_1$ is partitioned into smaller parts.

B.3 Conditional expectation

The objective of this section is to define the conditional expectation $E[X|\mathscr{G}]$ where $\mathscr{G}$ is a σ-algebra, which should be interpreted as the expectation of X given the information represented by the σ-algebra. However, we begin with the elementary definition of conditional expectation, given the probability space $(\Omega, \mathscr{F}, \mathbb{P})$ and two stochastic variables X and Z.

Definition B.7 (Conditional probability). *The probability of X conditioned on Z is given by*

$$\mathbb{P}(X = x_i | Z = z_j) = \frac{\mathbb{P}(X = x_i \cap Z = z_j)}{\mathbb{P}(Z = z_j)}. \tag{B.4}$$

The intuition behind this definition is as follows.

1. The probability of a given event x_i is the fraction of the total probability mass that is assigned to that event, e.g.,

$$\mathbb{P}(x_i) = \frac{\mathbb{P}(x_i)}{\mathbb{P}(\Omega)}. \tag{B.5}$$

2. When we have conditioned on the event z_j, we know that z_j has occurred, hence z_j now is the sample space. This explains the normalisation by $\mathbb{P}(Z = z_j)$ in (B.4).

3. The fraction of x_i that can occur, given the fact that z_j has occurred, is given by $x_i \cap z_j$.

The definition of the conditional expectation for discrete stochastic variables is

$$\mathbf{E}[X|Z = z_j] = \sum x_i \mathbb{P}(X = x_i | Z = z_j). \tag{B.6}$$

The (unconditional) expectation of a stochastic variable X is given by

$$\mathbf{E}[X] = \int_\Omega X(\omega) \mathrm{d}\mathbb{P}(\omega) \tag{B.7}$$

where the integration is taken over the entire sample space, with respect to the measure (distribution) $\mathbb{P}$. This covers the case where no prior knowledge of the outcome ω is available. Now assume that we know that $\omega \in B$, and $\mathbb{P}(\omega) > 0$. As a preliminary definition of conditional expectation we have the following:

Definition B.8 (Conditional expectation given a single event)**.** *Given a probability space $(\Omega, \mathscr{F}, \mathbb{P})$ assume that $B \in \mathscr{F}$ with $\mathbb{P}(B) > 0$. The conditional expectation of X given B is defined by*

$$\mathbf{E}[X|B] = \frac{1}{\mathbb{P}(B)} \int_B X(\omega) \mathrm{d}\mathbb{P}(\omega). \tag{B.8}$$

Note that this definition is very similar to the definition of conditional probabilities given in (B.4), and with a similar interpretation. This definition is now generalized to the case where the conditioning argument is a partition. Let $\mathscr{P} = \{A_1, \ldots, A_K\}$ be a partition of Ω with $\mathbb{P}(A_i) > 0$, then we know from Section B.2 that this could be interpreted as if we know in which set A_i the true ω lies. This leads to the following preliminary definition of conditional expectation:

Definition B.9. *Let $\mathscr{P} = \{A_1, \ldots, A_K\}$ be a partition of Ω with $\mathbb{P}(A_i) > 0$, then the conditional expectation is given by*

$$\mathbf{E}[X|\mathscr{P}] = \sum_{n=1}^{K} I\{\omega \in A_n\} \mathbf{E}[X|A_n] \tag{B.9}$$

where $I\{\cdot\}$ denotes the indicator function.

The problem with this definition is that it assumes that each set must have positive probability, which is a unnecessary restriction as we shall see. To give an idea of the interpretation of the final definition of conditional expectation, based on σ-algebras, consider the following.

Let $\mathscr{Z}$ be a partition of Ω into Z-atoms,[1] where the random variable Z is constant. The σ-algebra $\mathscr{G} = \sigma(\mathscr{Z})$ generated by this consists of exactly 2^n possible unions of the Z-atoms. It is clear from the elementary definition of

[1] If the sample space is finite an atom is a set which only consists of one element.

conditional expectation that the conditional expectation Y is constant on the Z-atoms, or to be more precise

$$Y \text{ is } \mathscr{G}\text{-measurable.} \tag{B.10}$$

Since Y takes the constant value y_i on the Z-atom $\{Z = z_j\}$, we have

$$\int_{\{Z=z_j\}} Y \mathrm{d}\mathbb{P} = y_i \mathbb{P}(Z = z_i). \tag{B.11}$$

Applying the elementary definition of conditional probability and expectation (B.4) and (B.6) we get

$$\begin{aligned}\int_{\{Z=z_j\}} Y \mathrm{d}\mathbb{P} &= \sum_i x_i \mathbb{P}(X = x_i | Z = z_j) \mathbb{P}(Z = z_j) \\ &= \sum_i x_i \mathbb{P}(X = x_i \cap Z = z_j) \\ &= \int_{\{Z=z_j\}} X \mathrm{d}\mathbb{P}. \end{aligned} \tag{B.12}$$

If we write $G_j = \{Z = z_j\}$, this says that $\mathbf{E}[Y I_{G_j}] = \mathbf{E}[X I_{G_j}]$, where I denotes the indicator function. Since I_G is a sum of I_{G_j} for every $G \in \mathscr{G}$ we have $\mathbf{E}[Y I_G] = \mathbf{E}[X I_G]$, or

$$\int_G Y \mathrm{d}\mathbb{P} = \int_G X \mathrm{d}\mathbb{P}, \qquad \text{for all } G \in \mathscr{G}. \tag{B.13}$$

This leads us to the final definition of conditional expectation.

Definition B.10 (Conditional expectation). *Let $(\Omega, \mathscr{F}, \mathbb{P})$ be a probability space, X a stochastic variable on this space and let $\mathscr{G} \subseteq \mathscr{F}$ be a σ-algebra on Ω. If Y is a stochastic variable such that*

1. Y is $\mathscr{G}$-measurable

2.

$$\int_G Y(\omega) \mathrm{d}\mathbb{P}(\omega) = \int_G X(\omega) \mathrm{d}\mathbb{P}(\omega) \qquad \text{for all } G \in \mathscr{G} \tag{B.14}$$

then $Y = \mathbf{E}[X|\mathscr{G}]$ is the conditional expectation of X given $\mathscr{G}$.

To give an intuitive understanding of conditional expectation given a σ-algebra consider the following example.

Example B.5. *Suppose we have a finite sample space $\Omega = (\omega_1, \omega_2, \omega_3, \omega_4)$ with four possible outcomes. Define three stochastic variables X, Y_1 and Y_2 $: \Omega \to \mathbb{R}$ with the following values*

	ω_1	ω_2	ω_3	ω_4
X	1	2	3	4
Y_1	1	2	1	2
Y_2	1.5	10	1.5	10

Since the stochastic variable X takes different values for all outcomes ω_i, the σ-algebra generated by that variable is given by

$$\begin{aligned}\sigma\{X\} &= \{\varnothing,\omega_1,\omega_2,\omega_3,\omega_4,\{\omega_1,\omega_2\},\{\omega_1,\omega_3\},\{\omega_1,\omega_4\},\{\omega_2,\omega_3\},\\ &\quad \{\omega_2,\omega_4\},\{\omega_3,\omega_4\},\{\omega_1,\omega_2,\omega_3\},\{\omega_1,\omega_2,\omega_4\},\\ &\quad \{\omega_1,\omega_3,\omega_4\},\{\omega_2,\omega_3,\omega_4\},\{\omega_1,\omega_2,\omega_3,\omega_4\},\Omega\} \end{aligned} \tag{B.15}$$

which corresponds to full information. The σ-algebra generated by Y_1 and Y_2 contains less "information" since these variables take the same value for ω_1 and ω_3 and the same values for ω_2 and ω_4. The two generated σ-algebras

$$\sigma\{Y_1\}=\sigma\{Y_2\}=\{\varnothing,\{\omega_1,\omega_3\},\{\omega_2,\omega_4\},\Omega\} \tag{B.16}$$

contain the same information about X despite the fact that Y_1 and Y_2 take different values. Assume that each outcome has probability $\frac{1}{4}$. By the elementary definition of conditional expectation we have

$$\mathbf{E}[X|Y_1=1] = \frac{1}{2}\cdot 1+\frac{1}{2}\cdot 3=2 \tag{B.17}$$

$$\mathbf{E}[X|Y_1=2] = \frac{1}{2}\cdot 2+\frac{1}{2}\cdot 4=3 \tag{B.18}$$

which summarize to

$$\mathbf{E}[X|Y_1](\omega)=\begin{cases}2 & \omega\in\{\omega_1,\omega_3\}\\ 3 & \omega\in\{\omega_2,\omega_4\}.\end{cases} \tag{B.19}$$

We shall now check whether the two conditions stated in Definition B.10 are fulfilled. Since $\mathbf{E}[X|Y_1](\omega)$ is constant on the two subsets $\{\omega_1,\omega_3\}$ and $\{\omega_2,\omega_4\}$ the conditional expectation (B.19) *is measurable with respect to $\sigma\{Y_1\}$.*
The other condition says that

$$\int_{\{\omega_1,\omega_3\}}\mathbf{E}[X|Y_1](\omega)\mathrm{d}\mathbb{P}(\omega) = \int_{\{\omega_1,\omega_3\}}X(\omega)\mathrm{d}\mathbb{P}(\omega) \tag{B.20}$$

$$\int_{\{\omega_2,\omega_4\}}\mathbf{E}[X|Y_1](\omega)\mathrm{d}\mathbb{P}(\omega) = \int_{\{\omega_2,\omega_4\}}X(\omega)\mathrm{d}\mathbb{P}(\omega) \tag{B.21}$$

which are also fulfilled. It is easy to show that $\mathbf{E}[X|\sigma\{Y_1\}]=\mathbf{E}[X|\sigma\{Y_2\}]$, since the generated σ-algebras are the same.

Some of the most important properties of conditional expectation are given in the following list, where $\mathscr{G}$ and $\mathscr{H}$ denote sub-σ-algebras of $\mathscr{F}$:

1. If X is $\mathscr{G}$-measurable, then $\mathbf{E}[X|\mathscr{G}]=X$ a.s.
2. $\mathbf{E}[a_1X_1+a_2X_2|\mathscr{G}]=a_1\mathbf{E}[X_1|\mathscr{G}]+a_2\mathbf{E}[X_2|\mathscr{G}]$ a.s.

3. If $\mathscr{H}$ is a sub-σ-algebra of $\mathscr{G}$, then

$$\mathbf{E}[\mathbf{E}[X|\mathscr{G}]|\mathscr{H}] = \mathbf{E}[X|\mathscr{H}] \quad \text{a.s.} \tag{B.22}$$

4. If Z is $\mathscr{G}$-measurable and bounded, then

$$\mathbf{E}[ZX|\mathscr{G}] = Z\mathbf{E}[X|\mathscr{G}] \quad \text{a.s.} \tag{B.23}$$

Remark B.1. *Intuitively, the statement that X is $\mathscr{G}$-measurable simply means that X is known, and thus $\mathbf{E}[X|\mathscr{G}] = X$ a.s. Item 2 simply states that the expectation operator is linear. Eq.* (B.22) *is often called the Tower Property, and it states that the most coarse sub-σ-algebra $\mathscr{H}$ overrules the finer sub-σ-algebra $\mathscr{G}$. Eq.* (B.23) *states that we can take out what is known (namely Z) from the expectation operator.*

B.4 Notes

Should you wish to pursue these (purely) mathematical topics, a number of books are available (Grimmett and Stirzaker [1992], Karatzas and Shreve [1996], Williams [1995], Royden [1988]). The first reference provides an excellent and readable introduction to stochastic processes and probability theory in general. The other references are given in an increasing order of difficulty and the topics considered herein are outside the scope and aim of these lecture notes.

Bibliography

Yacine Aït-Sahalia. Transition densities for interest rate and other nonlinear diffusions. *The Journal of Finance*, 54(4):1361–1395, 2002.

Yacine Aït-Sahalia. Maximum Likelihood Estimation of Discretely Sampled Diffusions: A Closed-form Approximation Approach. *Econometrica*, 70 (1):223–262, 2003.

Yacine Aït-Sahalia. Closed-form likelihood expansions for multivariate diffusions. *The Annals of Statistics*, 36(2):906–937, 2008.

Torben G. Andersen and J. Lund. Estimating continuous time stochastic volatility models of the short term interest rate. *Journal of Econometrics*, 77:343–377, 1997.

Jan Annaert, Anouk G.P. Claes, Marc J.K. De Ceuster, and Hairui Zhang. Estimating the spot rate curve using the Nelson–Siegel model: A ridge regression approach. *International Review of Economics & Finance*, 27: 482–496, 2013.

L. Arnold. *Stochastic Differential Equations*. Wiley, New York, 1974.

Hossein Asgharian, Ai Jun Hou, and Farrukh Javed. The importance of the macroeconomic variables in forecasting stock return variance: A GARCH-MIDAS approach. *Journal of Forecasting*, 32(7):600–612, 2013.

Richard T. Baillie, Tim Bollerslev, and Hans Ole Mikkelsen. Fractionally integrated generalized autoregressive conditional heteroskedasticity. *Journal of Econometrics*, 74(1):3–30, 1996.

Ole Barndorff-Nielsen. Exponentially decreasing distributions for the logarithm of particle size. *Proceedings of the Royal Society of London. A. Mathematical and Physical Sciences*, 353(1674):401–419, 1977.

Ole E. Barndorff-Nielsen. Processes of Normal Inverse Gaussian type. *Finance and Stochastics*, 2(1):41–68, 1997.

Ole E. Barndorff-Nielsen. Econometric analysis of realized volatility and its use in estimating stochastic volatility models. *Journal of the Royal Statistical Society: Series B (Statistical Methodology)*, 64(2):253–280, 2002.

Ole E. Barndorff-Nielsen and Neil Shephard. Power and bipower variation with stochastic volatility and jumps. *Journal of Financial Econometrics*, 2(1):1–37, 2004.

David S. Bates. Jumps and Stochastic Volatility: Exchange Rate Processes Implicit in Deutsche Mark Options. *Review of Financial Studies*, 9(1): 69–107, 1996.

Peter H. Baxendale. A stochastic Hopf bifurcation. *Probability Theory and Related Fields*, 9:581–616, 1994.

Denis Belomestny, John Schoenmakers, and Fabian Dickmann. Multilevel dual approach for pricing American style derivatives. *Finance and Stochastics*, 17(4):717–742, 2013.

A. K. Bera and M. L. Higgins. A survey of ARCH models; properties, estimation and testing. *J. Econom. Surveys*, 1993.

Alexandros Beskos, Omiros Papaspiliopoulos, Gareth O. Roberts, and Paul Fearnhead. Exact and computationally efficient likelihood-based estimation for discretely observed diffusion processes (with discussion). *Journal of the Royal Statistical Society: Series B (Statistical Methodology)*, 68(3):333–382, 2006.

Sara Biagini and Rama Cont. Model-free representation of pricing rules as conditional expectations. In *Stochastic processes and applications to mathematical finance*. 2006.

Bo Martin Bibby and Michael Sørensen. Martingale estimation functions for discretely observed diffusion processes. *Bernoulli*, pages 17–39, 1995.

Tomas Björk. *Interest Rate Theory - CIME Lectures 1996*. Department of Finance, Stockholm School of Economics, Stockholm, 1996.

Tomas Björk. *Arbitrage Theory in Continuos Time, Third Edition*. Oxford University Press, Oxford, 2009.

Tim Bollerslev. Generalized autoregressive conditional heteroskedasticity. *Econometrica*, pages 307–327, 1986.

Tim Bollerslev. Modelling the coherence in short-run nominal exchange rates: A multivariate generalized ARCH model. *The Review of Economics and Statistics*, pages 498–505, 1990.

Tim Bollerslev. Glossary to ARCH (GARCH). *CREATES Research Paper*, 49, 2008.

Tim Bollerslev and Hans Ole Mikkelsen. Modeling and pricing long memory in stock market volatility. *Journal of Econometrics*, 73(1):151–184, 1996.

Tim Bollerslev, Robert F. Engle, and Jeffrey M. Wooldridge. A capital asset pricing model with time-varying covariances. *The Journal of Political Economy*, pages 116–131, 1988.

G.E.P. Box and J.M. Jenkins. *Time Series Analysis: Forecasting and Control.* Holden-Day, San Francisco, 1976.

Søren Braes and Kent Stevens Larsen. Modellering af prisdannelsen på obligationsmarkedet (in Danish). Master's thesis, IMSOR, Lyngby, Denmark, 1989.

M.J. Brennan and E.S. Schwartz. A continuous time approach to the pricing of bonds. *The Journal of Banking and Finance*, 3:133–155, 1979.

Mark Briers, Arnaud Doucet, and Simon Maskell. Smoothing algorithms for state–space models. *Annals of the Institute of Statistical Mathematics*, 62(1):61–89, 2010.

Damiano Brigo and Fabio Mercurio. A deterministic–shift extension of analytically–tractable and time–homogeneous short–rate models. *Finance and Stochastics*, 5(3):369–387, 2001.

Damiano Brigo and Fabio Mercurio. *Interest Rate Models-Theory and Practice: With Smile, Inflation and Credit.* Springer, 2006.

P. Brockwell and R. Davis. *Time Series: Theory and Methods*. Springer, New York, 2nd edition, 1991.

Peter Bühlmann and Alexander J McNeil. An algorithm for nonparametric GARCH modelling. *Computational Statistics & Data Analysis*, 40(4): 665–683, 2002.

Olivier Cappé, Eric Moulines, and Tobias Rydén. *Inference in Hidden Markov Models*. Springer, 2005.

Lorenzo Cappiello, Robert F. Engle, and Kevin Sheppard. Asymmetric dynamics in the correlations of global equity and bond returns. *Journal of Financial Econometrics*, 4(4):537–572, 2006.

Peter Carr and Dilip Madan. Option valuation using the fast Fourier transform. *Journal of Computational Finance*, 2(4):61–73, 1999.

Marine Carrasco, Mikhail Chernov, Jean-Pierre Florens, and Eric Ghysels. Efficient estimation of general dynamic models with a continuum of moment conditions. *Journal of Econometrics*, 140(2):529–573, 2007.

George Chacko and Luis M. Viceira. Spectral GMM estimation of continuous-time processes. *Journal of Econometrics*, 116(1):259–292, 2003.

K.C. Chan, G.A. Karolyi, F.A. Longstaff, and A.B. Sanders. An empirical comparison of alternative models of the short-term interest rate. *The Journal of Finance*, XLVII:1209–1227, 1992.

Lin Chen. Stochastic mean and stochastic volatility - a three-factor model of the term structure of interest rates and its applications to the pricing of interest rate derivatives. *Financial Markets, Institutions, and Instruments*, 5:1–88, 1996.

Lindholm, Love (2014) Calibration and Hedging in Finance. Licentiate thesis in applied and computational mathematics, KTH School of Engineering Sciences, ISBN 978-91-7595-380-9.

Jens H.E. Christensen, Francis X. Diebold, and Glenn D. Rudebusch. The affine arbitrage-free class of Nelson–Siegel term structure models. *Journal of Econometrics*, 164(1):4–20, 2011.

Michael Christensen. *Obligationsinvestering, 3. Udgave*. Jurist- og Økonomforbundets Forlag, København, 1995.

Andrew A. Christie. The stochastic behavior of common stock variances: Value, leverage and interest rate effects. *Journal of Financial Economics*, 10(4):407–432, 1982.

Christian Conrad and Berthold R. Haag. Inequality constraints in the fractionally integrated garch model. *Journal of Financial Econometrics*, 4 (3):413–449, 2006.

Rama Cont. Empirical properties of asset returns: Stylized facts and statistical issues. *Quantitative Finance*, 1:223–236, 2001.

Rama Cont. Model uncertainty and its impact on the pricing of derivative instruments. *Mathematical Finance*, 16(3):519–547, 2006.

Rama Cont and Peter Tankov. *Financial Modelling with Jump Processes*, volume 133. Chapman & Hall/CRC, Boca Raton, 2004.

John C. Cox, Stephen A. Ross, and Mark Rubinstein. Option pricing: A simplified approach. *Journal of Financial Economics*, 7(3):229–263, 1979.

John C. Cox, Jonathan E. Ingersoll Jr., and Stephen A. Ross. A theory of the term structure of interest rates. *Econometrica*, 53(2):385–408, 1985.

Drew Creal. A survey of sequential Monte Carlo methods for economics and finance. *Econometric Reviews*, 31(3):245–296, 2012.

James Davidson. Moment and memory properties of linear conditional heteroscedasticity models, and a new model. *Journal of Business & Economic Statistics*, 22(1), 2004.

Freddy Delbaen and Walter Schachermayer. A general version of the fundamental theorem of asset pricing. *Mathematische Annalen*, 300(1):463–520, 1994.

Freddy Delbaen and Walter Schachermayer. The fundamental theorem of asset pricing for unbounded stochastic processes. *Mathematische annalen*, 312(2):215–250, 1998.

A. P. Dempster, N. M. Laird, and D. B. Rubin. Maximum Likelihood from Incomplete Data via the EM Algorithm. *Journal of the Royal Statistical Society, B*, 39(1):1–38, 1977.

Emanuel Derman and Iraj Kani. Riding on a smile. *Risk*, 7(2):32–39, 1994.

Susanne Ditlevsen and Adeline Samson. Parameter estimation in the stochastic Morris-Lecar neuronal model with particle filter methods. *Annals of Applied Statistics*, 8(2):674 – 702, 2014.

J.L. Doob. *Stochastic Processes*. John Wiley & Sons, New York, 1990.

Randal Douc and Eric Moulines. Limit theorems for weighted samples with applications to sequential Monte Carlo methods. *The Annals of Statistics*, pages 2344–2376, 2008.

Randal Douc, Aurélien Garivier, Eric Moulines, Jimmy Olsson, et al. Sequential Monte Carlo smoothing for general state space hidden Markov models. *The Annals of Applied Probability*, 21(6):2109–2145, 2011.

Darrell Duffie. *Dynamic Asset Pricing Theory, Second Edition.* Princeton University Press, Princeton, New Jersey, 1996.

Darrell Duffie. *Dynamic asset pricing theory*. Princeton University Press, 2010.

Darrell Duffie and Rui Kan. A yield-factor model of interest rates. *Mathematical Finance*, 6(4):379–406, 1996.

Darrell Duffie, Jun Pan, and Kenneth Singleton. Transform analysis and asset pricing for affine jump-diffusions. *Econometrica*, 68(6):1343–1376, 2003.

Garland B Durham and A Ronald Gallant. Numerical techniques for maximum likelihood estimation of continuous-time diffusion processes. *Journal of Business & Economic Statistics*, 20(3):297–338, 2002.

David Easley, MM Lopez De Prado, and Maureen O' Hara. The microstructure of the flash crash: Flow toxicity, liquidity crashes and the probability of informed trading. *Journal of Portfolio Management*, 37(2):118–128, 2011.

Paul Embrechts, Rdiger Frey, and Alexander McNeil. Quantitative Risk Management. *Princeton Series in Finance, Princeton*, 10, 2005.

Robert Engle. Dynamic conditional correlation: A simple class of multivariate generalized autoregressive conditional heteroskedasticity models. *Journal of Business & Economic Statistics*, 20(3):339–350, 2002.

Robert F. Engle. Autoregressive conditional heteroscedasticity with estimates of the variance of united kingdom inflation. *Econometrica*, 50(4):987–1007, July 1982.

Robert F Engle and Kenneth F Kroner. Multivariate simultaneous generalized ARCH. *Econometric theory*, 11(01):122–150, 1995.

Robert F. Engle, David M. Lilien, and Russel P. Robins. Estimating time varying risk premia in the term strucre: The arch-m model. *Econometrica*, 55(2):391–407, 1987.

T.W. Epps. Stock prices as branching processes. *Communications in Statistics - Stochastic Models*, 12(4):529–558, 1996.

Alvaro Escribano, J Ignacio Peña, and Pablo Villaplana. Modelling Electricity Prices: International Evidence. *Oxford bulletin of Economics and Statistics*, 73(5):622–650, 2011.

Fang Fang and Cornelis W Oosterlee. A novel pricing method for European options based on Fourier-cosine series expansions. *SIAM Journal on Scientific Computing*, 31(2):826–848, 2008.

Paul Fearnhead, David Wyncoll, and Jonathan Tawn. A sequential smoothing algorithm with linear computational cost. *Biometrika*, 97(2):447–464, 2010.

William Feller. Two singular diffusion problems. *Annals of Mathematics*, 54 (1):173–182, 1951.

Stephen Figlewski, William Silber, and Marti Subrahmanyam. *Financial Options - From Theory to Practice*. Irwin Professional Publishing, Illinois, 1991.

A. Ronald Gallant and George Tauchen. Which moments to match. *Econometric Theory*, 12(4):657–681, Oct. 1996.

Michael B. Giles. Multilevel Monte Carlo path simulation. *Operations Research*, 56(3):607–617, 2008.

Manfred Gilli, Stefan Große, and Enrico Schumann. Calibrating the Nelson-Siegel Svensson model. Technical Report WPS-031, COMISEF, 2010.

Lawrence R. Glosten, Ravi Jagannathan, and David E. Runkle. On the relation between the expected value and the volatility of the nominal excess return on stocks. *The Journal of Finance*, 48(5):1779–1801, 1993.

Clive W.J. Granger and Zhuanxin Ding. Some properties of absolute return: An alternative measure of risk. *Annales d'Economie et de Statistique*, pages 67–91, 1995.

Clive W.J. Granger and Roselyne Joyeux. An introduction to long-memory time series models and fractional differencing. *Journal of Time Series Analysis*, 1(1):15–29, 1980.

G.R. Grimmett and D.R. Stirzaker. *Probability and Random Processes*. Oxford Science Publications, Oxford, 1992.

Patrick S. Hagana, Deep Kumar, Andrew S. Lesniewski, and Diana E. Woodward. Managing smile risk. *Wilmott Magazine*, 2002.

L.P. Hansen. Large sample properties of generalized method of moments. *Econometrica*, 50:1029–1054, 1982.

Peter R. Hansen and Asger Lunde. A forecast comparison of volatility models: Does anything beat a GARCH (1, 1)? *Journal of Applied Econometrics*, 20(7):873–889, 2005.

Peter R. Hansen and Asger Lunde. Realized variance and market microstructure noise. *Journal of Business & Economic Statistics*, 24(2):127–161, 2006.

W. Härdle. *Applied Nonparametric Regression.* Cambridge University Press, Cambridge, 1990.

Wolfgang Härdle. *Nonparametric and Semiparametric Models.* Springer, 2004.

J. Michael Harrison and Stanley R. Pliska. Martingales and stochastic integrals in the theory of continuous trading. *Stochastic Processes and Their Applications*, 11(3):215–260, 1981.

Trevor Hastie, Robert Tibshirani, Jerome Friedman, T. Hastie, J. Friedman, and R. Tibshirani. *The Elements of Statistical Learning*. Springer, 2009.

Trevor J. Hastie, Robert John Tibshirani, and Jerome H. Friedman. *The Elements of Statistical Learning: Data Mining, Inference, and Prediction.* Springer, 2011.

David Heath, Robert Jarrow, and Andrew Morton. Bond pricing and the term structure of interest rates: A new methodology for contingent claims valuation. *Econometrica*, 60(1):77–105, 1992.

Olof Hellquist, Erik Lindström, and Jonas Ströjby. Likelihood Inference in Jump Diffusion driven SDEs. In *Symposium i anvendt Statistik*, volume 32, pages 269–278. 2010.

Erik Henricsson. Modelling Swedish Stock Data Using Regime Switching ARCH-Processes. Master's thesis, Lund University, 2002. (2002:E13) LUTFMS-3020-2002.

Steven L. Heston. A closed-form solution for options with stochastic volatility with applications to bond and currency options. *Review of Financial Studies*, 6(2):327–343, 1993.

Desmond J. Higham, Xuerong Mao, Mikolaj Roj, Qingshuo Song, and George Yin. Mean exit times and the multilevel Monte Carlo method. *Journal on Uncertainty Quantification*, 1(1):2–18, 2013.

Ali Hirsa. *Computational Methods in Finance.* CRC Press, 2013.

U. Holst, G. Lindgren, J. Holst, and M. Thuvesholmen. Recursive estimation in switching autoregressions with a Markov regime. *Journal of Time Series Analysis*, 15:489–506, 1994.

Peter Honoré. Estimation of a dynamic one factor continuous-time term-structure model. Presented at the Conference on Mathematical Finance, Aarhus University, June 1996.

Josef Höök and Erik Lindström. A fast adjoint-based quasi-likelihood parameter estimation method for diffusion processes. In *Proceedings to the 8th World Congress of the Bachelier Finance Society*, 2014.

Aijun Hou and Sandy Suardi. A nonparametric GARCH model of crude oil price return volatility. *Energy Economics*, 34(2):618–626, 2012.

Ronald Huisman and Ronald Mahieu. Regime jumps in electricity prices. *Energy Economics*, 25(5):425–434, 2003.

John Hull and Alan White. The pricing of options on assets with stochastic volatilities. *The Journal of Finance*, 42(2):281–300, 1987.

Henrik Hult, Filip Lindskog, Ola Hammarlid, and Carl Johan Rehn. *Risk and Portfolio Analysis: Principles and Methods*. Springer, 2012.

Nobuyuki Ikeda and Shinzo Watanabe. *Stochastic Differential Equations and Diffusion Processes*. North Holland/Kodansha, Amsterdam, 1989.

Edward L. Ionides, Anindya Bhadra, Yves Atchadé, and Aaron King. Iterated Filtering. *The Annals of Statistics*, 39(3):1776–1802, 2011.

E.L. Ionides, C. Bretó, and A.A. King. Inference for nonlinear dynamical systems. *Proceedings of the National Academy of Sciences*, 103(49): 18438–18443, 2006.

Joanna Janczura and Rafal Weron. An empirical comparison of alternate regime-switching models for electricity spot prices. *Energy Economics*, 32(5):1059–1073, 2010.

A.H. Jazwinski. *Stochastic Processes and Filtering Theory*. Academic Press, New York, 1970.

Morten B. Jensen and Asger Lunde. The NIG-S&ARCH model: A fat-tailed, stochastic, and autoregressive conditional heteroskedastic volatility model. *The Econometrics Journal*, 4(2):319–342, 2001.

Peter Engberg Jensen, Mogens Laursen, and Kaj Preskou. *Investering i aktier, obligationer og andre værdipapirer*. Borgens Forlag, Copenhagen, Denmark, 1994.

Søren Johansen. *Likelihood-based Inference in Cointegrated Vector Autoregressive Models*. Oxford University Press, Oxford, 1995.

P.L. Jørgensen. *American Option Pricing*. Department of Finance, The Aarhus School of Business, Aarhus, 1994.

Simon J. Julier and Jeffrey K. Uhlmann. A new extension of the Kalman filter to nonlinear systems. In *Int. symp. aerospace/defense sensing, simul. and controls*, volume 3(26), pages 3–2. Orlando, FL, 1997.

S.J. Julier, J.K. Uhlmann, and H.F. Durrant-Whyte. A new method for the nonlinear transformation of means and covariances in nonlinear filters. *Transactions on Automatic Control, IEEE*, 2000.

Ioannis Karatzas and Steven E. Shreve. *Brownian Motion and Stochastic Calculus, Second Edition*. Springer-Verlag, New York, 1996.

Mathieu Kessler and Michael Sørensen. Estimating equations based on eigenfunctions for a discretely observed diffusion process. *Bernoulli*, 5(2):299–314, 1999.

Rehim Kiliç. Conditional volatility and distribution of exchange rates: GARCH and FIGARCH models with NIG distribution. *Studies in Nonlinear Dynamics & Econometrics*, 11(3), 2007.

P.E. Kloeden and E. Platen. *Numerical Solutions of Stochastic Differential Equations, Second Edition*. Springer-Verlag, Heidelberg, 1995.

Steven G. Kou. A jump-diffusion model for option pricing. *Management Science*, 48(8):1086–1101, 2002.

Niels Rode Kristensen and Henrik Madsen. Continous time stochastic modelling: CTSM 2.3 mathematics guide. *Technical University of Denmark http://www2. imm. dtu. dk/ctsm/MathGuide. pdf*, 2003.

Hans R. Künsch. Recursive Monte Carlo filters: Algorithms and Theoretical Analysis. *Annals of Statistics*, pages 1983–2021, 2005.

H. Kushner. *Introduction to Stochastic Control*. Holt, Reinhart and Winston, New York, 1971.

D. Lando. *Investering og finansieringsteori*. University of Copenhagen, 1996.

Karl Larsson. General approximation schemes for option prices in stochastic volatility models. *Quantitative Finance*, 12(6):873–891, 2012.

Roger W. Lee. Option pricing by transform methods: Extensions, unification and error control. *Journal of Computational Finance*, 7(3):51–86, 2004.

Georg Lindgren. *Stationary Stochastic Processes: Theory and Applications*. CRC Press, 2012.

Erik Lindström. Model Validation for Diffusion Processes Using Generalized Gaussian Residuals. In J. Dhaene, Nikolai Kolev, and Pedro Morettin, editors, *First Brazilian Conference on Statistical Modelling in Insurance and Finace*, 2003.

Erik Lindström. *Statistical Modeling of Diffusion Processes with Financial Applications*. Ph.D. thesis, Centre for Mathematical Sciences, Lund University, 2004.

Erik Lindström. Estimating parameters in diffusion processes using an approximate maximum likelihood approach. *Annals of Operations Research*, 151(1):269–288, 2007.

Erik Lindström. Implications of parameter uncertainty on option prices. *Advances in Decision Sciences*, 2010, 2010.

Erik Lindström. A regularized bridge sampler for sparsely sampled diffusions. *Statistics and Computing*, 22(2):615–623, 2012a.

Erik Lindström. A Monte Carlo EM algorithm for discretely observed diffusions, jump-diffusions and Lévy-driven stochastic differential equations. *International Journal of Mathematical Models and Methods in Applied Sciences*, 6(5), 2012b.

Erik Lindström. Semiparametric lag dependent functions. *Applied Mathematical Sciences*, 7(12):551–566, 2013a.

Erik Lindström. Tuned iterated filtering. *Statistics & Probability Letters*, 83 (9):2077–2080, 2013b.

Erik Lindström and Jingyi Guo. Simultaneous calibration and quadratic hedging of options. *Quantitative and Qualitative Analysis in Social Sciences*, 7(1), 2013. ISSN 1752-8925.

Erik Lindström and Fredrik Regland. Modelling extreme dependence between European electricity markets. *Energy Economics*, 2012.

Erik Lindström and Johan Strålfors. Model Uncertainty, Model Selection and Option Valuation. In Peter Linde, editor, *34. Symposium i Anvendt Statistik*, pages 229 – 238. Copenhagen University, 2012. ISBN: 978-87-501-1975-3.

Erik Lindstrom and Hanna Wu. Fast Valuation of Options Under Parameter Uncertainty. In *Proceedings to the 21st International Forecasting Financial Markets*, 2014.

Erik Lindström, Jonas Ströjby, Mats Brodén, Magnus Wiktorsson, and Jan Holst. Sequential calibration of options. *Computational Statistics & Data Analysis*, 52(6):2877–2891, 2008.

Erik Lindström, Edward Ionides, Jan Frydendall, and Henrik Madsen. Efficient Iterated Filtering. In *IFAC System Identification*, volume 16, pages 1785–1790, 2012.

Andrew W. Lo. Maximum Likelihood Estimation of Generalized Itô Processes with Discretely Sampled Data. *Econometric Theory*, 4(02):231–247, 1988.

Francis A. Longstaff and Eduardo S. Schartz. Interest rate volatility and the term structure: A two-factor general equilibrium model. *The Journal of Finance*, XLVII, 4:1259–1282, 1992.

Francis A. Longstaff and Eduardo S. Schwartz. Valuing American options by simulation: A simple least-squares approach. *Review of Financial studies*, 14(1):113–147, 2001.

Hedibert F. Lopes and Ruey S. Tsay. Particle filters and Bayesian inference in financial econometrics. *Journal of Forecasting*, 30(1):168–209, 2011.

Per Lötstedt, Jonas Persson, Lina von Sydow, and Johan Tysk. Space–time adaptive finite difference method for European multi-asset options. *Computers & Mathematics with Applications*, 53(8):1159–1180, 2007.

Peter Lynggaard. *Investering og finansiering*. Handelshøjskolens Forlag, København, 1993.

Iain L. MacDonald and Walter Zucchini. *Hidden Markov and Other Models for Discrete- valued Time Series*, volume 70. CRC Press, 1997.

Dilip B Madan and Eugene Seneta. The variance gamma (VG) model for share market returns. *Journal of Business*, pages 511–524, 1990.

H. Madsen. Projection and Separation in Hilbert Spaces. Notes in Ph.D. course in multivariate system identification, 1992.

H. Madsen and J. Holst. *Modelling Non-linear and Non-stationary Time Series*. IMM-DTU, 1996.

H. Madsen and H. Melgaard. The mathematical and numerical methods used in CTLSM-a program for ml-estimation in stochastic, continuous time dynamical models. *Institute of Mathematical Statistics and Operations Research*, 1991.

Henrik Madsen. *Time Series Analysis*, volume 72. Chapman & Hall/CRC, 2007.

Henrik Madsen, Jan Holst, and Erik Lindstrom. *Modelling Non-Linear and Non-Stationary Time Series*. Informatics and Mathematical Modelling, The Technical University of Denmark, 2007.

Peter S. Maybeck. *Stochastic Models, Estimation and Control*. Academic Press, London, 1982a.

P.S. Maybeck. *Stochastic Models, Estimation and Control, Vol 1, 2 & 3*. Academic Press, New York, 1982b.

Daniel McFadden. A method of simulated moments for estimation of discrete response models without numerical integration. *Econometrica*, 57(5): 995–1026, 1989.

T.P. McGarty. *Stochastic Systems and State Estimation*. John Wiley & Sons, 1974.

Niels Rode Kristensen, Henrik Madsen, and Sten Bay Jørgensen. Parameter estimation in stochastic grey-box models. *Automatica*, 40(2):225–237, 2004.

R.C. Merton. *Continuous-Time Finance - Revised Edition*. Blackwell Publishers, 1993.

Robert C. Merton. Option pricing when underlying stock returns are discontinuous. *Journal of Financial Economics*, 3(1):125–144, 1976.

A. Milhøj. *Tidsrækkeanalyse for Økonomer*. Akademisk Forlag, 1994.

G. Milstein. Approximate integration of stochastic differential equations. *Theory of Probability and Applications*, pages 557–562, 1974.

C. Moler and C. van Loan. Nineteen dubious ways to compute the exponential of a matrix. *SIAM Review*, 20(4), October 1978.

Carlos M. Mora. Weak exponential schemes for stochastic differential equations with additive noise. *IMA Journal of Numerical Analysis*, 25(3): 486–506, 2005.

M. Musiela and M. Rutkowski. *Martingale Methods in Financial Modelling*. Springer, 1997.

E.A. Nadaraya. On estimating regression. *Theory Prob. Appl.*, 10:186–190, 1964.

C. R. Nelson and A. F. Siegel. Parsimonious modeling of yield curves. *Journal of Business*, 60(4), 1987.

Daniel B. Nelson. Conditional heteroskedasticity in asset returns: A new approach. *Econometrica: Journal of the Econometric Society*, pages 347–370, 1991.

Henrik Aa. Nielsen and Henrik Madsen. A generalization of some classical time series tools. *Computational Statistics & Data Analysis*, 37(1):13–31, 2001.

Jan Nygaard Nielsen. Nonlinear dynamics and time series analysis. Master's thesis, Department of Mathematical Modelling, Lyngby, Denmark, 1996.

J.N. Nielsen. *Chaos & Non-linear Time Series Analysis (in Danish)*. Institute of Mathematical Modelling, Lyngby, Denmark, 1995. Special course report.

Magnus Nørgaard, Niels K. Poulsen, and Ole Ravn. New developments in state estimation for nonlinear systems. *Automatica*, 36(11):1627–1638, 2000.

Peter Nystrup, Erik Lindstrom, and Henrik Madsen. Modelling Equity returns with a Continuous Time Hidden Semi-Markov Model. *Forthcoming in Quantitative Finance*, 2014. doi: http://dx.doi.org/10.1080/14697688.2015.1004801.

B. Øksendal. *Stochastic Differential Equations, 6th Edition*. Springer-Verlag, Heidelberg, 2010.

Jimmy Olsson, Olivier Cappé, Randal Douc, Eric Moulines, et al. Sequential Monte Carlo smoothing with application to parameter estimation in nonlinear state space models. *Bernoulli*, 14(1):155–179, 2008.

Greg Orosi. Improved implementation of local volatility and its application to S&P 500 index options. *The Journal of Derivatives*, 17(3):53–64, 2010.

N.J. Pearson and Sun Tong-Schen. Exploiting the conditional density in estimating the term structure: An application to the Cox, Ingersoll and Ross model. *The Journal of Finance*, XLIX, 4:1279–1304, 1994.

Asger Roer Pedersen. Maximum likelihood estimation based on incomplete observations for a class of discrete time stochastic processes by means of the Kalman filter. Technical Report 272, Department of theoretical statistics, University of Aarhus, 1993.

Asger Roer Pedersen. A new approach to maximum likelihood estimation for stochastic differential equations based on discrete observations. *Scandinavian Journal of Statistics*, pages 55–71, 1995.

Peter C.B. Phillips and Jun Yu. A two-stage realized volatility approach to estimation of diffusion processes with discrete data. *Journal of Econometrics*, 150(2):139–150, 2009.

Monika Piazzesi. Affine term structure models. *Handbook of Financial Econometrics*, 1:691–766, 2010.

Eckhard Platen and Nicola Bruti-Liberati. *Numerical Solution of Stochastic Differential Equations with Jumps in Finance*, volume 64. Springer, 2010.

M.B. Priestley. *Non-linear and Non-stationary Time Series Analysis*. Academic Press, London, 1988.

V.S. Pugachev and I.N. Sinitsyn. *Stochastic Differential Systems – Analysis and Filtering*. John Wiley & Sons, New York, 1987.

Fredrik Regland and Erik Lindström. Independent spike models: Estimation and validation. *Czech Journal of Economics and Finance*, 62(2), 2012.

P.M. Robinson. Nonparametric estimators for time series. *Journal of Time Series Analysis*, 4(3):185–207, 1983.

H.L. Royden. *Real Analysis, Third Edition*. Prentice Hall, New Jersey, 1988.

David Ruppert, Matthew P. Wand, and Raymond J. Carroll. *Semiparametric Regression*, volume 12. Cambridge University Press, 2003.

Tina Hviid Rydberg. A note on the existence of unique equivalent martingale measures in a Markovian setting. *Finance and Stochastics*, 1:251–257, 1997.

T. Rydén. *Parameter estimation for Markov modulated Poisson processes and Overload control of SPC switches*. Ph.D. thesis, Dept. of Mathematical Statistics, Lund Institute of Technology, Lund, Sweden, 1993.

Tobias Rydén, Timo Teräsvirta, and Stefan Åsbrink. Stylized facts of daily return series and the hidden Markov model. *Journal of Applied Econometrics*, 13(3):217–244, 1998.

Simo Sarkka. On unscented Kalman filtering for state estimation of continuous-time nonlinear systems. *Automatic Control, IEEE Transactions on*, 52(9):1631–1641, 2007.

Albert N .Shiryaev. *Probability*, volume 95 of *Graduate Texts in Mathematics*. Springer-Verlag, New York, 1996.

R. Shumway. *Applied Statistical Time Series Analysis*. Prentice Hall, London, 1988.

Annastiina Silvennoinen and Timo Teräsvirta. Multivariate autoregressive conditional heteroskedasticity with smooth transitions in conditional correlations. Technical report, SSE/EFI Working Paper Series in Economics and Finance, 2005.

Annastiina Silvennoinen and Timo Teräsvirta. Modeling multivariate autoregressive conditional heteroskedasticity with the double smooth transition conditional correlation GARCH model. *Journal of Financial Econometrics*, 7(4):373–411, 2009a.

Annastiina Silvennoinen and Timo Teräsvirta. Multivariate GARCH models. *Handbook of Financial Time Series*, pages 201–229, 2009b.

B.W. Silverman. *Density Estimation for Statistics and Data Analysis*. Chapman and Hall, New York, 1986.

Kenneth J. Singleton. Estimation of affine asset pricing models using the empirical characteristic function. *Journal of Econometrics*, 102(1):111–141, 2001.

Michael Sørensen. Estimating functions for diffusion-type processes. *Statistical Methods for Stochastic Differential Equations*, 124:1–107, 2012.

James C. Spall. *Introduction to Stochastic Search and Optimization: Estimation, Simulation, and Control*, volume 65. John Wiley & Sons, 2005.

Chris Strickland. A comparison of diffusion models of the term structure. *The European Journal of Finance*, 2:103–123, 1996.

Rolf Sundberg. Maximum likelihood theory for incomplete data from an exponential family. *Scandinavian Journal of Statistics*, pages 49–58, 1974.

L. Svensson. Estimating and interpreting forward interest rates: Sweden 1992–1994. Technical Report 579, Institute for Internation Economic Studies, Stockholm University, 1994.

S.J. Taylor. Financial returns modelled by the product of two stochastic processes-A study of the daily sugar prices 1961-75. *Time Series Analysis: Theory and Practice*, 1:203–226, 1982.

M. Thuvesholmen. Recursive estimation and segmentation in autoregressive processes with Markov regime. Technical report, 1994:E4, Dept of Mathematical Statistics, Lund University, Lund, Sweden, 1994.

H. Tong. *Threshold Models in Non-Linear Time Series Analysis*. Springer, Heidelberg, 1983.

H. Tong. *Non-linear Time Series – A Dynamic System Approach*. Oxford Science Publishers, Oxford, 1990.

Rudolph Van Der Merwe. *Sigma-point Kalman filters for probabilistic inference in dynamic state-space models*. Ph.D. thesis, University of Stellenbosch, 2004.

Aad W Van der Vaart. *Asymptotic Statistics*, volume 3. Cambridge University Press, 2000.

Charles F. van Loan. Computing integrals involving the matrix exponential. *IEEE Transactions on Automatic Control*, AC–23(3):395–404, June 1978.

O. Vasicek. An equilibrium characteriztion of the term structure. *Journal of Financial Economics*, 5:177–188, 1977.

Chunyan Wang. *Stochastic differential equations and a biological system.* Ph.D. thesis, Institute of Mathematical Modelling, The Technical University of Denmark, Lyngby, 1994.

Magnus Wiktorsson and Erik Lindström. Fast Simultaneous Calibration and Quadratic Hedging under Parameter Uncertainty. In *Proceedings to the 8th World Congress of the Bachelier Finance Society*, 2014.

David Williams. *Probability with Martingales.* Cambridge University Press, Cambridge, 1995.

Paul Wilmott, Sam Howison, and Jeff Dewynne. *The Mathematics of Financial Derivatives.* Cambridge University Press, New York, 1995.

Lan Zhang, Per A. Mykland, and Yacine Aït-Sahalia. A tale of two time scales. *Journal of the American Statistical Association*, 100(472), 2005.

Walter Zucchini and Iain L. MacDonald. *Hidden Markov Models for Time Series: An Introduction Using R.* CRC Press, 2009.

Index